Child Abuse: Understanding, Assessment and Response Strategies

Child Abuse: Understanding, Assessment and Response Strategies

Jonah Stewart

CLANRYE INTERNATIONAL
www.clanryeinternational.com

Clanrye International,
750 Third Avenue, 9th Floor,
New York, NY 10017, USA

ISBN: 978-1-64726-619-6

Cataloging-in-Publication Data

Child abuse : understanding, assessment and response strategies / Jonah Stewart.
p. cm.
Includes bibliographical references and index.
ISBN 978-1-64726-619-6
1. Child abuse. 2. Children--Crimes against. 3. Abused children. I. Stewart, Jonah.
HV6626.5 .U53 2023
364.155 54--dc23

For information on all Clanrye International publications visit our website at www.clanryeinternational.com

CLANRYE INTERNATIONAL

Contents

Preface

Child abuse is defined as any action that hurts a child. It can occur in a variety of ways such as emotional, physical and sexual abuse as well as exploitation and neglect. The abuser is frequently someone the child knows. It could be a relative, parent, a close family friend or caregiver. However, children are sometimes also abused by other adults on whom they are dependent such as day care workers, sports trainers and teachers. Child abuse assessment is performed to either assess claims of physical abuse, sexual abuse, or neglect in order to aid in legal decision making. The long-term impacts of child abuse can be lessened with proper mental and physical health care. This book presents the complex subject of child abuse in the most comprehensible and easy to understand language. Coherent flow of topics, student-friendly language and extensive use of examples make this book an invaluable source of knowledge.

The information contained in this book is the result of intensive hard work done by researchers in this field. All due efforts have been made to make this book serve as a complete guiding source for students and researchers. The topics in this book have been comprehensively explained to help readers understand the growing trends in the field.

I would like to thank the entire group of writers who made sincere efforts in this book and my family who supported me in my efforts of working on this book. I take this opportunity to thank all those who have been a guiding force throughout my life.

Jonah Stewart

1

Nordic Barnahus Model and its Application

Susanna Johansson, Kari Stefansen, Elisiv Bakketeig and Anna Kaldal

Introduction

Violence and abuse against children are serious threats to children's well-being, and the need for societies to take action is increasingly recognised, in both the Nordic region and internationally. Children

---

S. Johansson (✉)
School of Social Work, Lund University, Lund, Sweden
e-mail: susanna.johansson@soch.lu.se

K. Stefansen · E. Bakketeig
Norwegian Social Research, Oslo and Akershus University College of Applied Sciences, Oslo, Norway
e-mail: kari.stefansen@nova.hioa.no

E. Bakketeig
e-mail: elisiv.bakketeig@nova.hioa.no

A. Kaldal
Law Faculty, Stockholm University, Stockholm, Sweden
e-mail: anna.kaldal@juridicum.su.se

exposed to violence and abuse are vulnerable and often in need of multiple services, creating the risk of potential "secondary victimisation". This book targets a model that has been implemented in the Nordic countries for more than a decade, and that attempts to meet children's needs by offering multiple services in child-friendly premises and "under one roof"—*the Nordic Barnahus model.* The model was first introduced in Iceland and drew on experiences from Children's Advocacy Centres (CAC) in the USA. In this book, the Nordic concept of Barnahus will be used, as it acknowledges the process of translation and adaption that the implementation of the CAC model into the Nordic welfare state context encompasses, and that we will elaborate in this chapter.

In recent decades, violence and sexual abuse against children have been high on the political agenda in the Nordic countries, and a range of preventive as well as legislative efforts has been instigated. The implementation of the Barnahus model is linked to a long-lasting concern for the protection of children at risk and for the way children's needs are met during a criminal investigation, as well as a lack of coordinated follow-up services for children and families that need treatment or support related to the child's experiences.

What are considered legitimate measures for investigating suspected child abuse, including when and how to intervene in family life, differs between societies and over time (cf. Donzelot 1997; Hacking 1999). The introduction of the Barnahus model can be seen as the result of a long process of cultural change in the recognition of violence and sexual abuse against children as a real and widespread phenomena (e.g. Gudbrandsson 2010; Bakketeig 2000). This process of cultural change also encompasses a radical shift in the view of a parent's rights to discipline their children. Throughout the Nordic region, parental corporal punishment has been redefined as an illegitimate act of power and thus as violence. In Sweden and Norway, for instance, laws on parental violence were introduced in the 1970s, and in both countries, new amendments have set a very low bar for what is considered violence (Forsman 2013; Skjørten et al. 2016). Even though legislation may vary between countries, it seems reasonable to see the Nordic countries as characterised by very low and in a legal sense, zero tolerance for violence and sexual abuse of children. Both violence and the sexual abuse of children are today seen as a violation of children's basic human rights, in accordance with the UN Convention on the Rights of the Child (CRC) from 1989.

The Barnahus model has been described as one of the main policy ventures related to children as crime victims in the Nordic countries in recent years (Johansson 2012), and the diffusion process in the region has been rapid and extensive. In 2016, all the Nordic countries had implemented the model in some form or other; however, various measures similar to the Barnahus model had been tried out in several Nordic countries in the years before its introduction. In Sweden, for instance, this included a competence centre for child sexual abuse called "Bup-Elefanten" in Linköping, as well as consultation groups for suspected child abuse cases in many Swedish municipalities and recommended by the Swedish National Board of Health and Welfare since the 1990s (see, for example, Swedish National Board of Health and Welfare 2000). These earlier collaborative arrangements were typically not placed in child-friendly localities and under one roof, which are core elements of the Barnahus idea. The implementation of the Barnahus model can thus be seen as a manifestation of an ongoing development of multi-professional child protection interventions aiming at more integrated and child-centred models for handling suspected child abuse.

The establishment of the Barnahus model should also be seen as related to the partly overlapping development of broad policy packages to prevent all forms of domestic violence in their respective countries and thus not solely related to violence and abuse against children specifically. In Norway, for instance, the work in this field has been coordinated through a series of governmental action plans, and the current government is launching a wide-ranging plan to strengthen policies of domestic violence in 2016.

Barnahus is often referred to as an example of child-friendly justice, and the model is currently promoted at the European level by the Council of Europe (see, for example, Council of Europe 2010). Several European countries are now in the process of implementing multi-professional measures regarding investigations of child abuse, inspired by the Nordic Barnahus model. For example, a Barnahus was opened in

Lithuania in June 2016, following an initiative from the government.[1] In November 2015, the government in Cyprus decided to open a Barnahus, and a working group has been established for the implementation process. Initiatives have also been taken in the UK. Recently, we also learned that Barnahus may be tried out by UNICEF in Kazakhstan.

This situation warrants discussion. What are the characteristics of the Barnahus model? And what are the challenges and prospects of the Barnahus model within a Nordic welfare state context? Experiences and comparative knowledge from the different Nordic Barnahus contexts could, in turn, be of value when discussing the implementation of the Barnahus model (or similar integrated and multi-professional services) outside the Nordic welfare state context, as well as to further the development of collaborative and investigative Barnahus work within the Nordic countries.[2]

One perspective that will be put forward in this chapter and throughout the book is that the diffusion and implementation of the Barnahus model may be seen to be a continuous transformation of ideas rather than simple copying or imitation (Czarniawska and Sevón 1996; Røvik 2000, 2016; Johansson 2012). In this introductory chapter, we will use a contextual and comparative perspective to highlight how the model is shaped by the legal and organisational context into which it has been introduced. We start, however, by discussing the core elements encompassed by the Barnahus model—as an idea and as a distinct model of collaborative work in cases of violence and sexual abuse against children.

The Barnahus Idea

A first question for readers of this book, and for states, agencies or professionals discussing whether to implement the Barnahus (or a similar) model, would be what the Barnahus model is, and what core elements must usually be in place or regarded as necessary for an intervention to fall within the Barnahus category. In other words, what does the Barnahus idea consist of? And how does the Barnahus model relate to, and differ from, other measures and interventions for child victims of abuse participating in legal processes, such as the US Children's Advocacy Centres (CAC)?[3]

The concept "Barnahus" translates as "Children's House" in English and originates from Iceland, the first Nordic country to adopt the model in 1998. The Icelandic Barnahus took the CAC model as its inspiration, which developed as a response to child sexual abuse, starting in Huntsville, Alabama, 1985. The CACs currently number nearly 1000 centres across the USA (http://nationalcac.org). Both models build on the understanding that child abuse is a complex phenomenon, demanding highly specialised expertise and coordinated services.

A Multi-professional Approach

Both Barnahus and CACs represent multi-professional approaches to child victims of abuse with the double aim of facilitating the legal process and ensuring that the child receives necessary support and treatment. The multidisciplinary team concept is, for example, a core element of the CAC model. At both European and international levels, guidelines and policy documents on child-friendly justice stress the importance of close multidisciplinary collaboration in child-friendly facilities (Lanzarote Convention; Council of Europe 2010; FRA 2015; UN Economic and Social Council resolution 2005/20; CRC/C/GC/12). Some specifically mention Barnahus as an example of a promising practice to this end (see Council of Europe 2010).

The agencies involved most often encompass law enforcement, child welfare services and health care, and thus professionals such as social workers, psychologists, police and prosecutors, paediatricians and forensic doctors. The practice of consultation meetings around suspected child abuse cases is central when it comes to the organisation of multi-professional collaboration within the Barnahus model; however, it is important to note that there are variations regarding the agencies and professions involved—not only between the CACs and the Barnahus model, but also between different Nordic Barnahus models, as will be further discussed later in this chapter.

The One Door Principle

Both the CAC model and the Barnahus model are guided by the "one door principle" (or the "under one roof principle") meaning that professionals should come to the child and not the other way around. Barnahus has, for instance, been described as containing four rooms: the criminal investigation, protection, physical health and mental health, with a roof at the top representing knowledge (Landberg and Svedin 2013). Save the Children, as an important agent in promoting Barnahus in the Nordic countries, has argued that the establishment of Barnahus and the one door principle is necessary from a child rights perspective (e.g. Skybak 2004; Save the Children Sweden 2009; Landberg and Svedin 2013) . Barnahus would save children from the stress of being shuffled between public services, having to repeat their story over and over again, and often in environments that children experience as strange and sometimes even frightening. Such services were often poorly coordinated, suggesting that the investigations were not taking place at the premises of the child (Skybak 2004).

Avoiding Secondary Victimisation

Closely related to the one door principle is the idea of avoiding repeated contacts and interviews by multiple professionals in localities not adjusted to children's needs and thus to reduce the risk of "secondary victimisation". Both the CAC and the Barnahus models are thus supposed to be child friendly, or child centred, and sensitive, meaning that the measure shall not cause extra harm. Preventing the child being (re) victimised by the criminal process is often highlighted as important (see, for example, Skybak 2004). This core element is primarily materialised through the joint child investigative interview (see Gudbrandsson 2010) and thus the co-hearing of the interview in an adjacent monitor room at the Barnahus, where the idea builds on a multi-professional observation in order to avoid repeated interviewing, as well as making use of the specialised competences. Cross et al. (2007), for instance, describe how the joint interview is supposed to limit the number of interviews as well as interviewers (Cross et al. 2007).

A Safe Place for Disclosure and Neutral Place for Professional Interventions

Another core element of the Barnahus idea is that it is supposed to be a safe place for disclosing abuse (see Gudbrandsson 2010; Stefansen, Chap. 2), often interpreted as a child-friendly, child-centred and supportive setting, as well as a place that is safe from persons suspected of abuse. This is intended to provide the best possible circumstances for children to disclose abuse, and to feel safe, thereby avoiding secondary victimisation. Partly related to this core element, and partly to the one door principle, is also the localisation of Barnahus. There have been, for instance, ongoing discussions concerning the importance of Barnahus being localised in a residential area as opposed to a more office-like or agency-typical location. Similarly, there have been discussions concerning the importance of the medical examinations being held at the Barnahus as opposed to a nearby hospital (cf. Stefansen et al., Chap. 16).

In contrast to the CAC model, however, a specific characteristic of the Nordic Barnahus model is the fact that the child does not testify in court and therefore does not appear in court, as will be described further below. The Nordic Barnahus model thus represents a place away from the premises of the criminal justice system, while at the same time ensuring the child's right to participation and access to justice, without compromising the right to a fair trial for the suspected offender. The idea of Barnahus is thus, in addition, to represent a neutral space for professional interventions. The coordination of parallel and different professional investigations and interventions is, for example, to be balanced sufficiently, as are the partly conflicting interests of child-friendly justice and the principle of a fair trial. This element of the Barnahus idea is also concretely materialised in the Barnahus locality, through, for instance, the design of the interview room in a neutral but calming style, while other rooms are more stimulating.

A Broad Target Group and Definition of Child Abuse

The CACs, as well as Barnahus in Iceland, were launched as a measure for handling sexual abuse cases. Today, the Barnahus model within the Nordic countries most often encompasses both sexual abuse and violence cases. As illustrated in the appendix of this book, all Nordic countries, except Greenland, now include children being victims of both sexual abuse and physical (interpersonal) violence, in the target group of Barnahus. In fact, the majority of cases handled in Swedish and Norwegian Barnahus, for instance, involve suspicions of physical abuse where either one or both of the child's parents are suspected offenders (see, for example, Åström and Rejmer 2008; Kaldal et al. 2010; Bakketeig et al. 2012; Stefansen et al. 2012).[4]

In this chapter, and throughout the book, we will thus use "child abuse" as a generic term since it encompasses both violence and sexual assault, thereby including the target groups of all Nordic Barnahus models, and differentiate more specifically when relevant.

The Nordic Welfare State Context

We consider a description of the Nordic welfare state context important in order to understand the implementation process of the Barnahus model within the Nordic region. The Barnahus model can be understood as a service at the intersection of the child welfare system and the criminal justice system, making a description of these systems especially relevant. Since the implementation of the Barnahus model takes shape in relation to—and operates within—the distinct child welfare and criminal justice systems of the Nordic countries, the following section introduces the central characteristics of these systems within the Nordic welfare state context. This section also functions as a contextualising background for the next chapters of the book, as well as this chapter's comparative analysis of the implementation processes within the Nordic countries more specifically.

The Nordic countries are often described as well developed and similar when it comes to welfare and justice systems, for example, as belonging to a "Nordic welfare model", a "social democratic welfare regime" or "the Scandinavian model" (e.g. Esping-Andersen 1990; Lorenz 1994; Gilbert et al. 2011; Forsberg and Kröger 2011). Christiansen and Markkola (2006: 11) point out that "(…) some general assumptions are made about the Nordic welfare states. They are supposed to be characterised by a strong state, or more correctly, a large and expensive public sector; welfare benefits and services (…)". Even though the Nordic welfare model secures general benefits for citizens, it has primarily focused on the rights of adults or families, and not young people and children as independent actors in their own right (Backe-Hansen et al. 2013); however, this has been challenged by both a new understanding of childhood that sees children as competent agents and an increased focus and emphasis on children's rights through the development and ratification of the CRC (cf. James and Prout 2014 [1990]; Freeman 2012). The CRC has been ratified by all the Nordic countries and, for instance, been incorporated in full by Norway and suggested to be incorporated in Sweden.[5] The core message of the CRC is that the child is an individual holder of fundamental human rights that not only derive from their vulnerability but from a recognition of the child as a subject.[6]

The Child Welfare System

Child welfare systems in the Nordic countries are often described as "family service-oriented" in contrast to "child protection-oriented" systems in English-speaking countries such as the USA, Canada and the UK (Gilbert 1997; Gilbert et al. 2011). Since family service-oriented systems are primarily based on ideas about child welfare, they typically focus on early prevention and thus cover a broader target group. Services are mostly directed towards support for the family as a whole and based on voluntary measures and collaboration as a first option, and compulsory interventions as an exception. Child protection-oriented systems, on the other hand, have a more restricted focus, targeting abused or neglected children more specifically and not usually families in need of more broad support. Measures undertaken by child welfare services in child protection-oriented systems are usually introduced later and are typically more protective, controlling and legalistically based (e.g. in the sense of using investigatory and coercive means) (Gilbert et al. 2011). These differences also affect the number of cases that enter the child welfare system. In Norway, for example, a more family service-oriented system has resulted in a strong growth in the number of children who receive some kind of services from the child welfare system, thus increasing the potential to identify children in need of support at an earlier stage and to work more preventively. The increase in cases reaching the child welfare system has, in turn, been discussed in relation to the potential risk of developing a child welfare system with fewer resources left for children at greater risk, by contributing more to the general level of welfare than addressing children and families with more serious dysfunctions (Backe-Hansen et al. 2013; cf. Ponnert 2015).

In addition to the similarity in terms of a traditional family service orientation among the Nordic countries, there are also organisational differences between the respective child welfare systems (cf. Blomberg et al. 2011). This includes, for instance, whether child welfare is being regulated and organised as an independent body (as, for example, in Norway), or as part of a municipality's general social services system (as, for example, in Sweden). Being a specialised service may imply more targeted services (Backe-Hansen et al. 2013), but may also imply a risk of fragmentation in relation to dealing with social issues within the family. It may also affect the implementation of the Barnahus model in different ways, as several of the contributions in this book will illustrate.

The regulatory framework of mandatory reporting to the child welfare services among the Nordic countries means that there also are developed systems for child protection within the Nordic countries.[7] Several recent legislative changes have also been aimed at strengthening the protection of children at risk. This means that the child welfare systems within the Nordic welfare states tend to contain both elements of family service orientation and child protection orientation. Family service-oriented systems have been criticised for emphasising custodian rights at the expense of children's rights and needs (e.g. Kaldal 2010; Leviner 2011); however, it has been stressed that different child welfare systems, including the Nordic country systems, are moving towards the mix and convergence characterised by more "child-focused-oriented" systems (Gilbert et al. 2011). This convergence can be partly understood in the light of the strong standing of children's rights, because child participation has gained increased attention both in research and as an important element of child welfare work (Gilbert et al. 2011).

The Criminal Justice System

Child-Friendly Justice

The idea of child-friendly justice has developed and materialised in a number of international treaties and policy documents (see above) since the signing of the CRC. The idea is associated with two discourses: on the one hand, a discourse of protection that sees children as vulnerable, and on the other hand, a discourse that sees children as agents with the ability to act on their own behalf (Sandberg 2016). Both discourses are reflected in the Nordic legal systems.

A common characteristic of the criminal justice systems in the Nordic countries is that children do not give evidence in court. The best evidence rule and the adversarial principle are basic in legal procedure. These principles are sanctioned in the Convention for the Protection of Human Rights and Fundamental Freedoms article 6, the right to a fair trial. The core of the right to a fair trial is the defence's right to cross-examine a witness, art. 6.3d. According to this, evidence shall be given in court so that the accused can defend themselves against the charges. In the Nordic countries, when the aggrieved party is a child, their testimony is given outside of the court proceedings. The European Court of Human Rights has ruled in several cases that a testimony given in the pre-trial (criminal) investigation does not violate the defendant's right to a fair trial if the defendant's rights according to article 6 have been safeguarded in the pre-trial investigation (Danelius 2015; Hennum 2006; Sutorius and Kaldal 2003).

Historically, the child's need for protection has been a central justification for the child's testimony to be given outside of open court. In Norway, for instance, this practice was first implemented in sexual abuse cases. It has later expanded to cases involving physical violence and children witnessing violence. In Sweden, the Supreme Court ruled in 1963 (NJA 1963, 555) that a child's audio-documented statement from the police investigation could be used as evidence despite the breach of the fundamental principle of evidence immediacy. The Barnahus model can, against this background, be seen as part of a development aimed at protecting children against the burden that the investigation and court proceedings can represent for the child. In Barnahus, children give their testimony in child-friendly environments, and their testimony is video-recorded. Child-friendly environments can be seen as a way of orchestrating the best possible setting for the child to give their testimony, in accordance with the child's right to participation as stated in the CRC. The committee states that the hearing must be child friendly with regard to environment and procedures (CRC/C/GC/12). This brings us to the child rights perspective.

The Child Rights Perspective

The child rights perspective has influenced criminal law as well as other legal areas, such as child and family law and child welfare law. According to international law, children are granted legal protection from violence and abuse. This is stated in both the European Convention on Human Rights (art. 3), as interpreted by the European Court of Human Rights, and CRC, in, for instance, articles 19 and 34. Article 39 obliges states to implement measures to protect children from violence and abuse.

The child's right to participation is a basic right that follows from CRC article 12. Participation is one of the four main principles in the convention. It is an independent right, as well as a right integral to all the other rights that the CRC entails (Sandberg 2016). The right to participation applies to all issues concerning the child and includes the child right to access justice. The UN Committee on the Rights of the Child does not make any distinction as to whether the child is a witness to or a victim of crime. The child therefore has an independent right to be heard in cases of violence and abuse in a criminal case and in all stages of the legal process. The best interest of the child is another basic right and fundamental legal principle in the CRC (art. 3). This means that if a provision is open to more than one interpretation, the interpretation which most effectively serves the child's best interest should be chosen (CRC/C/GC/14). The principle of the best interest of the child is also a procedural principle. This means that when a decision relates to a specific child, the decision-making process must entail an assessment of the consequences of the decision for the child (CRC/C/GC/14).

The consideration of the child's need for protection (child-friendly justice) and participation (the child rights perspective) may conflict. Numerous studies have shown that the relationship between these two considerations is complicated. For instance, even though the child has a right to participate in all matters affecting them, several studies show that the child is not always heard (Bakketeig and Bergan 2013; Eriksson 2012; Kaldal et al. 2010). Protecting a child is often used as an argument for not hearing the child, even though this is not in accordance with the rights of the child. On the other hand, the right to participation does not imply a duty to participate; there must therefore also be consideration of the right of the individual child to not participate.

The Nordic Barnahus Model(s)

The fact that the Barnahus model has spread and is established in all Nordic countries could in one sense be interpreted as a sign of the similarities between the Nordic welfare states sketched above, but in the light of several completed as well as ongoing studies of Barnahus in the different Nordic countries (e.g. Åström and Rejmer 2008; Swedish National Police Agency et al. 2008; Kaldal et al. 2010; Johansson 2011; Bakketeig et al. 2012; Stefansen et al. 2012; Johansson 2012; Landberg and Svedin 2013), important variations regarding the implementation of the Barnahus model are crystallising. This actualises the importance of gathering knowledge from the different countries, as well as further developing an interdisciplinary, contextual and comparative understanding. In this section, we will compare how the Barnahus model has been implemented in the different Nordic countries on an overarching level, and address differences and similarities in aims and scope, as well as legal and organisational aspects of the different national models. We will thus identify key characteristics of the local adaptions of the Nordic Barnahus model that, in turn, will work as an introduction to the following chapters of the book.

Comparing Key Characteristics and Local Adaptions

The Nordic region consists of the five countries: Iceland, Sweden, Norway, Denmark and Finland, as well as their autonomous regions: the Åland Islands, Greenland and the Faroe Islands. In the following, we will address the key characteristics, as well as local adaptions, of the Nordic Barnahus models. Table 1.1 gives an overview of the key characteristics of the national Barnahus models in Iceland, Sweden, Norway and Denmark, based on the more detailed country model descriptions in the appendix of this book (which also include descriptions of the models in Finland and the autonomous Nordic regions). The main arguments for only including Iceland, Sweden, Norway and Denmark in the table are that they are the Nordic countries where Barnahus is most widespread and/or where most evaluations and research have been undertaken so far, so that the data available are robust and thus comparable. To some extent, however, all Nordic countries and regions will be part of the comparative discussion.

There are, of course, challenges when including comparable elements in a table like this one (Table 1.1). First, there are often discrepancies in data regarding how the Barnahus model on an ideological level is defined in the respective countries and how it functions in practice. For example, the target group could be defined more broadly in policy documents or regulations, while in practice reaching a more limited group of children, or vice versa. Secondly, there are difficulties in finding comparable data, resulting in various sources being used to describe the models in the different countries, even though we have tried to use additional sources in order to make the information as comparable as possible, as well as primarily focused on the four country models with most available data sources. Third, there are difficulties connected to the constant change that the collaborative Barnahus model is undergoing in respective countries, as well as local variations in implementation within countries (which applies more to some countries than others). Despite these difficulties, we have identified significant similarities and differences between the Nordic Barnahus models on an overarching level, which will be discussed in the following.

Table 1.1 Overview of the Barnahus models in Iceland, Sweden, Norway and Denmark

	Cases and target group			Coordination and collaboration			Regulation	
	Age group	**Type of abuse**	**Type of cases**	**Central co-ordination**	**Involved agencies**	**Barnahus staff**	**Mandatory use of Barnahus**	**Specific Barnahus regulation**
Iceland Since 1998 Currently one Barnahus	Below 15 years	Sexual abuse and since 2015 also physical violence	Police reported cases Child welfare cases when suspicions of abuse	Government Agency for Child Protection	Child welfare services Medical health services Police Prosecution Court judges	Psychologists, social worker, criminologist	Not Barnahus explicitly, but to run and use such facilities	No specific Barnahus law, but strong regulative support for the Barnahus operation in the Child Protection Act (no. 80/2002) and the Law on Criminal Procedure (no. 88/2008)
Sweden Since 2006 Currently ≈30 Barnahus	Below 18 yrs	Sexual abuse and physical violence National guidelines also include female genital mutilation; direct and indirect witnesses of violence; crimes of honour motives; children who sexually abuse other children (when appropriate) (+local variations)	Cases with parallel investigations by child welfare services and police and prosecutors	As a pilot: Ministry of Justice and an interagency coordination group on national level Currently: No central coordinating agency at a state level. National Barnahus network, first coordinated by Save the Children Sweden and since 2016 by National Competence Center in Child Abuse (Barnafrid) in cooperation with Save the Children Sweden	Child welfare services Police Prosecution Health care Forensic medicine	Social workers, also psychologists and/or police at some Barnahus	No	No specific Barnahus law. National guidelines and standards for Barnahus by the National Police Agency

(continued)

Table 1.1 (continued)

	Cases and target group			Coordination and collaboration			Regulation	
	Age group	**Type of abuse**	**Type of cases**	**Central co-ordination**	**Involved agencies**	**Barnahus staff**	**Mandatory use of Barnahus**	**Specific Barnahus regulation**
Norway Since 2007 Currently 11 Barnahus	Below 16 yrs and adults with intellectual impairment	Sexual abuse, direct and indirect violence, homicide and gender mutilation	Police reported cases only: aggrieved parties and witnesses	Police Directorate and state-level Barnahus committee	Police Prosecution Forensic medicine	Social workers and psychologists	Yes, for police and prosecutors	By law: Criminal Procedure Act and regulation on facilitated investigative interview (FOR-2015-09-24-1098)
Denmark Since 2013 Currently 5 Barnahus (+ 3 satellites)	Below 18 yrs	Sexual abuse and physical violence	Child welfare cases involving police and/or health care	National Board of Social Services	Child welfare services Police Prosecution Health care	Social workers and psychologists	Yes, for child welfare services if case also involves police and/or health care	By law: The Consolidation Act on Social Services (No. 1284) and Order on Children Houses (no. 1153 of 01/10/2013) Quality standards for Barnahus by the National Board of Social Services

Types of Abuse and Target Groups

As described above, most of the Nordic countries include children thought to be victims of both sexual and physical abuse as part of the target group. How the target groups of the different Nordic Barnahus models are more specifically defined differs to some extent between the Nordic countries, as well as the autonomous regions. While some have formally extended the types of abuse quite expansively (see Norway and Sweden in Table 1.1), other Barnahus models have even broader, but also much more demarcated, types of abuse as part of the target group for Barnahus. To illustrate, the Åland Island's Barnahus model generally targets crimes against children while in practice mainly handling (interpersonal) violence and sexual abuse cases, and the Faroe Island's Barnahus model in practice includes all criminal behaviour against children even though the primary target group is children who have suffered sexual or physical abuse. The Greenlandic Barnahus model, in contrast, focuses on cases where children have been sexually abused or been witnesses to sexual abuse (see appendix). Similarly, there are differences in whether Barnahus includes or excludes the child's family from the target group or eventual support and treatment services offered at Barnahus (see appendix). There are also variations regarding the age of the target group, with Sweden and Denmark receiving children under 18, while Iceland and Norway have age limits of, respectively, 15 and 16. The Greenlandic Barnahus model targets children and youths aged 0–18 years, but video-recorded interviews are only used with children up to 12 years of age (cf. also the Faroe Islands).

Implementation and Regulation

The comparison shows that there are variations in how the model has been implemented in the different Nordic countries, such as whether it was implemented as a pilot project, upon a decision of the government, or not. There are also variations in how the model is regulated, which to different degrees correspond to how it has been initiated.

In both Sweden and Norway, the Barnahus model was initiated as a pilot project by the Swedish Ministry of Justice in 2005 and the Norwegian Ministry of Justice and the Police in 2007. At that time, there was no specific Barnahus regulation in either Sweden or Norway. Today, there is still no specific Barnahus law in Sweden, even though there have been (not binding) national guidelines and criteria from 2009, issued a few years after the Barnahus pilot was initiated (Swedish National Police Agency 2009). In Norway, there was similarly no specific Barnahus regulation at the time of establishment, but in 2015 the Criminal Procedure Act was amended and new regulations of facilitated interviews were put into force (FOR-2015-09-24-1098). The new main rule states that Barnahus should be used for facilitated investigative interviews with children under the age of 16 and other vulnerable victims and witnesses in cases involving sexual abuse, direct and indirect physical violence, homicide and gender mutilation, thus making Barnahus mandatory for police and prosecutors in these cases. In Sweden, the use of Barnahus is not mandatory, which is also demonstrated by the local variations within the country, where, for instance, the child welfare services of 160 of the 290 municipalities in 2013 were connected to a Barnahus (Landberg and Svedin 2013).

In Iceland, there is no specific Barnahus law, and Barnahus is not explicitly referred to in any legal provision; however, there are regulations in both the Child Protection Act and the Law on Criminal Procedure that provide the legal basis for the Barnahus operation. The Child Protection Act mandates the Government Agency for Child Protection in Iceland to run special service centres with the objective of promoting interdisciplinary collaboration, and strengthening the coordination of agencies in the handling of cases of child protection (Art. 7; Child Protection Act). The Icelandic Government Agency for Child Protection has issued guidelines and standard settings for the local child welfare services, which are not mandatory but strongly normative for the practice of local child welfare services, not least since they may be sanctioned if a complaint is made and the standards are not met. These guidelines and standards address, for example, explorative interviews, medical examinations and therapeutic services provided by Barnahus. In 2015, there was also a legal change made in the Law on Criminal Procedure (nr. 88/2008) stipulating that investigative interviews of child victims up to 15 years shall be conducted under the auspice of a court judge in a facility specially designed for such purposes (Art. 9) and with the support of a specially trained person (Art. 123). These provisions are generally interpreted by court judges as mandating interviews with children below the age of 15 in Barnahus, even though this was the established practice years before the legal amendment.

In contrast, the implementation of Barnahus in Denmark followed a broad law reform that was brought into force in October 2013, called "the abuse package" , resulting in the simultaneous foundation of five Barnahus and three satellites covering the whole country. As part of the abuse package, several legal changes were made within the Consolidation Act on Social Services (No. 1284) that were of importance for the Barnahus model in Denmark. A specific Barnahus law was also passed (Order on Children Houses no. 1153 of 01/10/2013) authorising the Barnahus and providing guidelines for the tasks and duties of the Barnahus. These legislative reforms made it mandatory for municipality local child welfare services to use Barnahus in child welfare cases that involve the police and/or healthcare services and that relate to violence or sexual abuse (Consolidation Act on Social Services, §50b). It was also made mandatory for Barnahus to assist the local child welfare services in their child welfare investigations in these cases (Order on Children Houses no. 1153 of 01/10/2013 § 1). In addition to the legal provisions, the National Board of Social Services issued common professional quality standards for the Danish Barnahus model (see appendix).

It is interesting to note that in the countries where Barnahus is mandatory by law, the obligation to use Barnahus is directed towards different agencies: in Norway towards police and prosecutors, and in Denmark towards the municipality local child welfare services. In Iceland, the specific use of Barnahus is not mandatory; however, regulative support for the use of such facilities can still be regarded as strong and also well balanced in comparison with Norway and Denmark, due to the fact that there is a regulative support to be found in both child welfare and criminal procedural regulation.

Central Coordination and Collaboration

As a pilot project, Barnahus in Sweden was commissioned by the Swedish Ministry of Justice and coordinated by an interagency coordination group at state level. Since then, however, there has not been any central administrative coordinating agency for Barnahus in Sweden, except for the national Barnahus network established and for long coordinated by the non-governmental organisation Save the Children Sweden and since 2016 by the National Competence Centre in Child Abuse (Barnafrid) at Linköping University in cooperation with Save the Children Sweden.

In Norway, the Barnahus model is coordinated by the Police Directorate on behalf of the Ministry of Police and Public Security. Barnahus in Norway are organised as separate units within the police district where they are located, and the regular Barnahus staff are employed as civilians in the police districts. In Sweden, Barnahus do not constitute a governmental agency per se, which means that all agencies working in Barnahus are employed by their respective agencies, and the regular Barnahus staff are primarily employed within the municipality social welfare services. In Denmark, the five Barnahus are independent units that are supported and supervised by the National Board of Social Services. The administrative structure indicates a strong connection to the child welfare system in Denmark. This connection is apparently stronger than in many other Nordic Barnahus models; however, in Iceland, the Government Agency for Child Protection funds the general operation of Barnahus, employs the Barnahus staff and offers regular training in forensic interviewing and trauma-focused therapy (see appendix).

In Sweden, the Barnahus model is strongly associated with the coordination of parallel investigations (i.e. the pre-trial criminal investigation and the child welfare investigation) where Barnahus can be interpreted as a collaborative arena primarily for the child welfare services and law enforcement (police and prosecutors). Healthcare professionals, on the other hand, are not as central as in several other Nordic Barnahus models. In Sweden, the main role of Barnahus could thus be described as coordinating two parallel investigations with different objectives.

In Norway, the Barnahus model is strongly associated with the police, and in addition, the model is more health care oriented than in several other Nordic Barnahus models, offering support and follow-up by trained therapists. In Norway, the key role could therefore be interpreted as facilitating investigative interviews in a supportive environment. The child welfare services, on the other hand, are more peripheral than in many other Nordic Barnahus models, since they are not formally a part of the collaborative model, even though they can participate when necessary, which is often the case.

In Denmark, the Barnahus model is most strongly connected to the child welfare services, even though the Barnahus also facilitates the police and their child investigative interviews. The main role of Barnahus in Denmark could thus be interpreted as assisting the municipality local child welfare services, which are the responsible and key agency in the Danish model, and through which all cases are channelled.

If we look at some of the autonomous regions, we also see strong connections between Barnahus and the child welfare system. In the Faroe Islands, the Barnahus is an integrated part of the Child Protection Agency, and since spring 2016, the Barnahus in Greenland has become part of a larger Central Advisory Unit under the Ministry of Family, Equality and Social Affairs, which deals with child welfare in all of Greenland (see appendix).

In Iceland, several changes have been made since the start of Barnahus in 1998 and today, which have developed the collaboration within Barnahus in many ways. For example, the practice of explorative interviews, initiated by the local child welfare services, has developed in addition to the (forensic) child investigative interviews. Collaborative work has also developed, from being mostly characterised by direct communication in individual cases between the local child welfare services, the police and the medical professionals, towards strengthening the role of the Barnahus staff as coordinators. This has been materialised by setting up pre-interview conferences between local child welfare services, the police and the forensic interviewer, in connection with the interview with the child, addressing both the criminal and child welfare investigation. Regular consultation meetings in Barnahus have also been practiced since 2016, in order to coordinate and collaborate around complex cases, especially investigations of physical (interpersonal) violence. The collaboration in the Icelandic Barnahus model could be interpreted as moving towards an increasing coordination of both the criminal and the child welfare investigation as well as a strengthening role of the Barnahus staff as coordinators.

It is also evident that there are variations (between but also, to different degrees, within countries) when the Barnahus model is implemented locally, depending on pre-existing structures, regulatory frameworks and cultural, geographical or demographical differences. In Finland, for example, the development of the Barnahus model is connected to pre-existing collaborative structures, such as the Forensic Child and Adolescent Psychiatry Units at the five university hospitals and thus has a strong relationship to healthcare and child investigative interviews by forensic psychologists, although on request by the police.

Concluding Remarks

In relation to the differences in child welfare systems noted above, varying from family service oriented or child protection oriented to a convergence towards more child-focused-oriented systems (Gilbert et al. 2011), there is a need for reflection. The child welfare systems of the Nordic countries have traditionally been seen as family service oriented, but the implementation of the Barnahus model could in one sense be interpreted as part of an ongoing move towards a child protection orientation within Nordic child welfare systems, not least since Barnahus specifically handles cases of suspected child abuse with a strong focus on the suspected crimes and the investigatory processes. For instance, the Norwegian Barnahus model is primarily focused on facilitating (forensic) child investigative interviews in a supportive environment as explained above.

The family service orientation varies between the Nordic Barnahus models, partly due to differences in whether the family as a whole is included or excluded from the target group, or the support and treatment services offered. For example, it varies whether support is given to the closest caregiver accompanying the child to Barnahus (often a non-suspect), in order to be able to handle the situation and take care of the child, or whether treatment is offered to the family as a whole (cf. appendix).

The Barnahus model can also be seen as an indication of a convergence towards more child-focused or child-centred child welfare systems, since both the child-friendly settings and children's participation are central elements of the model. The implementation of Barnahus is an important part of the development towards more child-friendly justice in the Nordic countries and a strengthening of the children's rights perspective; however, the differences between the models, for instance, regarding affiliation, represent different conditions for balancing the interests of the criminal case in relation to the child welfare case. The structural affiliation of Barnahus within the police system, as in Norway, may, for instance, imply that the criminal case has higher priority (cf. Bakketeig, Chap. 13).

Evidently, there are several differences in how the implementation of the Barnahus model has taken shape in various national policy contexts. This leads to different conditions for interagency collaboration as well as more specialised investigation processes to evolve in practice, which the following chapters will elaborate further.

Outline of the Book

Themes and Chapters

The book is divided into four broad themes. The first theme relates to the idea of Barnahus as a *supportive context* for victimised children, which is an important part of the model's basic aim of being a child-friendly service for children. This part addresses the question of whether the Barnahus context and routines are actually experienced as supportive by children and their supportive adults. Kari Stefansen writes in Chap. 2 about the role of the material in staging a child-friendly atmosphere at Barnahus, using data from the Norwegian context. She analyses both professional views and the experiences of children and accompanying adults who have been at Barnahus because of a suspected crime against the child. Ann-Margreth Olsson and Maria Kläfverud from Sweden focus in Chap. 3 on children's understandings of Barnahus and the particularly difficult situation for children of being summoned to Barnahus when their parents or persons close to the parents are suspected of the crime—and thus are not informed about the child's visit to the Barnahus. An important part of offering a supportive context for children in Barnahus is also that the methods and tools for crisis intervention are evidence based. Drawing on a study in Sweden, in Chap. 4 Johanna Thulin and Cecilia Kjellgren introduce and discuss an intervention aimed at both children and parents in families where one or both parents have used physical violence against the child.

Theme II relates to *the (forensic) child investigative interview*. In Chap. 5, Trond Myklebust describes the Nordic model of handling children's testimonies and discusses today's interviewing procedures and the training provided for interviewers. Gunn Astrid Baugerud and Miriam Sinkerud Johnson present a revised version of the NICHD protocol in Chap. 6, which focuses on enhanced socio-emotional support from the interviewers in order to manage children's reluctance to reveal abuse. In Chap. 7, Julia Korkman, Tom Pakkanen and Taina Laajasalo present the framework for specialised university hospital units in Finland, used for investigating suspected crimes against children when requested by the police. Special attention is directed towards the use of forensic psychology expertise and a hypothesis-testing approach in relation to the (forensic) child investigative interview and pre-trial (criminal) investigation. In Chap. 8, Åse Langballe and Tone Davik discuss a new sequential interview model that is tailored to the needs of preschool children when they participate in investigative interviews in Barnahus.

The third theme covers different dimensions of *children's rights* in relation to Barnahus. In Chap. 9, Hrefna Fridriksdottir and Anni G. Haugen present a method for the analysis of interdisciplinary child rights justice systems, which aims to identify international principles and the main challenges in their practical application in handling cases concerning the sexual abuse of children. In Chap. 10, Anna Kaldal, Åsa Landberg, Maria Eriksson and Carl Göran Svedin discuss children's rights to information in a criminal investigation in Barnahus, from a child's rights perspective, according to both international law and Swedish national law. In Chap. 11, Maria Forsman discusses children's legal representatives in Sweden and their role in Barnahus.

The last theme (IV) addresses *professional autonomy and interagency collaboration*. These are core elements in Barnahus as a multi-professional collaborative model with the main aim of facilitating and improving interagency collaboration. As the chapters will show, professional autonomy and collaboration create tensions and challenges in an interagency model, which require balancing. Susanna Johansson relates to the Swedish context and shows in Chap. 12 how Barnahus collaboration spans different regulatory fields and brings together conflicting logics, creating an institutional tension between "justice" and "welfare". Her chapter analyses collaboration in Barnahus in a critical manner, drawing on institutional theory and a three-dimensional concept of power. Elisiv Bakketeig explores the issue of conflicting logics further in Chap. 13 by discussing whether, and how, juridification manifests in the Norwegian Barnahus model using the Swedish Barnahus model as a point of reference. She discusses factors that may stimulate or constrain processes of juridification in the Norwegian model. In Chap. 14, Lene Mosegaard Søbjerg explores how the establishment of Barnahus in Denmark has been perceived by child welfare workers in the local municipalities. More precisely she discusses how the establishment of Barnahus in Denmark affected the capability of child welfare caseworkers to work holistically with abused children and how this relates to Barnahus as an integrated service. Finally, in Chap. 15 Anja Bredal and Kari Stefansen discuss a pilot project in Norway called "project November" which involves adapting the main features of the Barnahus model with the aim of developing integrated services for adult victims of interpersonal violence. They highlight the importance of analysing the local landscape of services before new collaborative models are implemented.

In the concluding chapter, we comment on the contributions in the book and identify key challenges and potentials relating to the Barnahus model, both within a Nordic welfare state context and beyond. We also introduce Barnahus as an emerging organisational field and a corresponding field of research.

Notes

1. Lithuania is one of the Baltic Sea States, and the Council of the Baltic Sea States has received EU funding for a project aimed at promoting child-friendly multidisciplinary and interagency services for child victims of violence and sexual assault (the PROMISE project, www.cbss.org/promise-kick-meeting/).
2. We discuss the latter topic in the concluding chapter in this book.
3. The discussion below is informed by NGO and governmental reports, policy documents and guidelines on international and European levels, as well as commissioned research on the Barnahus model in the early phase after implementation (e.g. Skybak 2004; Diesen 2002; Landberg and Svedin 2013; Save the Children Sweden 2009; Gudbrandsson 2010; Norwegian Ministry of Justice and the Police 2006; Swedish Ministry of Justice 2005; Bakketeig et al. 2012; Stefansen et al. 2012; Åström and Rejmer 2008; Kaldal et al. 2010). The information on the CAC model stems partly from the National Children's Advocacy Center web page and partly from existing research and evaluation studies (see, for example, Wolfteich and Loggins 2007; Cross et al. 2007; Jones et al. 2007; Faller and Palusci 2007; Walsh et al. 2008; Miller and Rubin 2009).
4. In addition, the Nordic Barnahus models have a low threshold for cases in accordance with the definitions of sexual abuse and (interpersonal) violence in the criminal codes of the respective countries. Taken together, this means that the Barnahus model deals with a broader target group than the CAC and handles many cases with a high degree of uncertainty, not least when it comes to evidence for court proceedings.
5. In Sweden, the convention was ratified in 1990 and has since then been transformed through implementation in several areas of law. Today, there is a bill with a suggestion of an incorporation of the convention in Sweden (SOU 2016: 19*Barnkonventionen blir svensk lag*).
6. It is important to note, however, that the system categorisations are quite general descriptions of how the child welfare and criminal justice systems of the Nordic welfare states are designed and meant to work. It does not mean that the systems always work in the intended way. We are currently witnessing examples of "system-failures" within the Nordic countries due to, for instance, economic burdens or case overloads (see, for example, Backe-Hansen et al. 2016).

7. This is not the case in, for example, Belgium or the Netherlands. Note also that in Finland, mandatory reporting directly to the police has been enforced since 2015 in cases of suspected child abuse.

References

Åström, Karsten and Annika Rejmer. 2008. "Det blir nog bättre för barnen..." Slutrapport i utvärderingen av nationell försöksverksamhet med barnahus 2006–2007. Lund: Lund University.

Backe-Hansen, Elisabeth, Ingrid Höjer, Yvonne Sjöblom and Jan Storø. 2013. "Out of home care in Norway and Sweden—Similar and different." *Psychosocial Intervention* 22:193–202.

Backe-Hansen, Elisabeth, Ingrid Smette and Camilla Vislie. Forthcoming 2016. Kunnskapsoppsummering: Vold mot barn og systemsvikt. Report for the governmental committee on violence against children and system failure.

Bakketeig, Elisiv, Mette Berg, Trond Myklebust, and Kari Stefansen. 2012. *Barnehusevalueringen 2012, delrapport 1: Barnehusmodellens implikasjoner for politiets arbeid med fokus på dommeravhør og rettsmedisinsk undersøkelse.* Oslo: PHS Forskning.

Bakketeig, Elisiv. 2000. Rettsapparatet som sosialt system i saker om seksuelle overgrep mot barn. Avhandling levert til graden dr.philos ved Universitetet i Oslo. Oslo: Universitetet i Oslo.

Bakketeig, Elisiv and Lotte T. Bergan. 2013. Om ungdoms medvirking ved plassering i fosterhjem. Fosterhjem for barns behov. Rapport fra et fireårig forskningsprogram, ed. E. Backe-Hansen, Toril Havik and Arne Backer Grønningsæter. NOVA-rapport 16/13, 85–108. Oslo: NOVA.

Blomberg, Helena, Clary Corander, Christian Kroll, Anna Meeuwisse, Roberto Scaramuzzino and Hans Swärd. 2011. "A Nordic model in child welfare?" In: *Social work and child welfare politics. Through Nordic lenses*, ed. Hannele Forsberg and Teppo Kröger, 29–45. Bristol: Policy Press.

Christiansen, Niels Finn, and Pirjo Markkola. 2006. Introduction. In *The Nordic model of welfare: A historical reappraisal*, eds. Niels F. Christiansen, Klaus Petersen, Nils Edling, and Per Haave. Copenhagen: Museum Tusculanum Press.

Council of Europe. 2010. *Guidelines of the Committee of Ministers of the Council of Europe on child-friendly justice.* Strasbourg: Council of Europe Publishing.

Council of Europe Convention on the Protection of Children Against Sexual Exploitation and Sexual Abuse and Explanatory Report. (Lanzarote Convention). 2008. Strasbourg.

Cross, Theodore P., Lisa M. Jones, Wendy A. Walsh, Monique Simone and David Kolko. 2007."Child forensic interviewing in Children's Advocacy Centers: Empirical data on a practical model." *Child Abuse & Neglect* 31: 1031–1052.

Czarniawska, Barbara, and Guje Sevón. 1996. *Translating organizational change*. New York: Walter de Gruyter.

Danelius, Hans. 2015. *Mänskliga rättigheter i europeisk praxis: en kommentar till Europakonventionen om de mänskliga rättigheterna*. Stockholm: Norstedts juridik.

Diesen, Christian. 2002. *Child abuse and adult justice. A comparative study of different European Criminal Justice Systems handling of cases concerning child sexual abuse*. Stockholm: International Save the Children Alliance.

Donzelot, Jacques. 1997. *The policing of families*. London: Johns Hopkins University Press.

Eriksson, Maria. 2012. Participation for children exposed to domestic violence? Social workers' approaches and children's strategies. *European Journal of Social Work* 15 (2): 205–221.

Esping-Andersen, Gøsta. 1990. *The three worlds of welfare capitalism*. Cambridge: Polity Press.

European Union Agency for Fundamental Rights. FRA. 2015. Child-friendly justice—Perspectives and experiences of professionals on children's participation in civil and criminal judicial proceedings in 10 EU Member States.

Faller, Kathleen C.and Vincent J. Palusci. 2007. Children's Advocacy Centers: Do they lead to positive outcomes? *Child Abuse & Neglect* 31: 1021–1029.

Forsberg, Hannele, and Teppo Kröger. 2011. *Social work and child welfare politics. Through Nordic lenses*. Bristol: Policy Press.

Forsman, Maria. 2013. *Rättsliga ingripanden vid föräldrars våld och övergrepp mot barn*. Stockholm: Norstedts Juridik.

Freeman, Michael. 2012. *Law and childhood studies: Current legal issues*. New York: Oxford University Press.

Gilbert, Neil, Nigel Parton and Marit Skivenes. 2011. *Child protection systems. International trends and orientations*. New York: Oxford University Press.

Gilbert, Gilbert. 1997. *Combatting child abuse: International perspectives and trends*. New York: Oxford University Press.

Gudbrandsson, Bragi. 2010."Towards a child-friendly justice and support for child victims of sexual abuse." *Protecting children from sexual violence, a comprehensive approach*. Strasbourg: Council of Europe.

Hacking, Ian. 1999. *The social construction of what?*. Cambridge: Harvard University Press.

Hennum, Ragnhild. 2006. "Dommeravhør og menneskerettigheter – konvensjonspraksis om særlig sårbare vitner." In Festskrift til Carl August Fleischer, ed. Ole Kristian Fauchald, Henning Jakhelln og Aslak Syse. Oslo: Universitetsforlaget.

James, Allison and Alan Prout. 2014 [1990]. *Constructing and reconstructing childhood: Contemporary issues in the sociological study of childhood.* London: Routledge.

Johansson, Susanna. 2011. Rätt, makt och institutionell förändring. En kritisk analys av myndigheters samverkan i barnahus. Diss. Lund: Lund Studies in Sociology of Law 31, Lund University.

Johansson, Susanna. 2012."Diffusion and governance of 'Barnahus' in the Nordic countries: Report from an ongoing project." *Journal of Scandinavian Studies in Criminology and Crime Prevention* 13(1): 69–84.

Jones, Lisa, Theodore P. Cross, Wendy A. Walsh and Monique Simone. 2007. "Do Children's Advocacy Centers improve families' experiences of child sexual abuse investigations?" *Child Abuse & Neglect* 31: 1069–1085.

Kaldal, Anna. 2010. *Parallella processer. En rättsvetenskaplig studie av riskbedömningar i vårdnads- och LVU-mål.* Stockholm: Jure förlag.

Kaldal, Anna, Christian Diesen, Johan Beije and Eva F. Diesen. 2010. Barnahusutredningen 2010. Stockholm: Jure förlag.

Landberg, Åsa and Carl Göran Svedin. 2013. Inuti ett barnahus. En kvalitetsgranskning av 23 svenska verksamheter. Stockholm: Save the Children Sweden.

Leviner, Pernilla. 2011. *Rättsliga dilemman i socialtjänstens barnskyddsarbete.* Stockholm: Jure förlag.

Lorenz, Walter. 1994. *Social work in a changing Europe.* London: Routledge.

Miller and Rubin. 2009. The contribution of Children's Advocacy Centers to felony prosecutions of child sexual abuse. *Child Abuse and Neglect* 33: 12–18.

Norwegian Ministry of Justice and the Police. 2006. Barnas hus. Rapport om etablering av et pilotprosjekt med ny avhørsmodellfor barn som har vært utsatt for overgrep m.m. Oslo: Norwegian Ministry of Justice and the Police.

Ponnert, Lina (ed.). 2015. *Utredningsarbete i den sociala barnavården.* Malmö: Gleerups.

Røvik, Kjell A. 2000. *Moderna organisationer – trender inom organisationstänkandet vid millennieskiftet.* Malmö: Liber.

Røvik, Kjell A. 2016. Knowledge transfer as translation: Review and elements of an instrumental theory. *International Journal of Management Reviews* 18 (3): 290–310.

Sandberg, Kirsten. 2016. "Barns rett til å bli hørt" In Barnekonvensjonen, Barns rettigheter i Norge, eds. Njål Høstmælingen, Elin Saga Kjørholt and Kirsten Sandberg 3 ed., 92–122. Oslo: Universitetsforlaget.

Save the Children Sweden. 2009. *Gemensamma kriterier! Innehållet i ett barnahus i 10 punkter*. Stockholm: Save the Children Sweden.

Skjørten, Kristin, Mona Iren Hauge, Åse Langballe, Jon H. Schultz and Carolina Øverlien. 2016. "Å se det utsatte barnet." I: Barn, vold og traumer. Møter med unge i utsatte livsssituasjoner, eds. C. Øverlien, M.I. Hauge and J.H. Schultz, 93–107. Oslo: Universitetsforlaget.

Skybak, Thale. 2004. Barnas hus - et helhetlig og barnevennlig tilbud til barn som har vært utsatt for seksuelt misbruk. Oslo: Save the Children Norway.

Stefansen, Kari, Tonje Gundersen and Elisiv Bakketeig. 2012. Barnehusevalueringen 2012, delrapport 2. En undersøkelse blant barn og pårørende, samarbeidspartnere, ledere og ansatte. Oslo: NOVA, rapport nr. 9.

Sutorius, Helena, and Anna Kaldal. 2003. *Bevisprövning vid sexualbrott*. Stockholm: Norstedts juridik.

Swedish Ministry of Justice. 2005. Uppdrag att medverka till etablering av flera försöksverksamheter med samverkan under gemensamt tak vid utredningar kring barn som misstänks vara utsatta för allvarliga brott. (Government decision). Stockholm: Swedish Ministry of Justice.

Swedish National Board of Health and Welfare. 2000. *Sexuella övergrepp mot barn. En studie av samarbetet i samrådsgrupper*. Stockholm: Swedish National Board of Health and Welfare.

Swedish National Board of Health and Welfare,Swedish National Police Agency, Swedish Prosecution Authority and Swedish National Board of Forensic Medicine. 2008. Barnahus – försöksverksamhet med samverkan under gemensamt tak vid misstanke om brott mot barn. Stockholm: Swedish National Board of Health and Welfare.

Swedish National Police Agency. 2009. Progress report regarding a government commission to establish common national guidelines for multiagency collaboration in inquires relating to children who may be exposed to crime and standards for national Children's Advocacy Centres. (Official translation). Stockholm: Swedish National Police Agency.

United Nations Committee on the Rights of the Child. 2009. General Comment no. 12 on the right of the child to be heard. CRC/C/GC/12.

United Nations Committee on the Rights of the Child. 2013. General Comment no. 14 on the rights of the child to have his or her best interests taken as a primary consideration. CRC/C/GC/14.

United Nations Economic and Social Council Resolution 2005/20, Guidelines on Justice in Matters Involving Child Victims and Witnesses of Crime. (UN Economic and Social Council Resolution 2005/20).

Walsh, Wendy, Tonya Lippert, Theodore P. Cross, Danielle M. Maurice and Karen S. Davison. 2008. "How long to prosecute child sexual abuse for a community using a children's advocacy center and two comparison communities?" *Child Maltreatment* 13(1): 3–13.

Wolfteich, Paul and Brittany Loggins. 2007. "Evaluation of the Children's Advocacy Center Model: Efficiency, legal and revictimization Outcomes." *Child and Adolescent Social Work Journal* 24(4): 333–352.

Part I

Befriending, Supporting and Treating the Child

2

Child-Friendliness and Diverse Aspects of the Barnahus Model

Kari Stefansen

Introduction

In 2011–2012, I was part of a research team that evaluated the Norwegian Barnahus model (Bakketeig et al. 2012; Stefansen et al. 2012). For the purpose of the evaluation, we visited six Barnahus around the country. While the premises differed somewhat in size, layout and design, we were struck by the general welcoming feel of all the Barnahus. We could sense that great care had been taken to soften the impression of a formal and "adult" space. Furniture would often be bright colours, and there would be pillows and blankets, and soft rugs on the floor. In halls and other common areas, plants and pictures were used for decorative purposes. Some places had stuffed animals sitting around, and there might be a radio on with the sound turned low. Toys, books and a TV set were available in the designated waiting areas, and sometimes, there was a game

K. Stefansen (✉)
Norwegian Social Research, Oslo and Akershus
University College of Applied Sciences, Oslo, Norway
e-mail: kari.stefansen@nova.hioa.no

console and a massage chair. All the Barnahus we visited were clean and tidy, and the furniture and materials seemed to be of high quality. The picture below (Photo 2.1) is an apt illustration.

The nice interiors of the Barnahus are the institutional settings for children's testimony about difficult and possibly traumatising experiences of violence and sexual abuse, which sometimes involve close family members as the perpetrators. Prior to the establishment of Barnahus in Norway, children were summoned to such interviews either at the local police station or courthouse, and few if any special measures were taken to reduce the stress and possibly re-traumatising effect of participating in the legal process (Bakketeig et al. 2012, 121). The Barnahus premises clearly represent a very different physical environment for children's testimony. Against this background, I will highlight and discuss the "aesthetic-spatial support" (cf. Bjørnholt 2014) that the Barnahus locality, layout and design may represent for children and families. What is it meant to communicate, and how do children and their caretakers perceive it?

Part of the background to my analysis relates to discussions at the European level of the importance of child-friendly justice and the role of child-friendly environments in this respect (see Council of Europe

Photo 2.1 Waiting area, Oslo Barnahus.

2010; Kaldal 2015). My aim is to further the scholarly discussion on this topic: What does it mean to provide a child-friendly environment for children's testimony in cases involving violence and sexual abuse? Is child-friendliness related to aesthetics alone or also to other dimensions of the Barnahus activity?

It is worth mentioning here that concern has been voiced about the possible negative consequences of child-friendly aesthetics in Barnahus. In the final report from a comprehensive evaluation of the Swedish Barnahus model, Kaldal and colleagues (Kaldal et al. 2010, 146) concluded that Barnahus premises should be child friendly, but not invite to play and activity. In their opinion, Barnahus is a place for investigations and this should be reflected in the design of the premises: "It is certainly not wrong to make the setting nice and welcoming, but if overstated there is a risk of it being an over-stimulating environment for the child. *The environment should in other words be neutral, preferably warm and caring, but not stimulating for play and fantasy*" (p. 146, my translation, italics in original).

As part of the evaluation of the Norwegian Barnahus model (Bakketeig et al. 2012), lawyers and judges were interviewed. Some of the lawyers voiced concern that the informal atmosphere of the Barnahus in some ways contradicts the formal procedure that the investigative interview represents. Some of the judges expressed similar views. Others, however, took the opposite approach and argued that the Barnahus localities represent "safe environments and (…) a great place to interview children" (quote from Bakketeig et al. 2012, 76, my translation). These differing views suggest that the meaning of child-friendliness within the Barnahus model, and particularly the role of the material, is far from fixed. In my opinion, these differing views make an interesting background for the exploration of the layers of meaning that the material aspect of the Barnahus may hold for children and the professionals who are involved in Barnahus work.

In the following, and to facilitate discussion of the aesthetic-spatial element of child-friendliness, I will present two empirical analyses. First, I will explore how the notion of child-friendliness was articulated in key documents that were produced as part of the process of implementing

Barnahus in Norway. I will then explore the views of children and adult caretakers who have visited Barnahus in Norway as a result of a suspected crime—about the Barnahus idea in general, and the physical environment in particular. I follow the lead of Blundell-Jones (2014) who argues that buildings and interiors do not have fixed meanings, but offer users a framework for interpretation. It follows that different users may read the physical fabric of a space differently. This part of the chapter draws on survey data from children and adult caretakers.

Staging Atmospheres: Articulations of Child-Friendliness in Key Texts[1]

To follow the way that child-friendliness was discussed in the implementation phase of Barnahus in Norway, I have analysed a sample of key texts produced between 2004 and 2010. The sample includes texts written by NGOs, politicians and working groups at both the state level and local level. The documents can be seen as carriers of ideas that circulate in an ongoing discussion about child-friendly justice: What are the needs of victimised children during the legal process and beyond, and how should the Barnahus localities be arranged to accommodate them?

The idea of establishing the Barnahus model in Norway was introduced in a report published in 2004 by Save the Children Norway (Skybak 2004). In the report, the Barnahus model is described as a place that is "(…) child-friendly decorated with a child-oriented atmosphere that creates a sense of security for visiting children" (p. 6). In a later passage, what it means to create a sense of security for children is elaborated further: "(…) the Barnahus will be designed on children's terms with toys, small furniture, children's pictures on the walls, and colour. It will not have an institutional or office feel that makes the child feel insecure and alienated" (p. 15). The inspiration for the proposal was taken from the Barnahus in Iceland. The Icelandic Barnahus is described in the report as "a child-friendly house", and it is emphasised that it is located in an anonymous house in a residential area. According to the report, these surroundings mean that Barnahus is not scary and unfamiliar to children, in the way that public offices, hospitals, police stations and courts can be.

In this report, then, child-friendliness is linked primarily to children's feelings of safety. Safety is further connected to feelings of being in the right place, a place for children, and the presence of children's furniture and toys will communicate this. The suggestion to localise Barnahus outside established institutions follows from this construction of safety. The idea expressed here could be understood as an effort to stage what Edvardsson et al. (2005) define as a "supportive care setting" (related to nursing). They conceptualise supportive care settings as settings where patients are "sensing an atmosphere of ease" which facilitates the experience of being in familiar and safe surroundings. This further entails a feeling of "being seen, acknowledged and cared about" (p. 344).

Following the report from Save the Children, a private member motion for a pilot project with Barnahus in Norway was suggested in Parliament.[2] In the motion, Barnahus is described in a way that clearly links to the Save the Children's report and the core idea about safety, as achieved through "a neutral, child-friendly environment" (p. 2) in which investigative interviews and medical examinations can take place. The word neutral in this context refers to Barnahus as not linked to formal and possibly alienating institutions, such as hospitals, police stations and courts. A child-friendly environment is defined further as a "comfortable, private and child-oriented atmosphere that is secure both in the psychological and physical sense" (p. 3).

The suggestion of a pilot project with Barnahus was discussed in Parliament in March 2005, and the pilot project was recommended.[3] In a comment on the recommendation, the Standing Committee on Justice said that Barnahus should be designed to accommodate children in all age groups, introducing the idea that child-friendliness is age related. The committee also endorsed the idea of neutral surroundings as essential for achieving child-friendliness. The opposite view that placing the facility in a residential area and away from other ordinary activities such as shopping, and visits to cafes, restaurants and public offices, could underline the child's situation as special, was not mentioned, Research shows, however, that from the perspective of children and young people, an out-of-town location for special measures may be perceived as strange (cf. Stanley et al. 2016).

In 2006, the Ministry of Justice and the Police published a report from a ministerial working group on the implementation of a pilot project with Barnahus in Norway (Norwegian Ministry of Justice and the Police 2006). The working group endorsed the idea of a neutral location as part of the child-friendly approach, stating that the Barnahus premises should not be associated with either the police or a hospital. "The locale should not be institutional, and they should as far as possible be anonymous. (…) All rooms should be child-friendly and the waiting room should be equipped for children's well-being. Care must be taken to accommodate children in different ages" (p. 48). The report is inconclusive about the question of placing the Barnahus in a house in a residential area.

In this report, the idea of child-friendliness is expanded to children's well-being in a wider sense. The connection of well-being and how the rooms are "equipped" suggests that children's well-being relates to the activities the premises allow and invite, such as play, relaxation, being entertained or distracted from the issue at hand. Toys and equipment are not only important in the concrete sense, but also in the symbolic sense—they communicate to children that they are children and not only victims (see Olsson and Kläferud, Chap. 3).

From 2007, regional working groups were established to implement pilot projects with Barnahus at seven locations throughout the country. I have looked at the reports from such working groups and particularly the reports from Bergen (2007) and Oslo (2010). The Bergen report was the very first and therefore influential for later reports, and the Oslo report is interesting because it is the most elaborate in terms of discussions about the aesthetic-spatial environment. It also sets the bar high for the material aspect of child-friendliness within the Barnahus model, as I will explain later.

The Bergen report draws on the governmental report in many respects. It states that Barnahus should not be placed in a police station or hospital. It links child-friendliness to "calm surroundings" (p. 15) and mentions special waiting areas equipped for younger children and teenagers, respectively. This report is the first to link child-friendliness to the layout of the Barnahus interiors, the placing of rooms with different functions in relation to each other. It states, for instance, that the co-hearing room, the room where the judge and other involved agencies watch the investigative interview via direct video link, should not be placed next to the interview room. In this way, the child will not have to meet all the professionals involved in a Barnahus case prior to the interview. Another theme introduced in this report is the size of the interview room. It should not be too big. The thought behind this is that a small room feels more secure for the child and leads to less distraction. The interview rooms should also accommodate children of different age groups—a statement that also links child-friendliness to age appropriateness in the interview setting. This seems to have become the standard view in Norway. It is common in Norwegian Barnahus to have different interview rooms for young and older children. In interview rooms for the youngest children, the furniture is small and designed for children below school age, while the interview rooms for older children will have "normal" furniture, as illustrated in the pictures below (Photos 2.2 and 2.3).

The sparse decoration of the interview rooms in the pictures above is not mentioned in the working group reports, but is something we see in Barnahus in Norway. The child-friendly décor is reserved for

Photo 2.2 Investigative interview room for young children at Sandefjord Barnahus (picture by author)

Photo 2.3 Investigative interview room for older children at Oslo Barnahus.

waiting areas, kitchen, halls and the medical examination room. This use of décor is instructional for the child and suggests that different rooms have different purposes, something children seem to understand (cf. Olsson and Kläferud, Chap. 3). Interestingly, in theories of the therapeutic effect of buildings and interiors, the level of instruction that is built into, for instance, an institution such as a hospital is foregrounded as an important dimension for patient's well-being (Gesler et al. 2004).

In the Oslo report, elements such as light, sound and air quality are introduced, which further broadens the idea of child-friendliness within the Barnahus context. The locale should not only be neutral, accessible, suitable for children of different ages and generally child friendly, but also "bright", able to be soundproofed and have a good air ventilation. These elements add to the list of criteria for child-friendliness and set a high physical standard for Barnahus localities. The report also introduces suggestions from a professional interior decorator who was commissioned to suggest a design concept for Oslo Barnahus. This is an example of a professionalisation of the process of making the Barnahus localities child friendly, as the quote below illustrates:

> All painted planes have light colours and fabrics for chairs are chosen according to a holistic plan for the locale. Desks and bureaus are either

> white or birch and the fabrics are one-colored in blue and green tones. Emphasis is put on creating nice and friendly locations – something which is reflected in pictures and carpets (Oslo Police District 2010, 90).

What is also evident here and in the concrete implementation of Barnahus in Norway is that child-friendliness in time came to mean a child-friendly layout and interiors, and that the idea of establishing Barnahus as a separate house in a residential area was abandoned. Child-friendliness became an issue to be solved within mostly office buildings. In an analysis of the relationship between architecture and pedagogy in Waldorf education, Bjørnholt (2014) discusses how child-centeredness can be achieved through the manipulation of the physical environment and asks whether "the act of modifying and transcending the limitations of the given building structures may be as important as the architecture" (p. 120). The same question could be asked in relation to Barnahus.

In summary, aesthetic-spatial considerations were high on the agenda throughout the process of establishing the Barnahus model in Norway. The idea of the aesthetic-spatial dimension of child-friendliness that was launched in the early texts about Barnahus was linked to safety as a primary need for children who have been victimised. Safety was furthermore understood as linked to a feeling of being welcome as a child, and not a victim, hence the weight put on toys, décor and equipment that invites children to play or relax. One of the key ideas was also that any association with a formal institution—either police or hospital—would compromise the atmosphere of safety.

The concept of atmospheres is difficult to define, but can be understood as "a sensuous 'something' that takes place between things and people. Atmospheres may be ontologically difficult to grasp or contain, yet they play an important role in ordering spaces and social life" (Bille 2015, 257). The concept of making or "staging atmospheres" (Bille 2015; Bille et al. 2015; Böhme 2013) through locality and symbolic décor captures the thinking about child-friendliness in the texts referred to above. Staging atmospheres relates to "how people actively try to shape experiences and moods of selves and others through organizing objects, bodies and spaces" (Bille et al. 2015, 33).

In the key texts referenced above, there is no mention of children's voices. The ideas of child-friendliness that are discussed are all articulated by adults. The Barnahus is thus not an "invited space" in the sense that Gaventa (2006) writes about it, meaning a space that service users are invited to co-create by those in authority (see also Stanley et al. 2016). A key question is whether the thoughtful staging or orchestration of child-friendliness in the Norwegian Barnahus works—in the sense that children and accompanying caretakers feel welcomed, seen and cared for, key features of "supportive care settings" (Edvardsson et al. 2005).

Perceived Atmospheres: Children and Caretaker Experiences of Barnahus[4]

How do children and accompanying caretakers experience a day at the Barnahus, the atmosphere and the premises? Do they feel seen, welcome and safe? To explore these questions, I will draw on two surveys from 2012 conducted among children (aged 10 years+) and caretakers who visited six different Barnahus in Norway over a 2-month period. A total of 123 children and 198 accompanying adults answered questionnaires, setting the response rates at 62 and 69%, respectively.[5]

The questionnaires included questions about the day at the Barnahus, how the child and caretaker were guided through the process with the investigative interview, medical examination and the subsequent consultation with the Barnahus staff. We included questions about the investigative interview and medical examination, and about the waiting area, but refrained from asking about the child's experience with violence or sexual abuse. Most questions had fixed answers, but we also included some open-ended questions where the participants could write their answers in their own words. In the results section, we will present patterns related to both types of questions.

As I will explain in the following, children who visit Barnahus generally appreciate the atmosphere of the place, and the physical environment seems to play a key part in their positive evaluation (see also Rasmusson 2011).

It is important to take into account that for most children and caretakers, Barnahus is an unfamiliar place: they have not been there before and very few have talked with the police prior to the visit. Given the reason for the Barnahus visit, it is not surprising that children are anxious before the visit. In the survey, close to 60% of both children and parents indicated that they had been anxious (stated "yes, very" or "yes, somewhat" to a question about anxiety). Cross-tabulation of the answers by parents and the child's age revealed that it was more common for children aged 10 years or older (77%) to be anxious compared to younger children (43%).

We asked the children to describe in their own words why they were anxious. Almost half of the children ($n = 51$) replied. Most answers fell into three broad categories: The majority answered that they were anxious about talking about what had happened and about talking to the police, some wrote about being afraid to say something wrong and that they feared the response from the police, and some wrote about not knowing what to expect from the day at the Barnahus. Here are some typical quotes from the latter category:

- I thought it would be scary there (Boy, 10–12 years).
- I had not been here before (Girl, 10–12 years).
- I did not know what they would ask me (Girl, 13–15 years).

The insecurity that the children conveyed in these answers is an apt reminder of the need to create a safe and welcoming space at the Barnahus. The children's and caretakers' answers to the questionnaire as a whole suggest that their stay was better than the children feared. In the direct question about this issue, the majority of both children (66%) and caretakers (52%) indicated that the stay at the Barnahus had been better than expected and very few indicated that the stay had been worse (4% children, 3% caretakers). Among the children, 30% answered that the stay had been as they expected. The corresponding number of caretakers was 45%.

We also asked the children to explain in their own words what they thought about the Barnahus overall. Their answers suggest that children's feeling of safety relates to the child-friendliness of the Barnahus model in a broad sense, and that the aesthetical-spatial dimension is an integral part of this.

At the very end of the questionnaire, the children were encouraged to write a general comment: "Here you can describe what you think about the Barnahus all in all." Close to two-thirds of the children ($n = 78$) wrote a comment. A few were negative and some communicated that they thought that the Barnahus was ok—perhaps taking a neutral position. The majority of answers, however, were positive. Three themes emerged among the positive answers. A first theme related to the staff at the Barnahus and their approach to the children:

- I think it is a good place to talk about the experience and there were really nice people there (Girl, 13–15 years).
- Really good people. They really do everything to help you! (Girl, 13–15 years).

A second theme relates to the Barnahus model as a good idea for children in their situation and a good place to be:

- I think it is a really good house (Boy, 10–12 years).
- I think it is good what you do here (Boy, 16–18 years).
- The Barnahus is a good place for children who want to talk about how they feel (Girl, 10–12).

A third theme relates to the locale and the possibilities for both relaxation and activity:

- I like the Barnahus because it is nice there. Nice and decorated rooms (Boy, 13–15 years).
- That it is a nice and calm place. I also think the staff here is nice ☺ (Girl, 10–12 years).
- I liked the toys (Boy, 10–12 years).
- It is good to have food and drinks and activities while you wait (Boy, 13–15 years).

The three themes were represented at all the Barnahus in the study, which suggests that even where there are differences in routines, decoration and qualifications among the Barnahus (Stefansen et al. 2012), they all managed to convey child-friendliness to visiting children. This also suggests that children's sense of an "atmosphere of ease" (Edvardsson et al. 2005) at the Barnahus, while connected to the actual layout or décor, routines, food and drinks, toys and so on, also, or perhaps mostly, relates to the effort they sense has been taken to "soften" the experience of meeting the police and talking about very difficult experiences.

The most concrete expression of the effort that they sense has been made is perhaps the waiting room area. We asked both children and adults caretakers to indicate whether they liked the waiting room or not. More than half of the children (53%) and two-thirds of the caretakers (65%) answered yes, very much. Very few, and only children, indicated that they did not like it (6%). Cross-tabulation showed that adults who accompanied younger children were more positive than adults who accompanied older children. This accords with Rasmussen's (2008) qualitative study of Swedish Barnahus. Rasmussen interviewed 12 children of different ages, and some of the teenagers said that the Barnahus was equipped mainly for younger children; it felt childish. The children who participated in our study were asked to describe why they liked the waiting area or not. Three-quarters ($n = 92$) answered the question. A large majority described what they liked about the premises. Rasmussen's finding that teenagers felt that the Barnahus was too childish was not dominant in our sample. Only a few children voiced this opinion. Some older children even said that they valued the fact that the premises were suitable for younger children (also):

- The waiting room was nicely decorated, and young children would feel comfortable there. The woman who worked there was nice and easy to talk to. The room had a good energy, and it was not so big, so that the client feels safer (Girl, 13–15 years).

The remaining answers can be sorted into three broad categories: one typical answer was that the waiting area was nice and cosy. I take this to refer to the general feel or atmosphere of the room:

- It was big and nice and that is why I like the waiting room (Boy, 13–15).
- It is nice and very well suited and consoling for children who are struggling a bit (Girl, 13–15).
- It has nice furniture, drinks and a lot of cookies. Really cosy here! There is nothing negative about this room (Girl, 13–15 years).

Another typical answer related to the fact that children could do things in the waiting room—they did not have to sit passively and wait:

- There was a lot of toys here and that was nice. It's lots of things to do (Girl, 10–12 years).
- I like the waiting room because there are lots of fun things to do here, for instance play Wii, or relax (Boy, 10–12 years).
- You can do a lot here. I wish my room was like this! (Girl, 10–12 years).

A third quality that the children appreciated was the ability to relax in the waiting area.

- It is nice here, and there are no kids here so it is nice because it is mostly quiet. And I have relaxed and it was good so I really had a good time in the waiting room (Girl, 10–12 years).
- I liked the waiting room because of the [massage] chair. It was really good to sit in it while I relaxed and some of the people who work here talked to my mum so I sat in the chair (Girl, 10–12 years).

Referring to Rasmussen's (2008) study, Åström and Rejmer (2008) argue that children's responses in interviews suggest that they appreciate and notice the colours, toys and furnishing at the Barnahus. From the perspective of the children who participated in the survey on Norwegian Barnahus, child-friendliness is also connected to the activities that the waiting area invites and the choice between relaxation and play or entertainment. These possibilities are important in both the concrete and symbolic sense; they offer children a sense of agency and they can choose the level of activity that suits them in the situation.

In summary, children and caretakers see the Barnahus premises as welcoming and consoling in a difficult situation. They sense an "atmosphere of ease" (Edvardsson et al. 2005) at the Barnahus—across differences between Barnahus in actual layout, design and routines from the staff. The feel of the space seems to calm or distract the children, who in many cases are anxious about meeting the police and talk about their experiences with violence or sexual abuse.

The aesthetic-spatial dimension can be analytically separated as a core dimension of child-friendliness, but on the level of experience, this dimension blends in with the holistic approach to child-friendliness that also includes welcoming routines, the routines for the stay and the meeting with the police interviewer and other professionals at the Barnahus. Children's experiences point to how "place is constructed through relationships between people as well as through the physical environment" (Stanley et al. 2016, 86).

Concluding Thoughts

Barnahus was introduced in Norway as a means to support child victims of violence and sexual abuse during the legal process and to make sure that children's needs for psycho-social support and treatment were met. In the documents I have analysed, the importance of child-friendly premises is linked primarily to Barnahus as the institutional setting for the legal process. How child-friendliness could be achieved in the Barnahus setting was high on the agenda in the implementation process and revolved around the intent to create a child-friendly atmosphere where children can feel safe because they are seen as children and not (only) as victims of violence or sexual abuse. As the discussion proceeded, the idea of child-friendliness evolved to encompass the quality of the building, colour schemes and layout of the locale. Survey data from children and caretakers who had visited Barnahus as the result of a suspected crime show that the Barnahus premises is understood as welcoming and caretaking—and thus as child friendly. The analysis suggests that this is possible to achieve when Barnahus is placed in various types of office buildings and not conditioned on placement in residential areas as some of the key actors involved in the early discussions argued. Rather, the décor, layout and the interior design and physical quality of the premises transcend the institutional feel of such buildings (cf. Bjørnholt 2014): children understand and appreciate the care that has been taken to make sure that they feel welcome and seen. Drawing on Kolstad's (2001) reflections on the role of beautiful environments, it is possible to argue that the Barnahus setting may increase children's self-esteem, that they feel more valuable because they can identify with the environment they are offered (see also Cold 2003). The careful orchestrating of the Barnahus setting to accommodate children's needs can also be seen as a recognition of people's sensitivity to minor details when they are put in a vulnerable situation (Cold 2015). In this sense, the child-friendliness that permeates the material context of the Barnahus setting in Norway mirrors an idea by the Finnish architect Alvar Aalto, as presented by Pallasmaa (2001), that good design takes people at their most vulnerable as a starting point.

The child-friendly atmosphere of the Barnahus model is not linked to the aesthetic-spatial dimension alone, but is multidimensional (cf. Stanley et al. 2016). It is linked to the way the Barnahus staff behaves, how the day is organised and framed, as well as the layout and aesthetics of the premises, particularly the waiting area. One suggestion is that these dimensions combine to what Holopainen et al. (2014) talk about as a caring encounter (in nursing). They define a caring encounter as a "space of togetherness" based on recognition. One idea then is that a child-friendly environment is a necessary, but not sufficient factor for such a "space of togetherness" to emerge. One important role of the aesthetic-spatial dimension in creating a child-friendly atmosphere within the Barnahus involves how it influences the staff and other professionals that are involved in Barnahus work: the child-friendly environment is a constant reminder for the adults that Barnahus is a place where it is especially important to support the well-being of children. This could perhaps be thought of as a mediated effect of the child-friendly layout and décor: it works through the staff as well as directly on the children. Stanley et al. (2016) point to the same in a study on independent social work organisations that deliver services to children in out-of-home care and their families, claiming that

> the environment and location of social work services are relevant both for staff and for those who receive services, shaping service perceptions and perceptions of self as well as impacting on communication and relationships between practitioners and children and families (Stanley et al. 2016, 86–87).

My aim for this chapter was to enhance the understanding of the role of the material in achieving a child-friendly atmosphere in the Barnahus setting. The analysis has shown that child-friendliness related to the material can be understood at both a surface and a more extensive level comprising the material quality and layout of the premises in addition to child-friendly décor and artefacts. In the Norwegian Barnahus, child-friendliness related to the material is understood in the latter meaning, as something more than having toys and games available. To achieve and maintain child-friendliness in this meaning is a demanding and quite costly task. The expanded idea of child-friendliness that the Norwegian Barnahus represent in a sense reflects the willingness of the state to provide the necessary resources in the process of implementing Barnahus in Norway, and perhaps also shared cultural norms relating to material standards in the Norwegian or Nordic setting. I would argue that there is a general expectance that material standards should be high in public institutions, such as kindergartens, schools and hospitals. Neumann's (2012) work on the experiences of female prisoners regarding the material aspect of prisons is a relevant reference here. A key point in her analysis is that the meanings of the material aspects of an institution relate to the general material conditions in the specific society. Differences in material conditions in different societies may thus have an effect on how children experience the Barnahus environment. Translated to the Barnahus field, and following Neumann's argument, I would caution against a fixed template for child-friendly environments in Barnahus. I hope, however, to have demonstrated the importance of thinking about the meaning of child-friendliness related to the material environment and of allocating resources to this end.

Afterword

During my writing of this chapter, I presented an early version for my research group at NOVA. In the discussion, my colleague Svein Mossige, who is a clinical psychologist, talked about the most important institution for child psychiatry in Norway, Nic Waal's Institute, and explained that it is set in a building from the 1960s, meant to be child-friendly. I was curious about the thinking that had inspired the building and searched for books and articles about the institute. The thinking related to Nic Waal's Institute as presented in these texts makes an interesting parallel and contrast to the thinking about the aesthetic-spatial dimension of child-friendliness related to the Barnahus model. I include a brief introduction to it, also as a reminder of the value of the historical perspective in the exploration of present-day ideas of child-friendliness.

The institute and its founder, Nic Waal, played key roles in the development of child psychiatry as a professional field in Norway from the 1950s and onward (Ludvigsen and Seip 2009). The concrete building that houses the institute is placed on a large detached plot near the city centre and was drawn by architects Lund and Slaatto in 1968 (see Grønvold 1988, 213–217 for pictures and drawings). A key idea behind the building was to recreate some of the mysteries of children's play, writes Nic Waal's son, Helge Waal, in a biography about his mother (Waal 1991). Moe (2003) has also pointed out how the structure of the building, with a central atrium and adjacent towers for treatment rooms, was meant to facilitate a non-institutional feel (see also Grønvold 1988, 213), and also how the high placement of windows throughout the building is linked to ideas of sheltering: the outside world should be kept at a distance to avoid noise and distraction and allow for reflection and dialogue. While there are similarities in the weight put on child-friendliness between Nic Waal's Institute and the Barnahus model, how child-friendliness should be achieved is understood very differently. In Nic Waal's Institute, child-friendliness is linked to the structure of the building, the placement and size of windows and the dimensions of key architectural forms such as the cube (Grønvold 1988, 146), and not to the interior design, as it is in the Barnahus model.

Interestingly, the structure of the building was also meant to support multi-professional teamwork, a foundational element of the work model at the institute in the first decades (Grønvold 1988; Waal 1958). The idea of the building or locale as a facilitator for multi-professional teamwork is to my knowledge not mentioned in writings about the spatial elements of the Barnahus model. This is somewhat surprising given that Barnahus is essentially a model for collaboration between different professions and agencies. Perhaps, this chapter could also inspire discussion of the role of the material environment for professional work within the Barnahus model.

Notes

1. All quotes translated by author from the Norwegian language.
2. Private member motion: Dok 8:86, 2003–2004.
3. Recommendation to Parliament from the Standing Committee on Justice: Innst. St. nr. 123, 2004–2005.
4. Original analyses were presented in Stefansen et al. (2012), in Norwegian.
5. There were more girls (57%) than boys (43%) among the children. The accompanying adult was usually the mother or other relative (62%).

Acknowledgement I am indebted to Margunn Bjørnholt, Ingrid Smette, Susanna Johansson and my colleagues in the Domestic Violence Research Programme at NOVA for inspiring discussions and valuable suggestions on how to improve this chapter.

References

Åström, Karsten and Annika Rejmer. 2008. *Det blir nog bättre för barnen. Slutrapport i utvärderingen av nationell försöksverksamhet med barnahus 2006–2007.* Lund: Lund University.

Bakketeig, Elisiv, Mette Berg, Trond Myklebust, and Kari Stefansen. 2012. *Barnehusevalueringen 2012, delrapport 1: Barnehusmodellens implikasjoner for politiets arbeid med fokus på dommeravhør og rettsmedisinsk undersøkelse.* Oslo: PHS Forskning.

Bergen Police District. 2007. *Barnehuset region vest.* Bergen Police District: Rapport fra planleggingsgruppen. Bergen.

Bille, Mikkel. 2015. Hazy Worlds: Atmospheric Ontologies in Denmark. *Anthropological Theory* 15 (3): 257–274.

Bille, Mikkel, Peter Bjerregaard, and Tim F. Sørensen. 2015. Staging Atmospheres: Materiality, Culture, and the Texture of the in-Between. *Emotion Space and Society* 15: 31–38.

Bjørnholt, Margunn. 2014. Room for Thinking—The Spatial Dimension of Waldorf Education. *RoSE–Research on Steiner Education* 5 (1): 115–130.

Blundell-Jones, Peter. 2014. Foreword. In *Kindergarten Architecture. Space for Imagination*, ed. Mark Dudek, vi–x. London: Taylor & Francis.

Böhme, Gernot. 2013. The art of the stage set as a paradigm for an aesthetics of atmospheres.*Ambiances. International Journal of Sensory Environment, Architecture and Urban Space.* [Online], http://ambiances.revues.org/315.

Cold, Birgit. 2003. *Skoleanlegget som lesebok—synteserapport og fem delrapporter.* Trondheim: NTNU, Fakultetet for arkitektur og billedkunst.

Cold, Birgit. 2015. Estetikk, velvære og helse. In *Interiørarkitektur* ed. Ellen S. Klingenberg, 192–209. Oslo: Scandinavian Academic Press.

Council of Europe. 2010. *Guidelines of the Committee of Ministers of the Council of Europe on Child-friendly Justice.* Council of Europe.

Edvardsson, David, Per-Olof Sandman and Birgit H. Rasmussen. 2005. Sensing an Atmosphere of Ease: A Tentative Theory of Supportive Care Settings. *Scandinavian Journal of Caring Sciences* 19 (4): 344–353.

Gaventa, John. 2006. Finding the Spaces for Change: A Power Analysis. *IDS Bulletin* 37(6): 23–33.

Gesler, Will, Morag Bell, Sarah Curtis, Phil Hubbard and Susan Francis. 2004. Therapy by Design: Evaluating the UK hospital Building Program. *Health & Place* 10 (2): 117–128.

Grønvold, Ulf. 1988. *Lund & Slaatto.* Oslo: Universitetsforlaget.

Holopainen, Gunilla, and Anne Kasénand Lisbet Nyström. 2014. The Space of Togetherness–A Caring Encounter. *Scandinavian Journal of Caring Sciences* 28 (1): 186–192.

Kaldal, Anna. 2015. *Child Evidence. A Comparative Study on Handling, Protecting and Testing Evidence from Children in Legal Proceedings Within States in the Baltic Sea Region. Report Prepared for Council of Europe.* Strasbourg: Council of Europe.

Kaldal, Anna, Johan Beije, Eva F. Diesenand, and Christian Diesen. 2010. *Barnahusutredningen 2010.* Stockholm: Jure.

Kolstad, Arnulf. 2001. What Happens if Celeste Becomes an Architect? In *Aesthetics, Well Being and Health. Essays Within Architecture and Environmental Aesthetics* ed. Birgit Cold, 117–128. London: Ashgate.

Ludvigsen, Kari and Åsmund A. Seip. 2009. The Establishing of Norwegian Child Psychiatry: Ideas, Pioneers and Institutions. *History of Psychiatry* 20(1): 5–26.

Moe, Einar. 2003. *Nic Waals Institutt. Pioner og aktør i norsk barne-og ungdomspsykiatri gjennom 50 år*. Oslo: Nic Waals Institutt.

Neuman, Cecilie B. 2012. Imprisoning the Soul. In *Penal Exceptionalism? Nordic Prison Policy and Practice*, ed. Thomas Ugelvik and Jane Dullum, 139–155. London: Routledge.

Norwegian Ministry of Justice and the Police. 2006. *Barnas hus. Rapport om etablering av et pilotprosjekt med ny avhørsmodellfor barn som har vært utsatt for overgrep m.m.* Oslo: Norwegian Ministry of Justice and the Police.

Oslo Police District. 2010. *Sluttrapport Etablering av Barnehuset Oslo*. Oslo: Oslo Police District.

Pallasmaa, Juhani. 2001. The Mind of the Environment. In *Aesthetics, Well-Being and Health—Essays on Architecture and Environmental Aesthetics*, ed. Birgit Cold, 203–220. London: Ashgate.

Rasmussen, Bodil. 2008. *Det är ju inget dagis precis … Barns och föräldrars upplevelser av kontakter med barnahus. Delrapport 6 i utvärderingen av nationell försöksverksamhet med barnahus 2006–2007*. Lund: Lund University.

Rasmusson, Bodil. 2011. Children's Advocacy Centers (Barnahus) in Sweden. *Child Indicators Research* 4 (2): 301–321.

Skybak, Thale. 2004. *Barnas hus—et helhetlig og barnevennlig tilbud til barn som har vært utsatt for seksuelt misbruk*. Oslo: Redd Barna.

Stanley, Nicky, Cath Larkins, Helen Austerberry, Nicola Farrelly, Jill Manthorpe, and Julie Ridley. 2016. Rethinking Place and the Social Work Office in the Delivery of Children's Social Work Services. *Health & Social Care in the Community* 24 (1): 86–94.

Stefansen, Kari, Tonje Gundersen and Elisiv Bakketeig. 2012. *Barnehusevalueringen 2012, delrapport 2. En undersøkelse blant barn og pårørende, samarbeidspartnere, ledere og ansatte*. Oslo: NOVA.

Waal, Helge. 1991. *Nic Waal Det urolige hjertet*. Oslo: Pax Forlag.

Waal, Nic. 1958. Teamwork. In *Utvalgte faglige skrifter Dr. Nic Waal*, ed. Anne-Marie Auestad, and Borger Haavardsholm. Oslo: Nic Waals institutt.

3

Children's Perspectives on Going to Barnahus

Ann-Margreth E. Olsson and Maria Kläfverud

Introduction

This chapter explores children's perspectives on the institution of Barnahus and being summoned to a Barnahus in Sweden. The starting point for the chapter is a child's right to express their views and to be heard in all matters affecting them (cf. Alderson 2010; Barnombudsmannen 2007; Röbäck and Höjer 2009). Like adults, children have concerns and strategies of their own to help them cope with situations, which are important to identify and recognise (Brannen et al. 2000; Dencik and Jørgensen Schultz 1999; Qvortrup 1999; Lansdown 2010). In order to understand the world from children's point of view, researchers, as well as professionals

A.-M.E. Olsson (✉)
Kristianstad University, Kristianstad, Sweden
e-mail: ann-margreth.olsson@hkr.se

M. Kläfverud
Kristianstad University and Lund University,
Kristianstad and Lund, Sweden
e-mail: maria.klafverud@hkr.se

working in child welfare, need to be invited into children's life worlds and listen to how children explain and understand their experiences (Bell 2002; Olsson 2010; Sandbæk 1999). To capture children's understanding of Barnahus and of being summoned to Barnahus, we have interviewed children who have had these experiences and we have listened to and explored their narratives about being summoned to and visiting a Barnahus. Researchers have referred to this approach as research *with* children, rather than research about children (cf. Christensen and James 2008; Powell and Smith 2009). The children's narratives will be analysed, and in line with Bateson (1998), we will look for patterns, but also unique examples in the interviews, in order to capture participating children's understanding of Barnahus and of the emerging interaction, as well as why they were summoned to Barnahus.

The data that inform this chapter originate from an empirical study entitled 'Children in Barnahus: an interdisciplinary study into child perspectives'. The main study is a comprehensive systemic and dialogical participatory action research project (Olsson 2014a, b) approved by the Regional Ethics Board in Lund (dnr 2011/756; dnr 2014/84). A key focus in the project is exploring in dialogical interplay the meaning of the concept 'child perspectives' in use in the context of Barnahus and how the meaning is co-constructed (cf. Anderson 1999; Holland 2009; Olsson 2010; Shotter 2009). In this chapter, however, the aim is to make children's own voices heard, capturing 'children's perspectives' about being summoned to, arriving at and visiting Barnahus. The concept 'children's perspectives' is here used in the meaning of representing the voices of children, as *distinguished* from 'child perspectives' which here is used as an adult focus on the understanding that children have of experiences and actions (Halldén 2003; Sommer et al. 2011). The analysis is thus focused on the former, and on the children as acting subjects in their own life world, and making their voices heard.

Routines in Swedish Barnahus

A key purpose of Barnahus in Sweden is to improve the investigations and the collaboration of agencies involved in protecting children who might be victims of crimes of violence and abuse (Landberg and Svedin 2013).

Children are summoned to Barnahus for the purpose of a criminal investigation and to find out if they are in need of protection, and if so, to provide immediate support (Swedish National Police Board 2009). The collaborating agencies (police, public prosecution, forensic medicine, paediatrics, child psychiatry and child welfare services) are expected to put the children's rights into practice (Swedish National Police Board 2008; Johansson 2012; Rasmusson 2011).

A key question in the chapter is how children understand the meaning of the Barnahus institution. As a background to the children's statements, we briefly explain how a day at Barnahus is organised.

Arriving at Barnahus, the child and the accompanying person(s) are directed to a waiting room. The child investigative interview with the police takes place in a separate room with video cameras connected to a computer or TV screen in the co-hearing room. In this room, the prosecutor and the special representative for children are watching. With consideration of the child's perspectives and to be able to coordinate parallel ongoing investigations—criminal, social and medical—the prosecutor can decide to give the child welfare caseworker, a paediatrician and/or somebody from the child psychiatry services the right to be present in the co-hearing room (Swedish Prosecution Authority 2016). The objective of a joint interview is to protect children from unnecessarily telling their stories repeatedly to different persons in different places (Rasmusson 2011). After the interview, the child returns to the waiting room where accompanying persons (see below) are waiting. When the child welfare caseworkers decide that the child does not need immediate protection or support, the child leaves the Barnahus with their accompanying person(s). Otherwise, the children have to stay in the waiting room, while child welfare caseworkers take the necessary measures to protect and provide further support to the children.

Children visiting Barnahus are often accompanied by their parents (Kaldal et al. 2010); however, in cases where a custodian or someone with whom the custodian has a close relationship, is suspected of the crime, the child will be summoned to Barnahus without the knowledge or consent of the custodians (usually the parents, so henceforth in the chapter custodians are called parents). District courts can decide to temporarily remove and transfer custody rights to a special representative for children ('särskild företrädare', see Chap. 11 for further information about the special representative), usually a lawyer, who has the right to decide how the child should be summoned and about the child's participation in the interviews (Swedish Prosecution Authority 2016). In such cases, the child is approached outside of home, usually at kindergarten or at school. At the request of the special representative for the child, a person the child trusts (a safety person, 'trygghetsperson') asks the child to follow the safety person and the child's special representative to the Barnahus. The safety person accompanies the child to and from the Barnahus and stays there during the interviews (Landberg and Svedin 2013). Against this background, one issue explored in this chapter is children's experiences of being summoned and brought to Barnahus without the knowledge and presence of their parents.

Methods

The study was conducted at one Barnahus. Because children who are in contact with Barnahus often are in a vulnerable position (Rasmusson 2011), a key concern in the study was how children's participation and need for protection could be balanced (cf. Alderson 2010; Ost 2013). In consultation with the executive group of the Barnahus, including representatives from the collaborating agencies, it was decided that the Barnahus coordinator and the child welfare caseworkers were in the best positions to assess a convenient time in the investigation process for a research intervention, and when to ask children and parents if they wanted to participate. When parents and a child had agreed to participate, the researchers took over and obtained informed consent from both the custodians and the child. Eight children were interviewed in person: three children (girls) 6–8 years old and five children (two boys and three girls) 14–15 years old. In dialogue with the participating child, the interviewing researcher phrased questions based on an interview guide, and then followed up according to the responses, using so-called listening questions (cf. Olsson 2010). The interviews were recorded and transcribed by the interviewing researcher.

The data were subjected to thematic analysis, a method for identifying and reporting patterns within qualitative data that emphasise the content of what is being said (Katz 2013). Two main themes were identified in this process (1) children's understanding of Barnahus, and (2) children's experiences of being summoned without their parent's knowledge and presence. It is not possible to fully enter somebody else's lifeworld, but we can obtain glimpses into one another's social worlds through communication and dialogue (cf. Gergen 2009; Johansson 2003; Shotter 2009). Quotations and excerpts from the interviews are used to suggest how the children expressed themselves when inviting us into their world (cf. Kohler Riessman 1990). It should be noted that the translation from Swedish to English may slightly change the impression of their utterances.

Barnahus from Children's Perspectives: A House of Police

The children at first felt being summoned to Barnahus as something unpleasant. They became worried and felt uncomfortable. The invitation and accompanying persons gave them very little information. Parents and safety persons were often not familiar with Barnahus, and the others present when children were summoned, child welfare caseworkers and special representatives for children, did not seem to want to say much. The children felt that their questions were not answered.

> I could ask questions but I did not get much of an answer. They could answer: 'You have to wait and see' or 'You have to ask the person we will meet there'. (Sara 14 yrs)

Feelings of fear, nervousness and anxiety emerged for the children. As time went on, they understood that it was the police they were going to meet. In the view of the children, Barnahus now became a 'House of Police' [polishus], an impression they retained: this was a place to meet and talk with the police about serious matters.

Without being informed about why they were summoned, the children did not know what kind of meeting they were approaching or who was in trouble. Had something happened to somebody in their families? Was the child accused of something? Was the child going to be approached as a witness or victim?

> I was a little bit nervous or whatever you can say about it, because I didn't know what was going to happen. What if I had done something? What ever has happened causing this? (Sara 14 yrs)

Arriving at Barnahus, the children became both surprised and confused. The police who welcomed them did not wear a uniform, nor did the house look like a police station, rather quite nice and welcoming. Kajsa, 8 years old, remembers a house with brown bricks with a door with a name plate full of colours, a rainbow. At the entrance, there were steps, a railing, a lift, a potted plant, journals and newspapers. Inside the Barnahus, there was a hall with a toilet and a play room where they were directed to take a seat:

> Yes, there were armchairs, a sofa and a table with lemonade, three glasses and a jug, a drawing table, a box and a dollhouse [...] You can talk about what you want to [...] and do what you like in there [...] only the kids got to do what they wanted [...] open in another way than at a police station—that would be more scary. (Kajsa 8 yrs)

The youngest children in the interviews seemed to have some difficulties in remembering or understanding what was going on at Barnahus, but Kajsa, did, even if at first she found it difficult to understand what the police wanted to talk about. When the police disclosed who they were going to talk about, however, then Kajsa knew, as she explained:

> Otherwise, [when I am] not visiting the Barnahus, it is no problems with my understanding or memory. (Kajsa 8 yrs)

In our interview, she made several colourful drawings of the different rooms, giving detailed accounts of what a Barnahus could be from a child's perspective.

> I remember details of the Barnahus but I don't remember what we were talking about because I … (points to her head and make a wry face). (Kajsa 8 yrs)

Kajsa also revealed how she knew the difference between the playroom, as she called the room with the sofa and toys, and the room with the green thorny carpet, a sheep skin rug lying in one of the two green arm chairs and the two scary cameras, the room the children sit in during the interviews. Showing drawings of the two rooms she said: 'Here you talk and in there you play'.

Naemi, 7 years old, summarised her visit to Barnahus together with her father, in the following narrative: 'I talked to the police. Had coffee and watched Pippi on TV'.

She also remembered how her father had tested the chair in the interview room and how they could wave to each other through the video when she was shown into the next room where another policeman sat and watched.

Stina, 6 years old, visited Barnahus together with her mother. She summarised her experience with following words:

> A place with chocolate milk, no, lemonade and biscuits and dollhouse and video, Pippi Longstocking. (Stina 6 yrs)

Elisabeth, 14 years old, gave an account of what happens upon arrival and how important the support of the special representative for the children could be, including when you have to wait:

> … then I go into the room with the sofa and there sits [FirstName] a lawyer and then he tells us (…) all that is going to happen: I will go into the room and there will be cameras, they will film everything and I should not be worried about it or anything. (…) I thought that was very good. Because then you are prepared and know what is going to happen. Then I had to wait a while and then I went into the room where I was interviewed. (…) I felt comfortable going in there—felt good to go in—there are cameras and [her child welfare case worker's name] was in the other room. (…) She [the police] asked a lot of questions and she could bring

> them up over and over again to get a good enough response from me and then she went into [the other room] (...) and asked them if there was something they wanted to hear more about, or something like that, and then she came back and then there were a few more questions. (...) [Then I went] out of the room and went into the room with the sofa again and talked to [name of the special representative for children] who said 'it takes time before anything more happens'. I don't remember exactly what he said. And so, he said that I had been really good and brave because I dared to tell them everything and so ... (Elisabeth 14 yrs)

The special representative for children who participated in four of the cases, the children call "their lawyer". They talk about the lawyer as a person who was used to be at the Barnahus, knew what was going on and who could explain and assist them in understanding the processes of Barnahus. In three of the cases, the child welfare caseworker also assisted the child at Barnahus. The children talked about this approach by the special representative for children and the child welfare caseworker as helping them to calm down and settle for the interview with the police. This was important for the children. Eric, 14 years old, explained this in the following statement:

> You feel calm when you have settled there. Then it does not feel strange to go there. After all, it is something, a reason for you to be there—then it would not be good if there was something even more scary or sad or something like that there. It is necessary that you feel safe. (Eric 14 yrs)

In summary, to be summoned to Barnahus aroused feelings of worry and nervousness. When travelling to Barnahus, the accompanying persons either did not know or did not want to inform the children about what was happening or why. This strengthened the children's anxiety when approaching Barnahus and meeting the police. Upon arrival, Barnahus appeared to be a welcoming, nice and cosy house of police, where lemonade, biscuits, toys and videos were offered, co-creating feelings of safety and security. In the view of the children, Barnahus became a child-friendly 'House of Police', a place where children could talk about serious matters with the police.

Scary but Necessary: To Be Summoned Without Parent's Knowledge

Three of the children had been summoned and brought to Barnahus without their parents' knowledge and without any preparation, creating a sudden event from the perspective of the child. As Sara, one of the children, reported:

> The school welfare officer came for me in the school 20 or 2 min before the departure took place. She said we were going for a ride. (Sara 14 yrs)

About being surprised and not prepared Sara said:

> It was quite nice that we were 'picked up' like this:—'Let's go with this then ' Yes, it could have been 'you can decide whether you want to go with me or not', however it was much more comfortable that they just said: 'you are going with us now'. (Sara 14 yrs)

It seems to have been a relief for Sara that she did not have to take responsibility for choosing whether she should go to Barnahus or not. The travel to the Barnahus, however, became a hard time for Sara:

> Yes, a lot of thoughts spun in my head. What is happening now? What is going to happen? What have I done now? What has happened? Has something happened to my mum? Has something happened to my sister? Has something happened to dad? And so this … (Sara 14 yrs)

During the journey to Barnahus she asked questions:

> I didn't get much response from them […] To some questions, they said 'you must wait and see' and 'you may take it up with them when we meet them there' […] it was two policemen they said we were going to meet. I thought it was two policemen in full outfits, with uniforms and all that I was going to meet, but it was, well, two civilians or how do you put it, two ordinary people. (Sara 14 yrs)

Sara appreciated having the school welfare officer accompanying her, a person she recognised from school. She felt better with the information given by the special representative for children and the police after their arrival at Barnahus:

> You feel, that it felt … that we felt safe when we stepped in there. It felt like not at all rough […] more as soft to get into […] where you can act and become the child you are […] you don't need to be in any particular way or like this—you get to be yourself there […] We didn't have to feel and act as grown-ups, but be children. In school, at home and otherwise, it's easy to become and act as a grown-up. But here it was more like: 'Yes, well, but do what you want. If you're sitting here and are 14 years old playing with a dollhouse—we don't care—be yourself.' Like, be a child if you want to—be an adult if you want to. At the police station, it felt more like I had to be an adult […] it was more like this is for real now, it is really for real now, and serious. But at Barnahus it was not so. (Sara 14 yrs)

Vera, 14 years old, and Isac, 15 years old, also had experiences of being summoned and brought to Barnahus without their parents knowing. Vera was picked up by a child welfare caseworker at the school shortly after school began in the morning. Vera had never met the child welfare caseworker but a familiar teacher accompanied her, both during the journey to Barnahus and the entire day.

> I wasn't prepared for it happening, no, so first I was shocked and sad. So I don't know what really happened. Everything was going so damn fast. They came and picked us up and explained what it was and then we were there. […] I didn't want to at first, because I was scared. (Vera 14 yrs)

Isac knew something was about to happen soon because he was the one who had given away the secret of an abusing father to the police and had been asked by the school and the child welfare caseworkers to keep silent and not tell anyone about the report of the abuse. He had known for 3 days that something was going to happen making a change for the better for him and his younger siblings.

> It wouldn't have been good to reveal anything to (the brother's name) because he usually says things to our parents and if they had found out, we would never ever have gone to school or something that day. It felt good, knowing all that would disappear, however, I did know something was going to happen but not what—not that it would be to Barnahus, and I didn't know it existed. (Isac 15 yrs)

Knowing his father would become very angry when he received the information about the report of abuse, Isac kept silent. With no information during the journey to Barnahus, Isac had been worried about whether his father was going to be there when they arrived. That would have been a very difficult meeting, he said. He was also worried about what was going to happen afterwards. Isac and his siblings had to stay at the Barnahus for several hours, waiting for the result of the assessments of the child welfare service and necessary arrangements. Now and then somebody entered the room, giving information or asking questions and the children took the chance to ask questions. This gave them a feeling of hope and of being involved. They sat there the whole day, from arriving in the morning until half five or five, each with a teacher and the special representative, except for the interviews and a short visit to buy groceries, and the room became crowded. There were several opportunities for worries and uncertainties:

> I was hoping to avoid having to go home—my father had found out everything. He would probably not be too happy. They said perhaps we had to go home but they were trying to fix something else, a place where we could go [...]. It was quite difficult to find, and I think it was. Then they found [name of place] or what it was in [name of a city]. Then we went there and stayed there ... (Isac 15 yrs)

In summary, to be summoned to Barnahus without their parent's knowing aroused mixed feelings of worry and nervousness, but also of relief and hope of change. The children appreciated that they were listened to and given support. Although they had shown that they were ready for a change and to contribute, they were not consulted or given the information they needed and asked for until they arrived at the Barnahus.

Discussion and Conclusions

Children summoned to Barnahus in Sweden could be prepared and accompanied by a parent (Kaldal et al. 2010; Rasmusson 2008); however, in cases where the parents cannot become involved, a special representative for children is appointed. Instead of the parents, the special representative protects the child's rights in the legal procedures during the criminal investigation.

As the institution Barnahus has become established, the use of special representatives for children seems to have increased. In the beginning, a special representative for children was provided in 26% of the cases (Rejmer and Hansen 2008) and later in up to 50% of the cases (Gustafsson 2011; Holmsten 2009; Kaldal et al. 2010). As special representatives for children are primarily used when a parent is under suspicion, there are reasons to assume that many of the children summoned to Barnahus have been summoned without parents becoming involved. On the other hand, the special representative for children is usually a lawyer and, as the children in the study stated, the special representative had experience of, and knowledge about, the proceedings at Barnahus which parents cannot be expected to have. The special representatives chose not to give more detailed information until later, however, when the child has become a little more acquainted with the Barnahus.

The withholding of information when children are summoned, as well as at Barnahus, is based on the idea that information may influence the child and in consideration of what the child is going to disclose in the upcoming child investigative interview conducted by the police (Landberg and Svedin 2013). A key purpose of the concept of Barnahus is to improve child criminal investigations. The result of the police child investigative interview is crucial for the outcome of the investigation. The agencies collaborate in facilitating the child to disclose what has really happened and in not creating false stories in the police interview.

Not giving enough information to the child to help them feel comfortable with the situation, however, is also a way of influencing the outcome. This can, as heard in the study, create feelings of fear, uneasiness and insecurity in the child. When the child poses questions like:

'what is going on?', and these are answered evasively, it allows for many thoughts and wide scopes of imagination, including fearing the worst, as to both why the child is summoned to Barnahus and what is going to happen at Barnahus and afterwards. A child's understanding of what is going on could easily involve the assumption that something dangerous has happened to someone in the family. For example, one of the children summoned and brought to Barnahus without parental knowledge or consent became anxious that something might have happened to a family member or that she herself had done something wrong, especially when she did not get any answers to her questions. Would she not have been in better shape, approaching the police interview, if she had received enough information—thus avoiding this increased anxiety?

On the other hand, this non-involvement approach of the professionals can also be experienced and felt as a relief, as seen in the study. Being approached as a child, and not being expected to act and take any responsibility as 'an adult', allows children to respond as a child, to play with dolls and other toys, and not to have to make any (more) decisions. This transfer of responsibility, 'just do what you are told', is literally and in practice showing the child that the professionals are taking over because they take the child's experiences seriously and are ready to protect the child if necessary. This might relieve the negative stress the child might feel, but it also creates expectations of adaptation to what the adults are asking for.

At the same time, a child who is not given a reason for the summons, not even when they ask what is going on, is not respected as an acting subject with the right to information and support, in order to understand what is going on and why. When seen as a child living in a vulnerable situation, the child is approached as a victim in need of protection and a non-acting object (cf. Eriksson 2009; Eriksson and Näsman 2008). Gradually, the child starts to respond to the approach in use, accepting that they will be brought to and be at Barnahus without further questioning; however, soon, in the interview with the police, the child is expected to become an acting subject remembering details of experienced occurrences of violence and abuse. The impact of these preparations, aimed at getting a child ready for a police interview when there are suspicions of child abuse and violence, is an important area for further research including further inquiries about children's experiences of being summoned to Barnahus without their parents' consent, knowledge or presence.

Acting in the child investigative interview with the police is hard work for children. The older children explained that this was something they had to do if they wanted to put an end to the bad things that went on. In the middle of the cosy atmosphere, the child is expected to expose and disclose difficult memories. Entering the police interview room, the children are expected to transform into actors, answering questions and describing episodes in detail. Leaving the playroom, and entering the interview room, some of the children needed a reminder or a hint from the police before they understood what and whom they were going to talk about. We know very little about how the younger children understood Barnahus, except that all the children, including the youngest, associated Barnahus first and foremost with the police and second with biscuits, fruit drinks, toys and video films for young children. Kajsa, 8 years old, gave an account that showed that she knew the difference between play and the serious part of Barnahus: '—You play in the playroom, talk in the green room [police interview room]'. In the latter room, the children were supposed to perform hard work, which could feel stressful. This study did not address how successful the children were in becoming acting subjects in the investigative interviews, expected to give away secrets that they had so far very seldom, if ever, unmasked. No conclusions can thus be drawn about the influences of the preceding processes in the outcome of the police interviews. Further research exploring these presumed connections would be helpful in finding out whether existing procedures for summoning and bringing a child to Barnahus are warranted or whether there are reasons for making changes. According to what has been revealed in this study, the child's right to information and support in understanding what is going on and why is not fulfilled in existing routines and procedures (see also Chap. 10). Examples of where the child's right to participate and become respected as an acting subject, taking the child's view, ability and opinion into consideration, rarely appear in the children's narratives about becoming summoned to Barnahus, with one crucial exception—entering the room of the police child investigate interview. By entering the room with the police and the cameras, they were expected to stop being children at play, be able to focus and act as responsible subjects talking about serious matters—become the acting subjects they acted as and talked about being in the research interviews.

Funding This research was funded by the research group Research Platform for Collaboration for Health at Kristianstad University, the research group Children's and Young People's Health in Social Context (CYPHiSCO) at Kristianstad University, the Kempe-Carlgrenska foundation and the Letterstedtska foundation.

References

Alderson, Priscilla. 2010. Younger Children's Individual Participation in 'All Matters Affecting the Child'. In *A Handbook of Children and Young People's Participation. Perspectives from Theory and Practice*, eds. Barry Percy-Smith and Thomas Nigel, 88–104. New York: Routledge.

Anderson, Harlene. 1999. *Samtal, språk och möjligheter*. Mareld: Psykoterapi och konsultation ur postmodern synvinkel. Stockholm.

Barnombudsmannen [The Children's Ombudsman]. 2007. *The Right to be heard*. Stockholm: The Children's Ombudsman.

Bateson, Gregory. 1998. *Mönster som förbinder*. Stockholm: Mareld.

Bell, Margaret. 2002. Promoting Children's Rights Through the Use of Relationship. *Child and Family Social Work* 7: 1–11.

Brannen, Julia, Ellen Heptinstall, and Kalwant Bhopal. 2000. *Connecting Children. Care and Family Life in Later Childhood*. London: RoutledgeFalmer.

Christensen, Pia, and James, Allison. 2008. Introduction. Researching Children and Childhood. Culture of Communication. In *Research with Children Perspectives and Practice*, eds. Pia Christensen and Allison James, 1–9. New York: Routledge.

Dencik, Lars, and Jørgensen Schultz, Per (eds.). 1999. Børn og familie i det postmoderne samfund. København: Hans Reitzels Forlag.

Eriksson, Maria. 2009. Girls and Boys as Victims: Social Workers' Approaches to Children Exposed to Violence. *Child Abuse Review* 18: 428–445.

Eriksson, Maria, and Elisabet Näsman. 2008. Participation in Family Law Proceedings for Children Whose Father is Violent to Their Mother. *Childhood* 15: 259–275.

Gergen, Kenneth J. 2009. *Relational Being*. Beyond Self and Community. Oxford: Oxford University Press.

Gustafsson, Kaj. 2011. Utvärdering av Barnahus Gävleborg – slutrapport [Evaluation of Barnahus Gävleborg – final report]. Gävle: Fou Välfärd Region Gävleborg.

Halldén, Gunilla. 2003. Barnperspektiv som ideologiskt eller metodologiskt begrepp. [Child perspectives as a ideological and methodological concept. *Pedagogisk Forskning i Sverige* 8 (1–2): 12–23.

Holland, Sally. 2009. Listening to Children in Care: A Review of Methodological and Theoretical Approaches to Understanding Looked-after Children's Perspectives. *Children and Society* 23: 226–235.

Holmsten, Susanne. 2009. Barnahus Västmanland Omfattning, inriktning, sammanhang,: Utvecklings- och utredningsfunktionen Västmanlands kommuner & lansting.

Johansson, Eva. 2003. Att närma sig barns perspektiv. Forskares och pedagogers möten med barns perspektiv. *Pedagogisk Forskning i Sverige* 8 (1–2): 42–57.

Johansson, Susanna. 2012. Diffusion and Governance of 'Barnahus' in the Nordic Countries: Report from an On-going Project. *Journal of Scandinavian Studies in Criminology and Crime Prevention* 13: 69–84.

Kaldal, Anna, Christian Diesen, Johan Beije, and Eva Diesen. 2010. *Barnahusutredningen 2010*. Stockholm: Juridiska Institutionen vid Stockholms universitet.

Katz, Carmit. 2013. The Narratives of Abused Children Who Have Survived Attempted Filicide. *Child Abuse and Neglect* 37 (10): 762–770.

Kohler Riessman, Catherine. 1990. *Divorce Talk. Women and Men Make Sense of Personal Relationships*. London: Rutgers University Press.

Landberg, Åsa, and Svedin, Carl Göran. 2013. Inuti ett Barnahus. En kvalitetsgranskning av 23 svenska verksamheter.. Stockholm: Linköpings Universitet Hälsouniversitetet and Rädda Barnen.

Lansdown, Gerison. 2010. The Realisation of Children's Participation Rights: Critical Reflection. In *A Handbook of Children and Young People's Participation. Perspectives from Theory and Practice*, ed. Barry Percy-Smith and Thomas Nigel, 11–23. New York: Routledge.

Olsson, Ann-Margerth E. 2010. *Listening to the Voice of Children. Systemic Dialogue Coaching: Inviting Participation and Partnership in Social Work*. Luton: University of Bedfordshire.

Olsson, Ann-Margreth E. 2014a. Dialogical Participatory Action Research in Social Work Using Delta-Reflecting Teams. In *Promoting Change Through*

Action Research, eds. Franz Rauch, Angela Schuster, Thomas Stern, Maroa Pribila, and Andrew Townsend, 163–172. Rotterdam: Sense Publishers.

Olsson, Ann-Margreth E. 2014b. The Impact of Dialogical Participatory Action Research (DPAR): Riding in the Peloton of dialogical collaboration. In *Systemic Inquiry Innovations in Reflexive Practice Research*, eds. Gail Simon, and Alex Chard, 230–243. Farnhill: Everything is Connected.

Ost, Suzanne. 2013. Balancing Autonomy Rights and Protection: Children's Involvement in a Child Safety Online Project. *Children and Society* 27 (3): 208–219.

Powell, Mary Ann, and Anne B. Smith. 2009. Children's Participation Rights in Research. *Childhood* 16 (1): 124–142.

Qvortrup, Jens. 1999. Barndom og samfund. In Børn og familie i det postmoderne samfund, eds. Lars Dencik and Per Jørgensen Schultz, 45–75. København: Hans Reitzels Forlag.

Rasmusson, Bodil. 2008. Det är ju inget dagis precis … Barns och föräldrars upplevelser av kontakter med barnahus. Delrapport 6 i utvärderingen av nationell försöksverksamhet med barnahus 2006–2007. Lund: Lund University, Sociology of Law.

Rasmusson, Bodil. 2011. Children's Advocacy Centers (Barnahus) in Sweden. *Child Indicators Research* 4: 301–321.

Rejmer, Annika and Hansen, Helen. 2008. … känner du till skillnaden mellan lögn och sanning En analys av förundersökningar. Delrapport 5 i utvärderingen av nationell försöksverksamhet med Barnahus 2006–2007. Lund: Sociology of Law, Lund University.

Röbäck, Karin, and Ingrid Höjer. 2009. Constructing Children's Views in the Enforcement of Contact Orders. *International Journal of Children's Right* 17: 663–680.

Sandbæk, Mona. 1999. Children with Problems: Focusing on Everyday Life. *Children and Society* 13: 106–118.

Shotter, John. 2009. Listening in a Way that Recognizes/Realizes the World of 'the Other'. *International Journal of Listening* 23 (1): 21–43.

Sommer, Dion, Hundeide, Karsten, and Pramling Samuelsson, Ingrid. 2011. Introduktion: Barnperspektiv och barns perspektiv – den skandinaviska kontexten. In Barnperspektiv och barnens perspektiv i teori och praktik, eds. Dion Sommer, Karsten Hundeide and Ingrid Pramling Samuelsson, 17–43. Stockholm: Liber.

Swedish Prosecution Authority. 2016. *Handläggning av ärenden gällande övergrepp mot barn. Handbok*. Göteborg: Utvecklingscentrum Göteborg.

Swedish National Police Board, The National Board of Forensic Medicine, The National Board of Health and Welfare, and Swedish Prosecution Authority. 2008. *Barnahus – försökverksamhet med samverkan under gemensamt tak vid misstanke om brott mot barn.* Stockholm: Rikspolisstyrelsen, Rättsmedicinalverket, Socialstyrelsen, Åklagarmyndigheten.

Swedish National Police Board. 2009. *Delredovisning av regeringsuppdrag avseende gemensamma nationella riktlinjer kring barn som misstänks vara utsatta för brott och kriterier för landets barnahus.* Stockholm: Rikspolisstyrelsen.

4

Evidence-Based Intervention for Children and Parents in Cases of Physical Abuse

Johanna Thulin and Cecilia Kjellgren

Introduction

Even though corporal punishment has been banned in Sweden since 1979, 14% of children in the ninth grade report being subjected to physical abuse by their parents (Janson et al. 2011). Being exposed to parental violence increases the risk of trauma symptoms such as traumatic stress, depression and behavioural problems (Garbarino et al. 1991; Moffitt 2013). Child victims of physical abuse are also at increased risk of future eating disorders, conduct disorders, alcohol and drug abuse and sexual risk behaviour (Norman et al. 2012).

J. Thulin (✉) · C. Kjellgren
Linnaeus University, Växjö, Sweden
e-mail: johanna.thulin@lnu.se

C. Kjellgren
e-mail: cecilia.kjellgren@lnu.se

In Sweden, research has shown that children who experience parental physical abuse often continue to live with their parents, even after the abuse has come to the attention of the child welfare service (Lindell and Svedin 2006). Despite this, there has been a lack of specialised intervention for this group of families. The starting point for this chapter is the need for interventions aimed at preventing further violence and increasing the well-being of the child.

The national guidelines for Barnahus in Sweden state that "The goal of the collaboration is to ensure legal rights, good treatment and support, for children who it is suspected are victims of crime, and if necessary immediate crisis and treatment interventions" (The Swedish National Police Agency 2009, 7, author's translation).

Since the decision to introduce Barnahus in Sweden in 2005, the establishment of new Barnahus has been rapid; however, surveys show that a significant number of the Barnahus in Sweden do not adequately provide support, crisis and treatment interventions (Landberg and Svedin 2013).

In this chapter, we describe and discuss an evidence-based intervention that involves both abused children and their parents, in instances where one or both parents are perpetrators of the abuse. The intervention is Combined Parent–Child Cognitive Behavioural Therapy for families at risk of child physical abuse (CPC-CBT), which originates from the USA (Runyon et al. 2004; Runyon and Deblinger 2014) and that currently is being disseminated throughout Sweden in a research project where Linnaeus University and Linköping University collaborate. We argue that the intervention is well suited to the Barnahus context.

Thirty treatment units across Sweden currently offer the treatment, with additional teams being trained. The teams comprise 3–5 colleagues. Half of the trained teams consists of staff from a Barnahus. Some of these teams have social workers from other departments as co-workers in the treatment or cooperate with staff from child and adolescent psychiatric units.

If this treatment was used systematically, a higher percentage of Barnahus in Sweden would meet the criteria for Barnahus in the national guidelines. Through their collaboration with other professionals, Barnahus also has a unique opportunity to offer interventions to both children and their families in cases of suspected parental physical abuse.

Because the Barnahus staff meets families at a time of crisis, they are also strategically positioned to offer them voluntary forms of treatment.

In the following, we first present the basics of the CPC-CBT model and the Swedish version of the model named *Kognitiv integrerad behandling vid barnmisshandel* (KIBB). We then present the results from a large-scale dissemination project in Sweden and discuss possible implications for interventions in Barnahus.

Combined Parent–Child Cognitive Behavioural Therapy (CPC-CBT)

The CPC-CBT intervention was developed in the USA by Runyon and colleagues at CARES Institute (Child Abuse Research Education and Service) in New Jersey (Runyon et al. 2004). The method was evaluated with good results (Runyon et al. 2009; Runyon et al. 2010), and later, the manual was thoroughly presented (Runyon and Deblinger 2014). The method is unique in combining treatment for both children and parents in families where physical abuse has occurred (Runyon et al. 2004). The CPC-CBT is included in the National Registry of Evidence-based Programmes and Practices (NREPP) list of evidence-based practices in the USA. Cecilia Kjellgren, Ph.D., the second author of this chapter, introduced CPC-CBT in Sweden in cooperation with *Children's Welfare Foundation Sweden* (Stiftelsen Allmänna Barnhuset).[1, 2]

CPC-CBT is an intervention that aims to help the whole family, including the violent parent, according to the manual (Children's Welfare Foundation Sweden 2013; Runyon and Deblinger 2014). The child welfare services may refer families to treatment where physical abuse has occurred. Initially, child welfare services assess whether the intervention is appropriate in terms of both the needs of the family and the safety of the child. The aim of the treatment is to end all forms of physical abuse, including more severe child abuse. The child welfare service is responsible for the child's safety throughout the treatment and keeps in contact with the family and the therapists. Before treatment starts, the parents have to sign a non-violence contract. The therapist also informs parents about their professional obligation to the mandatory reporting of possible new abuse events to the child welfare services. Participation in treatment is voluntary.

The child receives treatment either individually or within a group of children, and the parents meet a therapist individually or join a group of parents for the sessions; consequently, the child meets one therapist and the parents meet another therapist simultaneously. Every treatment session ends with an integrated period where the family join together with one of the therapists, where parents can rehearse and practice new parenting strategies. Not all parents admit that they have been abusive, at least not in the beginning of the treatment. Initially, the child's story will be the starting point, sometimes a story that has been told by the child to the police. The parents usually admit having violent behaviour to some extent, such as being too harsh or grabbing the child too hard. Since the child holds the right to their own version and experience, the therapist will work with that story, both with the child and with the parents. Initially, the parents have to give the child permission to talk about the abuse. Further, they have to agree that there should be no more secrets, and this will be repeated several times during treatment to encourage the child to openly describe the details of their experiences and related thoughts and feelings.

CPC-CBT is an outpatient treatment intervention. Families attend approximately 16 sessions over a 16- to 20-week period, where therapists meet the family during a 2 h session weekly. Each week, specific themes are addressed according to the structured treatment manual (Runyon and Deblinger 2014). CPC-CBT has four phases: (1) engagement and psychoeducation, (2) effective coping skills, (3) family safety planning and continuation of skill building and (4) abuse clarification. Parenting skills are addressed across all phases.

Child Treatment

During the initial phase, engagement and psychoeducation, children learn about violence and abuse, and possible consequences in order to understand their own reactions and to acknowledge them. This is the beginning of a gradual process of exposing the child to abuse-related material to increase the child's comfort level in dealing with, and directly discussing, personal experiences of abuse.

During the effective coping skills phase, children learn to identify, regulate and appropriately express their emotions, and learn productive coping strategies for dealing with stress and anxiety in order to reduce their anxiety and to prepare them to manage to share the details of their abusive experiences. An essential part of the treatment is to help the child to understand and express their feelings. Some children lack the ability to regulate their feelings. The treatment is based on cognitive behavioural therapy, and the therapist tries to clear the connection between the child's thoughts, feelings and behaviour. Many children initially blame themselves for the abuse and may explain that it all happened because of their own behaviour. Such beliefs will be clarified later in treatment, together with the parents, and the parents can then take responsibility for acting wrongly. Considering the child's age and maturity, activities such as games, role-play and tools can be used as part of the therapy.

While safety is integral to every phase of CPC-CBT, the family safety planning phase focuses specifically on having family members develop and implement a safety plan that involves using the skills learned to date, in order to enhance the safety of all family members. The treatment starts with giving the child space and time to describe the specific occasion that led to the police report or the report to the child welfare service. This episode can be very frightening, and children may need to repeatedly talk it over, to explain what they have experienced and how their parents behaved. Children need to be reassured that they did not do anything that made them deserve to be hit or abused.

The final phase of therapy, the abuse clarification phase, involves the child developing a *trauma narrative*. This occurs after there is evidence in parent and child reports that the physical abuse has stopped and that positive parent–child interactions have increased. The therapist encourages the child to share a narrative about their specific experiences of abuse. The child will describe the situation, how they thought and felt. In this process, some children draw pictures or cartoons; other will play in sand or use dolls or character cards. The child and therapist will try to write the narrative down together and read it aloud to repeatedly expose the child to the anxiety-provoking memory in order to decrease anxiety and trauma symptoms. The therapist also assists the child with processing dysfunctional and self-blaming thoughts that may surface/occur during joint sessions with the parents. The child is asked whether they have questions concerning the abuse to ask their parents and whether they want the parents' therapist to forward the questions. When the child is ready, the story will be shared with the parents, and they will respond to it (see Section "Parent Treatment").

Parent Treatment

During the engagement and psychoeducation phase, parents discuss and process their personal experiences of abuse and violence, which can contribute to an increase in empathy for their children's experience of their relationship and current parenting style. They examine how children can be affected by growing up in a violent environment. Parents receive psychoeducation and learn more about the consequences of child abuse and maltreatment, about child development and the needs of a child.

Teaching parents alternative non-violent parenting strategies is a critical part of the treatment and is integrated into all phases. Parents learn active listening to strengthen communication with the child and to prepare them for the abuse clarification phase. The foundation of positive parenting skills is to encourage parents to express more appreciation, to affirm and praise their child. Parents are taught how to reinforce some behaviours and to reduce others.

During the effective coping skills phase, parents learn a variety of strategies for dealing with and expressing anger. They are also taught how to understand and express their own feelings in a different way. Many parents also need help to regulate their emotions, not least their anger. Anger management is a central part of the treatment. In the same way as the child, the parents will learn how thoughts, feelings and behaviours interact. They will practice how to communicate with their children, including how to listen.

In the final phase, abuse clarification, parents prepare an abuse clarification letter for their child which demonstrates that they take responsibility for their abusive behaviour and alleviate the child of blame. They also outline their commitment to parent their child in a more positive way. The child's trauma narrative is shared with the parent, and the parent can thus respond directly to any misconceptions, fears or concerns the child has about the abuse. This can be a very emotional moment, and the parent is prepared by first reading the child's narrative together with the therapist. When both parent and child are prepared, the child will share the narrative with the parent. The parent will also respond by writing a letter of clarification, where the parents will try to explain why they attended treatment, take full responsibility for the abuse situation(s) and explain how they feel about the child talking about the abuse. The parents will also try to describe what they have learned and how they hope to act differently from now on.

Joint Sessions

During joint sessions, children and parents will together create a security plan in order to avoid the escalation of future stressful situations and to prevent the risk of further abuse. The parents will also have opportunities to practice new parenting strategies. Both parents and children practice different skills, such as affirming and praising each other.

Implementation and Adaptions to the Swedish Context

Four teams participated in a pilot project during the initial CPC-CBT training in Sweden. The professionals had high expectations, but expressed doubts about the applicability of the model in the Swedish context due to cultural differences. The definition of physical abuse is not the same in Sweden as in the USA, where there is zero tolerance for parental physical violence in Sweden. This may indicate that victims of physical abuse are more severely abused and more burdened when being referred to treatment in the USA, compared to Sweden.

When the interventions were introduced in a Swedish context, minor adaptations were made in agreement with the programme developer (e.g. modification of language and exclusion of parenting strategies that are less relevant in the Swedish context) while maintaining the overall structure and constructs of the original model.

Initially, it was not known whether the method would integrate well with the work at the Barnahus. Three of the four teams in the pilot project were teams of Barnahus staff, and they reported valuable positive experiences while implementing CPC-CBT. The experience was positive for those teams who could present the treatment as an option at an early stage, provided they were in close cooperation with the child welfare caseworker. Later practice further confirmed these initial experiences.

A pilot study was conducted in 2010–2011 (Kjellgren et al. 2013), with a pre- and post-treatment design. The study had several positive results for children and parents. Children showed significantly reduced trauma symptoms and symptoms of depression at post-treatment. They also reported that parents had significantly improved in positive parenting and reduced corporal punishment. Significantly, fewer symptoms of depression were reported by parents at follow-up post-treatment as well as less use of violent parenting strategies and less inconsistent parenting behaviours (Kjellgren et al. 2013). Previous studies in the USA showed that similar effects of the treatment (more positive parenting, less physical abuse and increased emotional well-being for the children) persisted at follow-up, 3 months later (Runyon et al. 2010). Following such positive experiences of the pilot project, the intervention was further implemented by training a number of additional therapists across Sweden, starting in 2013. When the first invitation for training was announced, staff at the Barnahus were given priority. So far about one hundred therapists have been trained in the method in Sweden. A large-scale Swedish dissemination study to evaluate the outcomes associated with CPC-CBT was also planned. This study consists of three data collection periods, at pre-treatment before treatment has started, at post-treatment approximately 4 months later when treatment is completed and at a 6-month follow-up (see Fig. 4.1). The study is ongoing, and more than 50 children have participated in the first data collection period. The aim is to assess 50 children and their parents overall three data collection periods. We also intend to collect data from control families to

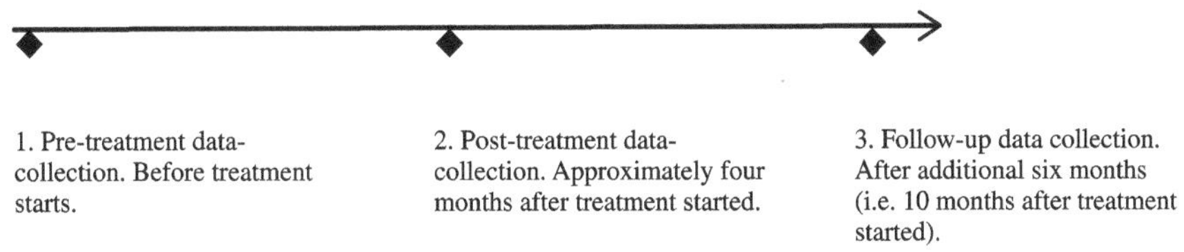

Fig. 4.1 Research design

make outcome comparisons possible. Families who have been assessed and offered CPC-CBT treatment by one of the teams previously mentioned were all informed about the study and asked whether they (parents and children) wanted to participate in the ongoing research.

Results

The results in this chapter have previously been published within a Swedish report (Thulin et al. 2015). This chapter presents the data of a subsample of 34 children and their parents ($N = 45$), from a total of 28 families, who have completed pre- and post-data collections. Slightly, more boys (58%) than girls (42%) participated in the study, and their mean age was 9.5 years (SD = 2.2). In the parent group, 50% were mothers and 46% fathers, and 4% were step-fathers. The parents average age was 39 years (SD = 6.7). Both children and parents completed self-assessment scales. The results were statistically analysed. Mean values were compared (the data from pre- versus post-treatment) using paired t tests in order to measure change at the individual level. Effect size was calculated and is presented using Cohen's d. The cut-off points for Cohen's d used in the analyses are ≥ 0.80 (indicating large effect), ≥ 0.50 (moderate effect) and ≥ 0.20 small effect).

Parenting Measurements

Trauma Symptoms

Parents were asked to estimate the child's trauma symptoms on the parent report scale *Trauma Symptom Checklist for Young Children* (TSCYC, Briere et al. 2001). The scale contains 90 items, and these

Table 4.1 Parents reporting differences in their children's well-being before and after treatment, $N = 36$

	Before treatment	After treatment			
Variable	*M* (SD)	*M* (SD)	*t*	*p*	*d*
Anxiety	12.89 (3.55)	11.31 (2.55)	3.75	0.001	0.52
Depression	13.15 (3.62)	11.24 (1.97)	3.56	0.001	0.71
Anger	14.37 (4.48)	12.20 (3.64)	3.67	0.001	0.54
PTS-intrusion	11.50 (2.83)	10.18 (1.66)	3.16	0.003	0.57
PTS-avoidance	11.12 (3.17)	10.18 (1.99)	2.06	0.047	0.35
PTS-arousal	13.56 (4.37)	12.38 (3.06)	2.39	0.023	0.32
Dissociation	12.94 (3.40)	11.29 (2.98)	3.27	0.002	0.50
Total trauma symptoms	120.46 (27.99)	106.43 (19.41)	3.65	0.001	0.61

were translated into Swedish and validated in a Swedish study (Nilsson et al. 2012). TSCYC contains eight subscales: anxiety, depression, anger, post-traumatic stress disorder (divided into three subscales), dissociation and sexual concerns. Parents rate whether the child shows symptoms using a four-point scale where 1 = *not at all* and 4 = *very often*. Due to the young age of the children participating in this study, the sexual concern subscale, which measures sexual thoughts and feelings, was not considered relevant.

The results showed that parents reported that the symptoms of the children had significantly decreased on all variables (see Table 4.1), from pre- to 4 months post-treatment. Parents reported that their children showed significantly less extrovert behaviour such as anger, as well as decreased introvert behavioural problems, such as anxiety, depression, post-traumatic stress symptoms and dissociation after treatment.

Parenting Strategies

Parenting strategies were measured by the *Alabama Parenting Questionnaire* (APQ, Frick 1991). The questionnaire measures five parenting strategies. The results for three subscales, *positive parenting, inconsistent discipline* and *corporal punishment* are presented in this chapter (see Table 4.2). Positive parenting includes praising and rewarding children, and the extent to which the parents show affection for

Table 4.2 Mean differences in parenting strategies after treatment (APQ-P), $N = 41$

	Before treatment	After treatment			
Variable	*M* (SD)	*M* (SD)	*t*	*p*	*d*
Positive parenting	24.37 (3.27)	24.20 (3.93)	0.42	0.680	0.05
Inconsistent discipline	14.11 (3.45)	12.95 (2.94)	2.18	0.036	0.38
Corporal punishment	3.56 (1.27)	3.05 (0.32)	2.64	0.012	0.63

the child. Inconsistent discipline regards to what extent their parent's behaviour is predictable to the child. The corporal punishment subscale includes items describing three kinds of punishing behaviour (spanking, slapping or hitting with an object).

The results reveal that parents became significantly more consistent and therefore more predictable for the children after treatment. This in turn can be interpreted as leading to a sense of security, when the child more easily understood the rules and how their parents might react. The results also revealed that parents significantly reduced their use of corporal punishment (the summarised value 3 indicates no use of physical punishment); however, parent responses did not suggest that they had been more positive in their parenting.

Parents' Psychological Well-Being

Parent's well-being changed after receiving treatment. The mean depression scores were significantly reduced, from $M = 12.37$ (SD $= 13.28$) to $M = 6.14$ (SD $= 7.63$) ($t = 3.69$, $p = 0.001$). The questionnaire used, *Beck Depression Inventory* (BDI, Beck, Steer and Brown 1996), is a well-established self-assessment scale for measuring symptoms of depression in adults. The total scores of symptoms are categorised into four levels: minimal, mild, moderate and severe depression (Beck et al. 1996). The share of parents who reported mild, moderate or severe depression was reduced after treatment. The treatment method does not explicitly aim to reduce depression, but the results suggest that treatment components affect depressive feelings. Previous feelings among parents, such as guilt about parental failure, are probably reduced by treatment when parents achieved alternative strategies such as improved consistent parenting. This could affect the reduction of symptoms.

Children and Trauma

Being subjected to abuse by a parent is serious and increases the risk of trauma symptoms, depression and behavioural problems in children (Garbarino et al. 1991; Moffitt 2013). Previous research has also shown that children who have been exposed to trauma are more likely to be exposed again; re-victimised (Gilbert et al. 2009) and also to be exposed to other types of trauma; and poly-victimised (Clarkson Freeman 2014). Children in this study completed the *Linköping Youth Life Experiences Scale* (LYLES) and were asked whether they had experienced various events. The scale is divided into three types of events: non-interpersonal events (nIPE), interpersonal events (IPE) and adverse childhood circumstances (ACC) (Nilsson et al. 2010). Examples of items concerning non-interpersonal events are whether the child has experienced a burglary or seen a fire. Interpersonal items include, for example, whether the child has been exposed to violence or sexual abuse. Items in the subscale of adverse childhood circumstances include whether the child has been subjected to bullying or has had a prolonged illness.

Our sample of children who have been physically abused experienced a mean of 13.1 (SD 6.1) potential traumatic events, with a range between 3 and 22. Some of the most prevalent forms of potential traumatic non-interpersonal events were the experience of a family member in hospital (85%) and experience of the death of a close person (72%). The most frequent interpersonal events were being hit or injured by an adult in the family (82%), being hit or injured by another adult (65%) and being the witness when another person was hit or injured (42%). The most frequent adverse childhood experiences were having experienced parents separation or divorce (44%), having been bullied (41%) and having been emotionally abused (33%).

Being exposed to such a high number of potentially traumatic events is categorised as being *poly-victimised* (e.g. Turner et al. 2010).

Children's trauma symptoms are also likely to increase according to the number of events (Turner et al. 2010). The result from our study confirms earlier studies, which revealed that physically abused children are a vulnerable group where the likelihood is strong that they have been exposed to other types of trauma in addition to the abuse.

Trauma Symptoms

The children completed the self-assessment scale *Trauma Symptom Checklist for Children* (TSCC, Briere et al. 2001). The results (see Table 4.3) revealed that the participating children significantly reduced their trauma symptoms after treatment for all tested variables: anxiety, feelings of depression, anger, post-traumatic stress and dissociation.

The results confirm those of previous research that the CPC-CBT method supports child victims of physical abuse.

Children's Experience of Parenting Strategies

Children were asked how they perceived the parenting strategies used by their parents before and after treatment (see Table 4.4).

Children, as well as parents, responded that the use of corporal punishment was significantly reduced after treatment (the summarised value 3 indicates no use of physical punishment). Although both children and parents reported that the violence had decreased significantly,

Table 4.3 Children's trauma symptoms before and after treatment (TSCC), $N = 25$

	Before treatment	After treatment			
	M(SD)	*M*(SD)	*t*	*p*	*d*
Anxiety	5.84 (3.14)	4.0 (2.38)	2.85	0.009	0.64
Depression	4.72 (3.49)	2.68 (2.21)	2.81	0.010	0.69
Anger	5.88 (3.86)	3.72 (2.42)	3.02	0.006	0.69
PTSD	7.32 (4.58)	5.44 (2.89)	2.22	0.036	0.50
Dissociation	5.72 (3.18)	4.08 (1.96)	2.46	0.022	0.62
Total trauma symptoms	29.48 (13.82)	19.92 (8.97)	3.70	0.001	0.84

Table 4.4 Children's reports of parenting strategies, $N = 33$

	Before treatment	After treatment			
Variable	*M* (SD)	*M* (SD)	*t*	*p*	*d*
Positive parenting	22.28 (5.00)	23.69 (4.00)	1.79	0.084	0.31
Inconsistent discipline	14.28 (3.73)	12.86 (3.30)	1.74	0.093	0.40
Corporal punishment	4.25 (1.68)	3.09 (0.39)	3.68	0.001	1.1

their responses differed. Children estimated that corporal punishment was more common at pre-treatment than did the parents. This difference highlighted the need to also talk to children when various conditions in a family are investigated. Previous studies have shown that parents tend to under-report children's experiences of abuse (Kjellgren et al. 2013; Svensson 2013; Litrownik et al. 2003).

Discussion

In this chapter, we have described how the CPC-CBT intervention aimed to reduce the risk of re-victimisation and to increase the well-being of children who have been exposed to parental physical violence. We have also described how the method has been implemented in Sweden. Some noteworthy results can be highlighted from the ongoing Swedish research.

We identified significantly reduced trauma symptoms in children at post-treatment, reported by children as well as parents. The abused children in the study reported high levels of various potentially traumatic experiences beyond being the victims of physical violence. The findings underline the need to organise relevant support and intervention for children so as to reduce traumatic stress. The treatment components in CPC-CBT seem to meet those needs and to support children by increasing their well-being. Parents reported significantly more consistency in their child-rearing and less use of corporal punishment after treatment. One of the aims of the treatment is to support parents in developing alternative, non-violent parenting skills and improved communication with their child. When parents achieve improved parenting skills and experience positive changes within the family, this may affect their well-being and probably affect the reduction of depressive symptoms in parents, as identified in the study.

The data from the previous Swedish pilot study (Kjellgren et al. 2013) reflected comparable pre- and post-treatment results as found in this study. When comparing Swedish data with US data (Runyon et al. 2009), the results of children as well as parents are very much the same regarding how children and parents report positive changes in parenting strategies and decreasing levels of depression and trauma symptoms in children. This could indicate the similarities of families where child physical abuse has occurred, despite several (other) differences when comparing the USA and Sweden.

The aim of the research project presented here was to explore the outcome of CPC-CBT compared to other interventions, by including a comparison group of children and parents receiving treatment as usual from child welfare services. Several attempts were made in different municipalities to recruit families to a control group. Despite the willingness of colleagues to assist, comparison data have not yet been collected due to difficulties in recruiting families. We could only speculate about the reasons. One reason could be that the staff at the Barnahus or child welfare services that do not offer specialised interventions might find it difficult to ask families to participate in research when the family is not offered an intervention designed for parental abusive behaviour.

Some of the treatment units reported serving a large number of immigrant families, using CPC-CBT. In one-third of the 28 families participating in this study, one or both parents had an ethnic origin other than Swedish. The post-treatment outcomes for these families are equally positive, but as a future goal when the treatment method serves families from other cultural contexts, the treatment programme as well as the therapists needs to be sensitive to religious beliefs and values that are central for the family, as concluded by a number of studies (Santa-Sosa and Runyon 2015; Partridge and Walker 2015; Damra et al. 2014). This could lead to an improvement in the treatment by using metaphors and beliefs that are more relevant to family values, beliefs and traditions and thus, more helpful for families. It is also necessary to approach families with respect by offering support to children and families from different cultural contexts in a sensitive way. It is important to identify the strengths associated with their values, beliefs and traditions, and to integrate these constructs into treatment to enhance family engagement throughout the treatment process.

Barnahus has an important role in, and potential to, identify and support families in need of further interventions. Since both child welfare services and child and adolescent psychiatric units collaborate within the Barnahus, there is a strong foundation for organising the support of families. Earlier evaluations have identified the need for further interventions (Åström and Rejmer 2008), but there has also been discussion about the role of the Barnahus in giving further support and long-term treatment (e.g. Stefansen et al. 2012; Chap. 16 in this book).

According to this ongoing research study, Barnahus is a suitable agency for providing treatment to families when physical abuse had occurred. The Barnahus staff meets families in crisis and could thus present the treatment as an option at an early stage. Barnahus staff are well experienced in assisting families where physical violence has been present and do not fear talking about the abuse. When meeting new families where physical abuse has been identified, the staff at Barnahus can also talk about the potential for change in a trustworthy way, because they have experienced such change in other families after treatment.

Conclusion

There have been a number of positive experiences in implementing CPC-CBT in Sweden for physically abused children and their families, which support the further dissemination of the intervention across the country. The experiences of the 10 teams from Swedish Barnahus participating in the project so far is that the method works very well in the Barnahus setting, as a possible early intervention when child physical abuse has been disclosed and the child welfare caseworkers have concluded that CPC-CBT is the right intervention with regard to child protection needs. The ongoing study confirms the previous research findings of traumatic stress associated with child physical abuse.

Given that child physical abuse has both short- and long-term consequences for the individual child, it is important that Barnahus, as well as other agencies, have the tools and ability to pay attention to abused children and provide interventions that meet the needs of families in crisis, as well as prevent further violence. The positive results of the study need to be further investigated in line with the research plan (Fig. 4.1). It is important to evaluate whether parents maintain the good, non-violent parenting strategies reported at post-treatment (4 months) and whether the increased well-being of the children is still present at the 6-month follow-up.

Notes

1. The Children's Welfare Foundation holds the Swedish rights to use the treatment manual that is provided for those who have participated in the CPC-CBT therapist training. There is no financial gain in providing the manual or disseminating the programme.
2. The Public Health Agency of Sweden (Folkhälsomyndigheten) supported the implementation of the intervention across the country.

References

Åström, Karsten and Annika Rejmer. 2008. Det blir nog bättre för barnen... Slutrapport i utvärderingen av nationell försöksverksamhet med barnahus 2006–2007. Lund: Lund University, Research Report in Sociology of Law 2008:7.

Beck, Aaron T., Robert A. Steer and Gregory K. Brown. 1996. Beck Depression Inventory, 2nd ed. Manual, Swedish version. Sandviken: Psykologiförlaget AB.

Briere, John, Kerri Johnson, Angela Bissada, Linda Damon, Julie Crouch, Eliana Gil, Rochelle Hanson, and Vickie Ernest. 2001. The Trauma Symptom Checklist for Young Children (TSCYC): Reliability and Association with Abuse Exposure in a Multi-Site Study. *Child Abuse and Neglect* 25 (8): 1001–1014.

Children's Welfare Foundation Sweden. 2013. KIBB – Kognitiv Integrerad behandling vid Barnmisshandel. Treatment manual. Stockholm: Children's Welfare Foundation Sweden.

Clarkson Freeman, Pamela A. 2014. Prevalence and Relationship Between Adverse Childhood Experiences and Child Behavior Among Young Children. *Infant Mental Health Journal* 35 (6): 544–554.

Damra, Jalal Kayed M., Yahia H. Nassar, and Thaer Mohammd F. Ghabri. 2014. Trauma-Focused Cognitive Behavioral Therapy: Cultural Adaptations for Application in Jordanian Culture. *Counselling Psychology Quarterly* 27 (3): 308–323.

Frick, Paul J. 1991. *The Alabama Parenting Questionnaire*. Unpublished Rating Scale, University of Alabama.

Garbarino, James, Kathleen Kostelny, and Nancy Dubrow. 1991. What Children Can Tell us About Living in Danger. *American Psychologist* 46 (4): 376–383.

Gilbert, Ruth, Cathy Spatz Widom, Kevin Browne, David Fergusson, and Elspeth Webband Staffan Janson. 2009. Burden and Consequences of Child Maltreatment in High Income Countries. *Lancet* 373 (9657): 68–81.

Janson, Staffan, Carolina Jernbro and Bodil Långberg. 2011. Kroppslig bestraffning och annan kränkning av barn i Sverige. En nationell kartläggning 2011. Stockholm: Stiftelsen Allmänna Barnhuset.

Kjellgren, Cecilia, Carl Göran Svedin, and Doris Nilsson. 2013. Child Physical Abuse—Experiences of Combined Treatment for Children and their Parents: A Pilot Study. *Child Carein Practice* 19 (3): 275–290.

Landberg, Åsa and Carl Göran Svedin. 2013. Inuti ett barnahus. En kvalitetsgranskning av 23 svenska verksamheter. Stockholm: Save the Children Sweden.

Lindell, Charlottaand, and Carl Göran Svedin. 2006. Social Services Provided for Physically Abused Children: A Four Year Follow-Up Study in Sweden. *Child and Adolescent Social Work Journal* 5–6: 597–616.

Litrownik, Alan J., Rae Newton, Wanda M. Hunter, Diana English, and Mark D. Everson. 2003. Exposure to Family Violence in Young at-risk Children: A Longitudinal Look at the Effects of Victimisation and Witnessed Physical and Psychological Aggression. *Journal of Family Violence* 18 (1): 59–73.

Moffitt, Terrie E. 2013. Childhood Exposure to Violence and Lifelong Health: Clinical Intervention Science and Stress-Biology Research Join Forces. *Development and Psychopathology* 25: 1619–1634.

Nilsson, Doris, Per E. Gustafsson, and Carl Göran Svedin. 2012. The Psychometric Properties of the Trauma Symptom Checklist for Young Children in a Sample of Swedish Children. *European Journal of Psychotraumatology* 3: 1–12.

Nilsson, Doris, Per E. Gustafsson, Jessica Larsson, and Carl Göran Svedin. 2010. Evaluation of the Linköping Youth Life Experience Scale. *Journal of Nervous and Mental Disease* 198 (10): 768–774.

Norman, Rosana E., Munkhtsetseg Byambaa, Rumna De, Alexander Butchart, James Scott, and Theo Vos. 2012. The Long-Term Health Consequences of Child Physical Abuse, Emotional Abuse, and Neglect: A Systematic Review and Meta-Analysis. *PLoS Medicine* 9 (11): 1–31.

Partridge, Kathrine J., and Donald F. Walker. 2015. Addressing Spiritual Struggles Using Spiritually Oriented Trauma-Focused Cognitive Behavioural Therapy: An International Case Study. *Journal of Psychology & Christianity* 34 (1): 84–88.

Runyon, Melissa K., and Esther Deblinger. 2014. *Combined Parent-Child Cognitive Behavioral Therapy. An Approach to Empower Families At-Risk for Child Physical Abuse. Therapist Guide.* Oxford: Oxford University Press.

Runyon, Melissa K., Esther Deblinger, and Christine M. Schroeder. 2009. Pilot Evaluation of Outcomes of Combined Parent-Child Cognitive-Behavioral Group Therapy for Families at Risk for Child Physical Abuse. *Cognitive and Behavioral Practice* 16: 101–118.

Runyon, Melissa K., Esther Deblinger, and Robert A. Steer. 2010. Group Cognitive Behavioral Treatment for Parents and Children at-risk for Physical Abuse: An Initial Study. *Child & Family Behavior Therapy* 32 (3): 196–218.

Runyon, Melissa, Esther Deblinger, Erika Ryan, and Reena Thakkar-Kolar. 2004. An Overview of Child Physical Abuse: Developing an Integrated Parent-Child Cognitive-Behavioral Treatment Approach. *Trauma, Violence & Abuse* 5: 65–85.

Santa-Sosa, Eileen, and Melissa Runyon. 2015. Addressing Ethnocultural Factors in Treatment for Child Physical Abuse. *Journal of Child and Family Studies* 24 (6): 1660–1671.

Stefansen, Kari, Tonje Gundersen and Elisiv Bakketeig. 2012. Barnehusevalueringen 2012, delrapport 2. En undersøkelse blant barn og pårørende, samarbeidspartnere, ledere og ansatte. Oslo: NOVA, rapport nr. 9.

Svensson, Birgitta. 2013. Barn som riskerar att fara illa i sin hemmiljö. Utmaningar i ett förebyggande perspektiv. Dissertation, Karlstad Universitet, Karstad.

Swedish National Police Agency. 2009. Delredovisning av regeringsuppdrag avseende gemensamma nationella riktlinjer kring barn som misstänks vara utsatta för brott och kriterier för landets barnahus. Stockholm: The Swedish National Police Agency.

Thulin, Johanna, Cecilia Kjellgren, and Doris Nilsson. 2015. Forskningsstudien. In *Slutrapport KIBB projektet. Kognitiv Integrerad Behandling vid Barnmisshandel 2013–2015*, ed. Carl Göran Svedin, Doris Nilsson, Cecilia Kjellgren, Johanna Thulin, Lotta Lindgren, and Ylva Söderlind Göthner. Stockholm: Stiftelsen Allmänna Barnhuset.

Turner, Heather A., David Finkelhor, and Richard Ormrod. 2010. Poly-Victimization in a National Sample of Children and Youth. *American Journal of Preventive Medicine* 38 (3): 323–330.

Part II

Interviewing Children for Forensic Purposes

5

Taking of Statements from Children under the Nordic Model

Trond Myklebust

Introduction

Barnahus performs investigative interviewing of children. Implementation of Barnahus in the Nordic countries is based on legal scrutiny of the taking of statements from children and the strong Nordic tradition of protecting children from the burden of being involved in legal proceedings.

Internationally, there are two parallel legal systems obtaining children's testimonies. The first system is often referred to as "examination-in-chief" or the "adversarial package", and the second has been called the "Nordic model" (La Rooy et al. 2015; Scottish Courts and Tribunals Service 2016; Spencer and Lamb 2012). The aim of this chapter is to describe the development of the Nordic model for each of the Nordic countries.

T. Myklebust (✉)
Norwegian Police University College, Oslo, Norway
e-mail: Trond.Myklebust@phs.no

The Adversarial Package

An *inquisitorial system* is a legal system where the court or a part of the court is actively involved in investigating the facts of the case, as opposed to an *adversarial system* where the role of the court is primarily that of an impartial referee between the prosecution and the defence. The adversarial package is a combination of the following legal traditions: firstly, that witnesses tell their tale in open court, in the presence of the defendant; secondly, the full narrative must be told under these conditions, meaning that the witness must tell the story in open court and must do so without incorporating or referring back to statements they have previously made; thirdly, submit to an adversarial cross-examination by someone whose agenda is to persuade the court that their account is incomplete, or that they are lying or mistaken (Spencer 2012).

For children, particularly young ones, these conditions often used to make it impossible for them to deliver their evidence at all. Modifications to the first element, "open court", have been implemented in most courts using the adversarial package as their basic judicial system. Special measures might include (Ministry of Justice 2011; Scottish Court Service 2015; Spencer and Lamb 2012):

- Removal of wigs and gowns: judge and barristers are asked to remove wigs and gowns when a vulnerable person gives evidence.
- Screen placed between the victim testifying and the defendant (jury and judge must be able to see).
- A live TV link from another room either within the court building, in another court building or from a remote location.
- The child giving evidence in a private chamber.
- Video evidence used as evidence-in-chief; the recorded child interview is presented for the court.
- Video evidence cross-examination: cross-examination is recorded prior to the trial.
- Accused cannot cross-examine the victim: in cases involving vulnerable witnesses or victims, the accused cannot cross-examine them if acting as their own counsel.

- Use of "Registered Intermediaries".
- Restrictions on questions regarding previous sexual behaviour.

Brennan (1994) discusses the difficulties experienced by child witnesses being cross-examined in court. He found that 85% of the time, across all ages [6–15 years] and ability groups, the tested children failed to hear and understand some questions. Critically, the study found that responses such as "*I don't know*" and "*I can't remember*" may indicate a failure to comprehend the question, rather than a lack of knowledge or ability to recall events. Such a failure might easily occur in the unusual surroundings of the courtroom and when the language usage is entirely unfamiliar to the child (Saywitz and Nathanson 1993). The list of features common to *courtroom language*, including complex structures (e.g. embeddings, negative questions and tag questions), difficult vocabulary (legalese, jargon, archaic structures) or speaking for another (including repeating the child's words), is, however, also commonly found in investigative interviewing conducted outside the courtroom (La Rooy et al. 2016; Rock 2007; Spencer and Lamb 2012).

Zajac et al. (2003a) found that children were frequently cross-examined using an inappropriate questioning style. The questions of defence lawyers included complexity to a significant degree, which caused as much as 75% of the children to change elements of their testimonies. Zajac and Hayne (2003) found that the accuracy of 5- and 6-year-old witnesses severely declined as a result of being interviewed in a cross-examination style where the language was too complicated to be readily understood by the children. According to Brennan (1995), cross-examination strategies used in court deny children any possibility of coming forward with their own experiences, as children are faced with questions that are hard to decode (for further discussions, see, for example, Spencer and Lamb 2012; Oxburgh et al. 2016; Lamb et al. 2011).

The combination of the legal traditions in the adversarial package might reduce the quantity and quality of investigation of relevant information obtained in the forensic interviews. If interviewees are not able to give their best evidence, this may affect the quality of both the investigation and court testimonies. This is why most adversarial countries have introduced additional precautions for the testimonies of vulnerable witnesses given in main hearings for the open court. An example of this could be England and Wales, where vulnerable witnesses are defined (in the Youth Justice and Criminal Evidence Act 1999) as all child witnesses (under 18 years), and any witness who has a mental health disorder has a significant impairment of intelligence and social functioning, or those with physical disability. England and Wales introduced Intermediaries in 2004 (Witness Intermediary Scheme) for both vulnerable child and adult victims with disabilities, and a national rollout was completed in 2008. According to Plotnikoff and Woolfson (2015), the role[1] of the Registered Intermediaries (RI) as highly trained communication specialists in England and Wales has been a great success. The RI have a variety of professional backgrounds (e.g. psychologists, speech and language therapists, teachers, social workers) . Their role is to assist the victims and witnesses of crime at police interviews and in court. The role of the RI in England and Wales and the staff at the Nordic Barnahus include several similar tasks. They both meet with the vulnerable person and assess their communication. In the police interview, they provide brief recommendations for the interviewing officer about how to communicate.

The "Nordic Model"

General

Criminal trials are based on oral proceedings in all adversarial systems, and evidence must be heard in court. Judges are therefore not permitted to see police records before the trial opens. The indictment is the only document that the court receives prior to the main hearing of the case. The "Nordic model" is a more inquisitorial pre-trial process, where the video of the child's interview is accepted in court as the evidence-in-chief, thus negating the need for the child to attend court, provide evidence or be cross-examined. The interview from the pre-trial investigation is accepted as evidence, as long as the interview is video-recorded, and the accused suspect has been given the opportunity to contradict the charges against them. In other words, the child's involvement in the judicial process almost always comes to an end after the pre-trial interview, even if the case is appealed (Oxburgh et al. 2016).

The development of a model focusing on the children's need started as early as 1913, in a motion put forward to the Norwegian Parliament by the Norwegian Women's National Council, to amend the law concerning investigative interviews of children who have fallen victim to sexual felonies. The Council's initiative brought about an amendment in the legislation, which came into effect in 1926 (Norske Kvinners Nasjonalråd 1957). To the author's knowledge, this made Norway the first country in Europe to statutorily outline how investigative interviews in child sexual abuse cases should be conducted.

In Iceland, the judge is still in charge and presents (monitors) the investigative interview of the children, while the police/prosecution are in charge in the other Nordic countries.

Unlike the adversarial model, the Nordic model demonstrates a fundamental shift towards the examination of the interviewee by a trained third party. During the police investigation, the parties' legal representatives (monitoring the interview) are indirectly questioning the interviewee through a specially trained interviewer. The video-recorded forensic interview will be the evidence-in-chief and potentially the only interview with the child (vulnerable witness) that will be required.

The Development of the Nordic Model

Despite a focus on children as vulnerable witnesses and children's rights since the early 1900s, the high-profile child abuse cases of the 1980s and 1990s [such as the McMartin preschool and Kelly Michaels case in the USA (State v. Buckey 1990; Garven et al. 1998; Myers 2009), and the Orkney inquiries in the United Kingdom (Clyde 1992)] did not gain the attention of psychological and legal professionals in the Nordic countries. They did pay attention, however, when the media and public were introduced to two well-documented Nordic cases where defendants were found not guilty due to inappropriate investigative interviewing protocols (see, e.g. Riksadvokaten 1994; Hennum 1999; Grothe Nielsen 1995). These injustices were found to have resulted from several decades of poor interviewing techniques, children's suggestibility and false memories (and the danger of therapist "interventions").

The two Nordic cases took place in Roum in Denmark (1989–1993) and Bjugn in Norway (1992–1994). In the Roum case, seven persons were convicted of sexual abuse on the testimony of three teenagers, two of whom were mentally retarded. The abuse allegations arose out of hours of therapy with the same therapist. The legal case it started in autumn 1989 and proceeded for four and a half years (though the closing legal arguments were only finalised in July 1996). Seven persons were convicted and sentenced to prison for a total of 14 years and had to pay immense damages. Through the efforts of defence attorneys and two journalists, the defendants were granted a new trial and eventually freed several years later (Grothe Nielsen 1995).

The Bjugn case involved seven adults who were arrested in 1992 under suspicion of sexual abuse and the rape of children. The police conducted more than 550 interviews of 220 witnesses and conducted 61 judicial hearings of 40 children. Charges were dropped for six of the seven suspects. After a two-and-a-half-month-long trial, the last defendant was acquitted in 1994 (Hennum 1999; Myklebust and Bjørklund 2006).

Following a review of the Bjugn case by the General Director of Public Prosecution in Norway, the following recommendations were made (Riksadvokaten 1994):

- The investigative interviews of children should be conducted by specialised trained police officers, instead of psychologists or social workers.
- The police interviewers should be given additional advanced training.
- New regulations specifying how these interviews should be conducted were introduced.

The allegations in the Roum and Bjugn cases and the criticism of the interviewers' competence, style of questioning and the time from the alleged abuse to the interview taking place, were similar to those in other highly publicised sexual abuse cases in earlier decades (Ceci and Bruck 1995). The subsequent development of interview protocols, guidelines and training was founded on research-based theories and proven structured communication models (Gamst and Langballe 2004; Korkman 2006; La Rooy et al. 2016; Melinder 2004; Myklebust 2012, 2009).

Interview Protocols and Guidelines

The scientific perspective of investigative interviewing backs to the German scientist William Stern (1903/1904). Stern was occupied with examining techniques that acquired the most valid information from children and introduced the distinction between *open* (bericht) and *closed* (verhör) questions. He demonstrated the superiority of *open* questions, showing that they gained more and a better quality of information compared to *closed* questions.

This benefit of using open questions is stated in nearly all interview guidelines used by the police internationally, highlighting the following three points (Oxburgh et al. 2010):

1. When children are encouraged to do most of the talking, this helps to transfer control from the interviewer to the child, which is more compatible with a witness-focused approach (Fisher and Geiselman 1992).
2. Elaborate responses during the rapport-building phase provide an opportunity for the interviewer to gauge the child's level of language competency, so that they can adjust the subsequent questioning style accordingly (Saywitz and Camparo 1998).
3. An open-ended rapport-building style sets up the expectation that the child will do most of the talking throughout the duration of the interview.

Central to the development of interview guidelines has been knowledge of how memory works, children's developmental capabilities and the conditions that improve a child's ability to discuss their abuse experiences. Today, we understand better the strengths, weaknesses and features of children's memory, and this knowledge has shaped professional recommendations about interviewing children.[2]

The guidelines presented are all generic; they cannot cater for every possible set of circumstances that might arise. Each witness is unique, and the manner in which they are interviewed and subsequently prepared for their court appearance must be tailored to their particular needs and circumstances; however, the core recommendations made by professional bodies worldwide share a remarkable consensus. Small differences in recommended procedures usually arise out of regional idiosyncratic legal constraints, rather than disagreements between scientists about the basic nature of memory and children's developing abilities.

The structured interview protocols used in all Nordic countries are remarkably consistent with the NICHD protocol. For a presentation of this protocol, see Chap. 6 (Bagerud and Johnsson) and La Rooy et al. (2015).

Interview Training and Professionalisation

Police interviewing has undergone a transformation in terms of professionalisation, due to scientific experimentation and analysis. Fisher et al. (1987) observed that an interviewer's level of competence directly affected responses in interviews of adult interviewees. The authors recommended the formal, scientifically based training of police officers at the institutional level. They also suggested that training programmes would be most successful if they were divided into intensive short, practical sessions, rather than longer sessions, with extended feedback to the individual interviewers (Fisher and Geiselman 1992).

Lamb and his colleagues argued that long-time improvement in the quality of investigative interviews is observed only when the training is distributed over time (Lamb et al. 2002a, b). In their studies, the length of training varied between 3 and 5 days of initial training, with follow-up supervision and feedback (Stewart et al. 2011). Knowledge about how to conduct the "optimal" interview is not automatically translated into practice. Continuous supervision and feedback are necessary and a prerequisite for efficient learning in general (Kahneman and Klein 2009), maintaining the quality and requested standard of the investigative interviews conducted.

Powell et al. (2005) outlined the elements of training that have been found to be the most successful. The core elements of success included the use of:

- Structured interview protocols;
- Multiple opportunities to practice over an extended period;
- Expert feedback and ongoing supervision; and
- The internal motivation of the interviewer to enhance their individual performance.

There has been much research showing that the complete transference of training into the workplace is rather elusive (e.g. Myklebust and Bjørklund 2006; Powell et al. 2005; Wright and Powell 2006). The more complex skills are particularly difficult to sustain over time (e.g. rapport, use of open questions) as opposed to more procedural interviewer behaviours, such as outlining persons present in the interview and giving legal rights (Griffiths et al. 2011).

The Nordic countries have all based their training of investigative interviewers of children around:

- Central national institution(s) providing the training.
- The nationally structured interview models being based upon empirically validated guidelines and/or communication models.
- The interview training being distributed over time with follow-up supervision and feedback to the interviewers.

Police training in the Nordic countries is vastly different to that of other European countries, where the police are provided with shorter basic training. Nordic countries train their police officers to become so-called generalists within their work as police officers. They are authorised for a multitude of responsibilities, from crime prevention via operational patrolling police duties to profound and scientifically based detective work (Birkeland 2007; Granhag 2010; Ministry of Justice and the

Police 2005). Focusing on the basic "generalist" training, the central police educational institutions in all the Nordic countries are heading (in the long term) towards a system of Police University Colleges. Norway was the first and founded the Norwegian Police University College (NPUC) in 1992, receiving their college charter in 2004. They comprise a three-year basic education which provides all police officers with a bachelor degree in policing before beginning patrol work or embarking on further specialised training and education.

Investigative Interviewers in the Nordic Model

The professionalisation of the investigative interviewers in each of the countries using the Nordic model will be described.

Norway

The investigative interviews of children, under 16 years, are only conducted by specially trained police officers. Assuming that specially trained police officers would elicit more information from children than officers without such training, substantial resources and effort have been invested in increasing the competence of the police officers conducting investigative interviews of children.

The training of child investigative interviewers is based on scientific and research-based techniques (Gamst and Langballe 2004; Norwegian Police University College 2012).[3] Child interviewers in Norway have the formal academic competence and are thus the interviewers most skilled in theory. The interviewers have dedicated most of their professional careers to interviews with children and cases involving children as victims. From 1992, the education and training of the interviewers have focused around the same theoretical principles based on a structured interview approach.

The basic education for all police officers in Norway is the NPUC's three-year bachelor's degree as a foundation level. Officers might apply for formal specialisation within investigation ("advanced level") after a minimum of a year's duty in the police service. Education at the advanced level starts with a 420 h (part-time) study in general investigation.[4] The study is worth 15 (ECTS) credits in the university accreditation system. From this advanced level, one of the formal specialisations an investigator could apply for is "investigative interviewing".

The investigators specialising in investigative interviews of children and minors are provided with a (15 ECTS) part-time study,[5] of approximately 420 h over a period of three-quarters of a year. The study is divided into face-to-face training at NPUC and self-study at the police district where the interviewer is employed.

After conducting at least fifty investigative interviews with children (under the age of 16 years), the interviewers are entitled to apply for further specialisation. This comprises (10 ECTS) 280 h of part-time study, focusing on vulnerable persons.[6]

In addition to the education, at foundation, advanced and specialist level, Barnahus and NPUC are involved in several joint projects handling children's testimonies and investigative procedures. One of these is the implementation and evaluation of the use of sequential interviews for the youngest (preschool) children under 6 years. Another upcoming area of concern is interviews with children (under the age of consent[7]) as suspects of offensive or intimidating behaviour against other children.

Iceland

Historically, all interviews outside of Reykjavík were conducted at the Barnahus, while the district court in Reykajvík had a specially designed interview suite, where the police conducted most of the interviews with children living in Reykjavík. Today, almost every interview with children is conducted in Barnahus, either by the police or by the Barnahus staff. The investigative interviews with children, under the age of 15, are conducted by both the psychologists at the Barnahus and specially trained police officers.[8] It is most common that specially trained forensic interviewers working at the Barnahus conduct the investigative interviews.

The system regarding forensic interviews has changed over time. According to the Code of Criminal Procedure, a judge is responsible for the interview of a child up to the age of 15. Children from 15 to 18 years are in most cases interviewed by the police at the police station and not at the Barnahus. If the case is taken to court, the youth will attend a separate court hearing. In the vast majority of cases, the judge contacts the Barnahus right after the case has been referred to them by the police, and asks for a forensic interview by a specialist at the Barnahus. The forensic interview (actual court hearing) is booked as soon as possible. On some rare occasions, the judge asks the police to conduct the forensic interview in the Barnahus. In Iceland courts, the judge decides who will conduct the interview and it is their decision whether it is a specialist from the Barnahus or a police officer.

The structured investigative interview protocol used at the Barnahus is the NICHD protocol with some minor adjustments. In February 2016, there were three forensic interviewers at the Barnahus, two of which are clinical psychologists and one with background in criminology and pedagogy (educational studies). They have worked in the field since 2001 and 2006. In addition to their formal clinical backgrounds, they have conducted further specialisation in investigative interviews of children in the USA, with the American Professional Society on the Abuse of Children (APSAC) and the National Child Advocacy Centre (NCAC), accordingly. Two of the interviewers have also completed the advanced investigative interview training at the NCAC. The two investigative interviewers from Reykjavik Metropolitan Police undertook their specialist training with the Greater Manchester Police in England. They attended their 3-week course in "Achieving Best Evidence in Criminal Proceedings" (Ministry of Justice 2011). The Icelandic courts (in general) have agreed that those police officers who finish the ABE[9] training in England and Wales are qualified to conduct investigative interviews of children in court.

In 2002, the Icelandic Barnahus was identified as a "best practice model" in a study of nine European states by the International Save the Children Alliance, generating international interest and inspiration (Guðbrandsson 2011).

Sweden

Video-recorded investigative interviews of all children under the age of 15 are conducted by the police.[10] The hearing is under control of the prosecutor. Also present in the monitoring room will be a police investigator, counsel for the complainer, substitute guardian for the child, defence lawyer, representatives from the child welfare services and/or an advisor from the Barnahus. There will also usually be a technician to operate the audio/video viewing and recording.

The training of interviewers is provided by the police college using a two-step approach.[11]

The first step is focusing on investigative procedures and methods in cases involving children and youths as victims of criminal offences. The course is provided by the University of Uppsala and lasts ten weeks, with five being lectures and teamwork at the University and 5 weeks of individual self-studies and assignments, at home or locally in the police district where the student is working (Police Academy 2014; Uppsala University 2014).

The second step focuses on "investigative interview methods and techniques". The education is provided by Stockholm University over a period of five weeks on a monthly basis. In this period, the students receive lectures about interview models (PEACE model and the NICHD protocol), conduct several interviews in criminal proceedings and are supervised and receive feedback from the lecturers and course administrators (Police Academy 2015; Stockholm University 2015).

Altogether, this stepwise educational approach takes just under a year to fulfil. The present model was introduced in 2008, and 20–25 students/police officers have attended each year.

Denmark

After the introduction of Barnahus in Denmark in 2013, the main rule is that all investigative interviews of children should be conducted by the police at the Barnahus.[12] In allegations of sexual abuse, investigative interviews of children under the age of 15 years are to be video-recorded

(Department of Justice 2015). The Danish police have conducted formal training of investigative interviewers in child sexual abuse cases since 2001. Before this, the training was more locally adapted (Danish National Police 2000). In December 2015,[13] there were approximately 115 specially trained investigative interviewers within the Danish police, conducting around 1200 interviews a year (Danish National Police 2016). The training of interviewers has, until 2016, been a two-week period (2 × 5 days) with lecturers within psychology, law and a structured communication model (equivalent to the PEACE model). It has been suggested that from 2016, this training is increased to 3 weeks (4 + 3 + 4 days), with at least 4 weeks between each week of face-to-face training, allowing more time to read the literature, visit Barnahus and fulfil assignments. Practical interview training, case studies and a reduced number of lectures will be prioritised at the face-to-face training (Danish National Police 2016).

Finland

In Finland, the investigative interview of a child is conducted by the police investigator or another person appointed by the police investigator to conduct the interview on their behalf.[14] Based on the EU directive on vulnerable victims and witnesses, the Finnish government ruled that from 1 July 2015 not only children up to 15 years, but also (adult) victims of sexual crimes up to 17 years old, *may* be video-interviewed during the pre-investigation. If a victim in the 15- to 17-year-old age group wishes, the recorded interview may be used as evidence-in-chief in court.

Since 2009, the Finnish National Police Board has annually offered one-year education to police officers and forensic psychologists conducting investigative interviews with children up to 15 years of age. The training includes ten days of lectures in psychology, including memory and the core issues related to testimonial psychology, child development, prevalence and features of various types of child abuse, decision-making procedures, the testing of relevant hypotheses and the relevant law.[15] The NICHD protocol is the structured interview protocol used in Finland. The students are taught the literature behind, and within their supervision groups, they are given feedback on their practical use of the protocol in real investigative interviews of children. The supervisions are given in small groups (6 × 3 h), spread throughout the year of training. The supervisors are all forensic psychologists with experience within the field of investigative interviewing. The final exam is an in-depth plan for an investigative interview conducted by the student themselves, transcribing, analysing and evaluating the interview against the NICHD protocol and other theory on the course, once the interview has been conducted.

Finnish instructors have conducted follow-up studies on the students who graduated, revealing positive changes in their questioning style, attitudes and beliefs. It is clear their level of professionalism has increased since 2006 (Kaunisto 2013).[16]

Conclusion

Historically, the forensic interviews of children have taken place at all times. Opinions about the reliability and validity of children's statements have changed as a result of the research and developments in law, psychology and linguistics, as academic disciplines. We have learnt about children's cognitive strength and limitations, and children's motivations and emerging abilities to communicate their experiences. Many elements of our current approach to interviewing children are now considered "conventional wisdom". One could argue that the basic communication principles, models and stepwise approaches that we teach and train our interviewers and students today are basically the same principles as those used by the Roman rhetorician Quintilian (c. 35–c. 100 CE) when he lectured and trained his students. Future developments in forensic interviews with children will involve the implementation of communication knowledge into practice.

Since the Norwegian Women's National Council pioneered effective investigative interviews with children in 1913, the Nordic model has been a realistic alternative to the more traditional and conservative ways of presenting and evaluating evidence in court. As discussed in other chapters in this book, there is enormous potential in Barnahus, as the point of contact for all professionals involved. Focusing on the forensic interview, Barnahus needs to be dynamic in its organisation and plan and prepare for several challenges. As an example, we cannot realistically expect investigators, members of the court and jurors, to be experts in communication assessments, cross-cultural linguistics and appropriate interventions with all groups of people. As such, Barnahus will play an important role in finding experts to assist in the forensic interview and investigative process.

Another international trend is the increase in the number of interviews being conducted through language and cultural interpreters due to global migration. This is another area where Barnahus, in the future, will have to supervise practitioners and the interview trainers. To be effective, such training has to be done by Barnahus in cooperation with the Nordic police colleges. The result could be a Nordic education programme in investigative interviews with children, provided for all the forensic interviewers in Nordic countries.

Protocols for forensic interviews of children tend to focus only on the interviews of those who are *victims* and/or *witnesses* of an alleged criminal offence. There are situations where the child (or another vulnerable person) is a suspect. Unfortunately, there is a dearth of literature regarding how best to interview such vulnerable suspects (Oxburgh et al. 2016). This is another area where Barnahus already is, and will be, challenged in the future.

To conclude, poorly conducted interviews have negative consequences. Misunderstandings and inaccuracies may lead to false convictions or family break-up. Alternatively, abusers may be left free to exploit other children. Justice can only be done when decision-makers are armed with reliable communication techniques. This chapter has focused on investigative interviews with children and how Barnahus is an important part of the Nordic model of investigative interviews with children. This chapter has also demonstrated some of the differences between investigation protocols and training, which have been embedded by local hierarchies. In order to continually improve, researchers and practitioners in all Nordic countries must work in closer partnership with each other through Barnahus. This will help to ensure all

Nordic countries continue the very proud tradition of supporting children through the justice system.

Notes

1. See: http://www.theadvocatesgateway.org.
2. See, for example, Achieving Best Evidence in Criminal Proceedings (Ministry of Justice 2011), Den Dialogiske Samtalemetoden [The Dialogic Communication Method] DCM (see Chapter 8: Sequential interviews with preschool children in Norwegian Barnahus, by Langballe and Davik, in the present book), National Institute of Child health and Human Development (NICHD) protocol (La Rooy et al. 2015; Sternberg et al. 2001), PEACE (National Crime Faculty 1998).
3. Inger Lise Brøste, The Norwegian Police University College. Personal communication 23rd June 2016.
4. Videreutdanning i etterforskning (Norwegian Police University College, 2015).
5. Videreutdanning i avhør av barn og ungdom (Norwegian Police University College, 2012).
6. Videreutdanning i avhør av sårbare personer (Norwegian Police University College 2014).
7. In Norway, the age of consent is 15 years (Norwegian Criminal Code §20).
8. Þorbjörg Sveinsdóttir at Barnahus, Reykjavik, and Einar Guðberg Jónsson, Lögreglan á Höfuðborgarsvæðinu [Reykjavik Metropolitan Police]. Personal communication and e-mail, 4th and 17th of February 2016; and Bragi Gudbrandsson, General Director, The Government Agency for Child Protection, Iceland. Personal communication 25th May 2016.
9. Achieving Best Evidence (ABE) in Criminal Proceedings (Ministry of Justice 2011).
10. Harriet Jakobsson Öhrn, Stockholm University. Previously in charge of the interview training at the Swedish Police Academy. Personal communication 23rd June 2016.
11. Britt Marie Therese Karlsson, The Swedish Police, Uddevalla. Personal communication and e-mails, 28 and 29 January 2016; Harriet Jakobsson Öhrn, see note 10 above.
12. Personal communication with Thomas Skou Roer, Special advisor and CIO, Danish National Police, 24th June 2016.

13. See note 12 above.
14. Professor Julia Korkman, Åbo University. Personal communication 1st February, 25th May and 23rd June 2016.
15. See note 14 above.
16. Personal communication with Jasmin Kaunisto, Oulun University Hospital, 23rd June 2016.

References

Birkeland, Åsmund. 2007. Politigeneralisten, den moderne staten og politiets legitimitet. In *Polisiær virksomhet, PHS Forskning 2007:7*, eds. Helene Gundhus, Tor-Geir Myhrer, and Paul Larsson, 31–48. Oslo: Politihøgskolen.

Brennan, Mark. 1994. The battle for credibility-themes in the cross examination of child victim witnesses. *International Journal for the Semiotics of Law* 7 (1): 51–73.

Brennan, Mark. 1995. Cross examining children in Criminal Courts: child welfare under attack. In *Language and the Law*, ed. John Gibbons, 199–216. Harlow: Longman Group.

Ceci, Stephen J., and Maggie Bruck (eds.). 1995. *Jeopardy in the Courtroom. A scientific analysis of children's testimony*. Washington: American Psychological Association.

Clyde, James John. 1992. *The report of the inquiry into the removal of children from orkney in February 1991*. Edinburgh: HMSO.

Danish National Police. 2000. Betænkning nr.1420: Gjennemførelse af straffesager om seksuelt misbrug af børn.

Danish National Police. 2016. Utdannelsesrapport: Videoafhøreruddannelsen 2016. Videoafhøring af børn og af voksne med varig funksjonsnedsættelse. På diplomniveau.

Department of Justice. 2015. *Betænkning 1554: Betænkning om videoafhøring af børn og unge i strafesager*. København: Justisministeriets Strafferetsplejeutvalg.

Fisher, Ronald P., R. Edward Geiselman, and D.S. Raymond. 1987. Critical analysis of police interview techniques. *Journal of Police Science and Administration* 15 (3): 177–185.

Fisher, Ronald P., and R. Edward Geiselman. 1992. Memory-enhancing techniques for investigative interviewing. The cognitive interview. Springfield, IL: Charles C. Thomas Publisher.

Gamst, Kari Trøften, and Åse Langballe. 2004. Barn som vitner—En empirisk og teoretisk studie av kommunikasjon mellom avhører og barn i dommeravhør. Utvikling av en avhørsmetodisk tilnærming. Doctoral dissertation. University of Oslo: Department of Education.

Garven, Sena, James. M. Wood, Roy S. Malpass, and John S. Shaw. 1998. More than Suggestion: The effect of Interviewing Techniques From the McMartin Preschool Case. *Journal of Applied Psychology* 83 (3): 347–359.

Granhag, Pär Anders (ed.). 2010. *Forensic Psychology in context. Nordic and international approaches*. Cullompton: Willan Publishing.

Griffiths, Andy, Rebecca Milne, and Julie Cherryman. 2011. A question of control? The formulation of suspect and witness interview question strategies by advanced interviewers. *International Journal of Police Science and Management* 13 (3): 1–13.

Grothe Nielsen, Beth. 1995. Straffesystemet i børneperspektiv. København: Jurist- og økonomforbundets Forlag.

Guðbrandsson, Bragi. 2011. Towards a child-friendly justice and support for child victims of sexual abuse. In *The Council of Europe Publication: Protecting children from sexual violence—A comprehensive approach*, 85–96. Strasbourg: Council of Europe.

Hennum, Ragnhild. 1999. Bevis i saker om seksuelle overgrep mot barn. Doctoral dissertation. Department of Criminology and Sociology of Law, University of Oslo.

Kahneman, Daniel, and Gary Klein. 2009. Conditions for Intuitive Expertise. American Psychologist 64 (6): 515–526.

Kaunisto, Jasmin. 2013. Kun se teki sulle niin Lapsen seksuaalinen hyväksikäyttö, hyväksikäyttöä koskevien oikeuspsykologisten haastatteluiden taso, kouluttautumisen vaikutukset ja osallistujien arviot koulutuksesta. Master's thesis. Joensuu, Finland [Department of Psychology University of Eastern Finland]. Retrieved 23rd June, 2016. http://epublications.uef.fi/pub/urn_nbn_fi_uef-20130256/urn_nbn_fi_uef-20130256.pdf.

Korkman, Julia. 2006. How (not) to interview children: Interviews with young children in sexual abuse investigations in Finland. Doctoral dissertation, Department of Psychology and Logopedics, Åbo Akademi University.

La Rooy, David, Sonja P Brubacher, Anu Aromäki-Stratos, Mireille Cyr, Irit Hershkowitz, Julia Korkman, Trond Myklebust, Makiko Naka, Carlos E. Peixoto, Kim P Roberts, Heather Stewart, and Michael E Lamb. 2015. The NICHD protocol: A review of an internationally-used evidence-based tool for training child forensic interviewers. *Journal of Criminological Research, Policy and Practice* 1 (2): 76–89.

La Rooy, David, Georgina Heydon, Julia Korkman, and Trond Myklebust. 2016. Interviewing Child Witnesses. In *Communication in Investigative and Legal Contexts. Integrated Approaches from Forensic Psychology, Linguistics and Law Enforcement* eds. E. Trond Myklebust Oxburgh, Tim Grant, and Rebecca Milne, 57–78. Chichester: Wiley.

Lamb, Michael E., Kathleen J. Sternberg, Yael Orbach, Phillip W. Esplin, and Susanne Mitchell. 2002a. Is ongoing feedback necessary to maintain the quality of investigative interviews with allegedly abused children? *Applied Developmental Science* 6 (1): 35–41.

Lamb, Michael E., Kathleen J. Sternberg, Yael Orbach, Irit Hershkowitz, Dvora Horowitz, and Phillip W. Esplin. 2002b. The effects of intensive training and ongoing supervision on the quality of Investigative interviews with alleged sex abuse victims. *Applied Developmental Science* 6 (3): 114–125.

Lamb, Michael E., David J. La Rooy, Lindsay C. Malloy, and Carmit Katz. 2011. *Children's testimony: A handbook of psychological research and forensic practice*. Chichester: Wiley.

Melinder, Annika Maria D. 2004. Perspectives on children as witness. Doctoral dissertation. Department of Psychology, University of Oslo.

Ministry of Justice. 2011. Achieving best evidence in criminal proceedings. Guidance on interviewing victims and witnesses, and guidance on using special measures. London: Ministry of Justice.

Ministry of Justice and the Police. 2005. Stortingsmelding nr. 42—Politiets rolle og oppgaver.[White Paper No 42. The role and duties of the Police]. Oslo: Statens Forvaltningstjeneste.

Myers, John E.B. 2009. Introduction: Improved forensic interviewing: the legacy of the McMartin Preschool case. In *The evaluation of child sexual abuse alegations: a comprehensive guide to assessment and testimony*, eds. Kathryn Kuehnle, and Mary Connell, XIX–XXV. NJ: Wiley.

Myklebust, Trond. 2009. Analysis of field investigative interviews of children conducted by specially trained police investigators. Doctoral dissertation. Department of Psychology, University of Oslo.

Myklebust, Trond. 2012. The position in Norway. In *Children and Cross-examination: Time to Change the Rules?*, eds. John R. Spencer, and Michael E. Lamb, 147–170. Oxford: Hart Publishing.

Myklebust, Trond, and Roald A. Bjørklund. 2006. The effect of long-term training on police officers' use of open and closed questions in field investigative interviews of children (FIIC). *Journal of Investigative Psychology and Offender Profiling* 3 (3): 165–181.

National Crime Faculty. 1998. A practical guide to investigative interviewing. Bramshill: Training and Development Unit.

Norske Kvinners Nasjonalråd. 1957. *Norske Kvinners Nasjonalråd 1904–1954 [Norwegian Women's National Council 1904–1954]*. Flisa: Flisa boktrykkeri.

Norwegian Police University College. 2012. Studieplan. Videreutdanning i avhør av barn og ungdom. 15 studiepoeng. Oslo: Politihøgskolen.

Norwegian Police University College. 2014. Studieplan. Videreutdanning i avhør av sårbare personer. 10 studiepoeng. Oslo: Politihøgskolen.

Norwegian Police University College. 2015. Studieplan. Videreutdanning i etterforskning. 15 studiepoeng. Oslo: Politihøgskolen.

Oxburgh, Gavin E., Trond Myklebust, and Tim Grant. 2010. The question of question types in police interviews: a review of the literature from a psychological and linguistic perspective. *The International Journal of Speech, Language and the Law* 17 (1): 45–66.

Oxburgh, Gavin E., Trond Myklebust, Tim Grant, and Rebecca Milne. 2016. Communication in investigative and legal contexts. Integrated approaches from forensic psychology, linguistics and law enforcement. Chichester: Wiley.

Plotnikoff, Joyce, and Richard Woolfson. 2015. *Intermediaries in the criminal justice system: improving communication for vulnerable witnesses and defendants*. Bristol: Policy Press.

Police Academy. Sweden. 2014. Utreningsmetodik med inriktning på brott mot barn och ungdomar, steg 1, HT 2014. Studieoversikt. 22.9.2014.

Police Academy. Sweden. 2015. Brott mot barn och ungdomar, Steg 2—Intervju- och förhörsmetodik, HT 2015. Datum 2015-08-10.

Powell, Martine B., Ron P. Fisher, and Rebecca Wright. 2005. Investigative Interviewing. In *Psychology and law: an empirical perspective*, eds. Neil Brewer, and Kipling D. Williams, 11–42, NY: Guilford Publications.

Riksadvokaten. 1994. Riksadvokatens gjennomgang av den såkalte Bjugnsaken. Oslo: Riksadvokaten.

Rock, Frances. 2007. *Communicating rights: the language of arrest and detention*. Houndmills: Palgrave Macmillan.

Saywitz, Karen, and Lorinda Camparo. 1998. Interviewing child witnesses: a developmental perspective. *Child Abuse and Neglect* 22 (8): 825–843.

Saywitz, Karen, and Rebecca Nathanson. 1993. Children's testimony and their perceptions of stress in and out of the courtroom. *The International Journal of Child Abuse and Neglect* 17: 613–622.

Scottish Court Service. 2015. Evidence and Procedure Review Report.White paper on the reform on investigative interviews of children. March 2015, 3–80.

Scottish Courts and Tribunals Service. 2016. Evidence and procedure review—next steps. White paper on the reform on investigative interviews of children. 26 February 2016, 1–31.

Spencer, John R. 2012. Introduction. In *Children and Cross-Examination. Time to change the rules,* eds. John R. Spencer, and Michael E. Lamb, 1–20. Oxford: Hart Publishing.

Spencer, John R., and Michael E. Lamb. 2012. *Children and cross-examination. Time to change the rules*. Oxford: Hart Publishing.

State v. Buckey, Superior Court, Los Angeles County, California, #A750900. (1990).

Stern, William L. 1903/1904. Beiträge zür Psychologie der Aussage. Leipzig: Verlag von Johann Ambrosius Barth.

Sternberg, Kathleen J., Michael E. Lamb, Yael Orbach, Phillip W. Esplin, and Susanne Mitchell. 2001. Use of a structured investigative protocol enhances young children's responses to free-recall prompts in the course of forensic interviews. *Journal of Applied Psychology* 85 (5): 997–1005.

Stewart, Heather, Carmit Katz, and David J. La Rooy. 2011. Training forensic interviewers. In *Children's testimony: a handbook of psychological research and forensic practice,* eds. Michael E. Lamb, David J. La Rooy, Lindsay C. Malloy, and Carmit Katz, 199–216. Chichester: Wiley.

Stockholms University. 2015. Kursbeskrivning. Brott mot barn och ungdomar. Steg 2—Intervju- och förhörsmetodik. 7.5 hp, grundläggande nivå, kvartsfart. Kurskod: UB104U. Høstterminen 205. 2015-05-15.

Uppsala University. 2014. Kursplan, uttagen 2014-08-22. Utredningsmetodik med inriktning på brott mot barn och ungdomar, steg 1 (uppdragsutbildning).

Wright, Rebecca, and Martine BPowell. 2006. Investigative interviewers' perceptions of their difficulty in adhering to open-ended questions with child witnesses. *International Journal of Police Science and Management* 8 (4): 316–325.

Zajac, Rachel, and Harlene Hayne. 2003. I don't think that's what really happened: The effect of cross-examination on the accuracy of children's reports. *Journal of Experimental Psychology: Applied* 9 (3): 187–195.

6

Investigative Interviews: Legal and Scientific Framework

Gunn Astrid Baugerud and Miriam Sinkerud Johnson

Introduction

One of the main challenges in cases where child sexual abuse or physical abuse is suspected is that the children are usually the only available sources of information about the experiences (Lamb et al. 1998). Definitive physical, medical or psychological symptoms are lacking or inconclusive in the vast majority of such cases (e.g. Lewis et al. 2014). Without any other witnesses or incontrovertible indications, the suspicion of abuse and the progress of the inquiry often rest upon the child's narrative and the interviewer's ability to maximise the quality and quantity of information obtained from the child.

Over the past 30 years, considerable resources have been invested in the development of professional guidelines for how investigative

---

G.A. Baugerud (✉) · M.S. Johnson
Oslo and Akershus University College of Applied Sciences, Oslo, Norway
e-mail: Gunn-Astrid.Baugerud@hioa.no

M.S. Johnson
e-mail: Miriam.Sinkerud-Johnson@hioa.no

interviewers should conduct interviews with children who are suspected victims of sexual or physical abuse, or witnesses to crimes. Considerable efforts have been made to understand how children's testimony can be made as useful and accurate as possible (Lamb et al. 2007).

An important change in child investigative interviewing within the Nordic countries was the establishment of the Barnahus model where interviews and medical examinations are delivered under one roof in a child-friendly environment. The Barnahus model is based on the principle that such child-friendly, interdisciplinary and multiagency responses to child abuse could enhance the quality of the investigative interviews (see the introduction chapter of this book). An important goal in order to enhance the quality of investigative interviews has been to take a closer look at interview practices and the techniques used in the interviews. The justice systems in Finland, Iceland and Sweden use methods inspired by the Protocol of the National Institute of Child Health and Human Development (NICHD) (Lamb et al. 2007; Orbach et al. 2000) when conducting investigative interviews of child witnesses. The NICHD protocol is based on research and expert professional consensus regarding children's memory, communicative skill and social knowledge, which has been translated into guidelines that aim to improve the quality of forensic interviews of children.

In this chapter, we will outline the main features and empirical background of the development of the NICHD Investigative Interview protocol. We also present a revision of the NICHD protocol, which has been designed to help interviewers to provide non-suggestive support to alleged victims who might be reluctant to make allegations of abuse.

Improving the Quality of Investigative Interviews with Alleged Child Victims

Since the early 1990s, highly publicised child sexual abuse cases, such as the McMartinand Kelly Michaels Cases in the USA, the Bjugn case in Norway and the Cleveland case in the UK, have drawn attention to inappropriate interview strategies and the counterproductive ways in which alleged victims are sometimes interviewed (Bruck 1999).

The lack of coordination among the agencies involved and the use of repeated interviewing with different interviewers, as well as stressful and compromising environments for the child when interviewed, were serious shortcomings in the field of investigative interview practice (Ceci and Bruck 1993; Cross et al. 2007). Researchers have shown that child investigative interviewing within Children's Advocacy Centres (CAC) seems to offer a more thorough child-focused response to children's reports, and the families involved seem to have more positive experiences (Cross et al. 2007). The American model (CAC) inspired the development of the Barnahus model in the Nordic countries to a large extent. The Barnahus model aims to reduce the stress of the legal process for children and their families, to increase the level of cooperation between professionals and to build and disseminate knowledge regarding victimised children (Bakketeig et al. 2012). Researchers have repeatedly shown that the quality of interviewing reliably improves dramatically when interviewers employ structured investigative interview protocols (e.g. Lamb et al. 2007). In Sweden, Iceland and Finland, where the Barnahus model has been implemented, police officers or psychologists are inspired by the NICHD protocol when conducting child forensic interviews. The NICHD protocol (Lamb et al. 1998, 2007; Orbach et al. 2000) is currently used in training of police officers and other criminal justice system practitioners in many different countries and is one of the most internationally used protocols for interviewing child witnesses.

NICHD Investigative Interview Protocol

A major purpose of the NICHD protocol was to translate the recommendations resulting from research into operational steps that would improve the organisation and quality of investigative interviews with children and increase the likelihood of obtaining complete and precise information. By helping interviewers conduct interviews that are more informative, the protocol is designed to promote children's well-being by facilitating the prosecution of offenders. The NICHD protocol was developed with reference to child development issues, including linguistic abilities, memory retrieval capacities, suggestibility, interviewer behaviour and the effects of stress and trauma. For example, the protocol integrates recent knowledge about memory functions and the suggestibility of children and is used with children who are suspected of having been sexually or physically abused.

Children's Memory Development

After children have disclosed the abuse, their memories of the event become very important if the case is going to court. Basic and applied research into children's memory development has been crucial in helping police and social welfare workers to conduct better child investigative interviews. Different factors influence a child's experience of an abusive event, and knowledge about how children encode, store and retrieve stressful events from the past is of vital importance (e.g. Lamb et al. 2011). Indeed, we all depend on our memory when we need to answer questions about experiences.

Memory is believed to be a multiple system composed of encoding arrangements or subsystems, storage and information recovery (e.g. Baddeley et al. 2011; Tulving 1985). In the past two decades, there has been growing consensus that memory is not a unified ability but rather a set of dynamic, integrated systems (e.g. Squire 2004).

The study of children's memory and factors influencing children's memory performance have been studied within a broad context in the past several years and is influenced by enhanced knowledge about cognitive maturity such as the development of language, perception, recognition and encoding (e.g. Lamb et al. 2011). Most theories distinguish between explicit and conscious memories, and memories not accessed by conscious recall (Goswami 2008). Autobiographical memory involves explicit memories of specific times and places in an individual's past (Fivush 2011) and depends on several factors such as language ability, neural structures, socio-emotional components, attachment orientation and cognitive development (Bauer and Fivush 2010). Differences in autobiographical memory across age groups have an important impact on memory capacity in terms of the memory retrieval strategies of preschoolers and older children. Fivush (2011) suggests that autobiographical memory is a system which develops gradually during childhood and depends on the individual's development of their sense of self. The awareness of self (i.e. "I" and "me") is first available around the age of two and facilitates what becomes an autobiographical memory (Howe 2003). Empirical studies have shown that events, including traumatic ones that occur before the age of 2–3 years are unlikely to be available for conscious verbal recall (Cordon et al. 2004; Newcombe et al. 2007; Simcock and Hayne 2002). This phenomenon is usually referred to as "infantile amnesia" and has been validated by over a century of empirical research (Bauer 2007; Josselyn and Frankland 2012). By the age of three, however, children's recall of stressful events can be consistent and robust (Peterson and Warren 2009), and they are able to recall stressful negative events over time, as well as reporting new correct information (Baugerud et al. 2014; Lamb et al. 2011).

Age Differences and Memory

The most important individual difference in children's memory is connected to their age (Schneider and Bjorklund 2003). In general, preschool children recollect less information, provide briefer accounts and tend to forget more rapidly than older children (Schneider and Bjorklund 2003; Ornstein et al. 1997). Preschoolers have more limited language comprehension and communication abilities due to more limited vocabularies and retrieval strategies than older children and adults (Schneider and Pressley 2013). Increasing age brings with it increasing sophistications in the exercise of strategic memory skills, such as rehearsal, use of mental imagery and semantic organisation (Schneider and Pressley 2013). That said, other causes such as experiences with abuse or concurrent stressors leading to psychopathology, lack of appropriate verbal stimulation from parents and the development of an overgeneral memory may all be factors involved in autobiographical memory problems (Greenhoot et al. 2008). Developmental differences are important, but the literature remains inconclusive and younger children may be as accurate as older children (see La Rooy et al. 2011 for a review).

Interviewer Techniques in Relation to the Quality and Quantity of Children's Response

Even if children as young as three years of age are able to give coherent verbal reports of both neutral and stressful experiences, research has repeatedly shown that the quantity and quality of children's reports are fundamentally affected by whether interviewers use interview techniques carefully (Brown et al. 2008). These findings have been important for the development of structured interview protocols, such as the NICHD protocol. The consensus among experts regarding how children should be interviewed is that it should involve as much use as possible of free recall and open-ended questions, rather than focused and suggestive prompts (Lamb et al. 2007). Responses to open-ended questions and eliciting free recall encourage more accurate and longer responses from children. On the other hand, suggestive questioning produces shorter reports, which are more likely to be erroneous and may also produce false reports, particularly in preschool children (e.g. Anderson et al. 2014; Craig et al. 1999; Davies et al. 2000; Lamb et al. 2007).

Suggestive Interviewing

A sizeable body of research has shown how suggestive interview techniques may negatively affect the dynamics of investigative interviews (see Bruck et al. 2002, for a review). Suggestive interviewing is strongly related to the concept of interviewer bias and the expectancy effects that emerge when interviewers with preconceived notions seek to confirm evidence in ways that are related to a priori beliefs and expectations (e.g. Ask and Granhag 2005; Bruck et al. 2002). Children may, for example, tailor their reports by confirming or rejecting information if they infer that interviewers would prefer certain responses (e.g. Bjorklund et al. 2000; Melnyk et al. 2007). Interviewer expectations may affect the way question types are used and explicitly or implicitly be communicated through a variety of option-posing and suggestive techniques that generally request children to confirm or reject options provided by the interviewer. Repeated suggestive questions and reinforcement questions (i.e. positive and negative consequences), for example, are believed to be question types that communicate to the child what response is expected and can quickly induce children to make persistent false allegations of wrongdoing (Bruck et al. 2002; La Rooy et al. 2010). Using co-witness information such as peer or parental pressure by telling the child that the interviewer has already received information from another person may also create pressures towards conformity (e.g. Ceci and Friedman 2000). An interviewer's expectations may also influence their nonverbal expressive behaviour (Andrews and Lamb 2014).

Although suggestive techniques might produce accurate abuse reports from otherwise silent children, the same techniques entail a risk of negatively shaping and contaminating children's reports, as the responses to such questions are more likely to be inaccurate. Contradictory or nonsensical responses, which can appear in response to suggestive questioning, may reduce the credibility of the children's account (e.g. Anderson et al. 2014; Howie et al. 2012; Lamb et al. 2013). The detrimental effect of suggestive techniques on children's accuracy is often misused in an attempt to discredit children's testimonies and is likely to be used against the child in court (Goodman et al. 1999).

People of all ages are susceptible to misinformation and can become confused over the source of their memories; however, a common finding across studies is that preschool children in general are more susceptible to the suggestion and distortion of their memories than are older children and adults (e.g. Ceci and Bruck 2006; La Rooy et al. 2009; Ghetti and Alexander 2004). Age differences in suggestibility have also been found in studies that included more realistic situations (e.g. Cassel and Bjorklund 1995; Eisen et al. 2002). During the past 10 years, there has been a shift in research characterised by refocusing on children's competence as witnesses and the conditions under which children's testimonies may be improved and suggestibility reduced. Researchers have shown that even young children can be resistant to suggestive questions and that children's compliance with suggestive techniques is related to the social demand characteristics of the situation (Schneider and Pressley 2013). Researchers have also suggested that interview factors are more important than children's individual characteristics in determining resistance to suggestion (Finnilä et al. 2003; La Rooy and Lamb 2011).

The Structure of the NICHD Protocol

The structure of the NICHD protocol, which is described in detail in several publications by Lamb and colleagues (e.g. Lamb et al. 2007), covers all phases of the investigative interview. In the *introductory phase*, the interviewer introduces themselves, clarifies the child's task ([a] describes events in detail and [b] asks them to tell the truth) and explains the ground rules of the interview, including the notion that the child can say, "I don't remember" or "I don't understand" or correct the interviewer when appropriate. The following *rapport-building phase,* which is designed to create a relaxed, supportive environment for children, is introduced with a section where the child is encouraged to describe a recently experienced neutral event in detail. Lamb and colleagues (2007) emphasise that this training section is designed to familiarise children with the open-ended invitations used in the substantive phase while demonstrating the specific level of detail expected of them. Additionally, in a transitional section between the presubstantive and the substantive phases of the interview, a series of prompts that are as open as possible are used to non-suggestively identify the target events under investigation. The interviewer moves on to some carefully worded and increasingly focused prompts only if the child fails to identify the target event/s. If the child makes an allegation, the free recall phase begins with an invitation ("Tell me everything…"), and other free recall prompts or invitations are recommended. As soon as the first narrative is completed, the interviewer prompts the child to indicate whether the incident occurred "one time or more than one time" and then proceeds to secure incident-specific information using follow-up prompts ("Then what happened?") and cued questions (e.g. "Earlier you mentioned a [person/object/action]. Tell me everything about that"), referring to details mentioned by the child to elicit uncontaminated free recall accounts of the alleged incident/s (Lamb et al. 2007, 1204–1205). Only after the exhaustive free recall, do prompting interviewers to proceed to focused recall questions that address details previously mentioned by the child and request information within specific categories. If crucial details are still missing, interviewers then ask limited option-posing questions, mostly yes/no or forced-choice questions referencing new issues that the child failed to address previously. Suggestive utterances, which communicate to the child what response is expected, are strongly discouraged (Lamb et al. 2007).

The NICHD protocol has been subjected to more empirical studies than any other interview protocols (e.g. Lamb et al. 2008). Overall, the findings obtained in field implementation studies in Canada (Cyr et al. 2012; Cyr and Lamb 2009) and in the UK demonstrate that when investigative interviewers employ recommended interview procedures by following the NICHD protocol, they generally enhance the quality of information elicited from alleged victims of sexual or physical abuse. Interviewers using the NICHD protocol use at least three times more open-ended and half as many option-posing and suggestive questions as they do without the protocol (Lamb et al. 2007). Specifically, the study by Cyr and colleagues (2012) revealed that application of the NICHD protocol effectively increases informative details about child sexual abuse provided by children in response to open-ended questions.

The Revised NICHD Protocol

When government employees interview children, many of them are reluctant to disclose abuse. This also happens in cases where the police have evidence that the children in fact have been abused (Leander 2007). Some researchers have pointed out that the Standard Protocol (SP) is most useful when children are "active disclosers", that is when children already have, for instance, told a parent or a teacher about sexual abuse (Faller and Everson 2012). Research has shown that disclosure rates have proved to be higher when children are formally interviewed, compared to adults with childhood histories of child sexual abuse, reporting the abuse in retrospective studies, even if there is great variation between different studies (London et al. 2008). This suggests that the skills of the interviewer and how to overcome a child's reluctance may be very important, and recent studies have just started to investigate the impact of enhanced socio-emotional support in the interview setting when children exhibit reluctance when interviewed (Ahern et al. 2014; Hershkowitz et al. 2013). It seems that interviewer support is particularly important when interviewing children unwilling to talk (Hershkowitz et al. 2006). Because of this, Herschkowitz and colleagues acknowledged the need for a revised NICHD protocol (RP) in order to enhance reports from alleged abused children (Herschkowitz et al. 2014). In the RP, it was important to raise the children's trust and cooperation and there is an increased focus on giving the children socio-emotional support through the interview. The order of the phases in the interview was changed, and the report-building phase precedes the ground rules phase instead of following it. More guidance was also provided to the interviewers to maintain and establish report building, and to encourage the children to disclose. The interviewers were trained to use more support in the presubstantive phase in a non-suggestible and non-leading way (e.g. asking children about their hobbies, what they like to do, etc.) before explaining ground rules (see nichdprotocol.com for a detailed description of the revised protocol). The RP was tested in a large study in Israel in which independent evidence that intrafamilial abuse had taken place was established. The results showed that children were significantly more likely to make allegations of abuse when the revised protocol was employed, compared to the SP (Herschkowitz et al. 2014). These results suggest that emotional support in forensic interviewing may be very important and facilitate accurate reports of abuse by children who might otherwise be reluctant to make allegations (Hershkowitz et al. 2014). In addition, it may be crucial in improving disclosures rates in child forensic interviewing to provide children with calm and supportive environments. Several factors, such as the interview itself, the child's age and gender and caregiver support, could all affect whether children disclose or not (Goodman et al. 2014) but the context in which the children are interviewed may also be very important and the Barnahus model provides a safe and child-friendly setting, which may lower children's stress and make them more relaxed. Studies have consistently shown that greater arousal during the retrieval of memories inhibits memory (Roozendaal et al. 2009; Smeets et al. 2008) and being interviewed at a Barnahus may reduce stress and make children more comfortable in the interview setting. This in turn may allow them to use cognitive resources to make a memory search and/or focus on the interviewer's questions (Goodman et al. 2014; Quas et al. 2004; Rush et al. 2014). The RP particularly highlights the importance of interviewers responding more sensitively and using supportive comments with reluctant children (Ahern et al. 2014). In summary, the high standards of the Barnahus that take the abilities, vulnerabilities and needs of child witnesses into account, combined with the use of RP in interviewing, may be very important in enhancing the disclosure rates of maltreated children.

In a recent study employing the RP, an extended training programme for interviewers was developed and tested (Hershkowitz et al. unpublished manuscript). The researchers used an evidence-based training programme which included more detailed guidance for interviewers and how they could support children reluctant to disclose. The format included a train—the trainer approach in which inexperienced interviewers received training from more experienced interviewers under the supervision of researchers. This training involves teaching interviewers to code their own interviews systematically as well as train, supervise and monitor the skills of others. A feedback system for self-identifying support was also included. This helped the interviewers recognise children's expressions of distress or reluctance (for a more detailed description see Hershkowitz et al. unpublished manuscript). The results showed that the level of support increased among the interviewers and instances of inadequate support and insensitivity to children's reluctance became less common. These effects can have important consequences for disclosure rates and avoid incidents of child abuse remaining unreported. The study shows encouraging results in that continued supervision and training might be very helpful in enhancing the competence of the forensic interviewers (Hershkowitz et al. unpublished manuscript). Several factors such as intrafamilial relations, loyalty to family members, fear, the severity of abuse, feelings of embarrassment and shame, perceptions of responsibilities and worries about legal consequences may prevent children from the disclosure of abuse. For example, research has indicated that children are less likely to disclose if the perpetrator is a close family member (Arata 1998; Goodman-Brown et al. 2003;

London et al. 2005). More supportive interviewing, through the use of the revised protocol, may reduce reluctance in these children and yield higher rates of allegations by young children, compared to children who still are interviewed with the SP.

It is important to continue to conduct more research with the RP model to further evaluate the model and to include physical as well as sexual abuse cases. All the different approaches that are endorsed for interviewing children should be evaluated and evidence based to ensure the quality in interviewing. Most important is that research-based guidelines are used when professionals are interviewing children.

Importance of Interviewer Training

There has been an awareness in the last 15–20 years of the importance of following the evidence-based recommendations and that interviewers should be trained in accordance with best-practice recommendations; however, a growing body of field studies that have examined investigative interviews conducted in Israel (Hershkowitz et al. 2005), the UK (Westcott and Kynan 2006), Australia (Agnew et al. 2006; Guadagno and Powell, 2009), the USA (Sternberg et al. 1996), Canada (Cyr and Lamb 2009), Sweden (Cederborg et al. 2000), Finland (Korkman et al. 2006; Santtila et al. 2004) and Norway (Johnson et al. 2015) suggests that investigative interviewers generally fall short of capturing best-practice evidence-based recommendations. In fact, regardless of country and investigative culture, the widespread tendency is for interviewers to rarely use open-ended questions that invite free narratives and instead rely heavily on option-posing, leading and suggestive prompts. Overall, studies have revealed a notably low frequency of open-ended invitations, ranging from 2 to 6%, regardless of the children's age and the nature of the alleged offences. The distribution of non-recommended techniques, such as option-posing and suggestive questions, was in turn quite high, often as high as 50% of the questions asked.

Although the use of suggestive interview techniques is generally assumed to be associated with untrained interviewers, similarly poor interviewing techniques have been observed in studies involving interviewers had received specialised training to improve their interview skills. Researchers have suggested that inappropriate questioning and poorly structured interviews are still dominant even when investigators have received specialised training and understand the conceptual issues of appropriate interviewing (e.g. Aldridge and Cameron 1999; Lamb 2016; Lamb et al. 1996; Sternberg et al. 2001; Warren et al. 1999). Brief initial training programmes appear to be insufficient even when police investigators are trained in knowledge such as the way human memory works, effective communication and proper interview techniques. These findings indicate that training programmes may not be as effective as presumed in reducing the amount of non-recommended questioning. Nevertheless, recent studies have shown that interviewer behaviour can be improved under systematic and intensive training conditions (e.g. Cederborg et al. 2013; Cyr and Lamb 2009; Davies et al. 2000; Lamb et al. 2011). For example, Lamb et al. (2002) concluded that organised feedback and follow-up sessions led to better investigative interviewing in terms of a significant reduction in unfortunate interviewing techniques.

In future studies, it will be important to carry out more evaluations using different approaches; however, despite the positive effects in terms of improved interviewer behaviour, few researchers have so far succeeded in showing enduring structural behavioural changes after the course of training has ended. In Norway, we will assess the interview model currently being used by evaluating the quality of a national sample of investigative interviews of suspected child sexual abuse and violence victims conducted at Barnahus during the past five years (2012–2017). After new regulations in Norway in 2015, all child forensic interviews are carried out at the Barnahus. It is possible that the Barnahus model contributed to children being less upset and stressed when the interviews are conducted and thus enhancing the quality of the interviewer practices, and thus led to more positive case outcomes. In line with similar studies, the quality of investigative interviews refers to the identification of the various elements of what takes place in these encounters, with special emphasis on analysing the content of interview strategies employed. This content analysis especially aims to measure the proportional differences between recommended and non-recommended questioning employed by interviewers in these situations, and how these relate to the content of the accounts provided by children. This will be addressed by examining different aspects of the responses by children in detail in relation to the forms of questioning employed in forensic interview situations. The quality of investigative interviews should also emphasise aspects of the social dynamics that develop in investigative interviews and the way these factors ultimately affect the quality of the information obtained from the child. The focus on developing interviewing skills in future training programmes of evidential investigative practice should emphasise aspects of interviewer behaviour and interviewer–respondent interaction in the interview setting, towards better compliance with internationally recognised guidelines. The quality of investigative interviews with vulnerable witnesses, such as preschool children and youths with intellectual disabilities, is entirely unknown. In future research, we need to know more about the ways in which vulnerable groups are interviewed and how these groups of witnesses provide information when interviewed about their abuse experiences.

The Barnahus: A Universal Model to Improve the Response to Child Abuse

The overarching goal of this chapter was to present the investigative interview protocol currently being used in most of the Nordic countries where the Barnahus model has been implemented.

The Barnahus model offers a child-friendly context that provides extended support to the children and their families, medical examinations, and the follow-up of treatment needs and mental health services that are important in taking care of abused children. The child-friendly facility that the Barnahus model provides may help the children be less distressed, as in providing more support the children typically become more comfortable and less aroused. This may create a better context than other arrangements for children when interviewed. Alleged offenders are not permitted to be in the area, interview rooms are private, and senior counsellors/psychology specialists from the Barnahus perform a monitoring role and assess the child's mental health as the interview is conducted, as well as ensuring that the child need only to describe their experience. There may also be follow-up interviews if needed. This is very important for determining what further treatment and follow-up are required. There is a reason to believe that the child-friendly environment in the Barnahus model can facilitate the use of structured interview protocols by providing optimal conditions for the children to talk about their own experiences.

Research findings have provided strong support for the effectiveness of the NICHD protocol. There are new promising findings for children who are unwilling to disclose abuse, using the revised protocol, and further research will show whether increased use of support will help children's reluctance to be less common; however, we must also recognise that children need to feel comfortable, and that creating a child-friendly setting is indeed important in order to provide the optimal conditions for children to provide accurate and detailed accounts of distressing and traumatic events. The Barnahus model ensures such environments and makes sure that children are cared for in the best way.

Contributions from three decades with practice and international research in relation to child investigative interviews have provided valuable knowledge when it comes to improving responses to child abuse in the Nordic countries. Future research should continue to evaluate the different models and adhere to evidence-based child interview strategies as this can optimise children's recall and as such have important implications for both legal and appropriate treatments of children.

References

Agnew, Sarah, Martine Powell, and Pamela Snow. 2006. An examination of the questioning styles of police officers and caregivers when interviewing children with intellectual disabilities. *Legal and Criminological Psychology* 11: 35–53.

Ahern, Elizabeth, Irit Hershkowitz, Michael Lamb, Uri Blasbalg, and Alice Winstanley. 2014. Support and Reluctance in the Pre-substantive Phase of Alleged Child Abuse Victim Investigative Interviews: Revised versus Standard NICHD Protocols. *Behavioral Sciences & the Law* 32 (6): 762–774.

Aldridge, Jan, and Sandra Cameron. 1999. Interviewing Child Witnesses: Questioning Techniques and the Role of Training. *Applied Developmental Science* 3: 136–147.

Anderson, Gwendolyn, Jessica Anderson, and Jane Gilgun. 2014. The Influence of Narrative Practice Techniques on Child Behaviours in Forensic Interviews. *Journal of Child Sexual Abuse* 23: 615–634.

Andrews, Samantha. J., and E. Michael Lamb. 2014. The effects of age and delay on responses to repeated questions in forensic interviews with children alleging sexual abuse. *Law and Human Behavior* 38: 171–180.

Arata, Catalina.M. 1998. To Tell or Not to Tell: Current Functioning of Child Sexual Abuse Survivors Who Disclosed Their Victimization. *Child Maltreatment* 3: 63–71.

Ask, Karl, and Pär-Anders Granhag. 2005. Motivational Sources of Confirmation Bias in Criminal Investigations: The Need for Cognitive Closure. *Journal of Investigative Psychology and Offender Profiling* 2: 43–63.

Baddeley, Alan D., Michael C. Anderson, and Michael W. Eysenck. 2011. *Memory*. PortoAlegre: Artmed.

Bakketeig, Elisiv, Mette Berg, Trond Myklebust and Kari Stefansen. 2012. Barnehusevalueringen. Delrapport 1. Barnehusmodellens implikasjoner for politiets arbeid med fokus på dommeravhør og rettsmedisinsk undersøkelse. PHS forskning 6. Oslo: PHS.

Bauer, Patricia, and Robyn Fivush. 2010. Context and Consequences of Autobiographical Memory Development. *Cognitive Development* 2: 303–308.

Bauer, Patricia. 2007. Recall in Infancy A Neurodevelopmental Account. *Current Directions in Psychological Science* 16 (3): 142–146.

Baugerud, Gunn Astrid, Svein Magnussen, and Annika Melinder. 2014. High Accuracy but Low Consistency in Children's Long-term Recall of a Real-life Stressful Event. *Journal of Experimental Child Psychology* 126: 357–368.

Bjorklund, David, S. William Cassel, Barbara Bjorklund, Rhonda Brown, Cynthia Park, Kim Ernst, and Felicia Owen. 2000. Social demand characteristics in children's and adults' eyewitness. *Applied Cognitive Psychology* 14: 421–433.

Brown Deirdre, Michael Lamb, Margaret-Ellen Pipe and Yael Orbach. 2008. Pursuing the Truth the Whole Truth and Nothing but the Truth Forensic Interviews with Child Victims or Witnesses of Abuse. In *Stress Trauma and Children's Memory Development Neurobiological Cognitive Clinical and legal perspectives*, eds. Mark L. Howe, Gale S. Goodman and Dante Cicchetti. Oxford: Oxford University Press.

Bruck, Maggie, and Stephen Ceci. 1999. The Suggestibility of Children's Memory. *Annual Review of Psychology* 50: 419–439.

Bruck, Maggie, Stephen Ceci, and Helene Hembrooke. 2002. The nature of children's true and false narratives. *Developmental Review* 22: 520–554.

Cassel, William, and David Bjorklund. 1995. Developmental patterns of eyewitness memory and suggestibility: An ecologically based short-term longitudinal study. *Law and Human Behavior* 19: 507–532.

Ceci, Stephen, and Maggie Bruck. 2006. Children's Suggestibility: Characteristics and Mechanisms. *Advances in Child Development and Behavior* 34: 247–281.

Ceci, Stephen, and Maggie Bruck. 1993. Suggestibility of the Child Witness: A Historical Review and Synthesis. *Psychological Bulletin* 113 (3): 403–439.

Ceci, Stephen. J., and Richard Friedman. 2000. The suggestibility of children: Scientific research and legal implications. *Cornell Law Review* 86: 34–108.

Cederborg, Ann-Christin, Charlotte Alm, Djaildes Lima da Silva Nises, and Michael Lamb. 2013. Investigative Interviewing of Alleged Children—An Evaluation of a New Training Programme for Police Officers in Sweden. *Police Practice and Research: An International Journal* 14: 242–254.

Cederborg, Ann-Christin, Yael Orbach, Kathleen Sternberg, and Michael Lamb. 2000. Investigative Interviews of Child Witnesses in Sweden. *Child Abuse and Neglect* 24: 1355–1361.

Cordón, Ingrid, Mararet-Ellen Pipe, Liat Sayfan, Annika Melinder, and Gail Goodman. 2004. Memory for Traumatic Experiences in Early Childhood. *Developmental Review* 24: 101–132.

Craig, Ron, A. Rick Scheibe, David C. Raskin, John C. Kircher, and David H. Dodd. 1999. Interviewer Questions and Content Analysis of Children's Statements of Sexual Abuse. *Applied Developmental Science* 3: 77–85.

Cross, Theodore, Lisa Jones, Wendy Walsh, Minique Simone, and David Kolko. 2007. Child Forensic Interviewing in Children's Advocacy Centers: Empirical Data on a Practice Model. *Child Abuse and Neglect* 31: 1031–1052.

Cyr, Mireille, and Michael Lamb. 2009. Assessing the Effectiveness of the NICHD Investigative Interview Protocol when Interviewing French-speaking Alleged Victims of Child Sexual Abuse in Quebec. *Child Abuse and Neglect* 33: 257–268.

Cyr, Mireille, Jacinthe Dion, Pierre McDuff, and Karine Trotier-Sylvain. 2012. Transfer of skills in the context of non-suggestive investigative interviews: Impact of structured interview protocol and feedback. *Applied Cognitive Psychology* 26: 516–524.

Davies, Graham, Helen Westcott, and Noreen Horan. 2000. The impact of questioning style on the content of investigative interviews with suspected child sexual abuse victims. *Psychology, Crime & Law* 6: 81–97.

Eisen, Mitchell, Jianjian Qin, Gail Goodman, and Suzanne Davis. 2002. Memory and suggestibility in maltreated children: Age, stress arousal, dissociation, and psychopathology. *Journal of Experimental Child Psychology* 83: 167–212.

Faller, Coulborn, and Mark Everson. 2012. Contested Issues in the Evaluation of Child Sexual Abuse Allegations: Why Consensus on Best Practice Remains Elusive. *Journal of Child Sexual Abuse* 21: 3–18.

Finnilä, Katarina, Nina Mahlberg, Pekka Santtila, kenneth Sandnabba, and Pekka Niemi. 2003. Validity of a Test of Children's Suggestibility for Predicting Responses to Two Interview Situations Differing in Their Degree of Suggestiveness. *Journal of Experimental Child Psychology* 85: 23–49.

Fivush, Robyn. 2011. The Development of Autobiographical Memory. *Annual Review of Psychology* 62: 559–582.

Ghetti, Simona, and Kristen Alexander. 2004. If it happened, I would remember it: Strategic use of event memorability in the rejection of false autobiographical events. *Child Development* 75: 542–561.

Goodman, Gail, Deborah A. Goldfarb, Jia Chong and Lauren Goodman-Shaver. 2014. Children's Eyewitness Memory: The Influence of Cognitive and Socio-Emotional Factors. *Roger Williams University Law Review* 19(2), Symposium: Child Witnesses in Sexual Abuse Cases. Article 7.

Goodman, Gail, Jodi Quas, Josephine Bulkley, and Cheryl Shapiro. 1999. Innovations for Child Witnesses: A National Survey. *Psychology, Public policy and Law* 5: 255–281.

Goodman-Brown, Tina, Robin Edelstein, Gail Goodman, and David Gordon. 2003. Why Children Tell: a Model of Children's Disclosure of Sexual Abuse. *Child Abuse and Neglect* 27: 525–540.

Goswami, Usha. 2008. The Development of Memory. In *Cognitive Development: The Learning Brain,* ed. U. Goswami, 250–293. Hove and New York: Psychology Press, Taylor & Francis Group.

Greenhoot, Andrea, Sarah Bunnell, Jennifer Curtis, Jennifer, and Alisa Beyer. 2008. Trauma and Autobiographical Memory Functioning. Findings from a Longitudinal study of Family Violence. In *Stress, Trauma, and Children's Development. Neurobiological, Cognitive, Clinical and Legal Perspectives*, eds. M.L. Howe, G.S. Goodman, and D. Cicchetti, 139–170. Oxford: Oxford University Press.

Guadagno, Belinda, and Martine Powell. 2009. A qualitative examination of police officers' questioning of children about repeated events. *Police Practice and Research* 10: 61–73.

Hershkowitz, Irit, Elizabeth Ahern, Michael Lamb, Uri Blasbalg, Yael Karni-Visel and Michael Breitman. (Unpublished manuscript). Changes in Interviewers' Use of Supportive Techniques During the Revised Protocol Training.

Hershkowitz, Irit, Dvora Horowitz, and Michael Lamb. 2005. Trends in children's disclosure of abuse in Israel: A national study. *Child Abuse & Neglect* 29: 1203–1214.

Hershkowitz, Irit, Michael Lamb, and Carmit Katz. 2014. Allegation Rates in Forensic Child Abuse Investigations: Comparing the Revised and Standard NICHD Protocols. *Psychology Public Policy and Law* 20 (3): 334–336.

Hershkowitz, Irit, Michael Lamb, Carmit Katz, and Lindsay Malloy. 2013. Does Enhanced Rapport-building Alter the Dynamics of Investigative Interviews with Suspected Victims of Intra-familial Abuse? *Journal of Police and Criminal Psychology* 30 (6): 6–14.

Hershkowitz, Irit, Yael Orbach, Michael Lamb, Kathleen Sternberg, and Dvora Horowitz. 2006. Dynamics of Forensic Interviews with Suspected Abuse Victims Who Do Not Disclose Abuse. *Child Abuse Neglect* 30 (7): 753–769.

Howe, Michael. 2003. When Autobiographical Memory Begins. *Developmental Review* 23: 471–494.

Howie, Pauline, Laura Nash, Nadezhda Kurukulasuriya, and Alison Bowman. 2012. Children's event reports: Factors affecting responses to repeated questions in vignette scenarios and event recall interviews. *British Journal of Developmental Psychology* 30: 550–568.

Johnson, Miriam, Svein Magnussen, Christian Thoresen, Kyrre Lønnum, Lisa Victoria Burrell, and Annika Melinder. 2015. Best Practice Recommendations Still Fail to Result in Action: A National 10-year Follow-up of Investigative Interviews in CSA Cases. *Applied Cognitive Psychology* 29 (5): 661–668.

Josselyn, Sheena, and Paul Frankland. 2012. Infantile amnesia: A neurogenic hypothesis. *Learning & Memory* 19: 423–433.

Korkman, Julia, Pekka Santtila, and Kenneth Sandnabba. 2006. Dynamics of Verbal Interaction Between Interviewer and Child in Interviews with Alleged Victims of Child Sexual Abuse. *Scandinavian Journal of Psychology* 47: 109–120.

Lamb, Michael. 2016. Difficulties Translating Research on Forensic Interview Practices to Practitioners: Finding Water, Leading Horses, but Can We Get Them to Drink? *American Psychologist* 71 (8): 710–718.

Lamb, Michael, Irit Hershkowitz, and Thomas Lyon. 2013. Interviewing Victims and Suspected Victims Who Are Reluctant to Talk. *APSAC Advisor* 4: 16–19.

Lamb, Michael, David La Rooy, Lindsay Malloy, and Carmit Katz. 2011. *Children's Testimony: A Handbook of Psychological Research and Forensic Practice*. London: Wiley.

Lamb, Michael, Kathleen Sternberg, and Phillip Esplin. 1998. Conducting Investigative Interviews of Alleged Sexual Abuse Victims. *Child Abuse and Neglect* 22: 813–823.

Lamb, Michael, Irit Hershkowitz, Yael Orbach, and Phillip Esplin. 2008. *Tell me what happened: Structured investigative interviews of child victims and witnesses*. Hoboken, NJ: Wiley.

Lamb, Michael, Irit Hershkowitz, Kathleen Sternberg, Meir Hovav, Talna Manor, and Liora Yidilevitch. 1996. Effects of investigative utterance types on Israeli children's responses. *International Journal of Behavioral Development* 19: 627–637.

Lamb, Michael, Kathleen Sternberg, Yael Orbach, Irit Hershkowitz, Dvora Horowitz, and Phillip Esplin. 2002. The Effects of Intensive Training and Ongoing Supervision on the Quality of Investigative Interviews with Alleged Sex Abuse Victims. *Applied Developmental Science* 6: 114–125.

Lamb, Michael, Irit Hershkowitz YaelOrbach, Phillip Esplin, Dvora Horowitz, and Dvora. 2007. A structured Forensic Interview Protocol Improves the Quality and Informativeness of Investigative Interviews with Children: A Review of Research Using the NICHD Investigative Interview Protocol. *Child Abuse & Neglect* 31: 1201–1231.

Lamb, Michael, Yael Orbach, Irit Hershkowitz, Dvora Horowitz, and Craig Abbott. 2007. Does the Type of Prompt Affect the Accuracy of Information Provided by Alleged Victims of Abuse in Forensic Interviews? *Applied Cognitive Psychology* 21: 1117–1130.

La Rooy, David, Carmit Katz, and Lindsay Malloy. 2010. Do we need to rethink guidance on repeated interviews? *Psychology, Public Police, and Law* 16: 373–392.

La Rooy, David, Lindsay Malloy and Michael Lamb. 2011. The Development of Memory in Childhood. In *Children's Testimony: A Handbook of Psychological Research and Forensic Practice*. eds. M.E. Lamb, D. J. La Rooy, L. C. Malloy, and C. Katz, 2nd ed, 49–68. New York: Wiley-Blackwell.

La, Rooy, Michael Lamb David, and Margaret-Ellen Pipe. 2009. Repeated Interviewing: Acritical Evaluation of the Risks and Potential Benefits. In *Child Sexual Abuse: Research Evaluation and Testimony for the Courts*, eds. K. Kuehnle, and M. Connell. New Jersey: Wiley.

Leander, Lina, Sven Christianson, and Pär-Anders Granhag. 2007. A Sexual Abuse Case Study: Children's Memories and Reports. *Psychiatry, Psychology and Law* 14 (1): 120–129.

Lewis, Tiffany, Bianca Klettke, and Andrew Day. 2014. The Influence of Medical and Behavioral Evidence on Conviction Rates in Cases of Child Sexual Abuse. *Journal of Child Sexual Abuse* 23: 431–441.

London, Kamala, Maggie Bruck, Daniel Schuman and Stephen Ceci. 2005. Disclosure of Child Sexual Abuse. What Does the Research Tell Us About the Ways That Children Tell? *Psychology, Public Policy and Law* (1): 194–226, doi:10.1037/1076-8971.11.1.194.

London, Kamala, Maggie Bruck, Daniel Wright and Stephen Ceci. 2008. Review of the Contemporary Literature on How Children Report Sexual Abuse to Others: Findings, Methodological Issues, and Implications for Forensic Interviewers. *Memory* 16 (1): 29–47. doi:10.1080/09658210701725732.

Melnyk, Laura, Angela Crossman, and Matthew Sculling. 2007. The suggestibility of children's memory. In *The Handbook of Eyewitness Psychology, vol I: Memory for Events*, eds. M.P. Toglia, J.D. Read, D.F. Ross, and R.C.L. Lindsat, 401–427. Mahwah, NJ, US: Lawrence Erlabuam Associates Publishers.

Michael, Lamb. Irit Hershkowitz, Kathleen Sternberg, Phillip Esplin, Meir Hovav, Talma Manor, and Liora Yudilevitch. 1996. Effects of Investigative Utterance Types on Israeli Children's Responses. *International Journal of Behavioral Development* 19: 627–637.

Newcombe, Nora, Marianne Lloyd and Kristin Ratliff. 2007. Development of Episodic and Autobiographical Memory: A Cognitive Neuroscience Perspective. In *Advances in Child Development and Behavior*, ed. R.V. Kail, vol. 35. 37–85. London, England: Elsevier.

Orbach, Yael, Irit Hershkowitz, Michael Lamb, Kathleen Sternberg, Phillip Esplin, and Dvora Horowitz. 2000. Assessing the Value of Structured Protocols for Forensic Interviews of Alleged Abuse Victims. *Child Abuse and Neglect* 24: 733–752.

Ornstein, Peter, Lynne Baker-Ward, Betty Gordon, and Kathy Merritt. 1997. Children's Memory for Medical Experiences: Implications for Testimony. *Applied Cognitive Psychology* 11: 87–104.

Peterson, Carole, and Kelly Warren. 2009. Injuries Emergency Rooms and Children's Memory: Factors Contributing to Individual Differences. In *Emotion and Memory in Development: Biological Cognitive and Social*

Considerations, eds. J. Quas, and R. Fivush, 60–85. Oxford: Oxford University Press.

Quas, Jodi, Amy Bauer and Thomas Boyce. 2004. Physiological Reactivity, Social Support, and Memory in Early Childhood. *Child Development* 75: 797–814. doi:10.1111/j.1467-8624.2004.00707.x.

Roozendaal, Benno, Bruce McEwen, and Sumatra Chattarji. 2009. Stress, Memory and the Amygdala. *Nature Reviews Neuroscience* 10: 423–433. doi:10.1038/nrn2651.

Rush, Elizabeth, Jodi Quas, Liona Yim, Mariya Nikolayev, Steven Clark, and Rakel Larson. 2014. Stress, Interviewer Support, and Children's Eyewitness Identification Accuracy. *Child Development* 85 (3): 1292–1305. doi:10.1111/cdev.12177.

Santtila, Pekka, Julia Korkman, and Kenneth Sandnabba. 2004. Effects of interview phase, repeated interviewing, presence of a support person, and anatomically detailed dolls on child sex abuse interviews. *Psychology, Crime & Law* 10: 21–35.

Schneider, Wolfgang, and David Bjorklund. 2003. Memory and knowledge development. In *Handbook of Developmental Psychology*, eds. J. Valsiner, and K. Connolly, 370–403. London: Sage.

Schneider, Wolfgang, and Michael Pressley. 2013. *Memory Development Between Two and Twenty*. New Jersey: Lawrence Erlbaum Associates.

Simcock, Gabrielle, and Harlene Hayne. 2002. Breaking the Barrier? Children Fail to Translate Their Preverbal Memories into Language. *Psychological Science* 13: 225–231.

Smeets, Tom, Henry Otgaar, Ingrid Candel, and Oliver Wolf. 2008. True or False? Memory is Differentially Affected by Stress-induced Cortisol Elevations and Sympathetic Activity at Consolidation and Retrieval. *Psychoneuroendorinologi* 33 (10): 1378–1386.

Smith, Daniel, Elizabeth Letourneau, Benjamin Saunders, Dean Kilpatrick, Heidi Resnick, and Connie Best. 2000. Delay in Disclosure of Childhood Rape: Results from a National Survey. *Child Abuse and Neglect* 24 (2): 273–287.

Squire, Larry. 2004. Memory Systems of the Brain: A Brief History and Current Perspective. *Neurobiology of Learning and Memory* 82: 171–177.

Sternberg, Kathleen, Michael Lamb, Graham Davies, and Helen Westcott. 2001. The Memorandum of Good Practice: Theory versus application. *Child Abuse and Neglect* 25: 669–681.

Sternberg, Kathleen, Michael Lamb, Irit Hershkowitz, Phillip Esplin, Allison Redlich, and Naomi Sunshine. 1996. The Relationship Between

Investigative Utterance Types and the Informativeness of Child Witnesses. *Journal of Applied Developmental Psychology* 17: 439–451.

Tulving, Endel. 1985. Memory and Consciousness. *Psychologie Canadienne* 26: 1–12.

Warren, Amya, Cara Woodall, Marney Thomas, Michael Nunno, Jennifer Keeney, Susan Larson, and Julie Stadfeld. 1999. Assessing the Effectiveness of a Training Program for Interviewing Child Witnesses. *Applied Developmental Science* 3: 128–135.

Westcott, Helen, and Sally Kynan. 2006. Interviewer practice in investigative interviews for suspected child sexual abuse. *Psychology, Crime and Law* 12: 367–382.

7

Legal and Theoretical Framework for Investigative Interviews

Julia Korkman, Tom Pakkanen and Taina Laajasalo

Preamble

In Finland, specialised university hospital units have taken on much of the role of the Barnahus in other Nordic countries, ensuring a child-friendly and expert environment for child interviews in cases of suspected crimes against children. The personnel consist of multi-professional teams including expertise in forensic psychology, paediatrics, child psychiatry and social work. There are units in the country's five university hospitals,

---

J. Korkman (✉) · T. Pakkanen · T. Laajasalo
Helsinki University Central Hospital, Helsinki, Finland
e-mail: jkorkman@abo.fi

T. Pakkanen
e-mail: tom.pakkanen@hus.fi

T. Laajasalo
e-mail: taina.laajasalo@hus.fi

J. Korkman · T. Pakkanen
Åbo Akademi University, Turku, Finland

thus covering the whole country. The units provide expert assistance when required by the police, in practically all cases involving preschool and young school-aged children as well as particularly vulnerable child victims. Finnish guidelines promote a hypothesis -testing approach and the use of expert interviewers (forensic psychologists with knowledge of human memory, child interviewing strategies, child development and suggestibility issues as well as the phenomena of child disclosure and trauma) within the pre-trial process, ensuring an evidence-based practice of investigating child abuse suspicions.

Introduction

In Finland, children under the age of 15 (and, as of 2016, in many cases 18) are not required to be present in court to testify. Instead, their testimony is usually recorded in the pre-trial (criminal) investigation. Interviews must be conducted according to best practice. Emphasis has been put on nationwide investigative interviewer training, including supervision and feedback. A particular feature of the Finnish system is the use of experts in forensic psychology within child abuse investigations. Another cornerstone within the Finnish system is the explicit use of a hypothesis-testing approach throughout the process.

Interviews with older children are normally conducted by the police, whereas preschool children, children with disabilities or communicational problems or children in cases that for other reasons are deemed to be particularly demanding are usually interviewed in the expert units. The units operate within the framework of the pre-trial investigation, and interviews within the units are monitored by the police in charge of the investigation but conducted by expert psychologists with training in forensic interviewing.

This chapter will present the legal and scientific framework of the units with a particular focus on the largest of these, the Child Forensic Psychology Unit at the University of Helsinki, founded in 2006 and inspired by the Icelandic Barnahus. The focus of the chapter is twofold: on the investigative interviews conducted by the forensic psychologists as well as the investigative process culminating in the expert statement delivered for the police and the court.

The Legal and Theoretical Framework for Assessing Allegations of Crimes Against Children in Finland

In a famous Finnish case in the 1990s, a preschool-aged boy, "Niko", played games, which were perceived as sexual in nature, with his preschool friends. This led to a concern that Niko might have been sexually abused. Niko was interviewed and taken into custody. He was not allowed to live with his parents until years later, when it was realised that the allegation was most likely unfounded and that the investigative interview with Niko had been severely suggestive.

At the beginning of the 2000s, analyses of Finnish investigative interviews in cases of suspected child sexual abuse (CSA) showed that these were often highly suggestive (Korkman et al. 2008b). Similar findings were made in other Nordic countries (e.g. Cederborg et al. 2000; Thoresen et al. 2006; Thoresen et al. 2009), showing that investigative interviews were often of poor quality.

As the child interview is often the most important piece of evidence in an abuse investigation, the importance of a high-quality interview cannot be too strongly emphasised. Interviews of poor quality might in many ways risk the well-being of the child; in cases where abuse has not occurred, children may be removed from their families without due reason (false-positive errors), while in actual cases of abuse, poor interviews may fail to recognise actually occurring abuse (false-negative errors).

In Finland, the realisation that investigative child interviewing warrants particular skills led to the development of guidelines (Taskinen 2003; Duodecim 2013; Ellonen 2013), training (Lahtinen et al. in press) and the creation of the specialised units, to ensure a child-friendly and expert setting for investigating crimes against children (Law 2009). It was decided that the investigations would be clearly separated from therapeutic processes and that mental health professionals assisting the judicial system be specially trained for this task.

As children in Finland give their evidence during the pre-trial investigation, all interviews are electronically recorded and transcribed word for word, enabling careful analyses of the information provided. In order to ensure the right to a fair trial, the defendant may watch the recorded child interview and pose questions to the child through the interviewer.

Evidence-Based Child Interviewing

> A forensic interview of a child is a developmentally sensitive and legally sound method of gathering factual information regarding allegations of abuse or exposure to violence. This interview is conducted by a competently trained, neutral professional utilizing research and practice-informed techniques as part of a larger investigative process (Newlin et al. 2015, 1).

Forensic child interviewing has been extensively researched, and there are widely endorsed best practice guidelines (e.g. Lamb et al. 2007). The most researched is the *NICHD interviewing protocol*, which is the standard in many countries (for an international review, including Finland and Norway, see LaRooy et al. 2015). The protocol improves the quality, and increases the amount, of reliable information in child interviews (e.g. Lamb et al. 2002, 2003; Sternberg et al. 2001), regardless of the child's age (Lamb et al. 2003). It is semi-structured and flexible and thus requires modification according to the suspicion at hand. This modification requires expertise on the part of the interviewer, and the interviews are thoroughly planned, bearing in mind the alternative hypotheses to the suspicion.

While the use of the NICHD protocol is associated with a lowered risk of false-negative errors (Lamb et al. 2007), the hypothesis-testing approach, and especially its application within the interview itself, may be considered a safeguard against false-positives errors and interviewer bias (Rohrabaug and London 2016). For instance, where the alternative hypothesis is that an abuse suspicion is the result of a parent coaching the child, the interviewer may pose questions about how the suspecting party found out about the allegation and how the child and this person have discussed the matter; especially in the case of older children, interviewers may also incorporate elements from other interview methods, in particular the cognitive interview (Memon et al. 2010; for an overview of different research protocols see, for example, Melinder and Korkman 2010).

Previous research (Korkman et al. 2008a; Lamb et al. 2003) has shown that the language used by child interviewers is often developmentally inappropriate. Children who witnesses in court have also reported that they didn't understand the language and that they experienced witnessing as traumatic (Plotnikoff and Woolfson 2004).

Needless to say, successful investigative interviews with children must fit the developmental level of the child. Children with problematic or developing communication skills may need expert assistance to communicate at their best level. An initial interview or linguistic assessment may be carried out with young children or children who have developmental difficulties, to assess the child's capacities as a witness. Tools (dolls, body diagrams) are not recommended or used in Finland (as recommended by research, see, for example, Poole et al. 2011; Poole and Dickinson 2011); however, the child may draw (e.g. an overview of the building) and write within the interview as a supplement to the verbal account.

While research previously cautioned against the repeated interviewing of children, underlining the risks associated with repeated *suggestive* interviewing (e.g. Bruck and Ceci 2004; Melnyk and Bruck 2004), recent research indicates that conducting more than one interview can have advantages in terms of an increase in information (LaRooy et al. 2008). One of the key concepts behind the Barnahus model is avoiding a secondary traumatisation of the child, which may occur, for instance, if the child is forced to talk about the abuse repeatedly to different agencies. This is also emphasised in the Children's Advocacy Centres (CACs) literature in the USA, stating that *"CACs have aimed to change the practice of forensic child interviewing by coordinating multiple investigations, limiting the number of interviews and interviewers children have, and providing "child friendly" locations for interviews"* (Cross et al. 2007, 1032). This evaluation of CAC interviews notes that children are usually interviewed once or twice in the CAC and in the vast majority of cases by the same interviewer.

Guidelines in Finland are flexible with regard to the number of interviews per child, and children in the Helsinki unit are (2006–2012) interviewed twice on average. Recent US recommendations suggest that more than one interview may be necessary to ensure children are given a real opportunity to communicate their experiences; however, importantly, they note that the risks associated with repeated questioning must be acknowledged and that potentially repeated interviews should always be conducted appropriately (i.e. not suggestively): *"However, some children require more time and familiarity to become comfortable and to develop trust in both the process and the interviewer. Recent research indicates that multiple interview sessions may allow reluctant, young, or traumatized children the opportunity to more clearly and completely share information"* (Cross et al. 2007, 11).

Conducting Child Abuse Assessments in University Hospital Units

University hospital teams consist of experts in forensic and developmental psychology, social workers familiar with child protection, child psychiatrists and paediatricians specialised in the field. The units serve as multiprofessional sites where all the information concerning a particular child can be shared among the police, health care and social work professionals in order to make informed decisions about how to proceed in a situation where an abuse allegation has been raised. The premises are child friendly, with a waiting room furnished with play areas with toys, books, games and magazines. The interview room itself is calm, with pleasant furniture but avoiding an abundance of stimuli (as recommended by, for instance, Poole and Lamb 1998, as these may distract the child).

The expert assistance can take many forms depending on the case under investigation. One of the central roles is to assist the police in conducting interviews with young children or children with disabilities. Psychologists with training in child development and forensic interviewing conduct the interviews within the units. The police and other professionals (e.g. the child's attorney, the prosecutor, a child psychiatrist, the defence lawyer) follow the interviews live through a video-link.

The police also turn to the units in particularly complicated cases, such as severe custody disputes. Custody disputes are arguably among the most complicated circumstances in which to investigate abuse allegations, it is necessary in virtually all cases to consider the possibility that the child(ren) *may* have been manipulated or coached (Hendershot and Bow 2013).

Since the founding of the specialised units, collaboration with the police has developed to include a wide range of collaboration forms. The unit can consult for or supervise the police in planning and conducting the interview as well as give feedback on interviews, something which has the long-term benefit of strengthening expertise within the police (Lamb et al. 2002).

In many cases, the units write expert statements for the purpose of the judicial process. Within these statements, the background of the allegation is detailed along with the alternative hypotheses formulated for the suspected abuse. The collected facts are then analysed, and the different hypotheses are weighed against these. The statements do not include opinions on whether a crime has occurred or not and are not binding in the court, but may serve as important information in the cases (see, for example, the Finnish Supreme Court decision 2014: 48).[1]

Cases at the Helsinki Unit Between 2006 and 2012[2]

During the first 6 years, 224 children were interviewed at the Helsinki unit.[3] The children were 3–16 years, with more than half (55%) below the age of 7. More than half of the interviewed children had psychological, neurological or developmental difficulties. In 25% of the cases, a custody dispute preceded the suspicion. Many of the families had problems related to substance abuse, mental health problems and/or a history with the child welfare services. The hospital units investigate both physical and sexual abuse allegations, although initially, emphasis was on child sexual abuse cases as these were deemed to be particularly challenging. Below is an overview of the child sexual abuse allegations assessed between 2006 and 2012.

In 45% of the suspected child sexual abuse cases, the suspect was the child's biological father, in 35% a person outside the family and in 5% a stepfather. It is important to note that according to research, child sexual abuse committed by a biological father is uncommon compared to other perpetrators (0.02%; Fagerlund et al. 2014 86–87). In cases of suspected physical abuse, the father was the most common suspect, followed by the mother.

When observing the outcomes of the assessments (Korkman et al. 2012), the child sexual abuse hypothesis was confirmed in ¼ of the cases, while in ½ of the cases, a rivalry hypothesis received more support (in the remaining ¼ of the cases, the outcome of the investigation remained inconclusive). The child sexual abuse cases which were least likely to be confirmed involved preschool (<7yrs) children, custody disputes, a suspected biological father and the non-existence of other evidence for the suspected abuse. Importantly, while more than 70% of the children interviewed were deemed in need of assessment or therapy, this need was equally great among children in cases assessed to be unfounded. This implies that rather than seeing psychological symptoms as indicators of abuse, they can also lead to or be the result of unfounded suspicions.

The Investigative Method at the Helsinki Unit

Key elements of the Finnish model of assessing child abuse allegations are explained below, along with case examples to describe the methods used in practice.

Formulating Alternative Hypotheses to the Allegation

It is recommended that investigators in Finland use a *hypothesis-testing approach* (Current Care Guidelines 2013; Ellonen 2013). After carefully assessing the available background information, alternative hypotheses to the suspected abuse are formulated (e.g. Poole and Lamb 1998; Rohrabaugh et al. 2016). The approach follows the principle stated by Dale and Gould (2014) who advocate for a "*neutral, objective, and even-handed hypothesis-testing stance*" by forensic experts and stress the need to use "*appropriate interviewing techniques, data collection from multiple sources, and consideration of multiple hypotheses*" (ibid., 171).

Within the initial assessment of the case, particular attention is paid to how the allegation came about, risk factors for abuse, identifying potential risks for pre-interview suggestion or misunderstandings, wrong interpretations or deliberate lies, and so on. Examples of alternative hypotheses in cases of suspected child sexual abuse may include (see Herman 2009):

- Child sexual abuse has occurred.
- The allegation has arisen from a misunderstanding (e.g. the suspect was helping the child wash).
- The child has seen porn/sexual material and, therefore, has knowledge about adult sexuality.
- The child's account is due to repetitive suggestive discussions with an adult (e.g. custody disputes).
- The child is lying (e.g. to cover up their own shame when getting caught masturbating).

In acute cases, where there are injuries or photo/video evidence, the focus is on interviewing the child as quickly as possible; however, in cases where a long time has passed since the alleged events, the need for thorough information collecting and analysis is stronger and the need to interview the child is not deemed as acute as in a recent case.

Acknowledging different possible hypotheses at the outset of the investigation is in the best interests of the child: if a suspicion is unfounded, the child will not be traumatised by, for instance, being unduly removed from their parents. Also, if all other relevant hypotheses to an allegation have been carefully addressed, the interview is more likely to be considered reliable evidence in court.

The case[4] below illustrates how alternative hypotheses are formulated in a case of suspected child physical abuse.

> A five-year-old boy, whose parents had separated, returned from a stay with his mother with a bruised cheek. According to the father, the boy

said his mother had hit him. The father filed a police report. The parents had divorced two years earlier, after which their relationship had been strained. A family court had ordered the boy to live with his mother with visits to his father. The parents had previously accused one another of physical abuse. Based on the initial information, three hypotheses were formulated: (1) the boy had been physically abused by his mother, (2) the suspicion was due to a misunderstanding between the father and the son, fuelled by the hostile relationship between the parents and (3) the child fabricated an account of physical abuse to gain attention or approval from his father. Because of the possible effect of the parent's tense relationship on the boy, it was decided that both parents would take turns to take the boy to his interviews.

The boy came to his first interview with his mother. When asked about the bruise on his cheek, he replied that he had fallen with his kick-bike and hurt his face. At his second interview with his father, the boy said his mother had hit him in the face. When the interviewer then asked if the hitting had left any marks, the boy referred to the bruise on the cheek. When confronted with the discrepancy in his accounts, the boy said the bruise was from his mother hitting him and that he didn't know why he had told the interviewer otherwise previously. In his third interview, when again brought by his mother, the boy told the interviewer that the bruise was from when he had fallen. When he again was confronted with the discrepancy in his accounts, he gave additional details about the situation where he had fallen. The conclusion was that all the tested hypotheses were supported to some degree, and thus, the outcome of the investigation was inconclusive. It should be noted that there were no reports made to persons outside the immediate family indicating physical abuse by either parent; instead, there was much concern about the effects of the difficult relationship between the parents on the boy's development. The parents were provided with psycho-education about the effects of an ongoing parental dispute on children and the means to handle their strained relation better.

In cases such as this, the possible contamination of the child's account needs to be taken into consideration when planning and conducting the interview. Had this child only been interviewed when accompanied by one particular parent, the investigation would possibly have been severely flawed. In many Barnahus (e.g. Stockholm), children are often accompanied by persons other than the parents (for instance, a support person from the school or similar) to the interview, which is likely to reduce the risk of immediate pre-interview contamination, at least to some extent.

Assessing the Emergence and Background Information of the Suspicion

Suspicions of child abuse form a diverse array of cases, and no one procedure can cater for all cases. Instead, investigations must be flexible and when necessary, very quick in operation. Some suspicions are vague and require thorough assessments of the background information. Information concerning the child and the suspicion provided by the child welfare services, healthcare information and information from the school or kindergarten and so on may differentiate long-lasting abuse and neglect from single instances of less severe forms of abuse. The background information helps direct the interventions undertaken in line with the best interests of the child. In acute cases, the priority is on hearing the child immediately, rather than gathering large amounts of background information.

One of the most important phases when investigating an abuse suspicion is the screening of background information to assess whether there is a cause for suspecting abuse. In cases of suspected child sexual abuse, Faust and colleagues state that "*the great majority of errors in the detection of sexually abused children occur during Phase 1 or screening. Every sexually abused child who is not referred is a certain error. Every nonabused child who is referred is a potential error, and some of these potential errors turn into actual ones during Phase 2 or evaluation. … there is essentially no question that a fairly substantial percentage of nonabused children referred for evaluation are misidentified as abused*" (Faust et al. 2009, 51).

Thoroughly taking into account alternative explanations for the abuse is also in the interest of all counterparts, not least the possible child victim. In cases where the child has indeed been victimised, a proper investigation should leave as little doubt as possible as to the events. Below is a description of a case where there was no other evidence for the sexual abuse than a little girl's account of a situation more than one year ago. A thorough examination of the alternative hypotheses and the background to the allegation, however, led to the conclusion that the child sexual abuse hypothesis was confirmed and no alternative hypotheses gained support. The court sentenced the suspected grandfather, largely based on the child's interview and the expert testimony.

> A five-year-old girl had lived at a children's home for almost a year, having been removed from her biological single-parent mother due to the mother's severe substance abuse. The girl had adjusted well to the children's home.
>
> When discussing fears one evening, the girl had spontaneously told a member of the personnel that she once was scared when visiting her grandfather, because he had locked her with him in the toilet and told her to suck his penis. As other children approached, the employee did not ask any further questions about this. Later, she asked the girl who she had meant when she said she had been scared in the toilet. The girl answered the name of her maternal grandfather, whom she hadn't seen for almost a year. The personnel consulted the Helsinki unit, and it was recommended that no further questions be asked. The police started an investigation, and the girl was brought to the unit for an interview within the following days. The alternative hypotheses formulated were (1) that the grandfather had sexually abused the girl (or attempted to), (2) that the personnel had misunderstood the girl's utterance or (3) that the girl had used words relating to adult sexuality without fully understanding what they meant.
>
> The girl's linguistic and memory skills were assessed through both practice interviews and with some neuropsychological testing, as the event in question was remote in time and the girl was very young. She had above average verbal and memory skills and was capable of giving detailed descriptions of events experienced months earlier. The topic of the interview was introduced by referring to her discussion of fears with the member of the personnel. The girl reported that around Christmas almost one year earlier, she had been left alone with her grandfather who took her to the toilet and tried to engage her in oral sex. The description was detailed and typically childish in its non-understanding of sexual elements, and the girl said she had told the mother at the time. When the police interviewed the mother, she confirmed this.

Screening the Cases: When Children Are not Interviewed

When the suspicion is deemed non-indicative of abuse, for instance, based on the behaviour that is age typical (see Poole and Wolfe 2009) or likely due to other factors in the child's life, children may not be interviewed at all. This is true also when the child does not have the developmental ability for an interview, or the abuse is suspected to have taken place in early infancy before autobiographical memories are formed (i.e. before language development; Greenhoot and Tsethlikai 2009).

In cases where the child has been repeatedly interviewed, re-interviewing may not be in their best interests. This may be the case particularly when there is evidence that the child has been subjected to suggestive questioning prior to the investigation. There are cases where caretakers provide agencies with their own recorded "interviews" (as proof of what the child has said), and these may at times be suggestive to the point that a child's statement is clearly contaminated (for an analysis of such cases, see Korkman et al. 2014). In some of those cases, the child has been asked the same leading questions (e.g. "did X touch you between the legs?") almost 20 times.

Below is a short description of a case where the child was too young to be able to give a full account of the worrying physical signs that led to a suspicion of severe physical abuse.

> The kindergarten noticed severe scratches on the arm of a boy who was almost four years old, which they thought looked like someone had grabbed the boy's arm. The boy was asked about the scratches. He said the family dog had caused them. The kindergarten did not believe him and reported a suspicion of physical abuse to the child welfare services. The child welfare services thought that the bruising looked like signs of physical abuse, and when asking the boy whether someone had hurt his arm, he had answered affirmatively (according to the child welfare services' files). When asked who had grabbed him, the boy replied "dad". The child welfare services filed a police report, and the boy was medically examined. At the first doctor's appointment, the boy told the doctor his father had grabbed his arm. The child welfare services took the boy into custody and the police referred the case to the Helsinki unit. Based on the available information, three alternative hypotheses were formulated:

> (1) the bruising on the boy's hand was due to physical abuse by the father, (2) the account of physical abuse had evolved as a result of suggestive questioning and (3) the scratches on his arm were due to (a) violent play with the family dog or with (b) other children (as the boy's mother had stated). When assessing the boy's linguistic capabilities, it became apparent that he did not possess the prerequisites to give reliable accounts of experiences. He also seemed prone to suggestion, answering questions he did not understand with "yes". While the child was unable to give a verbal account of how he had gotten the scratches, the plausibility of the hypothesis that the scratches were caused by the family dog could be tested. The police visited the boy at home and videotaped the boy playing with the dog. The dog (a dachshund puppy) made several lunges at the boy, biting his forearms where the scratches had been. It was concluded that the hypothesis about violent play with the dog and an account formed by repeated suggestive questioning (the initial response the boy had given was that the dog had caused the bruising) was most likely, and the outcome of the investigation was that the suspicion of child abuse was not founded.

As in this case, many of the children referred to the unit by the police are too young to possess the developmental prerequisites for giving a detailed enough account of their experiences. Here, the collaboration between different professionals and the thorough examination of other evidence is of crucial importance.

Support for the Children and Families

Assessments are made in close cooperation with the police and the child welfare services, guaranteeing timely interventions and support. After the assessment, the outcome of the interview and the assessment is discussed with the parents. Parents are informed about the continuation of the judicial process, and their worries about the child's recovery are discussed. Parents are also notified about where to find further support. The child's need for psychiatric support is assessed, and when necessary, the unit's child psychiatrist makes a referral to treatment (typically to family welfare units or child psychiatric units). In addition to the services provided outside the unit, the unit provides trauma-focused cognitive-behavioural therapy (Tf-CBT) for a number of children and their families. Tf-CBT is an evidence-based short-term treatment developed especially for victims of child sexual abuse (Ramirez de Arellano et al. 2014).

Concluding Remarks and Future Directions

While the Finnish system caters well for the youngest and most vulnerable witnesses, concern remains that older children who are interviewed by the police may not be directed to treatment or care, nor are police interviews necessarily done in child-friendly premises. There is currently a project (called Barnahus) that is ongoing in Finland, aiming to ensure that all children be interviewed in child-friendly settings, including older children and teenagers who are, at present, commonly interviewed by the police, at a police station, and that their possible need for further support be assessed.

Among the benefits of the Finnish system that the authors would like to stress, and which could easily be implemented into the praxis of other countries and to the different Barnahus developments, are *the use of (forensic) psychological expertise* within the pre-trial investigation and the *hypothesis-testing approach.*

Young children and children with special needs require particular expertise on the part of the interviewer. Children with developmental disorders such as ADHD or autism spectrum disorders particularly require an in-depth understanding of the neuropsychological elements of the children's functioning in order to facilitate their recollections. The opportunity to obtain assistance in complex cases has been greatly appreciated by the police, and collaborating with the expert unit has also served as a source of re-education for the police officers.

The fact that the expert units have the right to gather *all* information about the children is of vital importance. Only by closely examining child welfare services' reports, healthcare documentation and information by school or day care personnel, the risk of, for instance, long-term violent abuse can be assessed. The hypothesis-testing approach, when applied through the whole investigation—from the assessment of the emergence of the suspicion to the conclusions drawn based on all the gathered facts—minimises the risk of the critical problems of confirmation bias and leading interviewing styles. This helps guide investigators towards the truth behind a suspicion—be it founded or unfounded. It seems fair to assume that it is in the best interests of the child that criminal investigations rely on evidence-based practices, minimising the risk of wrong outcomes. When investigations are properly conducted, they can and should fulfil both the requirements of a fair trial and at the same time be sensitive to the particular needs of child witnesses and victims.

Notes

1. One weakness and point of critical discussion in the current Finnish system concern the availability of second opinions. Expert statements are not as readily available for all parties: only the police, prosecutor or the court can ask the units for an official statement.
2. The data were collected as part of an ongoing research project, which has been approved by the ethical committee of the Helsinki University Central Hospital and the National Police Board.
3. The following years have shown a steady increase in the number of cases and interviewed children as the unit has expanded from a personnel consisting of six professionals in 2006 to 19 in 2015. The number of investigations in 2011 was 118; in 2012, there were 145; in 2013, there were 151; in 2014, there were 203; and in 2015, there were 246.
4. All the case vignettes presented in this chapter have been thoroughly anonymised in order to protect the identity of all the parties involved.

References

Bruck, Maggie, and Stephen Ceci. 2004. Forensic developmental psychology. Unveiling four common misconceptions. *Forensic Developmental Psychology* 13: 229–232.

Cederborg, Ann-Christine, Yael Orbach, Kathleen Sternberg, and Michael E. Lamb. 2000. Investigative interviews of child witnesses in Sweden. *Child Abuse and Neglect* 24: 1355–1361.

Cross, Theodor P., Lisa M. Jones, Wendy A. Walsh, Monique Simone and David Kolko. 2007. Child forensic interviewing in Children's Advocacy Centers: Empirical data on a practice model. *Child Abuse and Neglect* 31: 1031–1052.

Dale, Milfred, and Jonathan W. Gould. 2014. Commentary on "Analyzing Child Sexual Abuse Allegations": Will a New Untested Criterion-Based Content Analysis Model be Helpful? *Journal of Forensic Psychology Practice* 14: 169–182.

de Arellano, Ramirez, A. Michael, Russell Lyman, Lisa Jobe-Shields, Preethy George, Richard H. Dougherty, Allen S. Daniels, Sushmita Ghose, Larke Huang, and Miriam E. Delphin-Rittmon. 2014. Trauma-Focused Cognitive Behavioral Therapy: Assessing the Evidence. *Psychiatric Services* 65: 591–602.

Duodecim (the Finnish Medical Society). 2013. *Current Care Guidelines: Investigating Suspicions of Child Sexual Abuse.* http://www.kaypahoito.fi/web/kh/suositukset/suositus;jsessionid=7E3A7E56839CC04A143BED0DA7F6BD97?id=hoi34040.

Ellonen, Noora. (ed.) 2013. Rikostutkinta lapsiin kohdistuvissa väkivalta- ja seksuaalirikoksissa (Investigating sexual and violent crimes against children). Poliisiammattikorkeakoulun oppikirjat 20.

Fagerlund, Monica, Marja Peltola, Juha Kääriäinen, Noora Ellonen and Heikki Sariola. 2014. Lasten ja nuorten väkivaltakokemukset 2013 (in Finnish). https://www.theseus.fi/bitstream/handle/10024/86726/Raportteja_110_lapsiuhritutkimus_web.pdf.

Faust, David, Ana J. Bridges and David C. Ahern. 2009. Methods for the Identification of Sexually Abused Children. Suggestions for Clinical Work and Research. In *The Evaluation of Child Sexual Abuse Allegations. A Comprehensive Guide to Assessment and Testimony*, ed. Kathryn Kuehnle and Mary Connell, 3–19. Wiley: Hoboken, New Jersey.

Finnish Supreme Court decision. 2014. A decision concerning a child sexual abuse allegation. http://korkeinoikeus.fi/fi/index/ennakkopaatokset/precedent/1404215595714.html.

Greenhoot, Andrea F., and Monica Tsethlikai. 2009. Repressed and Recovered Memories During Childhood and Adolescence. In *The Evaluation of Child Sexual Abuse Allegations. A Comprehensive Guide to Assessment and Testimony*, ed. Kathryn Kuehnle and Mary Connell, 203–244. Wiley: Hoboken, New Jersey.

Hendershot, Lesly, and James N. Bow. 2013. Investigating Sexual Abuse Allegations in Child Custody Cases. *American Journal of Forensic Psychology* 31: 37–53.

Herman, Steve. 2009. Forensic Child Sexual Abuse Evaluations. Accuracy, Ethics, and Admissibility. In *The Evaluation of Child Sexual Abuse Allegations. A Comprehensive Guide to Assessment and Testimony*, ed. Kathryn Kuehnle and Mary Connell, 247–266. New Jersey: Wiley.

Korkman, Julia, Aino Juusola, and Pekka Santtila. 2014. Who made the disclosure? Recorded conversations between children and caretakers suspecting child abuse. *Psychology, Crime and Law* 20: 994–1004.

Korkman, Julia, Pekka Santtila, Tove Drzewiecki, and N. Kenneth Sandnabba. 2008a. Failing to Keep it Simple: Language Use in Child Sexual Abuse Interviews with 3-8-Year-Old Children. *Psychology, Crime and Law* 14: 41–60.

Korkman, Julia, Pekka Santtila, Malin Westeråker, and N. Kenneth Sandnabba. 2008b. Interviewing Techniques and Follow-Up Questions in child Sexual Abuse Interviews. *European Journal of Developmental Psychology* 5: 108–128.

Korkman, Julia, Taina Laajasalo, Katarina Finnilä, Merja Oksanen and Eeva Aronen. 2012. *Investigating suspicions of child sexual abuse.* (Lapsen seksuaalisen hyväksikäyttöepäilyn selvittäminen). Suomen Lääkärilehti Duodecim 20/2012.

Lahtinen, Hanna, Julia Korkman, Aarno Laitila and Lauri Mehtätalo. In press. The Effect of Training on Investigative Interviewers' Attitudes and Beliefs Related to Child Sexual Abuse. *Investigative Interviewing: Research and Practice.*

Lamb, Michael E., Irit Hershkowitz, Yael Orbach and Philip Esplin. 2007. Tell Me What Happened: Structured Investigative Interviews of Child Victims and Witnesses. *Wiley Series in Psychology of Crime, Policing and Law.*

Lamb, Michael E., Kathleen Sternberg, Yael Orbach, Philip Esplin, and Susanne Mitchell. 2002. Is Ongoing Feedback Necessary to Maintain the Quality of Investigative Interviews with Allegedly Abused Children? *Applied Developmental Science* 6: 35–41.

Lamb, Michael E., Kathleen Sternberg, Yael Orbach, Philip Esplin, Heather Stewart, and Susanne Mitchell. 2003. Age Differences in Young Children's Responses to Open-Ended Invitations in the Course of Forensic Interviews. *Journal of Consulting and Clinical Psychology* 71: 926–934.

Lamb, Michael E., Yael Orbach, Irit Hershkowitz, Philip W. Esplin, and Dvora Horowitz. 2007b. Structured Forensic Interview Protocols Improve the Quality and Informativeness of Investigative Interviews with Children: A Review of Research Using the NICHD Investigative Interview Protocol. *Child Abuse and Neglect* 31: 1201–1231.

LaRooy, David, Michael E. Lamb and Margaret-Ellen Pipe. 2008. Repeated Interviewing: A Critical Evaluation of the Risks and Potential Benefits. In *The Evaluation of Child Sexual Abuse Allegations. A Comprehensive Guide to Assessment and Testimony*, ed. Kathryn Kuehnle and Mary Connell, 327–361. Hoboken: Wiley.

LaRooy, David, Sonja Brubacher, Anu Aromäki-Stratos, Mireille Cyr, Irit Hershkowitz, Eynkung Jo, Julia Korkman, Lindsey Malloy, Trond Myklebust, Moriko Naka, Carlos Peixoto, Kim Roberts, Heather Stewart, and Michael E. Lamb. 2015. The NICHD Protocol: A Review of an Internationally-used Evidence-Based Tool for Training Child Forensic Interviewers. *Journal of Criminological Research, Policy and Practice* 1: 76–89.

Law Concerning the Investigations of Sexual and Physical Abuse Against Children. 2009. 2013 (in Finnish: http://www.finlex.fi/fi/laki/ajantasa/2008/20081009).

Melinder, Annika, and Julia Korkman. 2010. Children's Memory and Testimony. In *Forensic Psychology in Context: Nordic and International Approaches*, ed. P.A. Granhag, 117–138. UK: Willan Publishing.

Melnyk, Laura and Maggie Bruck. 2004. Timing moderates the effects of repeated suggestive interviewing on children's eyewitness memory. *Applied Cognitive Psychology* 18: 613–631.

Memon, Amina, Chris A. Meissner, and Joanne Fraser. 2010. The Cognitive Interview: A Meta-Analytic Review and Study Space Analysis of the Past 25 Years. *Psychology, Public Policy, and Law* 16: 340–372.

Newlin, Chris, Linda C. Steele, Andra Chamberlin, Jennifer Anderson, Julie Kenniston, Amy Russell, Heather Stewart and Viola Vaughan-Eden. 2015. *Child Forensic Interviewing: Best Practices*. Juvenile Justice Bulletin, U.S. Department of Justice. http://www.ojjdp.gov/pubs/248749.pdf.

Plotnikoff, Joyce and Richard Woolfson. 2004. *In their own words: The experiences of 50 young witnesses in criminal proceedings*. Policy Practice Research Series, NSPCC Publications, London.

Poole, Debra Ann, Maggie Bruck, and Margaret-Ellen Pipe. 2011. Forensic Interviewing Aids: Do Props Help Children Answer Questions About Touching? *Current Directions in Psychological Science* 20: 11–15.

Poole, Debra Ann, and Jason J. Dickinson. 2011. Evidence Supporting Restrictions on Uses of Body Diagrams in Forensic Interviews. *Child Abuse and Neglect* 35: 659–669.

Poole, Debra Ann, and Michele A. Wolfe. 2009. Child Development: Normative Sexual and Nonsexual Behaviors That May Be Confused with Symptoms of Sexual Abuse. In: *The Evaluation of Child Sexual Abuse Allegations. A Comprehensive Guide to Assessment and Testimony*, ed, Kathryn Kuehnle and Mary Connell, 101–128. Hoboken, New Jersey: Wiley.

Poole, Debra Ann, and Michael E. Lamb. 1998. *Investigative Interviews of Children. A Guide for Helping Professionals*. Washington D.C.: American Psychological Association.

Rohrabaugh, Monica, Kamala London and Ashley K. Hall. 2016. Planning the Forensic Interview. *In Forensic Interviews Regarding Child Sexual Abuse.*

A Guide to Evidence-Based Practice, ed. W.T. O'Donohue and M. Fanetti, 197–218. Switzerland: Springer International Publishing.

Sternberg, Kathleen J., Michael E. Lamb, Graham M. Davies and Helen L. Westcott. 2001. The Memorandum of Good Practice: Theory versus application. *Child Abuse and Neglect* 25: 669–681.

Taskinen, Sirpa. 2003. *Recommendations by an Expert Group for Social Health and Welfare Personnel. Investigating Child Sexual and Physical Abuse (in Finnish)*. Gummerus Kirjapaino Oy.

Thoresen, Christian, Kyrre Lønnum, Annika Melinder, and Svein Magnussen. 2009. Forensic Interviews with Children in CSA Cases: A Large-Sample Study of Norwegian Police Interviews. *Applied Cognitive Psychology* 23: 99–1011.

Thoresen, Christian, Kyrre Lønnum, Annika Melinder, Ulf Stridbeck, and Svein Magnussen. 2006. Theory and Practice in Interviewing Young Children: A Study of Norwegian Police Interviews 1985–2002. *Psychology, Crime, and Law* 12: 629–640.

8

Norwegian Sequential Interview Model

Åse Langballe and Tone Davik

Introduction

This chapter presents and discusses a new sequential interview model —the Norwegian sequential interview model (SI)—that is tailored to the needs of preschool children aged about 3–6 years old, when they participate in investigative interviews in Barnahus. The model builds on the extended forensic interview protocol (EFI) from the USA. The Norwegian SI model is based on close collaboration between police interviewers and Barnahus staff and differs from the standard procedures of child investigative interviews in Norway—the dialogical communication method (DCM) (Gamst and Langballe 2004). DCM is

Å. Langballe (✉)
Norwegian Centre for Violence and Traumatic Stress Studies, NKVTS, Oslo, Norway
e-mail: ase.langballe@nkvts.no

T. Davik
National Criminal Investigation Service, Oslo, Norway
e-mail: tone.davik@politiet.no

consistent with international principles for scientific investigative interviews (Davies and Westcott 1999; Fisher and Geiselman 1992; Lamb 1994; Milne and Bull 1999). The differences between DCM and SI are highlighted in the chapter. The chapter concludes with suggestions for further research into investigative interviews with preschool children.

Two different evaluations of Norwegian legislation on child investigative interview have concluded that the legislation was not adapted to the needs of children when they testify about their experiences of violence and sexual abuse in investigative interviews (Ministry of Justice 2004, 2012). The evaluations pointed out the need for more child-friendly interviewing methods. It was particularly noted that preschool children may need more than one single interview to talk about their experiences. Regular investigative interview practice with children in Norway normally lasts about 1 h allowing only one short break during the interview. Against this background, changes were made to the Norwegian criminal code. The new amendments allowed the possibility of adjusting the investigative interview to the individual child's developmental and psychosocial needs during the interview, to a greater degree. The amendments expanded the opportunity for supplementary interviews. The law does not specify which methods must be used in child investigative interviews; however, other than that the interviews shall be conducted in accordance with currently approved interview methods taught at the Norwegian Police University College (Ministry of Justice 2014, see also Chap. 5 in this book).

The lack of satisfactory arrangements to meet the needs of preschool children in the interviews led to the development of the *Extended investigative interview project*. The project involved participants from the National Criminal Investigation Service (NCIS/KRIPOS), Barnahus and the police in the city of Bergen and Norwegian Centre for Violence and Traumatic Stress Studies (NKVTS). The authors of this chapter were members of the project group: Tone Davik from NCIS as the project leader and Åse Langballe from NKVTS as a researcher.

The aim of the extended investigative interview project was to combine practical experience with scientific research to achieve a more "tailored" investigative interviewing approach for preschool children in Norwegian Barnahus.

Below, we describe and reflect on the new procedures for interviewing preschool children in Norway that resulted from the project. First, we will summarise some of the most commonly described challenges in interviews with the youngest children. We will then describe the main elements of the interview method commonly used when older children are interviewed by the police in Norway [the dialogical communication method (DCM) as described by Gamst and Langballe (2004)] and present the extended forensic interview (EFI) (Carnes et al. 1999, 2001; Faller and Nelson-Gardell 2010), developed in the USA. Finally, we describe how the extended investigative interview project combined these two interview models in new procedures for interviewing preschool children as the SI method.

Challenges Encountered When Interviewing Preschool Children

There are important factors to assess when preschool children are interviewed in investigative interviews, including their language development, memory capacity, vulnerability to suggestibility and psychosocial aspects (Bruck et al. 2006, Lamb and Sim 2013). Research has shown that interviewers often fail to ask age-appropriate and understandable questions to children and that this may lead to incomplete information from them (Saywitz et al. 1990, 1993). It is well documented that the use of open-ended questions increases the chances of eliciting accurate and complete information from a witness (Mamon and Bull 1999; Christianson et al. 1998; Fisher and Geiselman 1992), but we also know that open-ended questions (*tell me about your father*) are experienced as problematic for preschool children, because they do not relate to a context that can help the child understand the intent of the question (Fivush 2002). Focused and context-related questions are alternatives. Focused questions can be defined as closed (yes and no) questions or choice questions. Several studies show that children's answers to closed questions (*are you afraid of your father?*) and choice questions (*did he hit you one time or more than one time?*) often lead to incomplete and incorrect answers (Lamb et al. 2007, 2003; Peterson et al. 1999).

How to adequately phrase questions in a legal context while still taking the child's developmental needs in account is challenging. The questions should be related to the child's reality and words that the child understands should be used. To achieve this, thorough preparations are required. This entails getting to know how the child expresses themselves and experiences the surroundings. This also involves making the child feel safe and giving them a feeling of mastery during the interview situation (La Rooy et al. 2009; Leander 2010; Sternberg et al. 1997).

From a witness psychological perspective, potential influence on the child is a central theme when children are asked to retell past events (Ceci and Bruck 1995). Forgetfulness, false memories and external circumstances are interrelated factors that can create unreliable testimony from a witness, and specifically from a child, as a result of developmental conditions (Tetzchner 2001). Memory is prone to be negatively affected by elapsed time, and the time from an event has occurred until it is communicated, especially concerning investigative interviews with preschool children (Ceci and Bruck 1995). This is why it is important to provide the child with the opportunity to disclose the incident as soon as possible after its occurrence. On the other hand, children also need time to remember and to be able to articulate traumatic experiences. If the child is allowed to talk over time and on several different occasions, it may facilitate memory and thus help with the difficulties encountered while remembering. Memories of an incident can be reinforced, not only by the child repeating what took place, but also because an adult can assist in helping to explain what has happened and clear up any misunderstandings (Christianson and Granhag 2008). Multiple interviews can thus be in the best interest of the child and needed in order to inform the case under investigation. This requires, however, that interviews be conducted by competent interviewers who use recommended methods (open-ended questions). Research shows that children underreport abuse rather than report abuse that has not happened (Cederborg et al. 2007; Leander 2010). Supportive adults make it easier for a child to talk about abuse. Such support involves time to establish trust and feelings of safety during the interview situation (Hershkowitz et al. 2006).

The Standard Model in Norway: The Dialogical Communication Method (DCM)

To fully comprehend the procedural differences between the regular interview model in Norway (DCM) (Gamst and Langballe 2004) and the sequential interview model for preschoolers (SI), an overview of the phases in DCM will be presented. In addition to the phases, DCM consists of following areas: *the interview setting* involving formal and physical factors, *verbal and non-verbal communication* and *topic development.* These areas are not described in this presentation. The first author of this chapter is one of the two researchers who developed DCM (Gamst and Langballe 2004).

The first phase in DCM is the *preparatory phase.* The objective of this phase is to reduce stress in the interview situation and to give—and collect—information in order to make the child and the interviewer as prepared as possible for the interview. Criteria towards obtaining this objective are to provide information about the interview to the child's caregiver, obtain information about the child, collect information about the reported offence and conduct a meeting with the legal participants in advance of the interview. The main objective of the second phase, *the rapport phase,* is to establish contact with the child and an atmosphere of trust, and try to relax the child. Other objectives are to estimate the cognitive level and emotional state of the child, to introduce dialogue as the form of communication during the interview, to explore the child's understanding of the concepts *truth* and *lies* and to obtain personal information from the child. The child should thus be allowed to express themselves personally and talk about personal interests and non-intrusive subjects freely. The interviewer also shows themselves and encourages the child to tell the truth. In the third phase, the *preliminary phase,* the objective is to motivate the child to talk about their experiences, to reduce the disparity of power between the interviewer and the child and to explain the rules of the conversation. To achieve this, the interviewer clarifies their professional role, generalises the situation, provides the child with an overview and structure of the interview and explains the most important rules of the conversation. The fourth phase is called the *introduction to the focused subject.* The objective is to introduce the focused theme in a neutral manner. The criteria for achieving this goal are to introduce the case by asking open questions stemming from several hypotheses of the suspected crime. The fifth phase, *free narrative*, aims to obtain as much spontaneous and coherent information from the child as possible. By practising open-ended questions and active listening, the child will be given the opportunity to express themselves in a free narrative. The sixth phase, the *probing phase*, aims to obtain detailed, comprehensive and consistent information and illuminate the case as deeply and broadly as possible. The child has the opportunity to go thoroughly into separate themes in the narrative by clarifying and expanding on elements in the story. The seventh phase, *closing the interview*, aims to support the child and establish a basis for a positive end. The aim is that the child should have a sense of being seen, understood and taken seriously.

Developing the Sequential Interview (SI) Model

Extended Forensic Interviews (EFI)

The extended forensic interview protocol for children was developed by the National Child Advocacy Centre in Huntsville, Alabama (Carnes et al. 1999, 2001), specifically for the youngest children and children with special needs. This protocol splits the interview into several sessions, thus allowing more time for the interview. This acknowledges that time is needed to establish rapport and allows the interviewer to make adjustments throughout the interview process. The USA has more than 15 years of experience with this method, and it appears that extended assessments disclose severe sexual abuse cases to a greater extent; however, it is stressed that more research on the extended approach is needed (Carnes et al. 1999, 2001; Faller et al. 2010; Faller and Nelson-Gardell 2010). The phases in EFI described by this research have many similarities with those in DCM.

The interviewer is responsible for planning and organising the session, allotting the time needed for each session and between sessions.

Normally, only one session is conducted a day. The EFI approach underlines the importance of careful preparation, including the collection of information about the child's language skills, cognitive development, family situation and possible trauma experiences. The method also allows the use of props such as pictures or drawing materials to encourage further verbal explanations from the child when needed.

Methodology

A project group was established in 2010 to apply EFI to preschool children by testing it in Barnahus. The Norwegian model of EFI was called *sequential interviews* (SI).

The first ten SIs were conducted by three different police interviewers and analysed by the Barnahus in Bergen to explore whether SI elicited more abuse-related information than normally practiced interview methods. The results showed positive changes in eliciting more abuse-related information from very young children in the SI interviews compared to the standard interview model, and that the new model was perceived positively by legal representatives and caregivers (project report after testing sequential interviews with preschoolers 2012) ("Rapport etter utprøving av sekvensielle avhør av førskolebarn 2012"). The same year, a pilot group was appointed, consisting of nine expert child interviewers from NCIS and three police districts, the specialist psychologist from Bergen Barnahus and the researcher who is the first author of this chapter. The nine expert child interviewers received SI method training from the project group as well as lessons in preschool children's developmental psychology and specific challenges encountered when communicating with them. This marked the beginning of a structured collaboration between the Barnahus staff and police interviewers in developing the SI model in Norway.

This project used qualitative methods. The investigative interviewers kept journals after each SI session. Minutes were also recorded from two group meetings running for 2 and 3 days, at two different time points, where representatives from the Barnahus staff and the nine experienced police interviewers were present. Group and open discussions based on observations of actual audio-taped interviews using the SI model were also held.

The authors also conducted semi-structured group interviews of four experienced police interviewers and four experienced counsellors from the Barnahus staff, to gain information about experiences from their collaboration with each other.

An overview of experiences from conducting SI in Norway, concentrating on preparations and the actual sequences in the interview, is presented below.

Key Differences Between the Standard Method (DCM) and Sequential Interviews (SI)

DCM procedures were both simplified and extended in the SI to suit the youngest children. It became clear that the following was needed: better preparation prior to the interview—for the child, the child's caregivers and the police; more time and breaks during the interview to enable the child to relax and feel secure; the use of various props and toys; and spending a considerable amount of time throughout the interview allowing the child real opportunities to disclose their experience(s) of violence or sexual abuse. This project also demonstrated new prospects for interdisciplinary collaboration within the context of Barnahus.

Preparations

SI emphasises the importance of thorough preparation. Information gathered from those who know the child well can assist the Barnahus staff and the police interviewer in adapting the situation to the child's needs. These adaptions could include making detailed plans for how the child is received at the Barnahus including:

- Who should greet the child?
- What to say during the initial meeting?
- Which playroom (waiting room) is best suited to making the child feel safe and calm?

Challenges regarding young children's language comprehension and memory functions can be solved by obtaining information about the child and their family, surroundings, daily life and experiences, and are needed for formulating questions suited to the individual child. By making a detailed plan of adequate questions, the risk of asking suggestive questions and thus eliciting incorrect information is reduced. The preparation phase of the SI is therefore extended compared with this phase in the DCM.

Legal Participants

It is important to ensure that all participants involved in the interview have scheduled enough time for the SI (4–5 h). It is necessary to inform those in the judicial and police field about what the SI approach entails. For this reason, the judge,[1] police advocate, defence lawyer[2] and the child's legal representative were provided with written information about the SI, and the challenges of interviewing the youngest children as described in an article written by the authors of this chapter (Davik and Langballe 2013). In this way, the participants had the opportunity to prepare and gain more knowledge about the interview situation.

Collecting Information

If one or both parents are the suspect(s), a person from the kindergarten or from the child welfare services will usually accompany the child to the Barnahus. The parents or the professionals who accompany the child receive advice from the interviewer on how they can explain the reasons for going to the Barnahus to the child, what happens on arrival and who accompanies the child. The child also receives information about the actual interview and what it will be about, which is adapted to the maturity and psychological needs of the individual child.

Due to the nature of violence and abuse against young children, the police investigators usually have little information concerning the reported offence. Investigators therefore often need to gather more information from witnesses who know the child—for example, kindergarten staff. Relevant background knowledge includes how and to whom the child disclosed the incident in question, how the person who obtained the child's story responded to the child and the kinds of questions that were asked when the child disclosed the abuse.

In line with DCM, the investigative interviewer will ask the child's caregivers for information about the child's daily life, specific interests, cognitive, verbal and social development. In SI, the caregivers may also be asked to provide information on significant or recent positive experiences that they believe the child would enjoy talking about. This information can be used in establishing rapport and to explore the child's ability to provide free narratives.

Information Sharing

Two meetings are usually held before the interview. The first meeting is commonly a telephone conference to plan collaboration and the practical conduct of the interview. It involves the police interviewer and a counsellor from the Barnahus. A police investigator, and often the police lawyer and a representative from the child welfare services, normally also attend the meeting.

The second meeting is held immediately prior to the actual interview. Those present at this meeting are the police lawyer (in charge of the interview), a police investigator, the police interviewer, other legal representatives (who follow the interview) and the counsellor from the Barnahus. The meeting discusses the challenges that are to be expected when interviewing young children, specific challenges concerning the particular child and the level of information that can be expected from the child. The interviewer's plan for the interview is also presented and discussed.

Interview Sessions

The First Session

The first session normally lasts about 20–30 min and includes the second and third phases of DCM. A break before the introductory phase provides the interviewer with the opportunity to focus on important elements in the rapport phase, such as building trust and making the child feel secure. Not having to rush, and knowing that the child's concentration span is limited, helps the interviewer stay calm and focused on the child, and able to observe the child's behaviour, language and reactions to questions, various tasks and topics. During this session, the child should also receive information about the reasons for the interview, preferably in a way that is not an invitation to start talking about the actual case.

Props like a picture book, a puzzle or drawing materials can be used in the first session, to help the child start talking. In DCM, drawing material is usually the only play material used. As in DCM, the child should be informed of the basic rules of communication for the interview, including that the child can say *I don't know* if there is something they simply do not know, and to correct the interviewer if they say something that may be incorrect. The props mentioned above can also be used to examine the child's knowledge of concepts such as quantity, size, colours and shapes. By talking about neutral matters while using props, the interviewer and the Barnahus counsellor explore the child's cognitive abilities.

In the first session, questions should primarily be open, to see if the child understands open questions. The interviewer will also use more specific questions, such as *what, who, where* and *how*, to explore the child's responses. In this session, it is also important to encourage the child to tell the truth. Young children's understandings of abstract concepts like "truth" and "lies" are complicated matters in a legal context. Here, however, the interviewer is only required to inform the child about the rules of telling the truth so that the interview meets legal requirements [Criminal Code § 128 (Straffeprosessloven§ 128)] and fulfils the regulations of child investigative interviews §10 [Forskrift om avhør av barn og andre særlig sårbare fornærmede og vitner (tilrettelagte avhør)].

Normally, the interviewer introduces a recent event the child has experienced, and the child will then be asked to say more about it—in order to explore the child's ability to master the free narrative form. If not, information collected in the preparation phase will be used to explore the child's abilities to narrate prior experiences.

The session ends when the child starts to get distracted or once the interviewer has an idea of the child's language and developmental level. In taking a break so early in the process, the child will normally experience the interview as something positive, combined with a feeling of mastery and control, and feel secure and more familiar with the interviewer and the interview situation.

The First Break

The first break usually lasts for 45–60 min. During the break, the child is allowed to relax, play and get something to eat—but too much stimulation should be avoided. The break also provides the interviewer time to receive feedback from the Barnahus counsellor and thus an opportunity to change the direction and strategy for the rest of the interview, if needed. The counsellor and the interviewer can also discuss their common experiences from the first session in detail, sharing their impressions of the child's emotional state, language skills and behaviour in the interview situation.

The Second Session

In the second session, preschool children will tend to have an attention span of approximately 15–20 min. The interviewer can decide whether it is appropriate to take breaks during this session. In this presentation of the SI, we choose to present only three sessions in an interview conducted over only one day. The model is flexible, and the numbers of sessions and the possibility of using several days for the interview must be considered by the interviewer and the police advocate, together with the counsellor at the Barnahus as the interview progresses, bearing in mind the best interest of the child.

The interviewer begins by repeating and explaining the reason for the interview to the child. After this, the interviewer introduces the topic of focus to the child. If the child is unable to talk about the experience(s), they can make some drawings together. This might be a good way of re-establishing contact after the break. The interviewer can also present photographs of the child's home and family, or other people related to the case. Using such props can help direct the preschool child's attention to the topic in focus. It is stressed that photographs are introduced in an open manner, such as: *Tell me about this house. Tell me who lives with you in this house.* To make themes tangible to the child, the interviewer may draw while talking with the child—for example, the child's house, parents, siblings, pets, etc.

If the child brings up abuse or other relevant topics for the case, the interviewer follows up with questions. The follow-up questions should be open ended, but concrete, and adjusted to the child's developmental level. For example, *You told me your father hits when he gets angry. Tell me more about your father hitting (or being angry)*. If this question is too open, a more focused question might be: *Tell me who your father hits when he gets angry.* If the questions are too advanced for the child, they might lose attention and thus their motivation to complete the interview. Difficult questions also increase the potential of incorrect or short answers, such as *yes/no* and *I don't know*.

As a rule, the interviewer should always follow the child's lead throughout the whole interview by not ignoring any conversational initiatives the child takes.

The Last Break

There is a short break of 5–10 minutes before the interview ends. This break offers legal representatives the opportunity to formulate any remaining questions to the child, to be asked by the interviewer. The interviewer is given the opportunity to discuss the case, if needed, with the counsellor. It is important that this break is not long to avoid the child becoming tired and unfocused.

The Last Session

It is often necessary to ask a few final questions on behalf of the legal representatives towards the end of the interview also allowing an opening for a second interview, in case new questions emerge. This last session is normally quite short, lasting 5–10 min.

Final Reflections

The most significant difference between "practice as usual" in Norway (DCM) and sequential interviews (SI) is first and foremost a new form of interdisciplinary collaboration that lasts throughout the whole interview process. In one of the group interviews, a Barnahus counsellor says:

> I define us as a team, and we will do this together when there is sequential interviewing. (…) Now we [the Barnahus staff] can contribute with our knowledge, working as a team throughout the whole procedure. Start-up isn't when the actual interview begins, but when it is scheduled.

The interviewees describe a productive collaboration during the preparations for the interview; however, there are challenges in balancing professional roles. In particular, one can question whether the specific child-oriented expertise may bias the investigation, by negatively influencing the potential to obtain objective and unbiased information from the child. The SI approach has given both the Barnahus staff and the police the opportunity to become familiar with each other's professional work. The counsellors describe it as a difficult but meaningful task to weave together the child-oriented and investigative perspectives within the framework and goal of the interview. The police interviewers, through cooperation with the Barnahus staff, describe the knowledge that has been mutually gained, and how this serves as a foundation in the development of a culture for cooperation.

Research has shown the importance of familiarity with a proper methodology for interviewing children, and that support and guidance are needed for this knowledge to be sustained (Lamb et al. 2002; Orbach et al. 2000; Powel et al. 2008). An investigative situation involving a young child will usually entail a high degree of systemic stress. Under such conditions, even an experienced and trained interviewer may not always manage to observe what is happening with the child, and between themselves and the child, and be able to find the best practices and solutions in the current situation. It is important that the interviewer receives feedback and good counsel based on interdisciplinary knowledge and a shared understanding of the tasks at hand. It is essential for the success of the collaborative effort that the main aim of the investigative interview is clearly defined, as are the tasks that this entails.

The informants pointed out that the assistance provided to the SI interviewers may differ greatly. They also described providing counselling for the interviewers as a complex task that requires specific expertise, and pointed out the need for a system to ensure continued expertise over time.

A central element of the SI model is the use of props. We have not, however, examined how the props are used and what effects they have on the children's narratives. In order for the props to be properly used, they should be used in a deliberate and structured manner. For example, preschool children may have difficulties relating pictures to a real object, while photographs and drawings can help children explain things (Cederborg et al. 2009; Hewitt 1999). According to Poole and Dickinson (2013), children aged 5–12 years can divide their attention between voluntarily drawing and talking about past events, but we know little about how younger children and those with cognitive impairments master such tasks (Poole and Dickinson 2013).

Extensive use of breaks can both strengthen the child's endurance and concentration and distract or exhaust the child. We have not systematically examined how the breaks are used and how they affect the children in SI.

Although this project has not been scientifically tested, we believe we have described important topics in assisting investigative interviews of preschool children in Barnahus, by systematising experiences of highly qualified and experienced Barnahus staff and police interviewers. The EFI approach is well proven in the USA, with positive results, as described earlier in this chapter. Because investigative interviews of preschool children are complex and require knowledge from multiple theoretical perspectives, there is a need for a combination of scientific, theoretical knowledge and systematically described experiences.

Our informants described their realisation that very young children, in difficult situations, were faced with unsuitable methods and procedures that simply did not work. They described how working together has paved the way for better interviewing practice. The project forms the basis of further research into the strengths and weaknesses of SI, and how this approach can best be implemented in Barnahus.

Notes

1. Under the former legislation, before October 2, 2015, a judge was the formal leader of the interview.
2. Under the former legislation, the defence lawyer had an expanded opportunity to also be present during the first investigative interview of the child.

References

Bruck, Maggie, Stephen J. Ceci, and Gabrielle. F. Principe. 2006. The child and the law. In *Handbook of child psychology*, eds. K. Ann Renninger, Irving E. Sigel, William Damon, and Richard. M. Lerner, 776–816. Hoboken, NJ: Wiley.

Carnes, Connie Nicholas, Charles Wilson, and Debra Nelson-Gardell. 1999. Extended forensic evaluation when sexual abuse is suspected: A model and preliminary data. *Child Maltreatment* 4 (3): 242–254.

Carnes, Connie Nicholas, Debra Nelson-Gardell, Charles Wilson, and Ute Cornelia Orgassa. 2001. Extended forensic evaluation when sexual abuse is suspected: A multisite field study. *Child Maltreatment* 6 (3): 230–242.

Ceci, Stephen, and Maggie Bruck. 1995. Jeopardy in the courtroom. *A scientific analysis of children's testimony.* Washington, DC: American Psychological Association.

Cederborg, Ann-Christin, Michael E. Lamb, and Ola Laurell. 2007. Delay of disclosure, minimization, and denial of abuse when the evidence is unambiguous: A multivictim case. In *Child sexual abuse: Disclosure, delay and denial, Margaret Ellen Pipe*, eds. Michael E. Lamb, Yael Orbach, and Ann-Christin Cederborg, 115–134. Mahwah, NJ: Lawrence Erlbaum.

Cederborg, Ann-Christin, Clara Hellner Gumpert, and Gunvor Larsson Abbad. 2009. *Att intervjua barn med intellektuella och neuropsykiatriska funksjonshinder*. Lund: Studentlitteratur.

Christianson, Sven Åke, Elisabeth Engelberg, and Ulf Holmberg. 1998. *Avanserad förhörs- och intervjumetodik*. Borås: Natur och Kultur.

Christianson, Sven Åke, and Pär Anders Granhag. 2008. *Handbok i rättspsykologi*. Stockholm: Liber.

Davies, Graham. M., and Helen L. Westcott. 1999. *Interviewing children under the Memorandum of Good Practice: A research review*. London: Home Office.

Davik, Tone, and Åse Langballe. 2013. Du får bare gjøre så godt du kan… Utfordringer og dilemmaer ved avhør av barn i førskolealder. Lov og Rett 52 (1): 3–20.

Faller, Kathleen Coulborn, and Debra Nelson-Gardell. 2010. Extended evaluations in cases of child sexual abuse: How many sessions are sufficient? *Journal of Child Sexual Abuse* 19 (6): 648–668.

Faller, Kathleen Coulborn, Linda Cordisco-Steele, and Debra Nelson-Gardell. 2010. Allegations of sexual abuse of a child: What to do when a single forensic interview isn't enough. *Journal of Child Sexual Abuse* 19 (5): 572–589.

Fisher, Ronald. P., and R. Edward Geiselman. 1992. *Memory enhancing techniques for investigative interviewing: The cognitive interview*. Springfield, IL: Charles C. Thomas.

Fivush, Robin. 2002. The development of autobiographical memory. In *Children's testimony: A handbook of psychological research and forensic practice*, eds. Helen L. Westcott, Graham M. Davies, and Ray Bull, 55–68. Chichester: Wiley.

Gamst, Kari Trøften, and Åse Langballe. 2004. Barn som vitner. En empirisk og teoretisk studie av kommunikasjon mellom avhører og barn i dommeravhør. Utvikling av en avhørsmetodisk tilnærming. (Doktorgradsavhandling). Faculty of Education, University of Oslo, Oslo.

Hewitt, Sandra. K. 1999. *Assessing allegations of sexual abuse in preschool children. Understanding small voices*. London: Sage.

Hershkowitz, Irit, Yael Orbach, Michael E. Lamb, Kathleen J. Sternberg, and Dvora Horowitz. 2006. Dynamics of forensic interviews with suspected abuse victims who do not disclose abuse. *Child Abuse and Neglect* 30: 753–769.

Justis- og politidepartementet. 2004. Dommeravhør og observasjon av barn. Evaluering fra arbeidsgruppe (2015 hefte 11). Retrieved from https://www.lovdata.no/dokument/SF/forskrift/2015-09-24-1098.

Justis- og beredskapsdepartementet. 2012. Særlig sårbare personer i straffesaker. Rapport fra arbeidsgruppen for gjennomgang av regelverket om dommeravhør og observasjon av barn og psykisk utviklingshemmede (Rapport 10.16.2012). Retrieved from https://www.regjeringen.no/no/dokumenter/avhor-av-sarlig-sarbare-personer-istraf/id712134/.

Justis- og politidepartementet. 2014. Endringer i straffeprosessloven (avhør av barn og andre særlig sårbare fornærmede vitner). Prop. 112L. (2014–2015). Proposisjon til Stortinget (forslag til lovvedtak). Retrieved from https://www.regjeringen.no/no/dokumenter/prop.-112-l-2014-2015/id2408302/.

La Rooy, David, Michael E. Lamb, and Margaret Ellen Pipe. 2009. Repeated interviewing: A critical evaluation of the risks and potential benefits. In *The evaluation of child sexual abuse allegations: A comprehensive guide to assessment and testimony*, eds. Kathryn Keuhlne and Mary Connel, 327–361. Hoboken, NY: Wiley.

Lamb, Michael E. 1994. The investigation of child sexual abuse: An interdisciplinary consensus statement. *Expert Evidence* 2: 151–156.

Lamb, Michael. E., Kathleen J. Sternberg, Yael Orbach, Irit Hershkowitz, and Phillip W. Esplin. 2002. The effects of intensive training and ongoing supervision on the quality of investigative interviews with alleged sex abuse victims. *Applied Developmental Science* 6 (3): 114–125.

Lamb, Michael E., Kathleen J. Sternberg, Yael Orbach, and Phillip W. Esplin. 2003. Age differences in young children's responses to open-ended invitations in the course of forensic interviews. *Journal of Consulting and Clinical Psychology* 7 (5): 926–934.

Lamb, Michael E., Yael Orbach, Irit Hershowitz, Dvora Horowitz, and Craig B. Abbot. 2007. Does the type of prompt affect the accuracy of information provided by alleged victims of abuse in forensic interviews? *Applied Cognitive Psychology* 21 (9): 1117–1130.

Lamb, Michael E., and Megan Py Sim. 2013. Developmental factors affecting children in legal contexts. *Youth Justice* 13 (2): 131–144.

Leander, Lina. 2010. Police interviews with child sexual abuse victims: Patterns of reporting, avoidance and denial. *Child Abuse and Neglect* 34 (3): 192–205.

Memon, Amina, and Ray Bull (eds.). 1999. *Handbook of the psychology of interviewing*. Chichester: Wiley.

Milne, Rebecca, and Ray Bull. 1999. *Investigative interviewing: Psychology and practice*. Chichester, UK: Wiley.

Orbach, Yael, Irit Hershkowitz, Michael E. Lamb, Kathleen J. Sternberg, Phillip W. Esplin, P. W., and Dvora Horowitz. 2000. Assessing the value of scripted protocols for forensic interviews of alleged abuse victims. *Child Abuse & Neglect* 24 (6): 733–752.

Peterson, Carole, Craig Dowden, and Jennifer Tobin. 1999. Interviewing preschoolers: Comparisons of yes/no and when-questions. *Law and Human Behavior* 23 (5): 539–556.

Poole, Debra Ann, and Jason J. Dickinson. 2013. Comfort drawing during investigative interviews: Evidence of the safety of a popular practice. *Child Abuse and Neglect* 38 (2): 192–201.

Powell, Martine B., Ronald P. Fisher, and Carolyn H. Huges-Scholes. 2008. The effect of intra- versus post-interview feedback during simulated practice interviews about child abuse. *Child Abuse and Neglect* 32 (2): 213–227.

Saywitz, Karen, Carol Jaenicke, and Lorinda Camparo. 1990. Children's knowledge of legal terminology. *Law and Human Behaviour* 14 (6): 523–535.

Saywitz, Karen, Rebecca Nathanson, and Lynn S. Snyder. 1993. Credibility of child witnesses: The role of communicative competence. *Topics in Language Disorders* 13 (4): 59–78.

Statens barnehus. 2012. Rapport etterutprøving av sekvensielle avhør av førskolebarn, 2012 [Unpublished]. Bergen.

Sternberg, Kathleen J., Michael E. Lamb, Irit Hershkowitz, Liora Yudilevitch, Y. Yael Orbach, Phillip W. Esplin, and Meir Horav. 1997. Effects of introductory style on children's abilities to describe experiences of sexual abuse. *Child Abuse and Neglect* 21 (11): 1133–1146.

Tetzchner, Stephen Von. 2001. Utviklingspsykologi. Barne og ungdomsalderen. Oslo: Gyldendal.

Part III

From the Viewpoint of Children's Rights

9

Interdisciplinary Child Rights Justice Systems and their Analysis

Hrefna Friðriksdóttir and Anni G. Haugen

Introduction

The first aim of this chapter is to introduce the method of interdisciplinary child rights justice systems analysis. The method aims to identify international principles and the main challenges in their practical application when handling cases concerning the sexual abuse of children. The method offers a way to create a holistic overview of the complicated collaboration between the different agencies required to ensure child-friendly justice. As such, it should be applicable in different countries and jurisdictions. The second aim of this chapter is to use the method to critically analyse and discuss the effectiveness of Barnahus in Iceland in ensuring child-friendly justice.

H. Friðriksdóttir (✉) · A.G. Haugen
University of Iceland, Reykjavik, Iceland
e-mail: hrefnafr@hi.is

A.G. Haugen
e-mail: annihaug@hi.is

The UN Convention on the Rights of the Child from 1989 (CRC) transformed the way we view children. It provides the standards necessary to protect the vulnerable status of children and to ensure their place as active members of society (Friðriksdóttir 2015). Article 3's concept of the child's best interests is aimed at ensuring both the full and effective enjoyment of all the rights recognised in the convention and the holistic development of the child. It places the obligation on member states to ensure that all judicial and administrative decisions as well as policies and legislation concerning children demonstrate that the child's best interests have been a primary consideration. Article 3 links directly to art. 12 on the right to be heard, as an assessment of a child's best interests must include respect for the child's right to express their views freely and due weight given to said views in all matters affecting the child (CRC/C/GC/12, 18; CRC/C/GC/14, 3).

Child sexual abuse is a particularly complex issue involving many different agencies. The Barnahus in Iceland has from the beginning played a major role in coordinating the complicated patterns of procedures that govern the process of dealing with a case concerning child sexual abuse. Today, Barnahus in Iceland and other countries play a similar role for other forms of abuse (see Chap. 1). The concept or model of Barnahus has thus been an inspiration for European instruments and standard setting, promoting child-friendly justice (Council of Europe 2010; Guðbrandsson 2011), founded on the principles enshrined in the CRC. Ensuring the effectiveness of the Barnahus model, however, requires an ongoing process of strengthening and furthering integrated knowledge and expertise on the workings of the justice system as a whole.

It has long been recognised that adapting justice to children is a challenge and difficulties encountered in implementing international principles are common (Council of Europe 2010, 37). In the wake of Iceland's 2008 ratification of the Council of Europe Convention on the Protection of Children against Sexual Exploitation and Sexual Abuse, signed in Lanzarote in 2007 (CETS No. 201, the Lanzarote Convention) , Iceland established a project called Raising awareness about sexual violence against children. The activities have since been expanded to also cover emotional and physical violence against children. Raising awareness was a collaborative project between the Ministry of the Interior, the Ministry of Education, Science and Culture and the Ministry of Welfare.

The purview of Raising awareness falls under Chap. 2 of the Lanzarote Convention which stipulates the responsibility of authorities to make necessary arrangements to ensure education and preventive measures in the field. It was clear at the outset that much was missing as regards accessible informative materials dealing with violence, and one of the main objectives of Raising awareness has been responsibility for the production of specialised educational material about violence against children (Ministry of the Interior, Ministry of Education, Science and Culture and Ministry of Welfare 2014, 1). Raising awareness commissioned the authors of this chapter, in collaboration with the University of Iceland's Ármann Snævarr Research Institute on Family Affairs, to undertake a project aimed at furthering practical knowledge and the implementation of international instruments within justice systems when dealing with child sexual abuse. The project resulted in new professional guidelines: *Child sexual abuse and the justice system—procedures and due process for children* (Fridriksdóttir and Haugen 2014). In preparing the guidelines, a method of analysis for interdisciplinary child rights justice systems was developed. The method and its application provide tools to identify and understand the complex interplay between different agencies involved with child sexual abuse and to identify strengths and weaknesses.

As mentioned above, the first aim of this chapter is to describe the development and explain the different elements of *the method of interdisciplinary child rights justice systems analysis*. The second aim is, by applying the method, to formally identify the role of Barnahus in Iceland within justice systems and to offer a critical discussion of the effectiveness of Barnahus in ensuring child-friendly justice. This chapter takes an interdisciplinary legal and social work perspective, with a focus on the rights of the child.

The Method of Interdisciplinary Child Rights Justice Systems Analysis[1]

Aim

The overall aim of developing the method of analysis for interdisciplinary child rights justice systems is to identify challenges in bridging the gap between international principles and their practical application.

The method provides different professions and agencies within justice systems with the opportunity to take a critical look at the complex patterns of procedures in dealing with child sexual abuse from a child rights perspective (Friðriksdóttir and Haugen 2014).

The Method Requires

1. analysis of the *main international instruments,* i.e. the CRC, the Lanzarote Convention and the Guidelines of the Council of Europe on child-friendly justice, with the aim of identifying the main principles governing the processes of handling child sexual abuse cases,
2. a step-by-step descriptive analysis of the main obligations of each agency within the justice systems in a broad sense, including Barnahus, and the agency collaboration, in order to provide an illustrative holistic overview,
3. an analysis of the views and experiences of major stakeholders, with the aim of identifying systemic weaknesses in practice,
4. a step-by-step normative analysis of how the aforementioned main principles of international instruments should be reflected in processes and procedures within the justice systems with the aim of identifying tensions and challenges and facilitating better practices.

An integral part of using this type of analysis to facilitate better practices is systematic follow-up through multidisciplinary and multiprofessional seminars with an emphasis on dynamic interagency interaction.

Data

In developing the method, the authors used different types of data collected in 2014. The following correlates with the requirements mentioned above.

1. Identification of the main principles requires a careful reading, analysis and categorisation of international and regional instruments.
2. The descriptive analysis of domestic processes and procedures relies on explanations and interpretation of domestic laws and regulations for the responsibility of different agencies. All police districts and

directors of child welfare services (CWS) in Iceland were contacted and offered the opportunity to present written supplementary information on work methods and comments they regarded as important.
3. The analysis of views and the experiences of major stakeholders rely mainly on semi-structured interviews with 33 key stakeholders and operative personnel using a purposive method (Karlsson and Þórlindsson 2003). Among those interviewed were the Director of the Government Agency for Child Protection in Iceland, the Director of Barnahus, directors and various personnel within CWS from different parts of the country, the Chief of the Metropolitan Police and leaders of the police specialised violence unit, the Prosecutor General and prosecutors from the Office of the Public Prosecutor, the Chairman of the Icelandic Judge's Association, the Chairman of the Judicial Council, the Director of the District Court of Reykjavík, the Director and other paediatricians from the Icelandic Children's Hospital, leaders from the two main Rape and Trauma Centres in Iceland, child advocates and leading academics in the field. At the final stages of developing, the method constructive comments were also gathered at a special seminar for major stakeholders as a focus group.
4. Finally, the normative analysis relies on the information above and was further supplemented by existing domestic and international research in the field.

It is further worth noting that using the results of the method through the offering systematic education with an emphasis on dynamic interagency interaction can provide an important platform for progressive analytical discussions and continuous improvements.

The Elements of the Analysis of Interdisciplinary Child Rights Justice Systems

International Instruments

One key dimension of the CRC is to safeguard the rights of the child to freedom from violence. Alongside the CRC general principles in art. 2,

3, 6 and 12, art. 39 specifically calls for a system of reporting, referring, intervening and supporting children.

The Lanzarote Convention is the most comprehensive legal instrument to date in the protection of children against sexual abuse. The aim is to adapt child-friendly judicial proceedings and measures to the needs of children. The Convention establishes common criteria to ensure an effective, proportionate and dissuasive punitive system. Chapter 7 in the Convention has detailed provisions covering the initiation of proceedings, investigations and court proceedings, emphasising multiagency response with a focus on where, how and who should interview the child victim.

The guidelines of the Council of Europe on child-friendly justice seek to interpret and build on the CRC and other instruments in order to enhance children's access to treatment and participation in justice in a broad sense (Council of Europe 2010). The guidelines promote and protect the rights to information, representation and the participation of children in judicial and non-judicial proceedings, and give a place and voice to the child in justice at all stages of procedures. They also present good practices and propose practical solutions to remedy legal tensions and inconsistencies. In preparing this document, the Council of Europe organised a direct consultation of children and young people which was the first attempt to directly involve children when drafting a legal instrument. Key themes to emerge included the importance of family, (mis)trust of authority, need for respect and the importance for children and young people of being listened to (Kilkelly 2010; Björgvinsson 2011).

Main Principles Governing the Processes of Handling Child Sexual Abuse Cases

The aforementioned international instruments include both general and more detailed principles and regulations. Through analysis and the classification of the overarching themes that these instruments present, the researchers identified four main principles that are considered pivotal in the process of handling child sexual abuse cases within the justice systems. These main principles are designed to draw our attention to the specific issues that are most important to child-friendly justice. The principles are intrinsically linked and best illustrated as in Fig. 9.1:

The principle of the *child perspective* is very extensive and as such may be said to encapsulate all aspects of child-friendly justice. Highlighting this as one of the main principles demands a clearer definition of child-centred processes, a focus on what information informs our knowledge of the best interests of the child, including the right to be heard, throughout all and any proceedings within the justice systems. A key element is to challenge our knowledge and perceptions of how a child experiences the judicial processes and how these processes respond to the needs and wishes of the child.

The principle of *safety* focuses specifically on themes such as immediately stopping the abuse, keeping the child secure at all times and reducing negative consequences and the danger of re-victimisation. A key question is how we can identify the elements that increase a child's feeling of insecurity and reduce them in the best possible way.

The principle of *efficiency* places emphasis on information, timely response and continuity. A key question is how to secure a coordinated flow of actions and information about who does what, when and how, which facilitates effective procedures.

The principle of *collaboration* relies on respect, knowledge, mutual understanding and the continuous willingness to adapt and change within a normative framework. A key question is how to identify, recognise and overcome known hindrances to effective collaboration at every level.

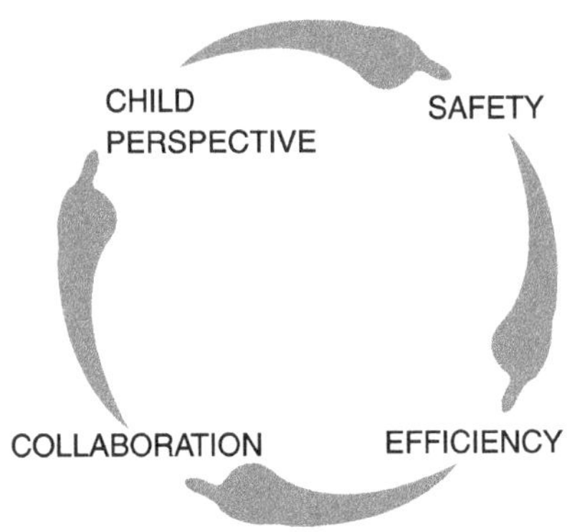

Fig. 1.1 The main principles

A Step-by-Step Descriptive Analysis—an Illustrative Process Diagram of the Justice Systems

The method of analysing interdisciplinary child rights justice systems then requires the identification of the different parallel procedures within the justice systems dealing with child sexual abuse. For this purpose, an illustrative process diagram was designed, identifying the different agencies and effectively signalling their roles and responsibilities. The illustrative process diagram includes a step-by-step analysis of all main processes and procedures (see Fig. 1.2).

The diagram embodies a broad definition of justice systems, including first and foremost agencies that play an important role in the processes or that have a responsibility to make decisions that can and may have a definitive outcome in a case concerning child sexual abuse.

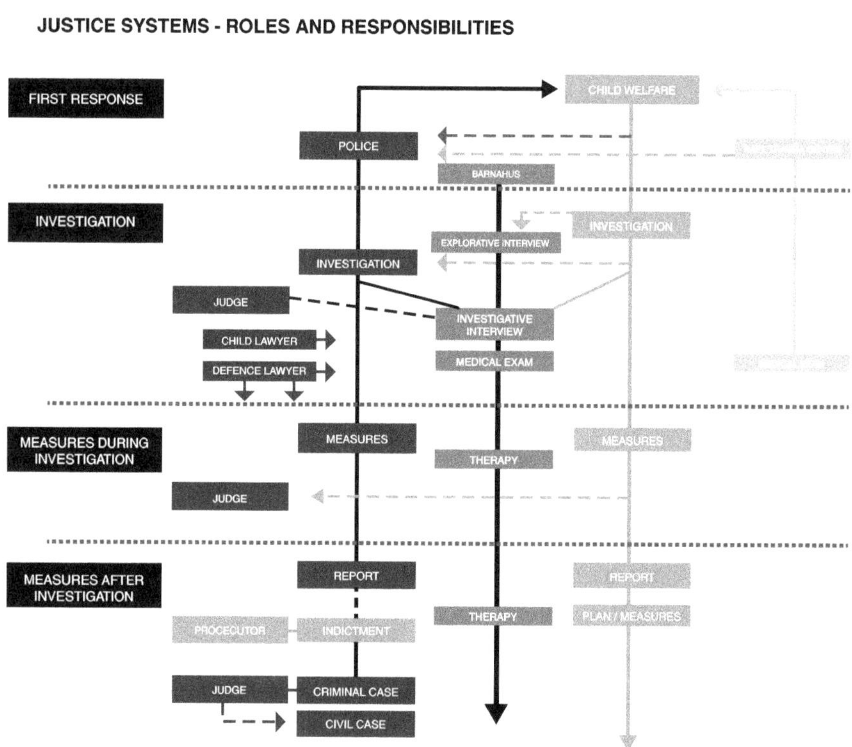

Fig. 1.2 The justice systems in Iceland—an illustrative process diagram

It shows Barnahus as a special agency and signifies its involvement in connection with the CWS and the police.

The diagram identifies four distinct steps in the processes deriving from various Icelandic laws and regulations: the first response, the investigation, measures during investigation and measures after investigation. The importance of an illustrative process diagram of this sort is to signal who is mainly responsible for particular actions at any given stage in the complex procedures.

The Views of Major Stakeholders and Focus Group

Interviews with major stakeholders further illuminate the state of knowledge and understandings of different agencies within the justice systems. The interviews provide information on how these agencies interpret their own and each other's roles, rights and obligations, and how they reflect on everyday practice. The input from a focus group provides further critical feedback. The above method thus provides an informative basis for the analysis of strengths and weaknesses.

Tensions and Challenges Within the Justice Systems

The method of analysing interdisciplinary child rights justice systems lastly embodies a normative analysis, taking a more critical look at procedures at each of the steps to identify challenges and tensions. This is done by using the main principles, articulated in Sect. 3.2, to scrutinise and classify themes that emerge from interviews with major stakeholders and comments from the focus group.

Barnahus in Iceland—Developments and Challenges

Critical Analysis

The importance of analysing the method of interdisciplinary child rights justice systems is in offering a systematic holistic overview of the complicated interactions between different agencies within justice systems.

The method also provides a tool to look more in-depth at the role of specific agencies.

The aim here is to use the method to look critically at the role, actions and successes of Barnahus as an integral part of a whole. This first and foremost requires a re-examination of semi-structured interviews with key stakeholders and operative personnel and the comments from the focus group, mentioned in Sect. 2.2. Using the lens of the four main principles of child-friendly justice described in Sect. 3.2 then allows us to identify and analyse themes that reflect both the positive developments and the challenges remaining. The following sections show how the main principles can be used to call attention to and articulate some of the main concerns. Some concerns reflect all of the main principles, while others correlate more strongly with a certain principle. Using the main principles also highlights the often sensitive issues of balancing rights and obligations in specific situations.

Parallel Processes

One of the fundamental ideals behind the model of Barnahus is to facilitate multiagency *collaboration* and *efficiency* considered essential for the successful handling of cases concerning child sexual abuse. Research indicates that this has been successful to some degree (Kaldal et al. 2010; Friðriksdóttir and Haugen 2014).

It is generally accepted that in most cases of suspected child sexual abuse in Iceland, the CWS starts the assessment of the child's safety and living conditions, and the police begin the investigation of the alleged sexual abuse. Our research suggested that the different agencies did not in general have a comprehensive knowledge of the parallel processes and many lacked sufficient knowledge of each other's roles and responsibilities. This may serve to hinder efficiency and necessary collaboration serving the needs of the child.

It is well established in research how lack of knowledge of each other's values and roles and the competing interests of different professions is likely to hinder effective collaboration (Sloper 2004), as well as how shared views and integrated knowledge and working methods provide a necessary foundation for a successful multiagency collaboration (White and Featherstone 2005).

Set Routines

A closer analysis of work routines raises specific concerns about active *collaboration* and questions as to the balancing of the *child perspective* and *efficiency*. Set routines have evolved to provide a certain amount of efficiency. Set routines involving Barnahus are on the one hand based in essence on a child-centred ideology but on the other hand may hinder the advancement of dynamic collaboration.

Most of the interviewees working directly with cases of child sexual abuse mentioned following a set of routines which, when looked at more closely, had mostly developed over time from the point of view of the agency applying them. The routines were thus mostly developed and adapted to the needs and resources of each agency with a limited account of the roles and responsibility of other agencies. Collaboration was limited to certain preset steps in the procedures, and there was a lack of a dynamic exploration as to how different agencies might cooperate in making sure that decisions served the overall best interests of the child. Other research has also shown how strict statutory guidance and the demands of bureaucracy can reduce the ability of professionals to stay child centred (Munro 2011).

The Focus of Collaboration and the Flow of Information

Our study indicated that the focus of *collaboration* between the agencies within the criminal justice system and the CWS seems to be first and foremost on how to conduct the child investigative interview. The general coordination and exchange of information between agencies raise many questions. Different agencies do not seem to have a mutual understanding of the need to, and positive effects of, sharing information, and lack a thorough understanding of their own or others sets of rules governing the exchange of information.

From the *child's perspective,* a shared understanding of the importance of multiagency collaboration in each case is vital to a better assessment of the needs of the child at every step in the procedures. The issue of *safety* is also of particular concern in this respect. Coordinating measures during an investigation, such as arrests, detainment and the removal of a child from the home, are of vital importance. Continuity in the flow of information to the child and the family also raises questions. There seems to be no extensive mutual understanding of who is responsible for giving the child and the family all the necessary and relevant information on all processes and procedures in a consistent and timely manner. One special issue here is the fact that the role of the child's legal representative is limited to the criminal procedure.

Long Distances

The location of Barnahus in Iceland raises concerns related to *all the main principles.* The fact that there is only one Barnahus in Iceland, situated in the capital Reykjavik, requires a careful balancing of the principles of *safety* and *efficiency* and the *perspective of children* living in other parts of the country. Questions were raised as to the existence of a uniform one-door policy in practice. This is also reflected in research from Norway indicating that the distance from a child's home to a Barnahus prevents the use of Barnahus in some parts of the country (Bakketeig et al. 2012). From the child's perspective, having to travel to Reykjavik, accompanied by parents (non-abusive), a child welfare caseworker, a policeman and a judge, can be overwhelming and stressful. This is also a safety issue, as it may challenge the child's right to privacy. The travelling furthermore takes time, effort and money, which may challenge the principle of efficiency. The question was raised whether this could be avoided by technical means, such as having the child travel to Reykjavik while others gathered in a courtroom using an electronic meeting system. This may provide a compromise, but the disadvantage is the loss of proximity in consultation and *collaboration.*

Child Explorative Interviews

One of the core elements of Barnahus is the interview with the child, strongly reflecting the *child perspective* and the principle of *safety*. The concept of child explorative interviews at Barnahus, solely for CWS in ambiguous cases, is a special feature of Barnahus in Iceland. Our study showed that there is an overall agreement that child explorative interviews are an important option from the child perspective and the principle of safety. It can facilitate optimal expression at an early stage and have a fundamental impact on further procedures. Findings from numerous studies have shown that more reliable information is gathered using a structured form for interviewing, like that used in Barnahus, the NICHD Protocol for Investigative Interviewers of Alleged Sexual Abuse Victims, which emphasises open questions (Lamb et al. 2007).

Child Investigative Interviews

All agencies involved with child sexual abuse cases in Iceland have been aware of a tension surrounding the child investigative interview, first and foremost regarding where, how and who conducts the interviews. Many interviewees and some members of the focus group complained that this tension has not reflected a general understanding of the fundamental ideology of the one-door policy from the *child perspective* and how this has created uncertainties, hindering *efficiency*.

In Iceland, the child investigative interview is under the auspices of a district court judge if the child is under 15 years, and the judges have the prerogative to choose where, how and who interviews the child. Judges have not been in agreement about choosing Barnahus over the years, and some have preferred using special facilities at courthouses. In 2015, the legislator adopted law no. 778/2015, amending the Code on criminal procedure no. 88/2008, requiring judges as a general rule to use a special facility for interviewing a child under the age of 15 years. It is worth noting that our data indicate that more and more judges used Barnahus in the year prior to the change in legislation.

When the child is over 15 years, the child investigative interview is under the auspices of the police. Our data show that the police have been strongly inclined to use police stations for these interviews without evaluating the needs or wishes of each child in question.

The child investigative interview is one of the most sensitive and important parts of the investigation, as the aim is to facilitate disclosure and to learn as much about the abuse as possible. The Guidelines of the Council of Europe on child-friendly justice highlight the importance of both methods and surroundings providing safe spaces for children (Council of Europe 2010).

Mutual Preparation and Follow-up After Interviews

Looking more closely at the child investigative interviews, our data raise particular concerns about *collaboration* in the preparation and immediate follow-up. Initially, when Barnahus started in Iceland, the intention was that the professionals involved had a meeting before the child investigative interview was conducted in order to coordinate their work as well as facilitating a mutual understanding of the case. This is also an integral part of the work methods in Barnahus in Sweden (samrådsmöten), and a similar procedure is present in a new regulation for the police and CWS in Oslo (Kaldal et al. 2010; Oslo Politidistrikt og Barneverntjenesten i Oslo 2015).

Our data indicate that, in practice today in Iceland, there is no strong focus on mutual preparation for the interview or a mutual understanding of the results and the way forward. More importantly, there is a lack of general understanding about who, how and where the child and the family are given necessary information in preparation for the interview. The working methods of CWS and child legal representatives vary, and in many instances, the child was brought into the CWS office and to the office of the legal representative before coming to Barnahus.

Participation of the Child

The concept of the dynamic participation of the child in all processes and procedures raises a critical question from the *child perspective.*

There is no doubt about the harmful effects of repetitive and unstructured interviews with children by many professionals in different locations, and that the concept of multiagency child investigative interviews securing successful disclosure can be the key to unlocking abuse.

The questions concern the fact that the child has a right, and often a need and a wish, to express their views on other elements of the process than the abuse itself. Our study, supported by further research, suggests a strong need for a more coherent strategy on who is responsible for securing the right of the child to participate and who provides the necessary assistance enabling the child to participate on all levels throughout the whole process from start to finish (Friðriksdóttir 2015).

Criminal Investigation and/or the Safety and Well-Being of the Child

Another crucial element from the *child perspective* and the principle of *safety* is the focus of justice system interventions. Our data clearly show that the focus on the criminal investigation of the alleged sexual abuse becomes strong during the investigation phase, threatening to overshadow other important child welfare case matters concerning the situation, care and well-being of the child.

Numerous studies have shown that a child who is sexually abused is also likely to experience other forms of abuse and/or neglect, and a careful assessment evaluating the child's overall need for safety and support is therefore essential (Devilly et al. 2008; Søftestad et al. 2012; Søftestad 2013).

Apart from the child investigative interview, Barnahus offers consultation and therapy for the child. Specialised therapy is of great importance to the child's social and psychological health and future well-being. There has also been a growing awareness and acceptance within the criminal justice agencies of the importance of evidence given by a therapeutic specialist. The strong focus on the services offered by Barnahus can run the risk of obscuring other important elements. Our data show that when a case is under criminal investigation, the CWS investigation is often confined to referring the case to Barnahus without further action. This runs the risk that the CWS investigation may not result in a comprehensive report followed by a plan for handling the case as required by law, giving sufficient attention to all the elements of the child's situation and needs. Our data thus reveal the same tendencies as noted in Sweden, outlining a focus on the growing juridification in child sexual abuse cases (Johansson 2011).

Conclusion

The first aim of this chapter was to introduce a method for the analysis of interdisciplinary child rights justice systems. Most countries in the world have committed to the challenge of creating and adapting justice systems to successfully handle cases concerning child sexual abuse. Most countries also respect international instruments that require the implementation of the rights of children. The method of analysing interdisciplinary child rights justice systems offers a systematic approach to qualifying, understanding and critically discussing the interwoven processes and procedures at play within justice systems dealing with child sexual abuse. The outlines of the process diagram offer an important tool to illustrate the role and responsibilities of different agencies and should as such be relatively easily adaptable to other jurisdictions. The four main principles embodying the themes most important for child-friendly justice offer a constructive way to critically analyse and hopefully improve each step in the procedures.

The second aim was to look more closely at Barnahus in Iceland and use the method to identify positive developments and remaining tensions and challenges. Our research confirmed, as other domestic research has also shown, that the establishment of Barnahus in Iceland was a radical improvement, strengthening the child perspective and in many aspects furthering safety, efficiency and collaboration (Newton et al. 2011). Research into the experience of establishing Barnahus in other Nordic Countries revealed the same results (see Bakketeig et al. 2012; Kaldal et al. 2010; Landberg and Svedin 2013; Walsh et al. 2008; Åström and Rejmer 2008). Overall, the situation of child victims in Iceland has thus developed in accordance with the main principles of international and regional instruments; however, cases concerning child sexual abuse are sensitive and complicated, and the concept of the best interests of children is dynamic and continuously evolving. The four main principles may seem familiar and self-evident, but bridging the gap between rhetoric and effective implementation is an ongoing challenge. Systematically analysing procedures through the lens of these main principles requires us to think critically about how the ideals of the child perspective, safety, efficiency and collaboration are understood, what knowledge informs their interpretation, and how this influences each and every decision made by the different agencies involved with Barnahus.

To summarise our main results, it is *firstly* important to acknowledge that Barnahus plays a role in connection with other agencies within justice systems as a whole. The aim of Barnahus is not to relieve other agencies of their responsibilities but to offer expert services that enhance and facilitate holistic, child-centred and effective processes in handling abuse cases. Our research indicates that careful consideration must be given to ensure that the focus of the investigative interview with the purpose of gathering evidence for the criminal investigation does not overshadow other child welfare concerns. *Secondly*, our research shows that in order to rise to the challenges of putting principles into practice, we need to strengthen the child perspective by ensuring that children are offered the chance to actively participate in all processes before, during and after the involvement of Barnahus. *Thirdly*, in order to fully realise the ideology of Barnahus, more efforts must be put into cultivating multiagency training and facilitating mutual understanding, respect and dynamic child-centred collaboration.

Notes

1. The authors both have varied experience working within the justice system, i.e. working for the Government Agency for Child Protection in Iceland, where we were both instrumental in setting up and organising Barnahus when it was established in 1998. It has been noted that this may have influenced the research, as there is a tendency to see things from only one point of view if the researcher knows the setting well. We are well

aware of how personal and professional experience can influence research (Taylor and Bogdan 1988) and took great care not to let our own perspective get in the way of looking at the data in an objective manner.

References

Åström, Karsten and Annika Rejmer. 2008. Det blir nog bättre för barnen. Slutrapport i utvärderingen av nationell försöksverksamhet med barnahus 2006–2007. Lund: Lund University.

Bakketeig, Elisiv, Mette Berg, Trond Myklebust and Kari Stefansen. 2012. Barnehusevauleringen 2012. Delrapport 1: Barnehus-modellens implikasjoner for politiets arbeid med focus på dommeravhør og rettsmedisinsk undersøkelse. Oslo: NOVA.

Björgvinsson, David Þór. 2011. "Alþjóðaskuldbindingar um vernd barna gegn kynferðisofbeldi." Hinn launhelgi glæpur Kynferðisofbeldi gegn börnum, ed. Svala Isfeld Olafsdottir, 23–57. Reykjavík: Háskólaútgáfan.

Council of Europe. 2010. *Guidelines of the Committee of Ministers of the Council of Europe on child-friendly justice.* Strasbourg: Council of Europe Publishing.

Devilly Grant James, Tracey Varker, Fallon Cook, and Marie Bee Hui Yap. 2008. Current empirical assessment methods. In *Handbook of social work in child and adolescent sexual abuse,* eds. Carolyn Hilarski, John S. Wodarski, and Marvin D. Feit, 119–153. New York: Routledge.

Friðriksdottir, Hrefna. 2015. Relational Representation: The empowerment of children in justice systems. In *Child-friendly Justice. A Quarter of a Century of the UN Convention on the Rights of the Child,* eds. Mahmoud, Pernilla Leviner, Anna Kaldal and Katrin Lainpelto, 55–75. Leiden: Brill Nijhoff.

Friðriksdóttir, Hrefna, and Anni G. Haugen. 2014. *Kynferðisofbeldi gegn börnum Málsmeðferð réttarkerfisins og réttarvernd barna.* Reykjavík: Bókaútgáfan Codex.

Guðbrandsson, Bragi. 2011. Að byggja brýr: Barnvænleg og þverfagleg málsmeðferð kynferðisbrota gegn börnum. In *Hinn launhelgi glæpur.Svala Isfeld Olafsdottir,* ed. 377–394. Reykjavík: Háskólaútgáfan.

Johansson, Susanna. 2011. Rätt, makt och institutionell förändring. En kritisk analys av myndigheters samverkan i barnahus. Dissertation. Lund: Lunds Universitet.

Kaldal, Anna, Cristian Diesen, Johan Beije, and Eva F. Diesen. 2010. *Barnhusutredningen.* Stockholm: Jure Förlag.

Karlsson, Þorlákur and Þórólfur Þórlindsson. 2003. Um úrtök og úrtaksaðferðir. In *Handbók í aðferðafræði og rannsóknum í heilbrigðisvísindum*, eds. Sigríður Halldórsdóttir and Kristján Kristjánsson, 51–66. Akureyri: University of Akureyri.

Kilkelly, Ursula. 2010. Listening to Children About Justice: Report of the Council of Europe Consultation with Children on Child-Friendly Justice. Strasbourg: Council of Europe CJ-S-CH 2010.

Lamb, Michael E, Yael Orbach, Irit Hershkowitz, Phillip W. Esplin and Dvora Horowitz. 2007. "Structured child investigative interview protocol improves the quality and informativeness of investigative interviews with children: A review of research using the NICHD Investigative Interview Protocol." *Child Abuse &* Neglect 31: 1201–1231.

Landberg, Åsa, and Carl Göran Svedin. 2013. *Inuti ett Barnahus En kvalitetsgranskning av 23 svenska verksamheter.* Stockholm: Linköping University and Save the Children Sweden.

Ministry of the Interior, Ministry of Education, Science and Culture and Ministry of Welfare. 2014. Report by Raising Awareness on sexual, emotional and physical violence against children 2012–2014. Reykjavík: Ministry of the Interior, Ministry of Education, Science and Culture and Ministry of Welfare.

Munro, Eileen. 2011. The Munro Review of Child Protection Final Report: A child-centred system. London: Department for Education.

Newton, Anna Kristín, Elín Hjaltadóttir and Heiður Hrund Jónsdóttir. 2011. Þjónusta Barnahúss: Reynsla barna og ungmenna á skýrslutöku og meðferð árin 2007–2009. Reykjavik: Rannsóknastofnun í barna- og fjölskylduvernd.

Oslo Politidistrikt og barneverntjenesten i Oslo. 2015. Samhandlingsrutine Vold og seksuelle overgrep mot barn. Oslo: Oslo kommune og politiet.

Sloper, Patricia. 2004. "Facilitators and barriers for co-ordinated multi-agency services." *Child Care, Health and Development* 30 (6): 571–580. doi: 10.1111/j.1365-2214.2004.00468.x.

Søftestad, Siri. 2013. Suspicion of child sexual abuse: Challenges in protection and care: A qualitative study exploring the perspectives of children, parents and child protection workers. Oslo: University of Oslo.

Søftestad, Siri, Ruth Toverud and Tine K. Jensen. 2012. "Interactive regulated participation: Children's perspectives on child-parent interaction when suspicion of child sexual abuse is raised." *Qualitative Social Work* 12 (5): 603–619.

Taylor, Steven J., and Robert Bogdan. 1988. *Introduction to Qualitative Research Methods. A guidebook and resource*, 3rd ed. New York: John Wiley & Sons Inc.

United Nations Convention on the Rights of the Child (1989).

Walsh, Wendy A, Tonya Lippert, Theodore E. Cross, Danielle M. Maurice and Karen S. Davisson. 2008. "How long to prosecute child sexual abuse for a community using a children's advocacy center and two comparison communities?" *Child Maltreatmen* 13 (1): 3–13.

White, Sue and Brid Featherstone. 2005. "Communicating misunderstandings: Multi-agency work as social practice." *Child and Family Social Work* 10: 207–216.

10

Criminal Investigations and Children's Right to Information

Anna Kaldal, Åsa Landberg, Maria Eriksson and Carl Göran Svedin

Introduction

The overall aim of the chapter is to investigate and analyse how children's rights to information are, or should be, met in a criminal investigation in Barnahus.

A. Kaldal (✉)
Stockholm University, Stockholm, Sweden
e-mail: anna.kaldal@juridicum.su.se

Å. Landberg
Independent Expert, Stockholm, Sweden
e-mail: asalandberg@hotmail.se

M. Eriksson
Ersta Sköndal Bräcke University College, Stockholm, Sweden
e-mail: maria.eriksson@esh.se

C.G. Svedin
Linköping University, Linköping, Sweden
e-mail: carl.goran.svedin@liu.se

The main aim of Swedish Barnahus is to adapt criminal proceedings to the child and let the best interest of the child be the primary consideration when a child victim or witness is the subject of a police investigation. This is stated in the Swedish national guidelines for Barnahus (RPS 2009). The guidelines also state the child's right to participation and the right to information:

> The child should be informed of measures concerning to him or her, and be given the opportunity to express his or hers views and opinions to the extent and the way his or her maturity allows.

As shown by the national guidelines, the child's right to information is interwoven with the child's right to participation. A corresponding view is presented by the UN Committee on the Rights of the Child, who describe the child's right to information as part of the child's right to participation according to art. 12 in the UN Convention on the Rights of the Child (CRC)[1].

In order to explore children's right to information in a criminal investigation in Swedish Barnahus, we will (i) describe and analyse the legal and normative basis for the child's right to participation and information; (ii) describe the Barnahus activities in the light of the right to information, with a focus on the criminal investigation; and (iii) analyse how the child's right to information in Barnahus is met in relation to the rights of the child.

Children's Right to Participation and Information: A Complex and Challenging Task

The Right to Participation and Access to Justice

The right of all children to be heard and taken seriously, CRC art. 12, is one of the fundamental values of the CRC.

The right to be heard is not a duty, but the fundamental right of every child to express their views without pressure. The right to participation requires that the child is informed concerning the matters, options and possible decisions to be taken, as well as the consequences of the arrangements and decisions (CRC/C/GC/12). The right to information is the precondition of the child's clarified decisions and ensures that the child receives all necessary information and advice in order to make a decision according to the child's best interests (CRC/C/GC/12; CRC/C/GC/14). Accordingly, participation is described as an ongoing process and an active dialogue between the child and the decision-maker, including information-sharing and dialogue between children and adults based on mutual respect, and in which children can learn how their views and those of adults are taken into account and shape the outcome of such processes (CRC/C/GC/12).

Under Swedish law, a child lacks procedural capacity until the age of 18, and therefore, the child's right of access to justice in Barnahus is exercised by the child's legal representative, normally the child's custodian. However, the custodian's right and responsibility to decide in the name of the child has limitations. One limitation is the child's right of self- and co-determination.[2] According to this principle, the child has a right to influence a decision concerning their own personal affairs according to age and maturity, and therefore in some cases make a decision independent of their custodian. Another limitation of the right of the custodian is when the child's right to participation is exercised through a specially appointed legal representative.

In the UN 'Guidelines on Justice in Matters involving Child Victims and Witnesses of Crime' (UN Economic and Social Council Resolution 2005/2020), it is pointed out that the participation of child victims and witnesses in a criminal proceeding is necessary for effective prosecutions. According to the Committee of Child's Rights, every effort has to be made to ensure that the child is consulted on relevant matters with regard to involvement in a case and be enabled to freely express views and concerns regarding the judicial proceedings. This is linked to the right to be informed about several issues, such as the availability of health, psychological and social services, the role of a child victim and/or witness in the criminal proceeding, the ways in which the 'questioning' is conducted, existing support mechanisms for children when submitting complaints and participating in investigations and court proceedings, the specific places and times of hearings, the availability of protective measures, the possibility of receiving reparation and the provisions for appeal (CRC/C/GC/12, 63–64).

In Swedish legal doctrine, it has been argued that the child's right to participation in legal proceedings is an ambivalent principle. The law emphasises, on the one hand, the child's right to express her or his view in legal proceedings and the importance of the child's perspective. On the other hand, the importance of the child to be spared from the burden it means to participate in a lawsuit is also emphasised, especially in family lawsuits (Eriksson 2012; Kaldal 2014). This ambivalence has been described as a tension between the vision of the child as a competent actor, *the competence-oriented perspective*, and the perception of the child as dependent on adults, *needs-oriented or protection perspective* (Singer 2000; Svensson 2005–2006; Ryrstedt and Mattsson 2007; Schiratzki 2014).

The Principle of Self- and Co-Determination According to Age and Maturity

The child's right to participation is expressed as a limitation to the custodian's right and responsibility to make decisions in the child's name in the Swedish Parents Act (Chapter 6 Section 11). The right and responsibility of the custodian to exercise the child's right is a part of the custodian's responsibility for the child's care, security and good upbringing (Chapter 6 Section 2). In exercising the right and duty to decide in the name of the child, the custodian shall take the child's views and wishes increasingly into account, keeping in mind the increasing age and maturity of the child. If the child has two custodians, both custodians share the right and the duty to make decisions (Chapter 6 Section 13).

The limitation of the parents' right to make decisions in the child's name also applies to decisions made by authorities concerning the child's affairs. An action concerning the child made by any agency can, and in some situations shall, when the child has reached a certain age and maturity, be made without the consent or even the knowledge of the child's custodian. The agency at hand (police, child welfare, school, etc.) therefore has the responsibility to assess the extent to which the child has reached the age and the maturity to make a decision independently. Information should therefore be provided to the child's custodian or to the child with the consent of the custodian, as long as the child has not reached the age and maturity to decide independently.

When interpreting the right to participation and information according to CRC art. 12, the reasoning will be similar to the Swedish principle of the child's right to self- and co-determination. One difference, however, is that the right to participation is highlighted and put forward as one of the fundamental principles of the convention, whereas the regulation of the child's right to self- and co-determination in Swedish law is regulated by indirectly expressing the child's right to participation by a limitation of the rights of the custodian. Similar to Swedish law, the convention states that the child's parents have the right and responsibility to provide appropriate direction and guidance in the exercise of responsibility to lead the child, as long as this is performed in a manner consistent with the evolving capacities of the child, (CRC art. 5). The parents' right and responsibility to lead the child must, however, always be in compliance with the rights of the child according to the convention as a whole and can only be limited if it is compatible with the (CRC/C/GC/12). Knowledge about the individual child, the child's maturity, special needs, experience of violence and situation concerning the child's family, safety and protection is therefore necessary. It is, however, clear that according to both the CRC and Swedish law, the rights of the custodian to determine what is in the best interest of child must be balanced/weighted in relation to the child's right to participation and in a wider sense, the child's right to integrity (Kaldal and Kankaanpää 2016).

The Right to Participation Through Representation

When a special legal representative is appointed, the right and responsibility of the custodian to decide in the name of the child is limited. This is the case when the child is a victim of crime and there is a reason to believe that an offence has been committed against the child by a family member. No such representation exists when the child is a witness of crime. Since the special legal representative enters into the role of the custodian, they are given the same responsibility as a custodian to exercise the child's right to participation and information. This means taking the child's views and wishes into account, bearing in mind the age and maturity of the child (the role of the special legal representative in criminal investigation in Barnahus is discussed in Chap. 11).

Needs- or Competence-Oriented Perspectives

Researchers in social studies have pointed out an ambiguity in current perspectives on children by constructing them, on the one hand, as subjects and, on the other hand, as objects (Qvortrup et al. 1994; Lee 1999; Qvortrup et al. 2009). Another way of framing the tension in the perspective of the child is to make a distinction between a care principle shaped by a needs-oriented perspective of children, constructing them as objects for adult care and control, and a principle of participation based on a view of children as citizens and social actors (Lee 1999; Neale 2002; Eriksson and Näsman 2008). This tension corresponds with the ambivalence in Swedish law and the tension between the needs- and competent-oriented perspectives discussed above. This tension and ambivalence create challenges for practise.

The perspective influences the degree of participation and the different dimensions of participation that become possible, for example, that the child is given information, is consulted or is allowed to take part in the decision-making (Hart 1992; Eriksson and Näsman 2008; Eriksson 2012). In a study of custody disputes, the overall tendency of professionals was to approach the child as a 'protected child' (approached in a child-oriented way but with a low level of participation) or a 'disqualified adult' (approached in an adult-oriented way and with a low level of participation). As a contrast, Swedish policy makers envision an approach that positions a child as a 'participating child' by encountering them in a child-oriented way while granting them a high level of participation (Eriksson 2009).

Not only attitudes can influence and limit children's participation but also organisation and resources. In a study about children in foster care suggests that even when the professionals are aware of the child's right to participation, the practical work situation contains a number of barriers to participation, for example, a full workload with responsibility for many children, limited opening hours and the disorganisation of work (Bakketeig and Bergan 2013). Jernbro et al. (2015) found that adolescents with experiences of child physical abuse often felt that professionals, especially social workers, showed a lack of a child perspective. Some adolescents reported that the police or child protection services were not available when needed, did not take action or that action was delayed.

Also, the ability to assess the maturity, and thereby to what degree the children can understand and able to influence their situation, can be especially challenging in cases where the child is potentially a victim or witness of crime. Maturity is a complex concept with many different elements. Some children may be early developers in one area, while late in another. Children with special needs may need extra support and specially trained adults to make their voices heard. Abused and traumatised children are less able to access and develop their potential. Van der Kolk (2005) introduced 'developmental trauma disorder', describing the multiple and severe effects of childhood trauma in a developing child, causing a wide array of symptoms.

Children's Right to Information in a Criminal Investigation in Barnahus: In Theory and Practise

Introduction

In this section, we will look closer into children's right to information in a criminal investigation in Barnahus. There are a number of questions that can arise when a child is subjected to a police investigation. For example: Do I have to testify? Do I have to take part in a medical examination? Why am I picked up from school? Who am I going to meet? What do they want to know? Why do they record my story and who will take part of the recording? What will happen to me if I tell? What happens next? Who is going to help me? Who is going to help my parents?

One way to describe a Barnahus is that it has four rooms, each of which contains a particular activity: criminal investigation, protection, physical health and mental health. In Sweden, different authorities have the primary responsibility for different 'rooms'; however, the lines of demarcation are not always clear, either legally or in practice (Landberg and Svedin 2013). The focus in this chapter is the room of the criminal investigation. We will therefore mainly discuss the child's right to information in this room, even if part of the situation is adjacent to the other rooms, child welfare protection, physical health and mental health.

In the room of the criminal investigation, the right to information will be analysed in three situations: when the child is brought to Barnahus, when the child visits Barnahus for the child investigative interview and medical examination and when the child leaves Barnahus after the child investigative interview. The general descriptions of the routines surrounding a criminal investigation in Barnahus are taken from Landberg and Svedin (2013), Kaldal et al. (2010) and the National Guidelines (RPS 2009).

There is no explicit regulation in the code of criminal proceedings that addresses children's right to participation in a criminal investigation, nor is the principle of the best interest of the child implemented in the Act of criminal procedure; however, the right of any witness or victim of crime also applies to children. These general regulations, however, must be interpreted in the light of the limited legal capacity of the child.

Information When the Child Is Brought to and Arrives at Barnahus

The right to know why you are summoned to the police is a right of any witness. This is the responsibility of the police. When the witness is a child, the summons with the information will be directed to the child's custodian or special representative. Legally, the decision to obey a summon and bring the child to Barnahus is made by either the child's custodian or the special representative;[3] however, the transportation of the child to Barnahus can be delegated and performed by someone else, such as the child welfare agency. The responsibility of the special representatives in this aspect is highlighted in the prosecutor manual (Åklagarmyndigheten 2016).

Even if the responsibility of informing the child of about why they are summoned to the police primarily lies with the police, and making sure this information is given to the child primarily lies with the custodian or the special representative, the responsibility of safeguarding the child's right to information would be a joint and overlapping responsibility according to the principle of the best interest of the child and depends on the individual child and the situation.

Landberg and Svedin (2013) explain that the routines surrounding how a child is brought to Barnahus differ among the Swedish Barnahus, especially when a special representative is appointed. In some Barnahus, it was always the child welfare agency that picked the child up from preschool or school and the special legal representative would then meet them at the Barnahus. Sometimes, they had a short meeting with the child before the police interview. In other Barnahus, the special representative picked the child up and therefore also spent time with the child before the child investigative interview. The way that the special representative handled their task differed. There were cases when the special representative had no direct contact with the child at all.

When a child is brought to Barnahus by their custodian, the custodian can tell the child where they are going and why in good time.

Kaldal et al. (2010) asked children in a survey whether they had been informed about whom they would meet at Barnahus before coming to Barnahus. Answers were provided by 111 children aged 3–17 from five Barnahus. The majority of children (78%) had received information beforehand about who they were going to meet at Barnahus. The children had usually received the information through a custodian. Some of them (19%) would have liked more information beforehand. The children who described not having received information beforehand (22%) said that they would have liked to be informed. Information that some children described as important to them included, for example, who would be listening to the interview, how many children had been to Barnahus, if there would be any food served and if there were guards.

The results from 2010 show that many children are given information in Barnahus. In the majority of cases, this is given to the child by the custodian, however, and not the special representative or agency. This suggests that children are in more vulnerable situations, where the custodian, perhaps for investigative reasons, is not informed about the police investigation. The lack of consistency in routines described by Landberg and Svedin indicates that there is a risk that the child's right to information may not be met. The studies imply that the responsibility of informing the child in practice firstly is placed on the custodian and secondly on the special representative. Since a custodian normally lacks in-depth information about what is going to happen in Barnahus, children are at risk of not getting enough information.

Information Concerning the Child Investigative Interview

The responsibility for giving a witness or victim of crime information concerning the investigative interview falls on the police and prosecutor. This responsibility concerns basic information such as how the interview will be conducted, the reason for the interview, whether the person suspected of crime is likely to take part of the statement and who is observing the interview. It also includes information concerning the right not to testify.

Landberg and Svedin (2013) explain that procedures for general information about the interview were similar across the country. The police officer conducting the interview meets the child at the door and shows the child around. The interview is run according to a manual, and the child is typically informed about how the interview is conducted, about the video-recording and the people in the observation room; however, there were differences in whether the child was informed about how the recording was going to be used, and whether the person suspected of the crime was likely to have access to the child's statement.

Some Barnahus staff expressed a fear that giving the child more detailed information concerning the purpose and the background of the interview could compromise the child's testimony. They explained a marked difference compared to the information given to adult crime victims and witnesses, in terms of how the person subjected to the interview was informed of its purpose. In order not to risk compromising the child's testimony, the child would not get information about the reason for being brought to Barnahus (Landberg and Svedin 2013).

There can be a number of people following the interview from the observation room, such as the prosecutor, defence lawyer, the special appointed legal representative and the child welfare caseworker, who is responsible for assessing the child's need of protection.

According to Kaldal et al. (2010), the information children received about the adults observing the interview varied between different Barnahus. Some Barnahus answered that it depended on the child's age and on how they thought the child would react to the information. It could not be excluded that some children did not receive any information at all, because they were perceived as too young or that they would react negatively because of the information. Usually, the child was informed about the people in the observation room and they were shown the video equipment and the observation room. The amount of information given about the people in the observation room varied. Some younger children could, for example, be told that it was 'people working with children', other children were told the names of the people observing and one Barnahus explained that everyone in the observation room was introduced to the child. According to the study, the fact that people are observing the interview did not disturb the children.

According to Swedish law, a witness has the right not to testify against a relative. This information is normally given at the main hearing, but since the child's testimony from the criminal investigation is used as evidence in the main hearing, the child needs to be informed during the criminal investigation in order to exercise this right. This information should be given to the child's custodian if the child has not reached the age and maturity to make an independent decision. According to the Swedish prosecutor guidelines, the consent of both of the child's legal custodians is needed in order to interview a child below the age of 15. A consequence of this is that if the child is a witness of crime, custodians can prevent a child below 15 from giving testimony, even when they have committed the crime themselves. Landberg and Svedin (2013) found that children as witnesses of domestic violence were rarely interviewed in Barnahus, which means that the question of how this dilemma is handled could not be studied empirically. On the other hand, the finding could also be a result of the fact that the consent of the custodian could not be obtained.

The studies show that general information concerning the interview is in many ways similar among the Swedish Barnahus. This concerns information about how the interview will be conducted and who is following the interview. When it comes to more complex questions that, for example, could affect the child's motivation for testifying, a more complex picture emerges. This involves, for example, more detailed information about the purpose of the interview and the fact that the suspect in most cases will see the child's testimony.

The dilemma that the consent of both of the child's legal custodians is needed in order to interview a child below the age of 15 seems to result in children who are witnesses not being heard in Barnahus. Child-friendliness must be questioned in this context, since it is a breach of the child's right to participation and access to justice; however, this is a question of how the law is interpreted by the Prosecutor Authority and may be an example of how a *needs-oriented or protection perspective* in practice can result in a breach of a child's right to participation according to art. 12 CRC.

Information About the Medical Examination

As a part of the criminal investigation, the child can be subjected to a medical examination. There are no coercive measures allowed in order to medically investigate a suspected victim of crime in a criminal investigation. The examination must therefore be undertaken with the consent of the victim. Medical law and ethics require that a patient must give informed consent for medical care and treatment. There is no fixed age limit for children's autonomy in this respect, but normally the right and responsibility applies to the child's custodian if the child is under the age of 15 (Kindström-Dahlin 2016). In the preparatory works, a fixed age limit was considered a risk, since some children would bear too much responsibility in relation to their capacity, while others could be denied self-determination in situations where they would be able to decide themselves. There would also be less scope to take into account the nature and urgency of the current healthcare measure. Instead, the importance of guidelines for healthcare professionals regarding how to make a maturity assessment was emphasised (proposition 2013/2014:106, 67; SOU 2013:2, 184 and 189 ff.). It has been argued that the Swedish health services legislation reflects a competence-oriented approach to children and their participation, unlike a needs- or dependency-oriented approach, which previously was the starting point in the law (Kindström-Dahlin 2016; Svensson 2007).

In a Barnahus context, this means that there is a wider scope for the child to consent to a medical examination than a police interview, which in this case includes the right to information in order to give informed consent.

Information After the Interview

After the police interview and possible medical examination, the child leaves Barnahus. At this point, if not earlier, the child welfare agency has the responsibility to assess whether it is safe for the child to go home. In severe cases, children are placed outside the home, but the most common scenario is that the child will go home to one or both parents, even though the parent may be suspected of crime against the child (Landberg and Svedin 2013; Kaldal et al. 2010).

According to the Social Services Act, the child has a right to participation and a right to information concerning a decision made by the child welfare agency (Chapter 11 Section 10). Child welfare agencies can neither send the child home nor take the child into care without informing the child about the measures taken and the reasons for this. Primarily, it is the responsibility of the police and prosecutor to inform the child's custodian that the child has been interviewed; however, it is the child welfare agency's responsibility to safeguard the child's need of protection and support, which means that the ultimate responsibility when it comes to the child's situation arriving at home lies with child welfare services.

There are no explicit regulations about to how to handle this situation, and research shows that in practice, the situation is handled differently in different Barnahus. According to Landberg and Svedin (2013), some Barnahus have a clear structure for collaboration after the interview. This included a follow-up case conference. Duties with regard to who is responsible for informing parents and children were allocated among the professionals. In other Barnahus, the routines for determining who informs the child after the interview were non-existent. Eight Barnahus (35%) had clear and consistent procedures for the return of the child and how the collaboration between the authorities worked after the police interview. Twelve (52%) had clear procedures that were not always followed. Three Barnahus could not describe any clear procedure. This means several professionals could inform the child or its parent, or none at all, with the consequence that a child could come home to the suspected parents without any support for either of them.

The lack of routines described above compromises the right of the child to be informed. This can have severe consequences since the child can be sent home to a potentially dangerous environment, and shows the need for a national standard of routines, including the need to ensure that the routines are followed.

Discussion and Final Comments

As the Committee on the Rights of the Child has stated, the right to participation requires that the child is informed about measures and the consequences of arrangements and decisions. The right to participation must therefore be looked upon as inseparable from the right to participation. The right to information must furthermore be assessed in accordance with the principle of the best interest of the child, seen in the light of the CRC as a whole.

The convention thus emphasises participation as a fundamental human right of the child, whereas participation according to Swedish law is described as an exception from the custodian right to represent the child. In other words, the scope of the extent to which a child can participate and be given information independently in relation to a custodian is likely to be wider according to the convention than to Swedish law.

Two core issues concerning the child's right to information have been put forward in this chapter. We have discussed how the child's right to information is interwoven with the custodian's right to make decisions in the child's name and how this principle is challenged when the interest of the custodian does not coincide with the interest of the child. In Swedish law, this dilemma has been addressed for a criminal proceeding when the child is a victim of crime and a conflict of interest is responded to by appointing a special representative for the child, who has the responsibility to assess how and when the child should be informed. When the child is a witness of crime, and no special representative can be appointed, the responsibility to handle a potential conflict of interest between the child and the custodian falls utterly on the agency at hand. According to Swedish law, the child's interest can be given precedence if the child has reached adequate age and maturity to make the decision independently. The guidance given in this aspect is the prosecutor's authority, which gives 15 years as the adequate age of self-determination as a witness in a criminal proceeding. According to the CRC, this guidance can be seen as a breach of the child's right to participation.

The child's maturity, background and earlier experiences of violence play an important part in assessing the child's best interest and need for information, and at the same time, the special legal representative and the authorities involved often have limited knowledge about it; especially in an urgent situation when a child is brought to the police for interviewing, there is not much time to get the information needed to make a thorough assessment. Despite this, there is no time to wait and the assessment must be made with the limited information that is at hand. The assessment is in reality often made from knowledge of what is best for *most children,* instead of what is *the individual child's best interest.* This leads to a potential risk that the personal values and opinions of the professionals influence their decisions more than they would have done if they had adequate information to work with.

The child's right to participation and information has a number of inherent complexities and challenges that do not seem to be of a mere legal character, and studies show that professionals fail to involve children even when the law is clear. This ambiguity seems to have several explanations that are closely linked to the complexity of the question of what is in the best interest of the child and how professionals view children and their capacity for participating. It is likely that such ambivalence and lack of clarity in the law contribute to a practice that is influenced or even dominated by personal attitudes.

So, how is the child's right to information in Barnahus met in relation to the rights of the child? Put in a Barnahus context, the child's right to participation and information must be seen as a strong right and a leading light, partly because the aim of Barnahus is adjusting the criminal proceeding to the best interest of the child and the child's right to information is emphasised in the national guidelines for the Swedish Barnahus. The multi-professional collaboration at the core of the Barnahus also speaks for the right of participation and information as a joint and overlapping inter-agency responsibility.

Some careful conclusions from the empirical findings include that children's right to information is firstly safeguarded by the child's custodian, especially information about what is going to happen at Barnahus and who the child is going to meet. The consequence of this is that a great number of children who are victims or witnesses of crime risk are not getting adequate information. Another result is that even when the child's right to information is clearly stated and therefore puts a direct demand on the agency at hand, there is a risk that the child's right to participation and access to justice is not respected. This seems to be a risk when the child is a witness: instead of involving the child and fully meeting the child's right to information the child is not heard. Another situation involves the child welfare agency responsibility to inform the child about measures taken by the agency. Empirical findings show that children are not informed about the child welfare assessment. This is not only a breach of the child's right to information and the law, but can have severe consequences for the child and lead to more severe abuse and a worse situation.

Conclusions

The challenges in practice show the complexity of a child rights perspective. There is not one solution for the issues we have raised concerning how children's rights to participation and their right to information are, or should be, met in Barnahus.

In Barnahus, as an inter-agency collaboration, different legal fields and organisational cultures come together and different notions and professional perspectives can therefore affect the child's ability to participate. The common notion of Barnahus as child friendly and child centred could work to promote children's rights to participation. On the other hand, without coordination, the inter-agency collaboration and the notion of a joint responsibility could lead to a lack of clarity as to what information, and by whom, should be given to the child. Since research has shown difficulties in involving the child even in child-oriented practices, the aim of Barnahus to safeguard the child's right to information is probably not enough in order to truly realise the child's rights in this respect.

We therefore believe that clearer regulation stating the child's right to participation and information in a criminal proceeding would make the scope of subjective approaches to children's participation less. We also believe that the lack of routines must be met by national guidelines. Otherwise, the child's right to participation and information will depend on either the custodian, the qualification and engagement of the special representative, or local engagement from professionals. The lack of clarity today must be questioned and is not compatible with the principle of non-discrimination (art. 2 CRC).

The aim of Swedish Barnahus to adapt the criminal proceedings to the child means that there must be room for individual adaptations, and at the same time, this allows individual interpretations by professionals. The risk of personal and subjective approaches to children's participation can be balanced by clear guidelines on how to inform and involve children of different ages, highly qualified personnel and the opportunity to consult experts regarding the assessment of maturity and special needs. Examples of how to formulate information for children of different ages and levels of maturity should be included. The guidelines also need to explain situations and the grounds on which information can be withheld from a child according to their best interest needs.

Notes

1. The convention was ratified in 1990 and has since then been transformed through implementation in several areas of law. Today, there is a bill with a suggestion of an incorporation of the convention, SOU 2016:19 *Barnkonventionen blir svensk lag.*
2. Authors' translation of 'själv- och medbestämmade'.
3. There are coercive measures to take a child to a police interview; these, however, very seldom come into practice and therefore will not be described in this chapter.

References

Åklagarmyndigheten. 2016. Handläggning av ärenden gällande övergrepp mot barnUtvecklingscentrum Göteborg, ÅklagarmyndighetenGöteborg.

Bakketeig, Elisiv, and Lotte T. Bergan. 2013. Om ungdoms medvirkning ved plassering i fosterhjem. In *Fosterhjem for barns behov. Rapport fra et fireårig forskningsprogram. Rapport 16/13*, eds. Elisabeth Backe-Hansen and Toril Havik. Oslo: Norsk institut for forskning om forskning, velferd og aldring.

Eriksson, Maria. 2009. Girls and Boys As Victims: Social Workers' Approaches to Children Exposed to Violence. *Child Abuse Review* 18 (6): 428–445.

Eriksson, Maria. 2012. Participation for Children Exposed to Domestic Violence? Social Workers' Approaches and Children's Strategies. *European Journal of Social Work* 15 (2): 205–221.

Eriksson, Maria, and Elisabet Näsman. 2008. Participation in Family Law Proceedings for Children Whose Father is Violent to Their Mother. *Childhood* 15 (2): 259–275.

Hart, Roger A. 1992. Children's Participation. From Tokenship to Citizenship. Innocenti Essays No 4. Florence: UNICEF International Child Development Centre.

Jernbro, Carolina, Gabriel Otterman, Ylva Tindberg, Steven Lucas, and Staffan Jansson. 2015. Disclosure of maltreatment and perceived adult support among Swedish adolescents. In *Barnmisshandel ur barn och ungas perspektiv,* ed. Jernbro Carolina, 2016. Omfattning, hälsa, avslöjande och stöd. Karlstad: Karlstads universitet.

Kaldal, Anna. 2014. Ombud och talerätt för barn i vårdnadstvister. In *Barnrätt en antologi*, ed. Ann-Christine Cederborg and Wiweka Warnling-Nerep. Stockholm: Norstedts juridik.

Kaldal, Anna, Christian Diesen, Johan Beije, and Eva Diesen. 2010. *Barnahusutredningen*. Stockholm: Jure Förlag.

Kaldal, Anna and Emelie Kankaanpää. 2016. Hedersrelaterat våld och förtryck mot barn och unga. Del I: En kränkning av barn och ungas rätt till integritet. Juridisk Tidskrift 4: 767–781.

Kindström-Dahlin, Moa. 2016. Att tvinga ett barn – om barns rättigheter i hälso- och sjukvården och behovet av en tydligare tvångsvårdslagstiftning. *Förvaltningsrättslig tidskrift* 2: 245–278.

Landberg, Åsa, and Carl G. Svedin. 2013. *Inuti ett Barnahus*. Stockholm: Rädda Barnen.

Lee, Nick. 1999. The Challenge of Childhood. Distribution of Childhood's Ambiguity in Adult Institutions. *Childhood* 6 (4): 455–474.

Neale, Bren. 2002. Dialogues with Children. Children, Divorce and Citizenship. *Childhood* 9 (4): 445–475.

Proposition. 2013/2014:106. Patientlag. Stockholm: Socialdepartementet.

Qvortrup, Jens, Marjatta Bardy, Giovanni Sgritta and Helmuth Wintersberger (eds.). 1994. *Childhood Matters: Social Theory, Practice and Politics*. Aldershot: Avebury.

Qvortrup, Jens, Wilhelm A. Corsaro, and Michael-Sebastian Honig. 2009. *The Palgrave Handbook of Childhood Studies*. London: Palgrave McMillan.

Rikspolisstyrelsen, R.P.S. 2009. *Progress Report Regarding a Government Commission to Establish Common National Guidelines for Multiagency Collaboration in Inquiries Relating to Children Who May Be Exposed to Crime and Standards for National Children's Advocacy Centres*. Stockholm: Rikspolisstyrelsen.

Ryrstedt, Eva, and Titti Mattsson. 2007. Barn och föräldrar – kan vi acceptera dem som motparter? *Svensk Juridisk Tidskrift* 4: 389–397.

Schiratzki, Johanna. 2014. Barnrättens grunder, uppl. 5. Lund: Studentlitteratur.

Singer, Anna. 2000. *Föräldraskap i rättslig belysning*. Uppsala: Iustus.

Statens offentliga utredning. SOU 2013:2. Patientlag - Delbetänkande av Patientmaktsutredningen. Stockholm: Socialdepartementet.

Svensson, Gustav. 2007. *Barns rätt i hälso- och sjukvård*. Lund: Studentlitteratur.

Svensson, Gustav. 2005–2006. Barns bestämmanderätt i medicinska frågor. *Juridisk Tidskrift* 4: 866–887.

United Nations Committee on the Rights of the Child. 2009. General Comment No. 12 on the Right of the Child to be Heard. CRC/C/GC/12.

United Nations Committee on the Rights of the Child. 2013. General Comment No. 14 on the Rights of the Child to Have His or Her Best Interests Taken as a Primary Consideration. CRC/C/GC/14.

United Nations Economic and Social Council Resolution. 2005/2020. Guidelines on Justice in Matters Involving Child Victims and Witnesses of Crime. (UN Economic and Social Council Resolution 2005/2020).

van der Kolk, Bessem. 2005. Developmental Trauma Disorder: Toward a Rational Diagnosis for Children with Complex Trauma Histories. *Psychiatric Annals* 35 (5): 401–408.

11

Child Abuse Criminal Justice Cases and the Role of Children's Lawyers

Maria Forsman

Introduction

It goes without saying that children who are victims of parental violence and abuse are in a highly vulnerable position. This is also true in the legal sense, as the alleged perpetrator(s) normally represent(s) the child in legal matters. In such cases, the child's rights must be independently safeguarded. This chapter offers a legal analysis of the roles of the "special representative for children", the child's lawyer in child abuse criminal justice cases. It will focus on the context of Swedish Barnahus.

In Sweden, a special representative can be appointed to safeguard the child's rights during a criminal investigation and subsequent trial (Act on Special Representatives for Children, Section 3). The legal

M. Forsman (✉)
Umeå University, Umeå, Sweden
e-mail: maria.forsman@umu.se

prerequisites for this are that a crime against a child is suspected which may carry a prison sentence, and the child's custodian is the suspect, or that a custodian may, on the basis of his or her relationship to the suspect, not protect the rights of the child (Act, Section 1). The purpose of this act, which entered into force in 2000, was twofold: to strengthen the rights of the child when victim of parental abuse *and* to improve the ability to investigate and prosecute such crimes (prop. 1998/1999:133).

The special representative for a child acts in the midst of a complex legal landscape with diverse legal responses regarding child abuse. In addition to constituting criminal offences and thus resulting in a criminal investigation and process, child abuse can also, at the same time, be the subject of a child welfare investigation with the primary aim of resolving the situation or ultimately, if needed and requirements are met, removing the child from his or her home environment under the Care of Young Persons (Special Provisions) Act. Essentially, in Sweden as in many other countries, child abuse is dealt with either as a social problem or as a crime, and sometimes both.

The legal landscape of child abuse interventions also encompasses the fact that it is increasingly common in these cases for the police and prosecutors and the social services—together with other involved professionals such as medical practitioners and (child and adult) psychiatrists—cooperate under the same roof, in Barnahus. When the Act on Special Representatives for Children was introduced, the Barnahus concept was in its infancy. The main interest of this act was, and still is, to facilitate the criminal justice process. The child-centred, inter-agency collaboration we know today was partly un(fore)seen.

In this chapter, I will scrutinise the act and its underlying values, focusing on the special representative's role(s) in the Barnahus context, from the point of view of the child's pathway through Barnahus and in relation to the agencies involved. The activities undertaken in Barnahus are sometimes, for illustration purposes, depicted as being divided into four rooms, each meeting a different need of the child (see the introductory chapter of this volume). In addition to focusing on the criminal justice room, this chapter will also consider child representation issues in the other rooms, in order to include the full Barnahus view of the topics of children's legal standing and representation. A legal analysis will be conducted, based on the legal sources which include the preparatory works of the Act (prop. 1998/1999:133) in particular[1], as well as the Code of Professional Conduct of the Swedish Bar Association (SBA) and disciplinary decisions from SBA's disciplinary committee.

Other sources, such as guidelines and evaluations of Barnahus, will also be used to shed light on the topics analysed. Follow-up studies of the Act have shown that the ability to investigate parental crimes against children has increased (RFR2:2005/2006); appointing a special representative is regarded as the strongest factor in facilitating a child abuse case to proceed in the criminal justice process (Swedish Prosecution Authority 2010). In relation to Barnahus, evaluations indicate that the role(s) of the special representative has become more prominent (Swedish National Police Board 2009) and that representatives are assigned more often where Barnahus collaborations exist than when they do not (Kaldal et al. 2010). Of particular interest is also that several questions and critiques regarding the special representatives and their roles have been raised in an evaluation (Landberg and Svedin 2013). This suggests the need for a closer look at this professional.

An overarching point of departure is that the special representative, in their capacity of being an independent legal representative for the child, forms an integral part of society's response to child abuse. In essence, no other single professional can have as full a picture of the child's views and circumstances as the one assigned to defend the child's rights and best interests. With this in mind, and building on the experiences of Swedish Barnahus, the goal is to identify and discuss challenges and possibilities of this piece of the child protection puzzle.

The Core Legal Issues

In this section, I will briefly outline topics I find integral to the understanding of the child lawyer's role(s) in Barnahus. These are the children's rights, family law and practical legal contexts of the issues studied. In exploring the role(s) of the special representatives, the relationship between the lawyer and the child client is also a core question, which will be highlighted.

The Child Victim's Rights

The special representative is, essentially, a means to realise the child victim's rights in the criminal justice process. This is critical, considering the difficulty, commonly recognised in research, of ensuring that rhetorics about rights translate into enforceable rights. This is evident with regard to children's rights (e.g. Smith 2013) as well as victim's rights (e.g. Groenhuijsen 2014). In the light of the strong link between rights-based issues of access to justice, the right to voice an opinion and, in practice, proper legal counselling, the right to an independent legal representative (in the child's own name) can be regarded as a relatively substantial right (see, for example, Council of Europe 2010). As such, the child's independent legal representation is also strictly linked to two fundamental principles of the UN Convention on the Rights of the Child (CRC), namely the child's best interest and the child's right to participation (art. 3 and 12).

It should, however, be noted that the setting in which the special representative works is the criminal justice process, and so the rights at hand are closely connected to those of an aggrieved party (målsägande). Procedurally, the rights of an aggrieved party include the right to information throughout the process, the right to assist the prosecutor's indictment and thus gain an independent right to appeal as well as the choice of individual actions or appeal to a superior prosecutor if the prosecutor decides not to prosecute (Träskman 2011). The aggrieved party's rights are, as indicated in victimological research, not very prominent in the criminal justice process (e.g. Burman 2011).

In relation to the target group for Barnahus, as defined in the joint guidelines for collaboration and criteria for Barnahus by the Swedish National Police Board (Swedish National Police Board 2009), the connection to legal standing as an aggrieved party inter alia means that children who have witnessed parental violence are excluded from independent representation unless they are (also) supposedly direct victims of a crime which may carry a prison sentence.

Independent Legal Representation

Children have limited legal capacity and are subject to their custodian(s) right and duty to decide in matters concerning the child, with account taken of the child's views and wishes according to the child's age and development (Parental Code, Chapter 6 Sections 2, 11 and 13). The need for an independent legal representative for the child in the criminal justice process stems from the fact that the alleged perpetrator(s) is the same person(s), or in a close relationship with the person, who legally represents the child. The child's statement is often crucial to a criminal investigation, and so the parental legal authority can constitute an acute obstacle to the investigation and consequently to the child's access to justice.

This legal problem can be solved in different ways. In the Nordic context, Iceland has a regulation that enables the independent legal representation of the child when they are at risk (and not as a priority to safeguard the child's right to participate and be heard in criminal proceedings), and in Norway and Finland, a legal representative can be appointed based on an assessment of whether the parent in question will safeguard the best interests of the child during the criminal investigation and whether there is a conflict of interest between the child's involvement in criminal proceedings and the interest of the parent (Kaldal 2015).

In Sweden, there are various solutions depending on the legal process at hand. In a child welfare investigation, the child welfare agency is given the power to decide whether and how the child is being interviewed, as well as whether the child should undergo a medical examination when the Care of Young Persons Act is applicable (Section 32, and Social Services Act Chapter 11 Section 10 para. 3). An independent legal representative for the child is not relevant until the child protection process reaches compulsory measures and court procedures (SOSFS 1997:15). This is a profound difference from the situation in the criminal justice investigation, where the decision-making power regarding investigative measures has, through the Act on Special Representatives for Children, been placed with an independent legal representative from the start of the investigation.

The independence of the child's legal representative is essential and built into the function and role of a lawyer as one fundamental principle in the Guiding Principles for Good Advocate Conduct. It should, however, be pointed out that the child is not always granted an *independent* representative. If the child has two custodians, who are not married or cohabitating, and one of them is not suspected of a crime against the child, or believed to have difficulties safeguarding the child's rights, then that custodian may be appointed by the court to represent the child (Act, Section 2). This exception is based on the principle that a custodian should not be excluded from the power of decision-making over a child to a greater extent than necessary (prop. 1998/1999:133). The regulation has one further exception, in cases where children are considered to have reached such an age that they can defend their own rights (Act Section 1 para 2; prop 1998/1999:133). Children who represent themselves, or are represented by one of their custodians, will not necessarily lack a legal counsel; however, they may be appointed an aggrieved party counsel[2] to ensure their procedural rights (i.e. to bring an action for damages) in the process. For this counsel, there is no regulation regarding particular suitability for representing children.

As the parental legal authority is restrained by the assignment of a special representative, the question at hand in the analysis of this chapter is mainly about the balance of power between the individual (child), the lawyer and the agencies (state power).

...in the Barnahus Context

It is crucial to the underpinnings of the analysis that there may also exist different, sometimes conflicting, interests between agencies involved in Barnahus. Research has shown that the collaboration implies a tension between a criminal law-oriented logic and a treatment-oriented welfare logic (Johansson 2012). In relation to the often-held aim of cooperation in Barnahus to "put the child in focus" (e.g. Thornblad 2006), such cooperation may also entail discord between the operational perspectives of the agencies involved on the one hand and the "child focus" on the other hand (Forsman 2013). The joint guidelines for Barnahus highlight that the collaboration should be characterised by a child perspective, *not* an operational perspective, and that the overall aim is for the child to be safe and supported from a holistic perspective (Swedish National Police Board 2009).

In this connection, it should be noted that, as regards the aims and functions of the investigations that are carried out in Barnahus (i.e. a criminal justice investigation and a social welfare investigation), the child victim is not essentially the main focus. Both investigations include the parents (custodians) as crucial participants, as they are, in relation to the processes, *key to change* in the home situation (e.g. by becoming motivated to work with their (in)abilities to fulfil the child's needs) and, also, *key information sources* regarding the crime(s) under investigation [the possibility that the suspect actually admits, acknowledges certain circumstances or at least provides new or more accurate leads in the investigation is believed to be underestimated (Diesen 2005; Swedish Prosecution Authority 2016)]. The implications of this overall focus of the investigations are thus that the child-centred elements, which are carried out in Barnahus, must not be separated but anchored in the investigation(s) as a whole, based on each involved authority's function, regulation and their independence in the exercise of authority (Swedish Instrument of Government, Chapter 12 Section 2). In relation to the special representative, however, the relevant investigative measures are Barnahus based, as the representation is centred solely on the child.

The Child as a Client

The Council of Europe Guidelines on child-friendly justice emphasises the importance of clarifying the exact role(s) of independent representatives for children. In the assignment studied, this legal professional functions, in general terms, both as an aggrieved party counsel and as a guardian ad litem (ställföreträdare[3]) for the child. As regards the former function, the special representative is to look after the child's interests as an injured party in the case, for example, in filing claims for damages and providing legal assistance and support throughout the process. In their function as a guardian, the special representative holds the decision-making power as to whether and how the child is to be interviewed, medically examined and so on, thus ensuring that all investigative measures are in the best interests of the child (prop. 1998/1999:133).

With their dual roles, and in view of the fact that the alleged perpetrator in the criminal justice process is the client's custodian, the special representative has to deal with a very sensitive situation that can often involve complex conflicts of interest and ethical concerns. Considering this, the act stipulates that only "an advocate, a legal associate at an advocate firm, or other" may be assigned to that role, who, on the basis of their knowledge and experience and personal skills, is particularly well suited for the assignment (the act, Section 5). The eligible group is not formally limited to lawyers, but considered a result of the experience needed in the field of criminal investigations and trials.

The duality of roles relates to what research has recognised as the "child lawyering dilemma" (e.g. Ventrell and Duquette 2005). Should the lawyer for the child (mainly) be guided by the child's expressed wishes or by the lawyer's determination of what is in the best interests of the child?

In Swedish Bar Association's memorandum on the lawyer's assignments for weak or vulnerable clients (SBA 2016), it is emphasised that the child's instructions should not always be followed: the special representative shall promote the child's best interests, and although this will include clarifying and paying regard to the child's own views, the lawyer shall *decide what is in the best interests of the child* following a comprehensive review. This may be related to, and partly inferred from, the lawyer's duty of loyalty, to act in an upright and honourable way, in the client's best interests, which may not always mean complying with the client's wishes but giving the client the advice and assistance that objectively will best benefit the client's cause. More specifically, the Swedish Bar Association emphasises, however, that in the case of a special representative having a different opinion than the child in matters relating to the criminal investigation or the trial, the lawyer should assert the idea that they believe is in the best interests of the child (SBA 2016).

Whereas the mainstream view in research and child law policies would be that lawyers representing children should put forward the opinion of the child and provide the child with all necessary information and explanations concerning the possible consequences of the child's views and opinions (e.g. Council of Europe 2010), the Swedish view seems particularly inclined to best interests representation. This model of lawyering in relation to children has inter alia been contested from the viewpoint that the lawyer may, subconsciously, insert their own views of what is best for children into the representation of an individual child. In the light of this, the international (American) discussion is heavily geared towards urging lawyers to get to know the child client as well as possible through frequent contact with the child (e.g. the Fordham Recommendations 1996). The *importance of discerning and presenting the child's voice* is also stressed, whilst viewing the child in multiple dimensions, such as developmental stages, language, culture, gender, class and disability (the UNLV Recommendations 2006). In the preparatory works of the Swedish Act, it is accordingly indicated that close contact with the child is fundamental in assessing the child's best interests, as is *valuing* the child's own opinions (prop. 1998/1999:133).

The role(s) of the special representative will now be further scrutinised in the Barnahus setting.

Role(s) in the Criminal Investigation Room

Initial Coordination Meeting: Assignment

One of the first steps in the Barnahus collaboration is the coordination meeting. During this, it is decided, in the light of investigative measures needed, whether a special representative for the child should be appointed (Kaldal et al. 2010).

The special representative is assigned to the child by the district court upon application of the prosecutor. If it appears necessary in order to safeguard the child's rights, for example, to enable an interview with the child without their custodian(s) impinging the investigation (prop. 1998/1999:133), the district court can appoint an interim special representative without the custodian(s) knowledge (Act Section 6). The timeframe for action in these cases is short, as the custodian(s) should be informed as soon as possible without it being detrimental to the investigation (Act, Section 7). This duty of information is normally conducted as soon as an interview or medical examination of the child has been undertaken, but no later than the fourth working day after the interim order (prop. 1998/1999:133, Ordinance on Special Representatives for Children, Section 2a). This urgency can mean that the interview with the child has already been scheduled when the prosecutor submits a request for a special representative to the court, and that the representative is appointed on the same day. The time available for the lawyer to get to know the child before the interview is thus limited.

A question worth considering in relation to the initial coordination meeting is the implications of the special representative not attending. The presence of the person who is assigned to safeguard the child's rights could be vital with regard to the child's best interests and to this person's ability to convey the child's views on the matters at hand. Such procedures would, however, need the criminal justice investigation to have a head start, so that it is established, before the coordination meeting, that the child will be interviewed in a criminal investigation and thus be in need of a special representative. Hence, this strict connection to the criminal justice process may be a significant element in how the legal representation of the child's rights might in the future be reinforced in and through Barnahus, which I will return to in the discussion.

Bringing the Child to Barnahus

In order to undertake initial investigative measures, such as an interview with the child, without the custodian's knowledge, bringing the child to Barnahus must normally be done in connection with the child spending time in kindergarten, school or the like (prop. 1998/1999:133). The special representative decides on the conditions surrounding the visit to Barnahus.

Given that the interests of the child are paramount, the child may be accompanied by a person who is known and safe for the child.

The special representative therefore needs to find out who is best suited to accompany the child (Swedish Prosecution Authority 2016). Although it is within the special representative's role to decide on different arrangements as regards the transportation of the child, on a case-to-case basis, the lawyers are never obliged to collect the child themselves (SBA 2016). It may not always be appropriate for the special representative to transport the child, inter alia by using public transport, for reasons of confidentiality (see, for example, the Journal of the SBA, no 3 2015, where this is discussed).

It is, however, of importance in this connection that the special representative has the opportunity to familiarise themselves with the child in question. As mentioned, the lawyer should decide what is in the best interests of the child following a comprehensive review. This may be a problematic element in the early, time-limited, stage of the process. It was also shown in a recent evaluation that other professionals involved in Barnahus reportedly sometimes felt that the special representatives were passive and seemed unaccustomed to talking to or associating with children. On occasions, the special representative neither greeted or talked to the child (Landberg and Svedin 2013) which of course is inconsistent with the lawyering roles and ethics as well as the demands regarding particular suitability.

Cooperation with Other Professionals

From the appointment and throughout the process, the special representative shall, within their independent role, consult and cooperate with professionals in kindergartens and schools, and other persons who may be close to the child. The same applies in relation to representatives of the child welfare services and the police. The preparatory works particularly emphasise that the representative's cooperation with child welfare services may mean that a child does not need to undergo more medical examinations and interviews than necessary (prop. 1998/1999:133). There were thus seeds of thought in the drafting of the Act as regards child-centred coordination measures, which are now exercised in Barnahus.

The Child Investigative Interview

A key undertaking in the criminal justice investigation and the Barnahus operations is the police interview of the child. Because multiple professionals collaborate, a time needs to be set when all (other) actors can join in, such as the prosecutor and the child welfare agency, the suspect's defence lawyer, as well as paediatricians and child psychiatry professionals who may be given the opportunity to follow the interview from an adjoining room (Swedish National Police Board 2009).

In connection with the investigative child interview, it is first worth stressing that the criminal justice authorities do not have any right to interview the child unless the child's custodians—or in their place, the special representative—consent. According to the preparatory works, it is generally in the child's interest that suspicions are investigated, but a special representative should not consent to an investigative measure if the child may be harmed, for example, due to strong fear. The special representative should thoroughly consider the child's views and wishes (prop. 1998/1999:133).

Secondly, *how* the interview is conducted is essential for the child, due to both legal rights and other interests. Earlier studies, and also more recent evaluations, have shown that police investigations of child abuse suffer from many systematic weaknesses, for example, that the child interviews are often substandard (Diesen and Diesen 2009) and the establishment of Barnahus operations has not eliminated these deficiencies (Kaldal et al. 2010). One key task for the special representative is to ensure that the interview meets high standards and is conducted in a child-friendly manner. One such example is to make sure that the interview is held by a person who is specifically competent for the task. If the child's testimony is of particular import to the investigation and it is warranted in view of the age and maturity of the child and the nature of the crime, someone with specific knowledge in child or interview psychology should assist with the interviewing of the child (Ordinance on Preliminary Investigations, Sections 18–19). Ensuring the quality of the interview is one way in which the special representative can safeguard the child's rights in relation to the investigative authority. The special representative has the opportunity and obligation to intervene and stop the interview if it is not in the best interests of the child, and this has also been done in Barnahus, although only in exceptional cases, according to an evaluation (Landberg and Svedin 2013).

Since it is common practice for interviews with younger children to be video recorded, and for these recordings to be later shown in court, it is essential that the interview meets high standards. Additional questions cannot be asked during the trial, so the quality of this investigative measure can be a determining factor in the child's safety and redress as a victim of crime.

Thirdly, it is within the special representative's role to give the child proper and age-adequate information and to support the child (prop. 1998/1999:133). The adversarial system entails that the suspect has the right to be told what he or she is accused of, in order to prepare his or her defence, and also that the child has the right to information about (the seriousness of) the situation. Balancing the child's right to information, whilst ensuring that the child is not frightened so that it becomes difficult for the child to talk in the light of the possible consequences, has been called a fundamental ethical dilemma (Edvardsen and Mevik 2014) and a "child-right" dilemma (Chap. 10 in this volume). If they are particularly suitable, the child lawyers—experienced and well trained in professional ethics and good advocate conduct—should be well placed to deal with this quandary, although difficult.

After the interview, it needs to be considered that the child might have to return home to one or both parents, even though they are suspects of crime. In relation to this delicate situation, the special representative thus needs to make sure that the agencies involved are coordinated in ensuring that the child is safe and properly informed.

Medical Examination of the Child

According to the joint guidelines for Barnahus, relevant medical expertise in paediatrics, gynaecology, child and adolescent psychiatry and forensics should be available under the same roof (Swedish National Police Board 2009). The role of the special representative in this part of the criminal investigation is, in place of the custodian(s), to consent or not consent to a forensic medical examination of the child. A medical examination constitutes a forced physical violation, from which everyone is safeguarded in the constitution (the Instrument of Government, Chapter 2 Section 6), and since there is a lack of a provision allowing an involuntary medical examination of a crime victim, the child, or the special representative in place of the child's guardian(s), needs to consent to this investigative measure.

In the preparatory works of the Act on special representatives, it is pointed out that the child's own opinion regarding the examination should be considered in case the child has reached such an age and maturity that her or his own will should be respected. There should be no question of forcing a child to undergo a medical examination even if the special representative would have consented to it (prop. 1998/1999:133 p. 44). As with interviews, it is indicated that an important task for the special representative is to be a support to the child and to ensure the creation of an atmosphere in the performance of the medical examination that minimises discomfort for the child. It is also noted that if a child feels very strong fear and discomfort before a medical examination, the special representative should decide to not consent (prop. 1998/1999:133).

A decision of the SBA's disciplinary committee (from 2008[4]) regarding a lawyer who had been appointed as special representative for a child is also of importance in this connection. The lawyer was given a disciplinary reminder after having consented to a forensic medical examination which showed that the crime of female genital mutilation had not been committed. Given that the child was subject to a gynaecological examination without the company of a support person, and experienced it as very unpleasant and intrusive, the disciplinary committee found that the lawyer had breached their duties as a lawyer, in not having, with due care, examined the need for the investigative measure nor taken any concrete measure to minimise discomfort for the child.

This disciplinary decision has been discussed in the Journal of the SBA (no 4, 2010) as the preliminary work offers unclear and somewhat inconsistent guidance. In the preparatory works, it is stated that it is not within the roles of the special representative to "make own assessments about the state of the evidence or other questions concerning the investigation" (prop. 1998/1999:133). Moreover, it is clarified that the representative cannot refuse to give consent because they have a different opinion on the position of the evidence of the case. The representative should carry out the assignment in close contact with the criminal justice agencies (prop. 1998/1999:133).

The Swedish Bar Association states in its memorandum on this topic that the special representative is obliged to carefully examine the need for a medical examination in each case and, in this regard, "assess the conditions for obtaining a specific result of the examination on the basis of the known circumstances of the individual case. If there are insufficient indications that the child has been subjected to a certain act, the child maybe should not be subjected to a medical examination" (SBA 2016).

This lawyering practice, going further than was envisaged in the preparatory works, defines the more independent role of the child's representative. There is an evident dilemma, however: acting (strictly) in accordance with the guidance of the preparatory works may collide with fundamental principles of lawyering. The advantage in relation to the child's rights may be a stronger legal position, but it also highlights the importance of the special representative obtaining a thorough knowledge of, and from, the child.

Role(s) in Relation to the Other "Rooms" in Barnahus

Child Protection

Since the special representative's assignment is limited to the criminal justice process, the lawyer cannot represent the child in child welfare matters, and insights into that investigation are thus limited. The representative has, however, the right to obtain information about the child and the child's situation, which may otherwise be confidential under the provisions on secrecy, if the information is needed in order to monitor and safeguard the child's interests in the criminal justice process. According to the main rule, secrecy is not applicable in relation to the individual themselves (the Public Access to Information and Secrecy Act Chapter 12 Section 1). In their capacity as special representative for the child, the lawyer exercises the child's powers as regards the right to receive and dispose of confidential information about the child to the extent that the information is necessary for the assignment. This right is reduced, however, in relation to the child's age and development, as with maturity the child's consent is needed in order to obtain such information. The social welfare agency may also find that information regarding the custodian(s) is protected by rules on secrecy and thus limits the special representative's insight. This was clarified in the preparatory works of the act (prop. 1998/1999:133).

The special representatives may thus be able to keep themselves somewhat informed of the child welfare investigation, but are legally speaking powerless to act on behalf of the child should the child's rights be violated.

The Child's Medical and Psychological Needs

In the remaining two rooms of Barnahus, it is the custodian(s) who hold the power of decision over matters concerning the child. In these rooms, which inter alia may involve crisis support, as well as having the needs for further support and treatment assessed (Swedish National Police Board 2009), the child lacks independent legal representation. The special representative's assignment includes paying attention to the child's needs for care and treatment, and conveying knowledge in those respects to the child welfare agency (prop. 1998/1999:133), but giving consent (or not) to medical or psychological measures is not included in the special representative's assignment (which is restricted to the criminal investigation and subsequent trial, Act, Section 3).

In the medical room, in addition to or resulting from a medical examination, there may be other medical needs detected that may warrant treatment. It is, however, at the custodian's discretion, considering the child's views and wishes according to age and maturity, to decide on such measures and thus govern the child's right to medical care.

Given that the custodians (joint) decision-making power could preclude a child from obtaining access to necessary psychological care and treatment, in particular in cases of suspected child abuse, the child welfare agencies have, however, (since 2012) been afforded the legal ability to execute an intervention measure with the consent of one custodian alone, if this is deemed necessary in view of the best interests of the child, as provided under the Parental Code (Chapter 6 Section 13a). This may, inter alia, apply to psychiatric or psychological assessment or treatment. The provision is intended to meet the child's right to support and care, and to counteract irrelevant considerations such as when a custodian's resistance to the measure is based on a fear that the suspicion might be strengthened because of what emerges when the child receives help to process their experiences (prop. 2011/2012:53).

The basis for application of the provision is that one custodian "takes sides" for the child and his or her needs, and a decision on a measure is required for the child's best interests. Against the background of the individual's right to protection against interference in their private and family life, the requirements for a decision of this kind must reasonably be set high and in each case considered proportionate to the intervention in the opposing interest (i.e. the rights of the custodian). Not least, there must be information to support the intrusion, which is why the provision can rarely be applied immediately. In these rooms, the child's ability to exercise his or her rights is weak.

Discussion

The issues dealt with in this chapter concern both principles and practicalities. From a children's rights perspective, it is crucial that the agencies involved prioritise a child focus *within* their operational perspectives; however, it is also important that the child is granted effective means to defend their rights when the agencies fail to do so. One reason to emphasise the potential benefits of independent legal representation of the child is that in the Nordic welfare states, there is often considerable (over)confidence that the agencies will, at all times, safeguard the child's rights and operate on the basis of the child's best interests.

In practice, the child victim's position is strengthened through the special representative since this professional has the potential to represent the voice of the child, facilitate the child's right to participation and ensure a child-friendly process. The representative has also some decision-making powers (e.g. to decide on the conditions surrounding an interview) and can, as an independent lawyer, act as a counterweight to the investigative interests of the criminal justice authorities if the child's rights and interests so require.

In determining the role(s) of the special representative, it is, in conclusion, important to consider and clarify (at least) the following two aspects:

(i) To what extent the child can instruct the lawyer. The regulation is somewhat ambivalent regarding the child's voice. The preparatory works mainly connect the role of the special representative with that of a custodian, that they shall take into account the child's views and wishes according to the child's age and development (Parental Code Chapter 6 Section 11). The motivation of the Act was thus to curtail parental legal authority over the child, rather than starting from the child's rights and interests. The Swedish Bar Association is correspondingly inclined to favour best interests representation, which makes it uncertain whether the child will be able to make use of their lawyer in practice.

(ii) The lawyer's discretion to act when the child has more and other interests than those assigned. This chapter has shown the child's right to independent representation is not adapted to the practical handling of child abuse cases nor to the child's legal needs. Quite the contrary, the legal representation of the child is connected to their legal standing in a (single) process, in this case as the aggrieved party in a criminal justice case. In the handling of these cases, the child is essentially a crucial source of evidence. The special representative makes the evidence available to the investigation, if it is in, and in a way that is in, the best interests of the child. The child has no independent legal representation in the other (medical and psychological health) measures in Barnahus, or representation only at a late stage in the process (in a child welfare investigation). The child might not benefit from having four different legal representatives (one in each room), but certainly from one, specialised in child abuse and children's rights, with the power to act on the child's behalf. If and when Barnahus operations are more thoroughly established in Sweden, the overall regulation of when and how the child is granted independent legal representation would benefit from the same holistic and coherent approach that underpins Barnahus operations as such.

Concluding Remarks

From a child('s) perspective, as far as it is possible to adopt such a perspective without asking the children themselves, as in Chap. 3 in this volume, it may be hard to grasp and understand what, if any, is the role of a lawyer (see, e.g. Buss 1996, "You're My What?"). The importance of the regulation allowing the lawyer time to build trust with the child client can thus not be overstated. Should the role be compared to that of a custodian (as is done), then age-adequate pedagogical approaches are paramount. In essence, when combining a "child focus" with a rights-based perspective, lawyering based on a thorough knowledge of the client in his or her context appears crucial to secure the child's future position as an independent rights holder.

Notes

1. Preparatory works are documents that precede a legal amendment. In Sweden, these documents are an important tool in interpreting legislation, i.e. in guiding those who implement the law. *Prop.* (proposition) is a government proposal.
2. An aggrieved party counsel, *målsägandebiträde*, is assigned to the crime victim in certain cases, usually cases of sexual offences, assaults, unlawful deprivation of liberty, robbery or other similar offences. The counsel is assigned to protect the interests of the victim in the process, e.g. in bringing action for damages if the prosecutor does not. See the Act (1988:609) on aggrieved party counsel.

3. The Swedish concept *ställföreträdare* roughly corresponds to the term "guardian ad litem" (or simply "guardian"). It is a person who acts on behalf of, i.e. who legally represents, a party to a case who themselves does not exercise control over the matter at hand, or is personally incompetent to enter into the legal relationship in question (Swedish Code of Judicial Procedure (1942:740) Chapter 11 Section 1).
4. For full text decisions from the disciplinary committee, see SBA's website [www.advokatsamfundet.se].

References

Burman, Monica. 2011. "Brottsoffer i straffrätten." In *Brottsoffret och kriminalpolitiken*, eds. Claes Lernestedt and Henrik Tham, 279–298. Stockholm: Norstedts juridik.

Buss, Emily. 1996. 'You're My What?' The Problem of Children's Misperceptions of Their Lawyers' Roles. *Fordham Law Review* 64: 1699–1762.

Council of Europe. 2010. *Guidelines of the committee of ministers of the council of Europe on child-friendly justice*. Strasbourg: Council of Europe Publishing.

Diesen, Christian. 2005. "Processrättsligt perspektiv. Om positiv och negativ särbehandling i straffprocessen." In *Likhet inför lagen*, eds. Christian Diesen, Claes Lernestedt, Torun Lindholm and Tove Pettersson. 183–390. Stockholm: Natur och kultur.

Diesen, Christian, and Eva F. Diesen. 2009. *Övergrepp mot kvinnor och barn—den rättsliga hanteringen*. Stockholm: Norstedts Juridik.

Edvardsen, Oddbjørg and Kate Mevik. 2014. "Vold mot barn i hjemmet: Hvordan ivareta barns rettigheter?" Tidsskrift for familierett, arverett og barnevernrettslige spørsmål, 3 (4): 317–333.

Fordham Recommendations. 1996. "Recommendations of the conference on ethical issues in the legal representation of children", *Fordham Law Review*, 64: 1301–1311.

Forsman, Maria. 2013. *Rättsliga ingripanden vid föräldrars våld och övergrepp mot barn*. Stockholm: Norstedtsjuridik.

Groenhuijsen, Marc. 2014. The development of international policy in relation to victims of crime. *International Review of Victimology* 20: 31–48.

Johansson, Susanna. 2012. Diffusion and Governance of 'Barnahus' in the Nordic Countries: Report from an On-going Project. *Journal of Scandinavian Studies in Criminology and Crime Prevention* 13: 69–84.

Journal of the Swedish Bar Association (SBA). 2010. "Ett beslut från disciplinnämnden om särskild företrädare för barn väcker förvåning", 4: 35–35.

Journal of the Swedish Bar Association (SBA). 2015. "Oenighet om rutiner för hämtning av barn till förhör", 3: 6.

Kaldal, Anna. 2015. *Child evidence. A comparative study on handling, protecting and testing evidence from children in legal proceedings within states in the Baltic Sea Region*, Strasbourg: Council of Europe.

Kaldal, Anna, Christian Diesen, Johan Beije, and Eva F. Diesen. 2010. *Barnahusutredningen*. Stockholm: Jure.

Landberg, Åsa and Carl Göran Svedin. 2013. *Inuti ett Barnahus. En kvalitetsgranskning av 23 svenska verksamheter*. Stockholm: Rädda Barnen.

Proposition 1998/1999:133 Särskild företrädare för barn. Stockholm: Justitiedepartementet.

Proposition 2011/2012:53 Barns möjlighet att få vård. Stockholm: Justitiedepartementet.

Report 2005/2006:RFR2 from the Swedish Government, Särskild företrädare för barn. Uppföljning om tillämpningen av lagen (1999:997) om särskild företrädare för barn.

Smith, Rhona. 2013. "The third optional protocol to the UN Convention on the rights of the child?—Challenges arising transforming the rhetoric into reality." *International Journal of Children's Rights*, 21: 305–322.

Socialstyrelsens allmänna råd om tillämpningen av lagen (1990:52) med särskilda bestämmelser om vård av unga. SOSFS 1997:15. Stockholm: Socialstyrelsen.

Swedish Bar Association. 2016. *Promemoria om advokatens uppdrag för svaga eller utsatta klienter, Revised April 2016*. Stockholm: Advokatsamfundet.

Swedish National Police Board. 2009. *Delredovisning av regeringsuppdrag avseende gemensamma nationella riktlinjer kring barn som misstänks vara utsatta för brott och kriterier för landets barnahus*. Stockholm: Rikspolisstyrelsen.

Swedish Prosecution Authority. 2010. *Tvångsmedelsanvändning och beslutsfrister m.m. vid vålds- och sexualbrott i nära relation och mot barn*, Göteborg: Utvecklingscentrum Göteborg.

Swedish Prosecution Authority. 2016. *Handläggning av ärenden gällande övergrepp mot barn*. Utvecklingscentrum Göteborg: Handbok. Göteborg.

Thornblad, Helene. 2006. *Därför Barnahus—så stärker vi rättigheterna för barn som utsatts för våld och övergrepp*. Stockholm: Rädda Barnen.

Träskman, Per Ole. 2011. Brottsoffret och brottmålsrättegången. In *Brottsoffret och kriminalpolitiken*, eds. Claes Lernestedt, and Henrik Tham, 299–310. Stockholm: Norstedts juridik.

UNLV Recommendations. 2006. "Recommendations of the UNLV conference on representing children in families: child advocacy and justice ten years after fordham" *Nevada Law Journal* 6: 592–605.

Ventrell, Marvin R., and Donald N. Duquette. 2005. *Child welfare law and practice: representing children, parents, and state agencies in abuse, neglect and dependency cases*. Colorado: Bradford.

Part IV

Collaboration between Agencies

12

Inter-Organizational Collaboration: A Study of Power Dynamics

Susanna Johansson

Introduction

Varying forms of inter-organisational collaboration in services for vulnerable children have grown rapidly during recent decades and enjoy an almost taken-for-granted status associated with consensus and synergetic decision-making (Horwath and Morrison 2007; Glad 2006; Wiklund 2007). Coercive legislation on collaboration regarding children at risk has also been imposed in Sweden (see, e.g. prop. 2002/03:53), implying increased demands on collaboration within the field. The incapacity of the justice system to meet children's rights as crime victims has, in addition, led to a variety of measures in order to improve children's access to justice and reduce secondary victimisation.

S. Johansson (✉)
School of Social Work, Lund University, Lund, Sweden
e-mail: susanna.johansson@soch.lu.se

These developments have contributed to the establishment of the Barnahus model in Sweden, with the dual goal of a more efficient judicial process on the one hand and improved protection and support on the other hand (see, e.g. Swedish Ministry of Justice 2005).

Collaboration in Swedish Barnahus can be seen as a development towards a more structured form of collaboration between agencies and professional actors from child welfare services, health care and law enforcement in investigations of suspected child abuse. The Barnahus collaboration includes overall collaboration, as well as collaboration in individual cases of child abuse. The agencies involved form a sort of 'hybrid organisation' spanning different regulatory fields and bringing together different institutional logics stemming from social welfare law on the one hand and criminal (procedural) law on the other (Johansson 2011a, 2013). In a Swedish context, there are two parallel investigations that are often coordinated in Barnahus: the child welfare investigation, which the child welfare services are responsible for, and the criminal investigation that is led and conducted by public prosecutors and police investigators. Other professional actors, such as child psychologists, forensic medicine technicians and paediatricians, can also be activated in relation to, or as a consequence of, the child welfare and/or criminal investigations. Police and prosecutor's (pre-trial) criminal investigations are focused on investigating whether a crime has been committed or not, and securing evidence, and are thus directed towards assessments of what has happened in the past, typically characterised by 'ex post-oriented' decision-making. The child welfare services investigation, on the other hand, is focused on ensuring the child's protection, welfare and development, which implies assessments of the child's present and future situation, typically characterised by 'ex ante-oriented' decision-making. These different decision-making logics may cause tensions in the collaborative practice (Johansson 2011a, b).

Even though collaboration is associated with consensus and synergy, conflicts and dilemmas often arise in collaborative practice. The purpose of this chapter is to analyse collaboration in Swedish Barnahus with a focus on the institutional power dynamics that may develop between the agencies and professional actors involved, and to discuss how the tension between 'justice' and 'welfare' is balanced.

Theoretical Framework

The importance and lack of a nuanced power perspective is stressed within organisational research (Clegg et al. 2006). This is also true for studies of inter-organisational collaboration more specifically (Phillips et al. 2000; Hardy and Phillips 1998). This chapter combines the institutional theory of organisations (see, e.g. DiMaggio and Powell 1991; Scott 2008a) with Steven Lukes' (2005 [1974]) three-dimensional power concept in order to facilitate a nuanced analysis of different power dynamics and institutionalisation processes activated in, as well as resulting from, collaboration.

Institutional Theory of Organisations

Within institutional theory, organisations are seen to be influenced and permeated by the surrounding institutional environment, which also creates interdependencies among organisations within an organisational field. According to Richard Scott (2008a), institutions consist of regulative, normative and cultural-cognitive elements (Scott 2008a, 48), affecting how organisations both think and act. Institutional theory emphasises the symbolic and legitimacy-seeking elements of organisational life and practice, often stressing the isomorphic tendencies among organisations within a field (DiMaggio and Powell 1983). By the end of the 1980s, however, the 'new institutionalism' had started to direct attention to organisations as active agents and not only passive reflections of their institutional environments. It was acknowledged that institutional environments are not homogeneous but rather contested and contradictory, often imposing conflicting demands on organisations. Attention was directed towards power, strategic action and translation processes (Czarniawska and Sevón 1996; Røvik 2000). The concept of *institutional logics* was defined as interpretative schemas associated with control structures and decision-making systems, or as organising principles, comprising material rules of conduct and symbolic structures, which can be linked to individual organisations in a specific context of collaboration (see Friedland and Alford 1991; Thornton and Ocasio 2008; Scott 2008a; Reay and Hinings 2009; Thornton, Ocasio and Lounsbury 2012). When a context of collaboration spans several fields and jurisdictions, such as in Barnahus, the collaborative processes are made more complex (Phillips et al. 2000, 30; Johansson 2013, 116). By viewing the interests of organisations as institutionally shaped, and the organisations as governed by different logics of action, it is possible to understand the conflicts and dilemmas that can arise in inter-organisational collaboration and the collaborative work in Barnahus more specifically.

Collaboration in the particular context of Swedish Barnahus is located in an area of contention between two regulatory fields, criminal (procedural) law and social welfare law. In relation to collaboration in Barnahus, the tension between justice and welfare, and more specifically the *criminal law-oriented* and *treatment-oriented logics,* is the most central, although there are also 'internal' tensions such as those between the crime victim and the suspect on the one hand, and between child protection and family support on the other hand (Johansson 2011a, b). The parallel investigations (i.e. the criminal and child welfare investigations), related to the criminal and child welfare regulatory fields, represent conflicting institutional interests and logics of decision-making. The Swedish Barnahus collaboration and coordination of the parallel investigations thus require that interests be balanced. This balancing is not undertaken by a single professional actor but through negotiations among the collaborative actors involved. The professional actor's authority and legitimacy are then based on their ability to argue in line with their respective logics, which creates frameworks for handling issues and making decisions that are addressed and negotiated in collaboration (Scott 2008b).[1]

Three Dimensions of Power in Collaboration

In order to analyse how and why the collaborative actors, as well as their respective institutional logics, affect and are affected by each other in collaboration, a nuanced concept of power is needed. Lukes (2005

[1974]) concept of power illustrates how power is contextually dependent and takes on different forms. He divides power into three dimensions: one-, two- and three-dimensional power. *One-dimensional power* relates to concrete action in decision-making on issues where there is an observable conflict of articulated interests, which could be labelled 'formal decision-making power'. According to Lukes, *two-dimensional power* also enables analysis of how decisions are prevented on issues where there is a conflict of interests. Two-dimensional power thus refers to the extent to which an actor or professional group (consciously or unconsciously) creates or reinforces barriers to conflicts being articulated in public, and the same actor or group possesses power (Lukes 2005, 20), which could be labelled 'non-decision-making power'. According to Lukes, the two-dimensional power view is still too narrow since it does not capture the ways in which latent conflicts are being oppressed (Lukes 2005, 58–59). Lukes therefore includes a *three-dimensional power* concept to acknowledge elements of power that are not directly visible. According to Lukes, power is at its most effective when least observable, in other words when it operates in disguise or is made invisible (Lukes 2005).

In my understanding, invisible power has to do with conflicting institutional interests being neutralised, avoided or completely concealed. In relation to collaboration, as in Barnahus, such a perspective is important. The idea of collaboration exerts a kind of 'cognitive power' that builds on the idea of consensus, which may conceal underlying conflicts of interests between the organisations involved. Subsequently, the collaborative actors might be unaware of these conflicts, both those exercising power and those upon whom power is exercised. In this way, the third dimension of power addresses 'the power over thought', that is, the capacity to influence actors ways of thinking in a certain direction, or to dominate or redirect their interests.[2] It is about 'setting the agenda' in a wider cognitive sense by making certain ways of thinking dominant. Three-dimensional power is thus about affecting the preferences of others in a way that makes them accept their role and position in the prevailing institutional order and, in that sense, ensure actors' voluntary compliance to dominance (Lukes 2005). As I interpret Lukes, however, the three-dimensional form of power does not replace the other two, but rather implies that power takes place one-, two- and three-dimensionally, and that these dimensions interact. Lukes also stresses that it is important to acknowledge that power in its (more open and visible) one- and two-dimensional forms has several three-dimensional effects (Lukes 2005, 121–122).

> Thus open, visible conflict between actors (one-dimensional power) can lead to asymmetric power relations in which those who prevail control the agenda (two-dimensional power) … are eventually able to count on the compliance of others in the absence of observable conflict of interests (three-dimensional power) (Lukes and Haglund 2005, 62).

In summary, one-dimensional power could be understood as a question of who holds the formal decision-making power over specific issues addressed in the Barnahus collaboration. Two-dimensional power relates to who possesses the power over 'non-decisions', such as which issues should be addressed and not, or who is included and excluded from collaborative arenas. Three-dimensional power relates to who, or rather what, has the power to 'set the agenda' in a broader cognitive sense, for example, when it comes to problem definitions, priority rights of interpretation and affecting (other's) institutional interests (Johansson 2011a). It might very well be that different actors possess different dimensions of power in a specific collaborative context and, in doing so, also affect and change the conditions for each other's abilities to exercise power, and therefore, it becomes important to analyse how the three dimensions of power interact and affect each other in the context of Barnahus collaboration.

Methodology and Empirical Material

Drawing on my doctoral thesis (Johansson 2011a), this chapter presents a theory-driven re-analysis of empirical material collected within the six first Barnahus in Sweden. The empirical studies comprised interviews with Barnahus staff, a questionnaire survey of the collaborating organisations, and observations of consultation meetings. The interview study included interviews with all Barnahus staff at the six Barnahus, amounting to 15 interviews with 22 interviewees, of which nine were carried out individually and six in groups. Apart from four interviewees, all participants in the interview study had social work as professional background and functioned as Barnahus coordinators and/or managers (i.e. not as child welfare caseworkers). The questionnaire survey was sent out to all agency members in the collaborative groups (i.e. steering-, referential- and working groups) and was subsequently directed to professional actors from child welfare services (including child welfare caseworkers) , health care (including child psychologists, forensic medicine technicians and paediatricians) and law enforcement (including police investigators and public prosecutors), amounting to 146 respondents, of whom 105 answered the survey (i.e. a response rate of 72%). Observations of consultation meetings at each Barnahus were made in connection with carrying out the interviews with the Barnahus staff.[3]

Analysis

Since both professional training and more specific organisational roles influence the power dynamics developing in the Barnahus collaboration, some clarifications are initially needed as a background to the following analysis. The Barnahus staff at the different Swedish Barnahus are primarily constituted of social workers who are coordinators that summon the different professional actors to 'consultation meetings' and 'co-hearings' for child investigative interviews.[4] The Barnahus coordinators lead the consultation meetings and make sure that the parallel investigations are coordinated in a suitable way. They often function as advisors for the child welfare caseworkers responsible for the child welfare investigations on matters such as how they should 'go about' the initial stages of the investigation process. The other actors, that is, child welfare caseworkers, police and prosecutors, as well as representatives from health care, generally attend Barnahus temporarily in connection with consultation meetings, co-hearings and/or when making different interventions in relation to either the child welfare or criminal investigations.

Perceptions of Power (Im)Balance

In the questionnaire survey sent to all the collaborating agencies, one question was 'Do you consider any agency representatives to possess more influence than others in your collaborative work?' Just over half the respondents stated that there were agencies possessing more influence than others in the Barnahus collaboration, and the child welfare services, police and prosecutors were clearly the three agencies (and professional groups) perceived as most influential, with an even distribution among them.

A first implication of this reply pattern would be to draw the conclusion that there seems to be an asymmetrical power relationship between child welfare services, police and prosecutors on the one hand and representatives from health care (including child psychologists, forensic medicine technicians and paediatricians) on the other hand. This result can be interpreted in relation to what Lukes calls one-dimensional power, or formal decision-making power. In this context, one-dimensional power can be understood as who holds formal decision-making power over the issues addressed in collaboration related to the parallel investigations. On the basis of the child welfare services, police and prosecutors being the agencies and professional actors possessing investigatory responsibility over the child welfare and criminal investigations, respectively, they subsequently hold a structurally based, formal decision-making power over several central and legally defined issues addressed in collaboration, which healthcare actors lack. For example, whether a police report will be filed by the child welfare services, or whether a criminal investigation will proceed and lead to a decision to prosecute.

A second implication would be to draw the conclusion that there seems to be a symmetrical power relationship amongst the representatives from the child welfare services, police and prosecutors, although the public prosecutors significantly less often considered any agency actors to possess more influence than others, compared to the other respondents. At the same time, the prosecutors themselves constitute one of the three agencies and professional groups perceived as possessing most influence by the others. In this light, it is important to recognise that the way power balances are distributed, perceived and used is not necessarily consistent. This can be interpreted in relation to Lukes' notion of power as being exercised both consciously and unconsciously. For example, you can be unconscious of how others perceive your actions, which in this case might explain the prosecutors' deviant reply pattern. In the same way, you can be conscious or unconscious of the consequences of your actions, and the 'real' intentions behind or the 'real' meaning of your actions.

The question addressed in the questionnaire survey was formulated in a way that is open to a broader interpretation. When agencies are considered to possess more influence than others in collaboration, it is not necessarily (only) connected to one-dimensional decision-making power. It can (also) relate to the actors that are considered to possess more influence than others concerning, for example, who is included in or excluded from collaboration, which issues to be addressed or not during consultation meetings or who has more influence than others over problem definitions. In other words, this could be interpreted as two- and three-dimensional power.

'Setting the Agenda' by Including and Excluding Actors from Collaborative Arenas

In relation to the permeating tension between the criminal law-oriented logic and the treatment-oriented logic, collaboration in Barnahus can be understood as characterised by competitions in 'framing' or 'setting' the agenda. In the questionnaire survey, for example, in response to the open question of what are considered to be the main difficulties with the collaboration, one respondent (forensic medicine) answered that there were '(…) different agendas among the agencies regarding what is of highest importance—the criminal investigation, the family or the child's mental well-being'.

An important issue when it comes to setting the agenda for the Barnahus collaboration turned out to be inclusions and exclusions of collaborative actors in relation to consultation meetings and co-hearings of child investigative interviews. The analysis of the empirical material shows variations between the different Barnahus regarding how these collaborative arenas were organised, which organisations were included and excluded from the arenas and, in turn, what content (related to which logics) the collaboration involved. Participation can thus be seen as a basic circumstance for the ability to exercise influence and power over different issues during a consultation meeting or in relation to co-hearings of child investigative interviews. At the same time, participation also implies the potential to be influenced and affected by others (and their institutional logics).

Consultation Meetings

Partly as a consequence of varied interpretations of rules of secrecy, the content of consultation meetings differed between the different Barnahus. For example, some Barnahus held consultation meetings between the child welfare services, police and prosecutors on the issue of whether a police report should be filed or not, while other Barnahus didn't hold consultation meetings with police and prosecutors attending until a police report had formally been filed from the child welfare service. In the latter case, consultation meetings were sometimes, instead, initially held between the child welfare services and child psychologists on partly different matters. The formal decision-making power over the question of police reports can, in this respect, be interpreted as being kept within the child welfare service's own organisation. These differences reflect variations regarding which collaborative actors were included or excluded from initial consultation meetings and how this, in turn, framed the issues that were addressed in the collaboration and the decisions made during, or in relation to, collaboration.

At those Barnahus where consultation meetings primarily considered the question of whether a police report should be filed or not, all agencies were included. In this case, the child welfare caseworker's formal authority and decision-making power over the question of filing police reports were affected by several collaborative actors. Both police and prosecutors, and the Barnahus coordinators leading the consultation meetings, were in this case regarded as specialists. They thus possessed a more diffuse two- and three-dimensional power over central issues related to the child welfare investigations, such as the question of police reports and the initial stages of the child welfare investigation process. At those Barnahus where consultation meetings were not related to the question of police reports, the collaboration rather revolved around questions such as in which order the different agency interventions should be made. Here, some respondents also had the ability to influence police and prosecutor criminal investigations by putting forward arguments about the importance of speeding up the judicial process from the perspective of the child's well-being and in relation to treatment and support interventions. Several police investigators also described how they, through the increased collaboration, had more opportunities to affect the prosecutor's decisions on whether a criminal investigation should proceed and lead to a decision to prosecute.

Co-hearings of (Forensic) Child Investigative Interviews

Variations were also identified between the different Barnahus regarding the organisation of 'co-hearings' of the child investigative interviews (taking place in an adjacent monitor room next to the interview room). Similar to the consultation meetings, these variations were partly connected to varied interpretations of rules of secrecy. Here, it was not the Barnahus coordinators who primarily decided which actors to include or exclude, even though it was the coordinators who in fact summoned the collaborative actors in both cases, but instead the public prosecutors who had investigatory responsibility and one-dimensional decision-making power over the criminal investigations that decided which actors were allowed to participate and not. At some Barnahus, all agencies and professional actors were included in the co-hearings of the child investigative interviews, while at others only some, or even none, of the collaborative actors were included.

In cases where the collaborative actors were allowed to participate in the co-hearings of the child investigative interviews, there were still other differences. Variations in the organisation of co-hearings can, then, be interpreted as the purpose of the co-hearing being sometimes related to the criminal law-oriented logic and at other times to the treatment-oriented logic. Consequently, the different collaborative actors possess different roles as institutional agents in relation to the co-hearings, sometimes related to the criminal law-oriented logic and other times to the treatment-oriented logic. For example, in some cases the purpose of the co-hearings was to constitute support for the criminal investigations, for example, when the police investigators consulted child psychologists about interpretations of the children's statements and expressions. In other cases, the purpose was to constitute support for the child welfare investigations, for example, when child welfare caseworkers used the information disclosed during child investigative interviews in their risk assessments.

At some Barnahus, neither the Barnahus coordinators nor the child welfare caseworkers were allowed to participate in the co-hearings due to the interpretations of the secrecy rules of the criminal investigations, as illustrated in this interview sequence with two Barnahus staff:

> **Interviewer:** These child investigative interviews that are being video recorded, are you also there and watching [in the adjacent monitor room for co-hearings]? **Interviewees A and B:** No. **Interviewer:** It's the police by themselves? **Interviewee B:** Yes, and the child's representative, and perhaps the prosecutor in some cases. So, we get as much information about the investigative interviews as the police and prosecutor decide to disclose. (Barnahus staff)

Viewed in this light, the prosecutor's one-dimensional power (related to the criminal investigations) can be interpreted as leading to an asymmetric power relationship where they (also) dominate control over the agenda concerning participation in the co-hearings (i.e. two-dimensional power), which, in turn, might lead to three-dimensional power effects.

The inclusions and exclusion of collaborative actors from the co-hearings of child investigative interviews and consultation meetings can be understood as a matter of controlling access to information and, subsequently, either enabling or preventing action from other collaborative actors in relation to their respective institutional interests and logics (based on this non/information).

Coordinator Influence on Formal Decision-Making Power

When it comes to the influence of the child welfare services, an important difference between the Barnahus staff functioning as coordinators at the Barnahus on the one hand and the child welfare caseworkers responsible for the child welfare investigations on the other hand is crystallised. Even though both are usually social workers and employed within the child welfare services, they exercise different forms of power based on which roles they possess in the Barnahus collaboration. The investigatory child welfare caseworkers possess a one-dimensional form of power and thus a formal authority, over central issues and decisions related to the child welfare investigations, while the Barnahus coordinators possess a more diffuse two- and three-dimensional power over the collaborative processes and over the child welfare caseworkers.

It is interesting to note that the social workers functioning as coordinators at the different Barnahus noted on several occasions that they do not possess any investigatory responsibility or decision-making power:

> Although, I have absolutely no investigatory responsibility, rather we can assist the child welfare services in some parts (…). (Barnahus coordinator)

While it was important for Barnahus coordinators to stress this, it was also noted as a complicating factor in relation to establishing collaboration:

> All agencies decide about themselves, so to speak. Yet, what is difficult (…) about collaboration is that nobody has an overall responsibility to go in and say to the prosecutor that this is what you have to do, or tell the police that you have to do like this, or to the child welfare services that you need to do this. That's what's difficult with collaboration. No one is mandated to decide for all agencies. (Barnahus coordinator)

By possessing roles as coordinators and functioning as specialised advisors primarily for the child welfare caseworkers (e.g. in matters such as decisions on filing police reports and other central issues related to the child welfare investigations), the Barnahus coordinators can be seen as exercising both two- and three-dimensional powers. These power forms can influence, affect and change the conditions of the one-dimensional decision-making power (and formal authority) of the child welfare caseworkers through consciously or unconsciously becoming dominated. For example, one coordinator at a Barnahus explained that:

> The most common situation is that the child welfare services call [the Barnahus], having received a report of suspected abuse. And after a short conversation over the telephone you decide quite quickly whether they should come here and present it to the police and prosecutor as well. And the psychologist. In consultation, that is. The biggest cases are handled in consultation [meetings] in order for everyone to have a say, to [express] their opinion. And then you do so. Sometimes things come up in the meantime so to speak, but the most common issues are: Should we file a police report in this case? How should we go about this? What do we need? They [the child welfare case workers] are often a bit worried about how serious it is, and so on, and which way they should go about in the case. And then, we sit gathered around the table and make these assessments. Police report and send it there and there, do this and that, write here and there. And take these and these contacts as part of the investigation process. After that, we await the police report and eventual child investigative interviews. If there is a queue, you might have to advise them [the child welfare case workers] to place [the child] and help them with the arrangement for that, then (Barnahus coordinator).

The analysis furthermore shows that this power, exercised by the Barnahus coordinators upon the child welfare caseworkers, in turn, is influenced by the police and prosecutor's criminal law-oriented logic, and the demands from police and prosecutors in relation to this logic.

> In accordance with the secrecy rules of the criminal investigations, we propose to the child welfare services that we do not want them to inform

> the custodians about a police report until investigative interviews with the children have been carried out (Barnahus coordinator).

These arguments and requests directed towards the child welfare caseworkers may impact and change how the caseworkers make assessments and decisions in relation to the child welfare investigations. For example, in the questionnaire survey, one child welfare caseworker described how the Barnahus collaboration had changed the working methods of the child welfare services:

> To a larger extent, you try to avoid informing the custodians (if they are suspected perpetrators) directly 1) that a child welfare investigation according to 11:1, 2 SoL [The Social Services Act] is initiated, 2) that a police report on suspected crime against the child will be/has been filed, and you, to a larger extent, are more concerned about having direct collaboration with [the Barnahus], police and prosecutor. (Child welfare caseworker)

As shown above, the Barnahus staff with specific roles as coordinators are powerful actors in the Barnahus collaboration. They can be interpreted as possessing strong influence and control over the collaborative processes and the decisions made (and not made), during collaboration, even though they (structurally viewed) lack one-dimensional decision-making power and formal authority in relation to the parallel investigations. For example, they determine which cases to hold consultation meetings around and which collaborative actors should be summoned. Other forms of power (which can be one-, two- and three-dimensional), exercised by other collaborative actors, can simultaneously influence and affect the coordinators' circumstances of exercising power.

The collaborative actors thus hold different positions and forms of power in collaboration 'from the start', due to the institutional structures that the specific collaboration is embedded within. At the same time, these positions are re-negotiated and changed to different degrees due to the more action-oriented power dynamics activated in collaboration. Prosecutors and child welfare caseworkers possess clear and visible one-dimensional decision-making power related to the parallel investigations; however, other more diffuse and partly invisible power dimensions can influence and affect these positions, with several three-dimensional power effects from the broader institutionalisation processes resulting from the Barnahus collaboration.

Juridification as a Three-Dimensional Power Effect

In a generalised sense, the analysis has shown how criminal law-oriented logic (focused on 'justice' and targeting a more efficient and improved judicial process) has gained priority at the expense of treatment-oriented logic (focused on 'welfare' and targeting improved and child-adapted protection and support). Expressed differently, the tension between 'justice' and 'welfare' has resulted in an unequal power balance between the agencies and their associated investigations and interventions. This change in power balance constitutes the process that I have called *juridification* (see Johansson 2011a, b). Juridification then is a process where the professional actors who are related to the treatment-oriented logic are letting themselves be influenced by, and adapts their working methods to, the criminal law-oriented logic. I interpret this as an institutional change resulting from the Barnahus collaboration.

The process of juridification was, among other things, reflected in how work assessments and interventions were prioritised, that is, in which sequence different interventions related to the child welfare and criminal investigations were conducted. Several child welfare caseworkers described how the Barnahus collaboration had resulted in them adjusting to police and prosecutor wishes to conduct their investigatory interventions before the child welfare services contacted custodians and informed them about the child welfare investigation. They described how this change affected and indeed complicated the initial and continuous contact and motivation work with the family, including accessing consent for support and treatment interventions for the children.

For example, one interviewee from the Barnahus staff explained the need for including, motivating and getting the family along in relation to the child welfare investigation process and the difficulties here of related to the judicial process:

> The goal is to – as quickly as possible after this disclosure – get in contact with the family. It is the nature of a case like this that it is difficult to make contact with the family. Most of the time it is someone in the family that is suspected of abusing the child. That is shameful, and many times when a police report has been filed they deny it. How are they supposed to admit to us that they hit their children, when it means admitting it to the police at the same time. It is very difficult to get this contact with the parents and the child. In order to get the child here [for support or treatment], we need to go through the parents. (Barnahus staff)

Another respondent from the survey stated that:

> The collaborative work has now a very clear focus on the judicial process. However, the child's/family's need for support, crisis counselling and so on has been pushed further into the background than what I had hoped for. (Child psychologist)

Even if some actors seemed aware, and to some extent even sceptical, about the stronger focus on the judicial process and adaption to the criminal law-oriented logic, the child welfare service representatives still accepted this way of thinking (and acting), as well as their roles and positions in the institutional order under making. In the questionnaire survey, child welfare services reported that they had changed their working methods the most as a consequence of the Barnahus collaboration; however, it is important to note, in relation to the criminal law-oriented logic rather than the treatment-oriented logic, what could be described as an 'adoption' of a contradictory institutional logic.

Conclusion

The analysis presented in this chapter, contextually based on the six first Barnahus in Sweden, has shown how Barnahus coordinators can be seen as exercising two- and three-dimensional power, partly over the organisation of the collaborative practices within Barnahus (such as consultation meetings) and partly over the child welfare caseworkers in relation to how they should 'go about' the child welfare investigations. On the other hand, the coordinators themselves are subjected to three-dimensional power in the sense of being 'carriers' of the police and prosecutor's institutional interests rather than interests stemming from a treatment-oriented logic. In that sense, they can be interpreted as being dominated by the criminal law-oriented logic and, in turn, argue on the basis of this logic when influencing the child welfare caseworkers about matters connected to the child welfare investigations.

Juridification can be understood as a move towards a new institutional power order, which includes a modification in power balance between the treatment-oriented and the criminal law-oriented logics, implying a content-wise focus on justice rather than welfare. More concretely, this implies a primary focus on the suspected crimes rather than investigating how the future situations of children and families can be improved by support and treatment interventions.

Juridification can be understood as an on-going institutionalisation process, wherein this Barnahus setting, and the different agencies and actors involved in this collaboration, have come to develop increasingly towards a common field (cf. Stefansen et al. Chap. 16). Juridification can be interpreted as a three-dimensional power effect, as an institutionally tied exercise of power, which might increasingly come to be taken-for-granted as something 'natural': in other words become institutionalised. By seeing collaboration as something undergoing constant negotiation and change, however, this power (im)balance does not have to be seen as static, since it might be re-activated and re-negotiated and, in turn, lead to a new power balance and institutional order in the field of tension between justice and welfare. The balance between justice and welfare could, subsequently, be of different character; conflicting, contested, dominated or - perhaps- equally balanced.

Notes

1. According to Scott (2008b) some professionals, understood as institutional agents, primarily possess formal authority (e.g. based on regulative power), others normative authority (e.g. based on normative principles of 'how to act') and yet others cultural-cognitive authority (e.g. based on knowledge claims and competence).
2. Cf. Stein Bråten on 'model power' and 'model monopoly' (Bråten 1973).
3. For a more detailed description of the methodological approach and empirical materials, see Johansson (2011a). The study was approved by the Regional Ethical Review Board in Lund. In the analysis section, all quotes from the empirical material are translated from Swedish into English by the author.
4. At some Swedish Barnahus, however, also psychologists and/or police investigators work as Barnahus staff (cf. Johansson et al. chap. 1).

Acknowledgements I would like to thank my co-editors Elisiv Bakketeig, Kari Stefansen and Anna Kaldal for valuable discussions and improving comments in the process of finalizing this chapter.

References

Bråten, Stein. 1973. Model Monopoly and Communication: Systems Theoretical Notes on Democratization. *Acta Sociologica* 16 (2): 98–107.

Clegg, Stewart, David Courpasson, and Nelson Phillips. 2006. *Power and Organizations*. London: Sage Publications.

Czarniawska, Barbara, and Guje Sevón (eds.). 1996. *Translating Organizational Change*. New York: Walter de Gruyter.

DiMaggio, Paul J., and Walter W. Powell. 1983. The Iron Cage Revisited: Institutional Isomorphism and Collective Rationality in Organizational Fields. *American Sociological Review* 48 (2): 147–160.

DiMaggio, Paul J., and Walter W. Powell (eds.). 1991. *The New Institutionalism in Organizational Analysis*. London: The University of Chicago Press.

Friedland, Roger, and Robert R. Alford. 1991. “Bringing Society Back. In: Symbols, Practices, and Institutional Contradictions.” In *The New Institutionalism in Organizational Analysis*, eds. Paul J. DiMaggio, and Walter W. Powell, 232–263. London: The University of Chicago Press.

Glad, Johan. 2006. Co-operation in a Child Welfare Case: A Comparative Cross-national Vignette Study. *European Journal of Social Work* 9 (2): 223–240.

Hardy, Cynthia, and Nelson Phillips. 1998. Strategies of Engagement: Lessons from the Critical Examination of Collaboration and Conflict in an Interorganizational Domain. *Organization Science* 9 (2): 217–230.

Horwath, Jan, and Tony Morrison. 2007. Collaboration, Integration and Change in Children's Services: Critical Issues and Key Ingredients. *Child Abuse and Neglect* 31(1): 55–69.

Johansson, Susanna. 2011a. Rätt, makt och institutionell förändring. En kritisk analys av myndigheters samverkan i barnahus. Lund Studies in Sociology of Law 35: Lund University.

Johansson, Susanna. 2011b. Juridifiering som institutionell förändring. Om mötet mellan straffrätt och socialrätt vid interorganisatorisk samverkan. Retfærd. *Nordic Journal of Law and Justice* 34/135: 38–59.

Johansson, Susanna. 2013. Institutions and Norms in Collaboration: Towards a Framework for Analysing Law and Normativity in Inter-organizational Collaboration. In *Social and Legal Norms*, ed. Matthias Baier, 107–120. Aldershot: Ashgate Publishing.

Lukes, Steven. 1974. *Power: A Radical View*. Basingstoke: Palgrave Macmillan.

Lukes, Steven. 2005. *Power: A Radical View*. The original text with two major new chapters. Basingstoke: Palgrave Macmillan.

Lukes, Steven, and Ladawn Haglund. 2005. Power and Luck. *Archives européennes de sociologie* 46(1): 45–66.

Phillips, Nelson, Thomas Lawrence, and Cynthia Hardy. 2000. Inter-Organizational Collaboration and the Dynamics of Institutional Fields. *Journal of Management Studies* 37 (1): 23–43.

Proposition 2002/03:53 Stärkt skydd för barn i utsatta situationer. Stockholm: Government bill.

Reay, Trish, and C.R. Hinings. 2009. Managing the Rivalry of Competing Institutional Logics. *Organization Studies* 30 (6): 629–652.

Røvik, Kjell Arne. 2000. Moderna organisationer: trender inom organisationstänkandet vid millennieskiftet. Malmö: Liber.

Scott, Richard W. 2008a. *Institutions and Organizations. Ideas and Interests*. London: Sage Publications.

Scott, Richard W. 2008b. Lords of the Dance: Professionals as Institutional Agents. *Organization Studies* 29: 219–238.

Swedish Ministry of Justice. 2005. Regeringsbeslut. Uppdrag att medverka till etablering av flera försöksverksamheter med samverkan under gemensamt tak vid utredningar kring barn som misstänks vara utsatta för allvarliga brott. Stockholm: Ministry of Justice.

Thornton, Patricia H. and William Ocasio. 2008."Institutional Logics." In *The SAGE Handbook of Organizational Institutionalism*, eds. Royston Greenwood, Christine Oliver, Kerstin Sahlin-Andersson and Roy Suddaby. London: Sage Publications.

Thornton, Patricia H., William Ocasio, and Michael Lounsbury. 2012. *The Institutional Logics Perspective. A New Approach to Culture, Structure, and Process*. New York: Oxford University Press.

Wiklund, Stefan. 2007. United we stand? Collaboration as a means for identifying children and adolescents at risk. *International Journal of Social Welfare* 16: 202–211.

13

Juridification and the Barnahus Model of Norway

Elisiv Bakketeig

Introduction

Improving services through inter-agency collaboration in cases of child abuse has been a challenge since violence and abuse against children were set on the national agenda in Norway in the late 1970s and early 1980s. Improving collaboration has been an aim in every strategy or action plan the Norwegian government has made in the last two decades (Jonassen 2013). In their latest action plan, the government states: "*Good preventive work and comprehensive services regarding help and treatment depends on services collaborating well across boundaries*" (Ministry of Justice and Public Security 2014, 27)[1].

The Barnahus model may be seen as an answer to these challenges, as an inter-agency approach to children being victims of crime with a double aim of facilitating the legal process and ensuring that the child and

E. Bakketeig (✉)
Norwegian Social Research, Oslo and Akershus University College of Applied Sciences, Oslo, Norway
e-mail: elisiv.bakketeig@nova.hioa.no

family receive the necessary help to cope with the child's experiences, but this presupposes that both aims are fulfilled. The double aim of the model risks tension between competing aims instead of having aims of equal significance. Results from a study of the Swedish Barnahus model (Johansson 2011a) suggest that "the penal perspective" in some respects has been prioritised at the expense of securing necessary help and treatment for the child and family. Johansson interprets this as a case of juridification. In this chapter, I will focus on analysing juridification tendencies within the Norwegian Barnahus model[2]. *My aim is to explore whether and how juridification manifests in the Norwegian Barnahus model using empirical results from juridification from the Swedish Barnahus model as a point of reference. A second aim is to discuss factors that may stimulate or constrain processes of juridification, as well as possible implications.*[3]

As noted, the double aim in Barnahus creates potential tensions. How do these relate to the extensive national and international research-based knowledge that already exists about important conditions for successful inter-agency collaboration? We know that good communication and a clear understanding of professional roles and responsibilities are important prerequisites, as well as mutual trust and an understanding of each other's duties and responsibilities (Darlington et al. 2004). Formal agreements regulating collaboration are also important, in addition to having enough resources in terms of time and financing to be able to collaborate successfully (Darlington et al. 2005; Katz and Hetherington 2006).

There is also extensive knowledge about the conditions that inhibit successful collaboration. Conflicting professional aims and mandates cause tensions and challenges (Darlington et al. 2005). In the Barnahus context, it is especially the tension between the criminal case and a need to ensure the child's well-being and psychological treatment that represents a challenge. The Norwegian and Swedish Barnahus models (as well as all the Nordic Barnahus models) have the double aim of facilitating the legal process and ensuring that the child and family receive the necessary help in order to cope with the child's experiences. By including different perspectives and interests that may conflict each other, the double aim implies potential tension. At the same time, the basic idea of Barnahus is that a child will receive help from different agencies "under one roof" which avoids having to repeat their story over and over again to different agencies. This means that tensions between professional aims and mandates within the model may be a potential threat to the model itself.

Juridification

"Juridification" is an ambiguous concept defined in various ways among researchers and within different disciplines. It is, for instance, used about new legislation being implemented in new areas (Debaenst 2013; Aasen et al. 2014), or to suggest that law as a profession is given too much influence in society (Norwegian Official Report 2003), that social problems are redefined as legal problems, or that legal regulation limits professional discretion and may imply a bureaucratisation of welfare services (Aasen et al. 2014; Bærøe and Bringedal 2014). Blichners and Molanders (2008) have deconstructed juridification to include five dimensions that cover many of the above meanings: "*...constitutive juridification, juridification as law's expansion and differentiation, as increased conflict solving with reference to law, as increased judicial power and as legal framing*".

Johansson (2011a, b) has specifically used the term "juridification" in a Barnahus context, as part of an analysis of how institutional power between different professions is negotiated in Barnahus[4]. One of the tendencies she identifies is the influence of "criminal law-oriented" logic on professionals with duties other than those related to the criminal case. This may include influences on professional attitudes as well as work practices, but not necessarily both. She found that child welfare services adapted their practice to the tasks of the police and the prosecutor. According to Johansson, this shows that criminal law-oriented logic dominates "the treatment-oriented logic". She also found that professions that traditionally have belonged to the treatment-oriented logic are influenced to a greater degree by the criminal law-oriented logic in their practice than vice versa. She therefore concludes that this may be seen as a general process of juridification representing an institutional change as a result of participating in inter-agency collaboration within Barnahus.

Johansson develops her analysis of the process of juridification further in an article where she looks closer at the relationship between the criminal law- and the treatment-oriented logic. Johansson argues that differences in the power of criminal law-oriented logic and treatment-oriented logic are related to differences in power between laws regulating these areas. The criminal code is based on a normative rationality that limits the space for discretion, while social law targets specific goals and thus leaves more room for discretion. Tensions between these create conflicts of norms which again have consequences for organisation, negotiations and practices of collaboration (2011b). Johansson sees this change as part of a process of juridification.

The term "juridification" may thus be used about a situation where the criminal law-oriented perspective is given priority at the expense of other perspectives; however, it may be argued that the term "juridification" is imprecise, since it refers to *jura* and thus laws in general. It is important to stress that it is the process of the criminal case and the influence this has on the professions in Barnahus with other primary responsibilities than those related to the criminal case that is subject for analysis here. In this chapter, the term "juridification" will therefore be used about the situation where the penal way of reasoning influences the way of thinking and practice of professionals with other primary tasks in Barnahus than those involving the criminal case. The penal way of reasoning reflects considerations and assessments related to the criminal case and I will refer to this as "the penal perspective".

Juridification in the Swedish Barnahus Model

Johansson's (2011a) empirical results concerning juridification in the Swedish Barnahus model will be used as a point of reference for the analysis of the Norwegian model. Since my intension is not to scrutinise juridification processes as such, but to explore whether and how juridification manifests in the Norwegian Barnahus model, I will not draw on her theoretical framework (institutional theory of organisations and power theory, see Chap. 12) but only refer to her empirical results regarding juridification. I will therefore elaborate on some of her findings. In her study, she found that representatives of all the different professions had been influenced by each other; however, she also found that there were differences in the extent of the influence between the different professions. Representatives from the child welfare services were influenced the most by the others. Representatives from the police and forensic medicine were also influenced, but to a smaller degree than the child welfare workers. Representatives from the prosecuting agency were influenced the least.

The influence that the child welfare workers experienced resulted in changes to their work practice. The sequence of tasks was organised in a way that gave the criminal case priority at the expense of the responsibilities of the child welfare workers in the child welfare case. Johansson found that the changes made were justified by means of a reasoning that reflected the criminal case and was not in line with the professional mandate of the work of the child welfare workers.

An example of a change of practice concerned the notification of the child's parents. From a child welfare perspective, it is important for child welfare professionals to notify parents quickly, because it is important in child welfare cases that the caseworkers establish a good relation with the family at an early stage; however, the criminal investigation and the criminal case require that the parents are not notified so as to avoid the risk of reducing the evidential value of witness statements or tampering with evidence. Johansson found that the child welfare caseworkers postponed notification of the parents to avoid this risk, and her interpretation is that the interests of the criminal case were given priority at the expense of the child welfare case.

Different Contexts for Analysing Juridification

Using the Swedish Barnahus model as a point of reference for an analysis of manifestations of juridification in the Norwegian model is not without problems. There are important differences between the models. First, practice in Barnahus in Sweden seems to vary to a greater extent than Norwegian practice due to differences in implementation processes (see Chap. 1) and makes it more difficult to write about a unified Swedish practice. This means that when I write about how the model generally functions in Sweden, there will be local variations that, to some degree, differ in practice from the general model described here.

Second, there are differences between the Norwegian and Swedish models that relate especially to the role of the child welfare services. This touches upon an important point of reference, since Johansson (2011a), as previously noted, found that child welfare workers were the profession in Barnahus most affected by the penal perspective. A core question in my analysis is whether there is a similar tendency in the Norwegian model, despite the differences between the models, regarding the role of child welfare services?

In the Swedish model, the child welfare investigation and the criminal investigation follow parallel paths in Barnahus. This is not the case in the Norwegian model, where the child welfare investigation is not formally a part of the Barnahus model. In Norway, a case in Norwegian Barnahus implies that the alleged abuse has been reported to the police. It is the police who contact the Barnahus and make an appointment for the child investigative interview. In this sense, the case is police-initiated and the focus is primarily on the child investigative interview and thus the criminal case. This organisational difference implies a stronger presence of the child welfare case in the Swedish Barnahus compared to the Norwegian model and a stronger focus on the criminal case in the Norwegian model.

A third difference concerns the professional background of the Barnahus staff. This relates to the question of who is influenced by the penal perspective in the two models. In the Swedish model, it is primarily child welfare workers who are functioning specifically as permanent Barnahus staff and coordinators, while in Norway the Barnahus staff consists of employees with different professional backgrounds, for example, within pedagogics, psychology and child welfare[5]. The Norwegian Barnahus staff thus represent a more diverse group of professionals than in the Swedish model. This means that we compare models that involve different conditions for being influenced by the penal perspective. Diversity in professional backgrounds may be a factor of significance for how susceptible they are to influence from the penal perspective, since it may imply that assessments and decisions are based on a broader professional basis, and may thus represent a stronger resistance to influence.

Systemic differences could also imply an expectation that the child welfare perspective is more pronounced in the Swedish model due to the stronger involvement of both the child welfare services and the child welfare case. We might also expect the penal perspective to be stronger in the Norwegian model due to the case being police-initiated, or even police-focused or driven. Based on this, we might expect to see more traces of juridification in the Norwegian model compared to the Swedish. I will now go on to explore whether and how juridification manifests in the Norwegian Barnahus model.

Juridification in the Norwegian Barnahus Model

Methods

The analysis of the Norwegian model is based on data from an electronic survey conducted in 2011 with professionals in Barnahus who participated in child investigative interviews, and which included data from legal personnel (police, lawyers and judges). The number of respondents was 273 in total, with a response rate of 53% of the professionals who were invited to participate in the survey. Our study did not include an in-depth analysis of juridification, but we did include a question about how they assessed the balance between the interests of the child's well-being and the penal perspective. This question may give information to suggest whether such an effect is present in Norwegian Barnahus; however, due to limited data and the relatively low response rate, we have to be careful not to draw overly strong conclusions from these results.

The analysis is also based on interviews with leaders and other employees at six Norwegian Barnahus from 2011. These interviews were conducted as individual interviews (leaders) and focus group interviews (employees) using open-ended questions. The interviews included questions about the Barnahus concept, activities and organisation (i.e. professional background of the staff, the staff tasks in the different phases of the case, the number of child investigative interviews and medical examinations, collaboration with other agencies and organisational affiliations). A sample of these interviews, involving three randomly selected Barnahus, has been reanalysed for this chapter. The specific aim of this analysis has been to look for descriptions of practices and assessments that inform us about the relationship between the criminal case and the other activities in Barnahus. Special attention has been given to identify reflections among professionals that inform us about how they prioritise the interests of the criminal case in relation to other aspects of the case, such as treatment or safe-guarding well-being of the child and family.

Finally, I have included new data, based on the analyses of interviews conducted in 2015–2016 with Barnahus staff at five Barnahus in different parts of Norway. These interviews concerned inter-agency collaboration between four different services (crisis shelters, Barnahus, family therapeutic services and child welfare services). In these interviews, we included a question to the Barnahus staff about the relationship between the penal perspective and offering treatment and support for the child. All quotations from the interviews have been translated into English by the author.

Empirical Results Regarding Juridification in the Norwegian Barnahus Model

When Barnahus was implemented in Norway, there was concern among public authorities that the inter-agency model would result in role conflicts; however, when Norwegian Barnahus was evaluated in 2012, the results suggested that this was not a problem. Legal professionals were, for example, asked how they assessed the balance between the interests of the child well-being and the penal perspective. Seven out of ten lawyers and police representatives reported that they experienced the child and the penal perspectives as well balanced. Nine out of ten also reported that the Barnahus staff had a good understanding of their role (Stefansen et al. 2012).

The Barnahus leaders and staff also reported in the interviews that they found it very important to have a clear understanding of their role. A major impression after reanalysing the interviews was also that the Barnahus staff were very much focused on describing their specific role within the Barnahus as being facilitators for the other professionals. They also emphasised the clarity of roles when they described how they relate to welfare services outside the Barnahus model. A good balance between the different perspectives and a clear understanding of professional roles, at least as the professionals themselves experienced them, may imply that juridification is less widespread in the Norwegian Barnahus model.

Our results about this point were surprising because the double aim in the Norwegian and Swedish model should imply that the tensions between taking care of the well-being of the child and the penal perspective would be the same in both models. It is therefore necessary to look closer at this result. I will start with possible explanations for why we may find fewer traces of juridification in the Norwegian model compared to the Swedish, and then discuss some factors that in contrast may suggest a juridification effect in the Norwegian model as well.

Factors that May Suggest Less Influence from the Penal Perspective in the Norwegian Model

One factor that may imply less influence from the penal perspective on child welfare caseworkers in the Norwegian model may be that they are not formally a part of the Norwegian Barnahus model. As noted earlier, the child welfare case and child welfare professionals are more strongly involved in the Swedish Barnahus model compared to the Norwegian model. This implies that representatives from child welfare services are less exposed to the influence of the penal perspective in the Norwegian, compared to the Swedish model and may imply a stronger potential to maintain their professional autonomy. This may make it less likely that the penal perspective influences assessments in the child welfare case.

Another factor of significance for juridification is the clarity of roles within the Barnahus model. Clarity of roles may be a barrier to juridification and, as noted earlier, was also emphasised as important in the interviews by several of the leaders of the Barnahus. There are some factors that may suggest that a clarity of roles is more distinctive in the Norwegian than the Swedish model. This is due to differences regarding the implementation of Barnahus in the two countries.

The Barnahus model in Sweden was introduced as a new service, but as part of the pilot project, partly implemented in existing services for abused children and their families. This implied that the Barnahus model was implemented into services with variations in organisation and practice, including in existing practices of collaboration. As in Sweden, Norwegian Barnahus was introduced as a new measure, but was not implemented into existing services. Instead, the Barnahus was built from scratch, as part of the Norwegian pilot project. Building the model from scratch may have resulted in more unified practice and facilitated a clarity of roles in the Norwegian Barnahus.

Another factor that may affect the clarity of roles is the resistance many of the Barnahus experienced during the implementation process. Implementation of Barnahus in Norway meant that the child investigative interview of the children was to be conducted in Barnahus instead of at the police stations or the courthouses where these interviews were conducted prior to the establishment of Barnahus. In the initial phase, there was resistance to this change of practice, especially from members of the justice system. Some judges and leaders in the police were against having the interviews conducted at Barnahus partly because they found it unnecessarily time-consuming to travel to the Barnahus (Bakketeig et al. 2012). There was also scepticism about the role of the Barnahus staff and their presence during the child investigative interview. The interviews with representatives from the Barnahus staff showed that they found some lawyers and judges to be hostile in the early days after the implementation (Stefansen et al. 2012); however, this gradually changed when the legal personnel understood the benefits of conducting the interviews in Barnahus[6]. The Barnahus staff was also very aware of this resistance and worked systematically to reduce it. They succeeded in overcoming this resistance partly because they were very clear about defining their own role in relation to the other professional roles in Barnahus. They stressed that they would *not* take over any of the other profession's tasks in these cases, and that their primary role was to facilitate the child investigative interview and the medical examination, and to make sure that the child and their families received necessary help in order to cope with their experiences, including psychological counselling. Thus, the initial resistance in Norway may have contributed to a clarity of roles in the model, which may again have constrained juridification.

Factors that May Imply a Juridification Effect in the Norwegian Model

I have suggested some factors that may explain why we find less traces of juridification in the Norwegian model compared to the Swedish model; however, there are factors that may suggest a juridification effect in the Norwegian model as well, although expressed in other circumstances, and partly due to changes in the institutional, organisational and legal framework for Norwegian Barnahus.

First, the affiliation of Barnahus with the police system (see Chap. 1) could imply a strong influence from the penal perspective, resulting in a reduced focus on treatment and securing the child and family's well-being. This risk of bias was also underlined in the evaluation of the Norwegian model, where the authors pointed out the need for a stronger involvement from the ministries with political responsibilities for treatment and securing the child and family's well-being, in this case the Norwegian Ministry of Health and Care Services and the Norwegian Ministry of Children, Equality and Social Inclusion. The authors state: "*A steering model that makes the relevant ministries accountable will also secure the balance between the different elements in the Barnahus model: The criminal track, the treatment track and the comprehensive principle of the child's best interest*" (Stefansen et al. 2012, 156.)[7].

Our interviews, however, showed that the Barnahus staff was aware of the implications of being employed by the police organisation, and found it important to be clear that Barnahus was an independent unit and different from the police. Being employed by the police organisation also naturally affects how they see their responsibilities, however, partly because of organisational demands, but perhaps also due to a closer identification of the Barnahus staff with the aims of the police organisation over time as a result of being affiliated with the police system. The following statement from a member of the Barnahus staff in 2016 illustrates the significance of the affiliation when comparing her own role to the police interviewers:

> Also I am employed in the police organisation(…), so I am also concerned about the child's involvement in the criminal case, but my primary concern is the child's well-being. To balance these two elements can be a bit challenging.

Finally, affiliation with the police system may imply that issues relevant to the penal process may receive more attention in the political and administrative system than issues for which other ministries are responsible, and may therefore promote juridification.

I have emphasised that a clarity of roles may inhibit juridification; however, clarity of roles does not exclude juridification. It is possible to have clarity of roles within an organisation, but for one perspective to still be given priority at the expense of others. A reanalysis of our interviews with employees at the Barnahus may illustrate this point, as we found several examples of similar statements. A leader underlines that the Barnahus staff:

> *… always confers with the police to make sure that they can continue to follow up the child, because sometimes, if they are going to do another police interview (…), then we (…) can't go in and do anything. Therefore, we have a very open dialogue with the police, so we don't ruin the penal case.*

Another employee says:

> *...we never talk to the child and family before we have asked the investigator if it is ok. (...) so we make sure that we do not go in and ruin the investigation.*

On the one hand, this reflects a clear definition of roles, but on the other hand it is also clear that the criminal case is prioritised and that the immediate follow-up and treatment of the child have to wait. This implies that in the Norwegian model too, the penal perspective influences the sequence of tasks, as Johansson found in the Swedish model (2011a). This may be necessary for the Barnahus model to function according to its aims, but it also shows that the penal perspective is given priority at the expense of other perspectives in the Norwegian Barnahus. This may also imply that there is a mismatch between the *conception* among the professions in the Barnahus that the different perspectives are well balanced on the one hand and their *work practice* on the other hand. It may be that it has become so common in the Barnahus to be careful not to interfere with the criminal case that they are not aware of the fact that one perspective is given priority at the expense of others (cf. Johanssons's discussion of three-dimensional power in Chap. 12 in this volume).

The Norwegian legal framework is also of relevance, because Barnahus is undergoing changes. New regulations about child investigative interviews have been adopted and came into force in October 2015.[8] The amendments mean that child investigative interviews will now be led by the police and no longer by a judge. One of the consequences of the changes in legislation is that the defendant no longer has to be notified prior to the first interview of the child. The obligation to notify the perpetrator has formerly suggested challenges, which are referred to in the preparatory works of the amendments (Prop 112 L). To avoid notification of the alleged perpetrator, child welfare caseworkers sometimes postponed reporting suspected abuse to the police in consideration of the child welfare case (to be able to maintain good relations with the parents). When the case was later reported to the police, the value of the evidence of the child's statement was impaired because there was a risk that it had been influenced by the child welfare investigation. The ministry therefore argues that the amendment about not having to notify the perpetrator before the first interview of the child will improve collaboration between the police and child welfare services and avoid delays in reporting cases to the police. The ministry also emphasises the importance that the procedures are followed in the correct sequence to avoid destruction of evidence. If we turn back to the example of juridification that Johansson (2011a) identified in her study, where the child welfare caseworkers postponed notifying the child's parents in consideration of the criminal case, the legal changes in the Norwegian code of criminal procedure actually suggest a similar juridification effect. On the other hand, not having to notify the alleged perpetrator may mean that the first interview of the child is taken more rapidly after the case is reported to the police and may in fact reduce the potential conflict of interests between the criminal and the child welfare case.

Finally, the Norwegian Barnahus reports of 2016 show that they are cutting back on the psychological treatment of children and their families due to an increased number of police interviews at the Barnahus. For instance, the Barnahus in Stavanger treated 167 children and families in 2014, and only 55 in 2015. The interviews with Barnahus employees in 2015–2016 showed that four out of five Barnahus were currently very pressed for time and resources because of the increased number of interviews. The consequence is that they have to cut back on the treatment of children and their families. The strong increase in child investigative interviews is a result of the amendments in the Norwegian criminal procedure legislation. Moving from interviews led by a judge to police interviews may have lowered the threshold for conducting child investigative interviews but also led to an increased number of interviews due to the fact that supplemental interviews may be required by the defence attorney if the first police interview has substantiated the concerns about the abuse of the child. The time limit for undertaking interviews has also been reduced. In some cases, the interview has to be taken within one week of the case being reported to the police (Norwegian Code of Criminal Procedure §239 e). Compliance with these limits is a target within the police organisation. Overall, this creates strong pressure on the Barnahus, forcing them to prioritise the child investigative interviews and reduce treatment as a consequence of limited resources. It may seem as if the Barnahus ends up in a "crossfire" of competing expectations. Since the Barnahus staff are employed by the police, they feel that the Barnahus has to serve the police in order to fulfil the demands of new time limits. On the other hand, the Barnahus are very conscious of the fact that treatment and support of the child and family are just as important. In an interview from 2016, a Barnahus employee describes the pressure of crossing expectations:

> *...yes, we have been very accommodating [towards the police]. Now we are more explicit that we have two tasks: the interrogation of the child and the follow up afterwards. Both are equally important.*

The Barnahus employees describe this as a struggle about resources within the police organisation. A member of the Barnahus staff says that when the police require them to set up a second interview room which demands extra financial resources, they make sure to ask for the financial means to employ more therapists to be sure to increase their capacity for offering treatment at the same time.

The reduction in treatment due to the increase in the numbers of child investigative interviews is thus a strong indication that the interests of the criminal case are also being prioritised at the expense of securing the necessary treatment for the children and their families in Norway, but it also suggests that Barnahus is making a strong effort to secure treatment and the well-being of children and families.

Conclusion

In this chapter, I have explored whether and how juridification manifests in the Norwegian Barnahus model using empirical results regarding juridification from the Swedish Barnahus model as a point of reference. I have also discussed factors that may promote or inhibit penal perspective being given priority within the model. Factors that may suggest *less* juridification in the Norwegian model include the experience of roles as well balanced between the Barnahus staff and the majority of the judicial respondents in our study. Well-balanced roles may be due to a clarity about roles. This clarity of roles may have developed as a result of implementing Barnahus as a service built from scratch and not, as in Sweden, partly implemented within existing services. A clarity of roles may also have developed as a response to the resistance initially expressed in parts of the legal community to the establishment of Barnahus in Norway. Clarity of roles may inhibit juridification. Even more important, however, is that the lower formal involvement of child welfare services in the Norwegian model, compared to the Swedish model, may suggest a stronger potential to maintain their professional autonomy.

I have also discussed factors that may suggest a juridification effect in the Norwegian model. A closer look at the data through reanalyses of the interviews with Barnahus leaders and employees gave examples where the criminal case influenced the sequence of tasks. The effect of the organisational affiliation of Barnahus in the police organisation and recent developments after the Norwegian model was evaluated also strongly suggest a juridification effect. This is related to the effect of Barnahus staff being organised as part of the police organisation, of changes in the Norwegian criminal procedure legislation and the implications of these changes for the Barnahus.

As of today, we have limited research-based information about the level of juridification in the Norwegian Barnahus. It is therefore necessary to initiate research in Norway to scrutinise the degree to which such an effect is present and to obtain a deeper insight into the implications of juridification. It would, for instance, be interesting to compare the degree and implications of juridification on child welfare services in Norway compared to other countries with a stronger formal involvement of child welfare services in the Barnahus model, as in Sweden and Denmark (see Chap. 1).

It may be argued that organising the tasks in Barnahus in a way that does not reduce the value of evidence from the child's statement does not necessarily imply that the different aims of the model are not fulfilled. On the contrary, it may be necessary to organise the sequence of tasks in order for the different professional aims to be accomplished. It is when the Barnahus model is put under pressure to prioritise the child investigative interview at the expense of treatment and taking care of the well-being of the child and family that it becomes a problem, but problems may also occur if professional aims are incompatible, for instance, when the child is in need of immediate treatment. If the interests of the criminal case are prioritised at the expense of immediate treatment of the child, it could put the child at risk. Even though an important part of the Barnahus obligation is to facilitate the child's best interest in the criminal case, it is important to remember that the official aim of the criminal case is primarily based on the public interest of pursuing a criminal offence and is not primarily based on the interests of the child. Prioritising the interests of the criminal case at the expense of treatment can also challenge the basic presumptions for the Barnahus model. Ensuring the necessary help and treatment for a child and their family based on the child's individual needs is an independent and important aim in Barnahus. Putting less emphasis on these perspectives, due to considerations of the criminal case, could imply a reduced quality in services offered to children and families in Barnahus.

It is also necessary, however, to recognise that tensions between the different perspectives in Barnahus are unavoidable, and this is a situation that professionals in Barnahus will have to live and cope with. This is a natural consequence of working within an inter-agency model that operates at the intersection of the criminal justice system, treatment and securing the well-being of children and their families. Competence, good communication skills, mutual understanding and respect between the professionals, as well as clarity of roles when working with the individual child and their families, are important conditions under which to manage the balance between the different professional aims and perspectives. As Johansson concludes in her analysis of power dynamics in Swedish Barnahus collaboration, the balance of power will also be subject to continuous negotiations. Finding a balance that fulfils the separate aims of the model is necessary in order to secure good services for children and their families.

Notes

1. Author translation.
2. This chapter relates to a project about inter-agency collaboration between welfare services in cases of domestic violence conducted within the framework of the Domestic Violence Research Programme (2014–2019) at NOVA, funded by the Ministry of Justice and Public Security.
3. I would like to thank my co-editors and especially Susanna Johansson and Kari Stefansen for very constructive comments.
4. Johansson's reanalysis of collaboration in Swedish Barnahus (2011a) builds on her evaluation of collaboration in the Swedish national trial project of the Swedish Barnahus model (2008). Also, see Johansson's chapter (12), Power dynamics in Barnahus collaboration.
5. In some Barnahus, in Sweden there are also police and/or psychologists employed as part of the permanent Barnahus staff, for instance, at Stockholm Barnahus; however, as far as we know, it is also practice within these Barnahus that mainly child welfare workers work as coordinators. These child welfare workers are not the same as the child welfare workers visiting Barnahus in relation to their work with specific child welfare cases (case workers). Both groups of child welfare workers are formally employed by social services, but only the first group works as part of the permanent staff at the Barnahus.
6. In 2011, 69% of the child investigative interviews were conducted in Barnahus.
7. Translated by the author of this chapter.
8. Amendments have been made to the Code of Criminal Procedure 4. September 2005 no 91. Ref. also Regulations concerning interviews of children and other vulnerable aggrieved parts and witnesses (facilitated interviews) of 24. September 2015 no. 1098.
9. According to the Code of Criminal Procedure §239 b, section three and four, if facilitated interviews are conducted without notifying the alleged perpetrator, the assessment of whether to charge them shall be made as soon as possible. If charged, the alleged perpetrator and their attorney shall have the opportunity to see the documents and the video-recording of the interview. They shall also be informed about the right to ask for a supplementary interview of the child.

References

Aasen, Henriette Sinding, Siri Gloppen, Anne-Mette Magnussen and Even Nilssen. 2014. "Introduction." In *Juridification and Social Citizenship in the Welfare State*, eds. Henriette Sinding Aasen, Siri Gloppen, Anne-Mette Magnussen and Even Nilssen, 1–20. Cheltenham, UK: Edward Elgar Publishing.Inc.

Bakketeig, Elisiv, Mette Berg, Trond Myklebust and Kari Stefansen. 2012. Barnehusevalueringen 2012. Delrapport 1. Barnehusmodellens implikasjoner for politiets arbeid med fokus på dommeravhør og rettsmedisinsk undersøkelse. Oslo: Politihøgskolen.

Bærøe, Kristine, and Berit Bringedal. 2014. "Professionalism, discretion and juridification: social inequality in health and social citizenship." In *Juridification and Social Citizenship in the Welfare State*, eds. Henriette Sinding Aasen, Siri Gloppen, Anne-Mette Magnussen and Even Nilssen, 146–161. Cheltenham, UK: Edward Elgar Publishing Inc.

Blichner, Lars Christian and Anders Molander. 2008. "Mapping juridification." *European Law Journal* 14 (1): 36–54.

Darlington, Yvonne, Judith.A. Feeney, and Kylie Rixton. 2004. Complexity, conflict and uncertainty: Issues in collaboration between child protection and mental health services. *Children and Youth Services Review* 26 (12): 1175–1192.

Darlington, Yvonne, Judith A. Feeney, and Kylie Rixton. 2005. Practice challenges at the intersection of child protection and mental health. *Child and Family Social Work* 10 (3): 239–247.

Debaenst, Bruno. 2013. "A study on juridification. The case of industrial accidents in nineteenth century Belgium." *The Legal History Review* 81 (1–2): 247–273.

Johansson, Susanna. 2008. Myndighetssamverkan i barnahus – organisering, innehåll och process. Delrapport 4 i utvärderingen av nationell försöksverksamhet med barnahus 2006–2007. Research Report 2008:4. Lund: Universitetet i Lund.

Johansson, Susanna. 2011a. Rätt, makt och institutionell förändring. En kritisk analys av myndigheters samverkan i barnahus. Lund studies in sociology of law. Lund: Lunds universitet.

Johansson, Susanna. 2011b. "Juridifiering som institutionell förändring. Om mötet mellan straffrätt och socialrätt vid interorganisatorisk samverkan." *Retfærd. Nordic Journal of Law and Justice* 34:4(135): 38–59.

Jonassen, Wenche. 2013. «Fra kvinnemishandling til vold i nære relasjoner. Regjeringens handlingsplaner mot vold.» Tidsskrift for kjønnsforskning 37 (1): 46–62.

Katz, Ilan and Rachael Hetherington. 2006. "Co-Operating and Communicating: A European Perspective on Integrating Services for Children." *Child Abuse Review* 15 (6): 429–439.

Ministry of Justice and Public Security. 2014. Et liv uten vold. Handlingsplan mot vold i nære relasjoner 2014–2017. Oslo: Justis- og beredskapsdepartementet.

Norwegian Official Report. 2003. Makt og demokrati. NOU 2003:19. Oslo: Arbeids- og administrasjonsdepartementet.

Prop.112 L. (2014–2015). Endringer i straffeprosessloven (avhør av barn og andre særlige sårbare fornærmede og vitner). Oslo: Justis-og beredskapsdepartementet.

Stefansen, Kari, Tonje Gundersen and Elisiv Bakketeig. 2012: Barnehusevalueringen 2012. Delrapport 2. En undersøkelse blant barn og pårørende, jurister og politifolk, samt ledere og ansatte. Oslo: NOVA.

14

Building Barnahus in Denmark

Lene Mosegaard Søbjerg

Introduction

Providing a multidisciplinary and comprehensive response to child abuse is the fundamental core of the Nordic Barnahus model. In Denmark, five Barnahus were established by law in October 2013. The establishment of Barnahus was one of the several outputs of a broad legislation called "the assault package" (in Danish "*overgrebspakken*"), implemented as a response to the disclosure of a number of shocking cases of child neglect and abuse in Denmark during the 2010 (Glassow 2015). There were high expectations of Barnahus from politicians, experts and child welfare caseworkers (Damsgaard and Christiansen 2012). The gathering of expertise in one organisational unit and the concept of ensuring multidisciplinary and interagency collaboration between professionals and agencies dealing with the child and the child's

L.M. Søbjerg (✉)
VIA University College, Aarhus, Denmark
e-mail: LMOS@VIA.DK

family in particular were thought to improve work with abused children (Sundhedsstyrelsen 2012).

Work with abused children not only takes place within the Barnahus but also between the Barnahus and collaborating agencies. In Denmark, there is an important collaboration between the Barnahus and the child welfare services in the local municipalities where the children and their families live. As described in the introductory chapter, the responsibility for Barnahus is in the Danish National Board of Social Services, which suggests a strong connection with the social welfare system. The child welfare services in municipalities have the overall legal responsibility for the children and their well-being before, during and after a case has been handled in the Barnahus. This strong connection with the child welfare system is apparently stronger in Denmark than in most of the other Nordic Barnahus models, for example, in Norway, where Barnahus is organised within the judicial system (Stefansen et al. 2012).

The Barnahus model and cooperation inside the Barnahus have been analysed in other Nordic countries (see, for instance, Conte 2014; Johansson 2012; Stefansen et al. 2012). Less attention has been given to collaboration between Barnahus and other agencies[1], and consequently, it is appropriate to investigate the role of Barnahus in a broader context.

Based on the empirical study, this chapter will discuss the collaboration between the Danish Barnahus and local child welfare services, departing from a holistic perspective on social work. A holistic perspective is central to social work in Denmark, as will be explained later in this chapter. The key question explored in the chapter is, *How the establishment of Barnahus has affected the experience of child welfare caseworkers regarding their ability to work holistically with an abused child and his/her family?* The understanding of holism will be analysed from the perspective of caseworkers in local child welfare services who have collaborated with Barnahus in specific cases.

Initially, the chapter explains the responsibilities of Barnahus and the child welfare services in municipalities in Denmark. A set of theoretical perspectives and definitions of a holistic approach to social work are then presented before the methodology of the study undertaken among the municipalities of one Danish Barnahus is introduced. The empirical data for the study is finally analysed in light of the theoretical approaches of holistic social work. The focus of the analysis is the cooperation between child welfare services and Barnahus as seen from the perspective of the child welfare caseworkers dealing and cooperating with the Barnahus.

Responsibilities of Barnahus and the Local Child Welfare Services

The role of Barnahus in Denmark is to coordinate cases and assist the local child welfare services, who are responsible for providing the necessary and correct help for an abused child. If the child welfare services suspect that an assault has taken place and it is necessary to involve at least two public agencies in the case (most often this involves the police, health care system and child welfare services), the child welfare services are obliged by law to contact the local Barnahus. The involvement of Barnahus is mandatory under these circumstances, regardless of the resources and expertise of child welfare services in relation to cases of abused children[2]. When a suspicion of child abuse is raised, a child welfare investigation has to be made[3]. This child welfare investigation is made by the child welfare services who have full responsibility for the case, while the role of the Barnahus is to provide expertise, coordinate initiatives and assist in child psychiatric evaluations. This division of responsibility fits well with the general organisation of the Nordic Barnahus model, where each participating agency is responsible for its own part (Landberg 2009, 17).

Theoretical Perspectives on Holistic Social Work

A central concept in Danish social work is what will be termed "holism" or "holistic social work" in this chapter; however, holism does not completely translate and explain the core values of the terms "*helhed*" (meaning "whole") or "*helhedsorientering*" (meaning "orientation towards the whole") which are often used in Danish social work. A characterisation and explanation of the importance of holism to social work in Denmark are consequently appropriate.

Holism is a central aspect of social work because all children, young people and adults are part of a whole, of something bigger than the individual. A holistic approach is based on the understanding that the problems of a child or young person cannot be viewed separately from the rest of the individual (Ejrnæs and Guldager 2008; Guldager 2015). Working holistically means working with all the aspects of a person's life that are important to a case, based on the assumption that all the aspects are interconnected (Harder 2011). Not all elements are equally important, but they are all significant and nothing can deliberately be left out. A holistic approach is by definition multidisciplinary, as one profession cannot be profoundly knowledgeable about all the aspects of a case (Guldager 2015).

Holism is central to social work, as explained in the words of Ferguson, because social work includes the

> combination of a value base of respect, empowerment and social justice, the emphasis on a relationship between worker and service user founded on trust and non-judgmental acceptance; a knowledge base which embraces both developmental psychology and also an understanding of social structures and social procedures, and a repertoire of methods ranging from individual counselling to advocacy and community work; all these give social work a holistic perspective which makes it unique among the helping professions (Ferguson 2008).

Putting all the different concerns and topics mentioned by Ferguson together is the core of holistic social work.

Uggerhøj (2011) defines holism as "*being able to see a case in as big a perspective as possible and being able to view a problem from as many angles as possible*". A holistic perspective is consequently the ability of the child welfare caseworker to see a case from a broader perspective: to see a case in multiple dimensions and to act according to these multiple dimensions. The purpose of working holistically is to be able to find the right solution(s) to the child's problems. An unintended consequence of not working holistically is attempting to solve the wrong problem or trying to make a solution fit the problem rather than letting the problem(s) define the solution.

In the case of abused children, working holistically means viewing the child not only as an abused child, but also as an individual with a multitude of possibilities and challenges which can affect the child's ability to deal with, and react to, the abuse. It is also important to acknowledge that the abused child is part of a larger whole, first and foremost a family, but also a circle of friends, a neighbourhood, a town or city and a society. In a holistic approach, the abuse cannot be viewed alone, and the child cannot be treated without consideration of the child's immediate environment. Although it is clear that the sexual or physical abuse is the central issue in a case of child abuse, the abuse is typically not the child's only concern. In a study of the effect of group therapy for sexually abused children in Denmark, the background data on the participating children showed that their life circumstances were difficult, and the children had a number of challenges in addition to the abuse. Many of the families had problems with alcohol or drug abuse, mental illness and/or unemployment (Lægsgaard and Søbjerg 2012). The fact that abused children often have multiple problems that social caseworkers have to include in their dealings with the child accentuates the importance from a social work perspective of using a holistic approach in cases of child abuse.

The opposite of holism is reductionism. Reductionism occurs when a case is viewed from a more simple or reduced perspective. From a theoretical perspective, two of the core elements of Barnahus, the cooperation of multiple professionals and specialised knowledge, pose a contradiction when analysed as part of a holistic approach. Gaining specialised knowledge on one issue inevitably leads to less focus on other issues. This can be termed reductionism, which is the opposite of holism. Laursen (2011) argues that if a holistic approach is not used, some form of reductionism is inevitably taking place; however, social problems are often complex and sometimes even wicked (meaning impossible to solve) (Rittel and Webber 1973), and in order to handle or tame these complexities, it can be necessary to employ a certain degree of reductionism. Despite the inevitable need to reduce the complexity in the field of social work, the ideal is to work holistically (Laursen 2011).

The Barnahus model also includes holistic aspects. Johansson argues that the main goals of Barnahus are "*to improve the criminal investigations and make the judicial processes more efficient* on the one hand, *and to improve protection, support, and treatment* on the other hand" (Johansson 2012). This involves a combination of criminal law-oriented logic and treatment-oriented welfare logic. The combination of several logics in the Barnahus is an example of multi-professional cooperation, which contributes to holistic social work, because the main objective is to use a multidisciplinary effort to help the child with all aspects of the abuse. There are consequently holistic elements integrated within the Barnahus model; however, working multi-professionally is not the same as using the theoretical perspective of holistic social work presented above, because the theoretical foundation of holistic social work focuses on the child (or in more general terms, the citizen) and not the logic of organisations or professionals working with a case.

The difference between the instinct of child welfare caseworkers to see a case of child abuse from a holistic perspective and the Barnahus' more organisational objective of providing multidisciplinary specialised expertise poses a conundrum worth investigating. An ambition to analyse this dilemma was the main inspiration behind the research question presented and analysed in this chapter.

Methodology and Strategy of Analysis

The chapter draws on data from a study conducted at one of the five Barnahus in Denmark, in 2014, approximately one year after the establishment of Barnahus in Denmark.

The study included a quantitative survey distributed to all nineteen child welfare services connected to this Barnahus and semi-structured qualitative interviews with twelve child welfare caseworkers in eight municipalities. Seventeen municipalities answered the survey, which gave a response rate of 89%. The quantitative data of the study provided a basis of knowledge about the Barnahus and the cooperation between the municipalities and the Barnahus; however, the written answers of the questionnaire did not elaborate on the holistic perspective on the cases, and the data included in the analysis are thus primarily based on the qualitative study.

Eight municipalities were chosen for the qualitative part of the study, based on the size of the municipality and the number of Barnahus cases in each municipality. The municipalities represented four categories: large and small municipalities with relatively high numbers of cases, and large and small municipalities with relatively low numbers of cases. The intention was to include municipalities with variation in the numbers of Barnahus cases, not only because of differences in the size of the municipality. Two child welfare services from each of the four categories were contacted, and qualitative interviews with a child welfare caseworker and/or a manager from the child welfare services were carried out.

Five interviews were single interviews and three interviews involved two or three respondents. All interviews were recorded and transcribed verbatim. The interviews were undertaken in Danish and followed a semi-structured interview guide. The quotes in this chapter have been translated by the author. All interviews are treated anonymously.

The data were analysed in an iterative process using both a deductive and an inductive approach (Kvale 2007). First, all transcriptions were read and the identified patterns of statements led to the construction of a coding framework based on the research question. Second, an inductive reading, in which unexpected themes were discovered, was conducted. Finally, systematic coding identified recurring themes and patterns.

The analysis identified two divergent perceptions of the establishment of Barnahus. One perception was a positive reaction to the increase in expertise and attention given to child abuse. A contradictory perception was the expression of a number of dilemmas encountered when working with abused children in the child welfare services. The essence of the dilemmas is connected to the holistic approach to social work and will be analysed and discussed below.

Centralisation of Competences Challenges Holism

A holistic perspective on abused children was evident in all interviews undertaken in the study. Several child welfare caseworkers explained how an abused child is more than just the abuse, and it is important to have a holistic perspective in cases of child abuse. "*It [the abuse] fits into a set of events in the child's life and the abuse is only a part of it*" (Interview 1). The acknowledgement that the abuse is only one of many problems in an abused child's life makes it very important for the child welfare caseworkers to be able to work with the complete child.

Many caseworkers described positive expectations regarding the establishment of Barnahus. One child welfare caseworker stated that "*the establishment sends an important signal that child abuse is not acceptable*", and this gives the child welfare caseworkers an increased incentive to act on suspicions of child abuse (Interview 7). Several child welfare caseworkers also explained that the establishment of Barnahus gives them more confidence because they know there is a place where they can ask for help and advice. One caseworker said: "*We actually have these world champions in child abuse who we can work together with*" (Interview 3). There is consequently no doubt that the child welfare caseworkers had high expectations about the establishment of Barnahus and the ability of the Barnahus staff to assist the local child welfare services in their handling of cases of child abuse. The child welfare services were also very satisfied with the advice and help they received from Barnahus.

Despite an acknowledgement that the concentration of expertise leads to a higher level of knowledge and expertise, and that the quality of the services from Barnahus is very high, about half of the child welfare services participating in the qualitative study argued that the centralisation has negative side effects related to the holistic understanding of social work. One concern is that the concentration of expertise in Barnahus may drain the knowledge of local child welfare services about cases of child abuse. One child welfare caseworker said outright:

> One disadvantage with the Barnahus is the centralisation. You move resources and competences away from the child welfare services (Interview 3).

Another said:

> The thought of securing a systematic approach in these cases is good but securing the expertise within the child welfare services instead of

centralizing it outside the child welfare services could have been considered (Interview 1).

Since the handling of an abused child is moved away from child welfare services to Barnahus, some child welfare caseworkers fear that there will be fewer and fewer employees in the child welfare services who actually have experience in dealing with abuse cases. They fear that a weakening of local expertise in child abuse will affect the ability of child welfare caseworkers to work holistically, because there is a risk that the focus on child abuse will be downgraded due to inadequate knowledge. Viewed from a holistic perspective, the consequence may be a sort of reductionist approach to the child, where issues of abuse are ignored, and this is not in line with a holistic perspective. This can make it more difficult to detect and expose new cases of abuse since signs of child abuse are in danger of being overlooked or ignored by the local child welfare services. An unintended negative effect could be that fewer abused children actually receive the help they need.

There is a dilemma here between holism and reductionism. The child welfare caseworkers, who work holistically, need to have knowledge about child abuse in order to do their job properly; however, it is important to recognise that half of the child welfare services interviewed did not make a direct connection between the centralisation of expertise and their ability to work holistically[4].

Improvement in Cooperation with Other Public Agencies

The child welfare services greatly appreciate the close cooperation with the police which was established in relation to Barnahus and to a certain degree administered by Barnahus.

What we experience as a positive effect of this is that the cooperation with the police and the sharing of information has become much better. All of a sudden we get a lot more information about the family which we can use when we continue the work with the family afterwards (Interview 2).

As part of the legislative assault package mentioned in the introduction, which included the establishment of Barnahus, child welfare services now have the legal right to share information about cases across different public agencies. Several child welfare caseworkers explicitly emphasise the added value of cooperating and sharing information with the police, but information can also be shared with hospitals and other medical agencies. The right to share information is not a direct consequence of the establishment of Barnahus; however, Barnahus coordinates the meetings where information is exchanged and the meetings often take place in Barnahus, which provides Barnahus with an obvious role in this improvement of cooperation. "*The sharing of knowledge has really meant a lot. It is easier to hold on to cases and follow them, when you have more information*", one child welfare caseworker argued (Interview 2). The sharing of information consequently strengthens the ability to work holistically with abused children.

Dilemmas of Involving the Police

Although the close cooperation with other public agencies is greatly appreciated, some child welfare caseworkers see a dilemma in the involvement of the police because it can result in the fragmentation of social work with the family. Involving the police often means pressing charges, and sometimes, the child welfare caseworkers feel that involving the police clashes with the best interests of the child. The dilemma is that when the police are contacted about the suspicion of a crime against a child, the legal system steps in, child investigative interviews are conducted, and the alleged abuser and perhaps others are interviewed by the police. At times, the conclusion of these interviews is that there is not enough evidence to actually press charges, or the public attorney does not believe that a trial will end in a conviction, so the case is dismissed. If this happens, the whole family has been disrupted and the child welfare services have to continue working with the family in order to ensure the well-being of the child. One caseworker argued that "*It may not be a case for the legal system, but there is something in the family which they need help with*" (Interview 7). Another caseworker said "*Our goal is to help this child. The Barnahus can help us [if the police is contacted], but sometimes the best thing is not to press charges*" (Interview 5).

The predicament is that according to the legislation establishing Barnahus, a Barnahus cannot get involved if there is only one public agency involved in the case. If the child welfare services do not involve the police (which is the second public agency in most cases), the case cannot involve Barnahus. This again means that the child welfare services in the municipalities do not have access to the expertise offered in Barnahus, and this becomes an unintended effect of this predicament. Sometimes, the child welfare services would like to obtain guidance, assistance and psychological treatment in cases that they see as being in a grey zone, cases that should not be tried in a court of law, but where a child shows signs of failure to thrive and the municipality has to deal with the family. This poses a dilemma which is related to the opposition between holism and the reductionism of specialised knowledge. On the one hand, the child welfare services appreciate the opportunity to receive assistance from experts with knowledge about child abuse. On the other hand, the legal framework of Barnahus states that it is necessary to involve the police or health services in order to involve Barnahus in the case. Involving the police is often very important, but in some cases, the child welfare caseworkers found that involving the police and engaging with all the legal issues of interrogation was the wrong way to deal with a particular child and the child's family.

> It is against the law to hit your child, but should the police be contacted when a child says something or only when the child has bruises, because then the police has evidence? Or should the police be contacted because you think it will help the child if the parents are punished? Sometimes when I contact the police, they are also in doubt (Interview 5).

Approaching the family from a holistic perspective and looking at the strengths and potential of the family may be a more constructive way of working with the family, according to the child welfare caseworkers.

Conflicting Approaches to Working with the Family

The acknowledgement that abuse is one of several problems in an abused child's life, makes it very important for the child welfare caseworkers to be able to work with the child. In many child welfare services, this implies working with the whole family, not just the child. This is especially difficult in cases of child abuse, since many cases of abuse take place within the family or the child's immediate circle of trust. "*Of course there are families where someone from the outside has abused the child but the majority of cases happen within the family*" (Interview 8). Several caseworkers, however, argue that working with the whole family is not an integrated part of the work in a Danish Barnahus.

> The coordination is around the child but the child is part of a unit called a family. When the child welfare services look at the whole picture, it [the case in Barnahus] becomes a bit fragmented compared to how we deal with the family. We cannot take care only of the child. It is not in the interest of the child if we don't take care of the family (Interview 6).

The interviews indicate that there may be a tension between the approach of child welfare services and that of Barnahus in working with the families. Several child welfare services argue that the extent of work in Barnahus is sometimes too narrowly defined, because their focus is exclusively on the abused child. The child welfare caseworkers find it challenging that Barnahus does not work holistically with the child and the child's family. "*If the whole family received a collective offer of help [from Barnahus] then it would make sense, when we work to heal the family again*" (Interview 6). This statement shows how child welfare services are focused on working with the child and its family rather than just the child. It was not expressed as an intended critique of Barnahus, but rather as an expression of frustration because the perspective and focus of Barnahus do not match the perspective of the child welfare caseworker. A Swedish book on Barnahus describes how the cooperation between all relevant professionals in a Barnahus will lead to "*an unbroken chain of support where the child and its parents receive the help they need*" (Landberg 2009, 79, author's translation). This description of an unbroken chain is in many ways what many Danish child welfare caseworkers are asking for, but the chain appears to have weak links because the child welfare services do not feel that the whole family receives all the help they need in Barnahus.

Concluding Discussion: Common Agenda, Different Perspectives

The simple but also multifaceted answer to the research question of how the establishment of Barnahus has affected the ability of child welfare services to work holistically is that it has affected them in several ways. The core elements of multiple professionals working together on a case, as in Barnahus, is in some ways an example of holistic social work because the child's case is viewed from several angles. The centralisation of expertise in cases of child abuse in Barnahus has clear advantages because it can provide the caseworkers with room to engage more holistically with the case at hand. Conversely, the centralisation of expertise is viewed by some as a weakness, because it drains the local child welfare services of knowledge on child abuse which may lead to a fragmentation in the treatment of the cases. Barnahus and the legislation implementing Barnahus provide productive closer cooperation between public agencies, which improves the ability to work holistically with the child. At the same time, the mandatory involvement of the police or health services in order for Barnahus to become involved leads to dilemmas about how to best protect the interest of the child, because sometimes the best interest of the child is not to involve the police. Finally, the holistic perspective means that child welfare caseworkers wish to work with the whole family which is not possible within the framework of the legislation initiating the Danish Barnahus. Consequently, child welfare caseworkers at times disagree with the focus of Barnahus. Analysed from the theoretical perspective of holistic social work, the conclusion is that while Barnahus contributes to holistic social work with abused children, Barnahus and the child welfare services do not embrace the same type of holistic approach to abused children. While Barnahus has an organisational holistic perspective, child welfare services have a more comprehensive child-centred holistic perspective.

The divergent perspectives on holism can be illustrated using a metaphor. Treating abused children in Barnahus is like using a pair of binoculars to view the child. Barnahus zooms in on the case of abuse and sees certain parts of the child and the child's problems clearly and in detail. Barnahus staff all see the same problem, and from this perspective, it is possible to initiate treatment and procedures to deal with the problem in focus. As long as the binoculars can retain this focus, the problem is dealt with in the best possible way. The initiatives in Barnahus are greatly appreciated and are of high quality, which is acknowledged by the child welfare services responsible for the children's well-being.

However, a large part of the child and the child's problems cannot be seen when zooming in with the binoculars. The majority of the child and the child's difficulties are outside the perspective of the binoculars. The child welfare services work closely with the child and the family and they do not use binoculars, but try to see all of the children in front of them. Child welfare services can consequently see problems and nuances that are outside the scope of Barnahus binoculars. Child welfare services see the problems that are addressed in Barnahus but they often also see a wider picture. They view this wider, more holistic perspective on the child as very important in work with abused children, and while they appreciate the knowledge obtained by using binoculars, they also argue that blocking out large parts of the child's life has unintended consequences for their social work with the abused child and its family.

Some of the differences between Barnahus and child welfare services in Denmark are not just theoretical but practical. The Danish Barnahus has been given specific tasks with a specific budget to fulfil these tasks. It is, for instance, not within the statute of Barnahus to offer services to the child in relation to problems other than the abuse, nor is it possible to offer actual family counselling or a larger degree of family support; however, these frameworks for the work undertaken within Barnahus are not necessarily unchangeable. Barnahus in Denmark is still a young institution, and the experiences of Barnahus are being continuously gathered in order to improve the help given to abused children (Ankestyrelsen 2015; Børnerådet 2015; Socialstyrelsen 2015). It is very important to include the perspective of the local child welfare services in discussions about an elaboration of the mandate of Barnahus in Denmark. Offering specialised help on one particular subject (the abuse) is exactly what Barnahus is meant to do, according to the legislation establishing Barnahus. At the same time, the local child welfare services continue to hold overall responsibility for the well-being of the child, implying a holistic approach. Barnahus and the child welfare services thus have a common agenda of helping children but different perspectives on how to implement and improve the assistance to abused children.

Notes

1. One exception is Johansson (2008), which looked at the external cooperation of Barnahus during the pilot of the Swedish Barnahus.
2. An alternative form of Barnahus involvement is through consultative cases. These are cases where child welfare services contact Barnahus and ask for advice, but the interaction does not lead to an actual Barnahus case. The cases included in this chapter are actual Barnahus cases.
3. In Denmark, a child welfare study is called a §50 study due to the section in the legislation (LBK no. 1284 17/11/2015) authorising the study.
4. Theories of holism and reductionism cannot explain all the wariness about the centralisation of expertise. Other aspects, such as a discussion of independence and autonomy between local authorities and the central government of Denmark (see, for instance, Bømler 2012), can play its own part in comments on centralisation and loss of local expertise (Bømler 2012).

References

Ankestyrelsen. 2015. *Evaluering Af overgrebspakken.* Copenhagen. Retrieved from http://sim.dk/media/1001951/ankestyrelsens_unders_gelse_af_evaluering_af_overgrebspakken.pdf.

Bømler, Tina. 2012. Fra specialisering og tilbage til specialisering: Organisering af socialt arbejde i kommunerne. *En kort historisk, sociologisk baggrundsanalyse* 13(24): 4–13.

Børnerådet. 2015. *Erfaringsopsamling: Børns oplevelser af børnehusene.* Børnenotat 2/15. (April): 15.

Conte, Jon. 2014. *Child Abuse and Neglect Worldwide*. Retrieved from http://kbdk.eblib.com/patron/FullRecord.aspx?p=1693459.

Damsgaard, Signe and Michael Ørtz Christiansen. 2012. *Regionale børnehuse til misbrugte børn høster ros.* Berlingske Nyhedsbrev.

Ejrnæs, Morten, and Jens Guldager. 2008. *Helhedssyn og forklaring i sociologi, socialt, sundhedsfagligt og pædagogisk arbejde*. København: Akademisk Forlag.

Ferguson, Iain. 2008. *Reclaiming Social Work: Challenging Neo-Liberalism and Promoting Social Justice*. Los Angeles: Sage Publications.

Glassow, Trine. 2015. Socialt arbejde med børn og unge udsat for seksuelle overgreb - en praksisnær grundforståelse. In *socialt arbejde med børn, unge og familier*, eds. Maiken Hougaard, and Lisbeth Ravn Højbjerg, 453–477. København: Hans Reitzel.

Guldager, Jens. 2015. Helhedssyn - teori og modeller på børnefamilieområdet. In *Udsatte børn - et helhedsperspektiv*, eds. Karen-Asta Bo, Jens Guldager, and Birgitte Zeeberg, 16–59. København: Akademisk.

Harder, Margit. 2011. Helhedssyn - et begrebs udvikling In *Helhedssyn i socialt arbejde, Professionsserien*, eds. Margit Harder, and Maria A. Nissen, 288. Kbh.: Akademisk Forlag.

Johansson, Susanna. 2008. *Myndighetssamverkan i barnahus – organisering, innehåll och process. Delrapport 4 i utvärderingen av nationell försöksverksamhet med barnahus 2006–2007*. Research Report in Sociology of Law. vol. 4. Sociology of Law, Lund University.

Johansson, Susanna. 2012. Diffusion and Governance of 'Barnahus' in the Nordic Countries: Report from an On-Going Project. *Journal of Scandinavian Studies in Criminology and Crime Prevention* 13 (sup1): 69–84.

Kvale, Steinar. 2007. *Doing Interviews*. Retrieved from https://www.statsbiblioteket.dk/au/#/search?query=recordID%3A%22sb_4346788%22. Los Angeles: Sage Publications.

Landberg, Åsa. 2009. *Boken om barnahus: Samverkan med barnet i centrum*, 1. uppl. Stockholm: Gothia.

Laursen, Finn. 2011. Mennesket fra alle sider - Helhedssyn i et figurationsperspektiv. In *Helhedssyn i socialt arbejde, Professionsserien*, eds. Margit Harder, and Maria Appel Nissen, 111–130. København: Akademisk Forlag.

Lægsgaard, Mett Marri and Lene Mosegaard Søbjerg. 2012. Evaluering og effektmåling af gruppebehandling for børn/unge, der har været udsat for seksuelle overgreb. *Midtvejsrapport*. Aarhus: CFK—Center for Kvalitetsudvikling.

Rittel, Horst W. J. and Melvin M. Webber. 1973. Dilemmas in a General Theory of Planning. *Policy Sciences* 4(2): 155–169.

Socialstyrelsen. 2015. *Erfaringsopsamling af børnehusene*. Socialstyrelsen, September 2015 http://socialstyrelsen.dk/udgivelser/erfaringsopsamling-af-de-danske-bornehuse.

Stefansen, Kari, Tonje Gundersen, and Elisiv Bakketeig. 2012. *Barnehusevalueringen 2012*. Delrapport 2. Oslo: NOVA.

Sundhedsstyrelsen. 2012. *Etablering af børnehuse i Danmark - Styrkede rammer for det tværfaglige og tværsektorielle samarbejde i sager om overgreb mod børn*. Retrieved from http://www.sst.dk/publ/Publ2012/10okt/EtablBoernehuseDK.pdf.

Uggerhøj, Lars. 2011. Kan helhedssyn ligesom kartofler gå til det hele? Om helhedssyn og perspektiver i socialt arbejde. In *Helhedssyn i socialt arbejde, Professionsserien*, eds. Margit Harder, and Maria Appel Nissen, 239–264. København: Akademisk Forlag.

15

Adult Victims and the Barnahus Model

Anja Bredal and Kari Stefansen

Introduction

The idea of a "Barnahus for adults" was launched by the Norwegian government in 2013 (Ministry of Justice and Public Security 2013). Two years later, Project November, as it is called, officially opened in Oslo. Based in a police station, this pilot project is inspired by both the Barnahus model and a Swedish multi-agency model for adult and child victims of domestic violence, called Project Karin. As a case of diffusion and translation, Project November thus cuts across both age and national borders. As with the Barnahus model, the overall aim is to improve social and legal interventions through increased multi-agency and multi-professional collaboration. In this chapter, we describe how

A. Bredal (✉) · K. Stefansen
Norwegian Social Research, Oslo and Akershus University College of Applied Sciences, Oslo, Norway
e-mail: anja.bredal@nova.hioa.no

K. Stefansen
e-mail: kari.stefansen@nova.hioa.no

this Norwegian project has developed during the early phase of its implementation. What kind of collaborative model does November set out to be, and how are these ideas negotiated and brought into practice? The key purpose of this chapter is to identify challenges in terms of reinterpreting the Barnahus model to accommodate adult victims of domestic violence in the current landscape of policies and measures against domestic violence in Norway. This analysis of Project November may highlight important issues to consider for the implementation of other types of collaborative models, such as the Barnahus model. The discussion will be linked to theoretical concepts on multi-agency and multi-professional collaboration (Atkinson et al. 2007).

The chapter is based on results from the first part of an ongoing process evaluation of the November project.[1] Empirically, we draw on different types of data: Written material that includes initial project plans describing the model and process documents from the implementation phase and qualitative interviews with 21 key stakeholders and operative personnel within November. The interview material is central to our analysis but as anonymisation is complicated, we will refrain from direct quotations.

Conceptual Framework

In both Norway and Sweden, a key motivation for the original Barnahus models as well as the subsequent models for adults, November and Karin, was to facilitate coordination between the different agencies and services involved in police-reported incidents of violence and sexual abuse. The concept of inter- or multi-agency collaboration is often used to explain such models (for instance, Johansson 2011, 2012); however, the meaning of multi-agency collaboration is rarely spelled out. Several scholars point to the confusing terminology used to describe collaborative arrangements and multi-agency activity, which makes classification and comparison difficult (Atkinson et al. 2007; Percy-Smith 2006; Blacklock and Phillips 2015). Different researchers use words such as partnership, joined-up, coordinated, integrated, co-located, and more for such arrangements. We also note that the concepts linked to multi-agency collaboration are all positively connoted. Multi-agency work can, of course, result in professional competition and conflict, and the analysis also needs to be sensitive to this (see Johansson, Chap. 16 in this book).

Atkinson et al.'s (2007) differentiation between multi-agency and multi-professional working is fruitful for our purpose. According to their definitions, *multi-agency* or *cross-agency working* represents situations where professionals from more than one agency work together, and service is provided by agencies acting in concert and drawing on pooled resources or pooled budgets. *Multi-professional* or *multidisciplinary working* denotes situations where staff of different professions, background and training work together within the same agency. Our question then relates to how the Barnahus model, Project Karin and Project November may be classified according to these concepts.

Given that Project November is inspired by two other collaborative models, Barnahus and Project Karin, the implementation of November can be seen as an act of translation (cf. Johansson 2012). It is an example of how organisational ideas circulate or travel between actors and places. Czarniawska and colleagues designated the study of such processes as the "sociology of translation" (in Røvik 2016, 291). A key understanding from this perspective is that ideas are transformed while being transferred from one organisational context to another. From this perspective, Barnahus and Karin represent "source" models, meaning organisations that are "performing a practice and possessing knowledge about it that someone attempts to transfer to another organisation (recipient unit)" (Røvik 2016, 290). Project November represents the recipient unit in this framework. Røvik points to the need for process data to capture what happens to ideas after their formal adoption, suggesting that ideas are shaped and reshaped as part of implementation processes. Local translations often lead to the emergence of new versions, and significant variation in structures, routines and practices (Røvik 2016, 291). In terms of Project November, such variation could be expected given that the project was designated from the beginning as a pilot version of two different, albeit linked, institutional models for inter-agency working.

The analysis in this chapter will focus on two interrelated processes of reinterpretation: the translation of two related, but in some respects different, source models for multi-agency collaboration, and the translation of such models across different national contexts, as well as different target groups. First, however, the next section briefly presents the two source models, Barnahus and the Karin, followed by an outline of the Norwegian context.

Background

The Source Models: Barnahus and Project Karin

As noted, Project November originates in the current national action plan against domestic violence (Ministry of Justice and Public Security 2013). In both the plan as well as in the main project documents, the project is described as a "Barnahus for adults" on the one hand and as a Norwegian pilot version of the Karin model on the other.

As explained in more depth in other chapters of this book, the remit of a Norwegian Barnahus is to facilitate and coordinate the process of forensic documentation in cases where there is a suspicion that a child has witnessed or been the victim of violence or sexual abuse. A core idea is to bring the relevant professionals together under one roof and in a child-friendly setting. Other core activities include the child investigative interview performed by specially trained police personnel and medical examinations by specialist doctors and nurses from cooperating paediatric departments. Barnahus staff coordinate the process and provide follow-up/treatment on a short-term basis, and work with child welfare services to ensure seamless referral to local agencies.

The Norwegian Barnahus model includes a permanent staff of psychologists and social workers, and police investigators, medical staff and representatives of child welfare services and other agencies are present on a case-by-case basis. This is in contrast to the Swedish Barnahus model, where child welfare services are part of the Barnahus organisation (cf. Bakketeig, Chap. 13). Through the use of link workers, it is nevertheless a coordinating facility. The Swedish Barnahus thus qualifies as a multi-agency model in Atkinson et al.'s (2007) understanding of this as more than one agency working together with pooled budgets. The Norwegian Barnahus, on the other hand, cannot be considered a fully developed multi-agency model in this sense. Multi-professional working seems to be a more applicable categorisation. Still, the model involves some sense of bringing together agencies through the provision of a common physical space and collaborative routines. As pointed out in the introductory chapter and by Johansson in Chap. 12, the Norwegian Barnahus organisation is perhaps most accurately described as a multi-professional competence centre. Institutionally and in terms of budgets, Norwegian Barnahus belong to the relevant police districts and are most often located in separate buildings, although a few are part of a police station.

Project Karin in Malmö Sweden on the other hand has a broader remit than the Barnahus, in terms of both target groups and organisational structure. It is a police station that specialises in helping women, men and children who are the victims of violence or sexual abuse by a closely related person. The project also supports children who have witnessed violence, and it can assist people who have been reported to the police (suspected perpetrators). Notably, in terms of being a collaborative model, Karin is the result of a joining of forces by two specialist units working with domestic violence in the municipality of Malmö: one in social services and one in the police force. As social workers and criminal investigators respectively, they have retained their affiliation with their mother institutions, but at Karin they collaborate closely and liaise with other organisations and public authorities. Shelter services for adults and a children's service similar to Barnahus are also organised in conjunction with Project Karin (BRÅ 2013). The physical environment is designed to create an atmosphere of security and comfort, much like the Barnahus (see Stefansen, Chap. 2). In other words, Karin is a more comprehensive, and in some respects more self-sufficient, model than the Barnahus in terms of target groups, facilities and services offered in one location. As personnel are employed in two different agencies (social services and police), it qualifies as a multi-agency model in Atkinson et al.'s (2007) terminology.

The Norwegian Context: Public Policies and Services in the Field of Domestic Violence

Following years of awareness raising and capacity building, the current government action plan (2014–2017) confirms that domestic violence has become a mainstream policy issue and that service provisions are in place. According to the plan, the main challenge is now to improve coordination between services and agencies, creating a more coherent and efficient chain of services. Testing a multi-agency model inspired both by Project Karin in Sweden and by Norwegian Barnahus is among the measures introduced in the plan.

Other previous and recent reforms include a system of special domestic violence coordinators in the police districts (from 2002), the introduction of Barnahus (from 2007), municipal action plans and a law on shelters for victims of domestic violence (implemented in 2010, see Bakketeig et al. 2014). The shelter law is particularly relevant to our analysis of Project November as a translation of collaborative models in a new context, as from 2010 it is a statutory municipal duty in Norway to provide shelter services to victims of domestic violence, irrespective of gender. This special law goes beyond shelter services in the traditional meaning of a safe house for victims in need of immediate protection and peer support, however (Stefansen 2006). In fact, the law sets out a comprehensive range of duties for local authorities, including the following services, all free of charge: a 24-h telephone helpline, shelter or equivalent safe, temporary accommodation, a day service including support and counselling, and assistance during the re-establishment phase. The latter includes guidance in establishing contact with social services and other relevant agencies. In providing such services, the law obliges municipal authorities to pay special attention to children's needs and, most notably in the context of this chapter, to coordinate different services. This coordination duty is closely connected to municipal action plans that are not mandatory, but strongly encouraged by central authorities and supported by guidelines. In sum, these policies mean that the role of Norwegian shelters is considerably different from shelters in Sweden and other European countries, where they more often belong to the third sector. In a Norwegian context, domestic violence shelters have become part of the public sector on a par with other contracted services. In fact, the majority of shelters are today run by municipalities (Bakketeig et al. 2014).

Major achievements notwithstanding, there is considerable diversity among public agencies regarding domestic violence competence and priorities. While the police force has made considerable progress, the health and social services are often claimed to be less informed about and sensitive to issues of domestic violence (Grøvdal et al. 2014). Shelters vary, however, in their evaluation of collaboration with social services. Collaboration is rated as good in some municipalities and as difficult in others (Bakketeig et al. 2014). All in all Project November was introduced into a complex institutional landscape of already existing service provisions for adult victims of domestic violence. A key question we address in this chapter involves the extent to which this is recognised in the translation and implementation process of the model.

Analysis

Project November

Initiated as a measure in the national action plan against domestic violence, the overall aim of Project November is to provide better, more holistic and coordinated services to adult female and male victims of domestic violence. From the ministry's point of view, the idea was to bring agencies together "under one roof", allowing victims to access services through "one door" (see Chap. 1), or as in the wording of the plan, in the same locality:

> Establishing "Karin" (Barnahus for adults) as a pilot project. A collaborative project equivalent to Karin in Malmø, where the police and other agencies offer assistance to victims of violence in the same locality, will be tried out. (The Ministry of Justice and Public Security, 2013, p. 28)

In terms of aims, there are clear resemblances to the Barnahus model and the discussions prior to implementation. A multi-agency project group worked together to design the model in the preliminary phase, but the project was placed firmly within the police sector with only limited participation from the municipality in the steering group.

Project November is set in Stovner police station, which houses the centralised family domestic violence unit of the Oslo police district. It is located in a designated part of the police station building that has been designed specifically for this purpose, including a room dedicated to investigative interviews with audiovisual equipment and with an adjacent co-hearing room. Aesthetically, the furniture and interior decoration have much in common with the Oslo Barnahus (see Chap. 2) and Karin, described above, and it is very different from the other parts of the police station.

So far, the November staff consists of seven people who have been recruited specifically for the project. All are employed in the police district. The staff is divided into two teams: a police team with two police specialists in domestic violence risk analysis and a psycho-social team with two social workers (one clinical specialist and one with experience in the social services) and a psychologist. It should be noted that the Oslo police distinguish between risk analysis on the one hand and criminal investigation on the other, in order to cultivate risk management as separate expertise. In contrast to Karin then, police investigators are not included as such, but the November staff cooperate with investigators and prosecutors from the regular police station. The project is headed by a police leader, assisted by the leader of the psycho-social team.

The psycho-social staff partly assist the police and partly work on their own initiative. In particular, the psychologists, but also social workers, assist the police in risk assessments of perpetrators. In other words, one added value of November is directly related to improving police work. The psycho-social support that was previously offered to some extent by the police is now taken care of by specially trained social workers. In this sense, Project November relieves the police of their workload and thus contributes to freeing more time for investigative and preventive work.

In addition to assisting the police team in risk assessments, the psycho-social team engages in a range of victim support and counselling, including outreach work. They provide psycho-social support, stabilise victims in acute situations, inform them about the police process, give advice on how to approach other agencies, assist and follow them to the social services and housing offices, and in short do advocacy work in line with common definitions. Hoyle and Palmer (2014, 14), for instance, offer this definition of advocates: "Advocates 'direct, guide, and support battered women while confronting and challenging obstacles to their safety (Shepard 1999, 115)'. They counsel, provide access to resources, represent victims in other institutional settings, such as the court, but more importantly they help women to better understand their options and how to make choices." In this sense, the advocacy work of the November staff resembles the advocacy work of the staff at domestic violence shelters (see Bakketeig et al. 2014). A central concern for the November staff is to motivate victims to file a police report and to contribute to the investigation and punitive process. Victims who are not yet part of a criminal investigation can obtain information and motivational support.

If cases involve children, either as victims of, or witnesses to, violence, they are referred to the Oslo Barnahus according to ordinary procedures. Perpetrators, on the other hand, are part of Project November's target group, in contrast to Norwegian Barnahus but similarly to Project Karin. The tasks relating to perpetrators include motivating them to seek treatment, typically in terms of anger management and treatment for alcohol and substance abuse. The psychologist and the clinical social worker also offer short-term treatment sessions, and the psychologist refers victims to the psychiatric services and perpetrators to specialist therapy for perpetrators of domestic violence.[2]

In sum, there is no doubt that November represents a more extensive support service for victims and perpetrators, than the ordinary police station, and in particular in terms of social work. One example described in an interview at November is that of a woman whose former partner had been violent and had also taken out loans in her name. A police report was filed, and he had violated his restraining orders. The social worker at November spent a considerable amount of time asking different creditors to freeze these loans pending the police investigation. There was also a general consensus among the staff that social services were particularly important but also reluctant to take on domestic violence as part of their expertise and remit, much in line with Grøvdal et al.'s (2014) findings.

Victims of domestic violence are also offered more qualified psycho-social support in the context of a police investigation and, to some extent, beyond. Our interviewees from the psycho-social team stressed the benefits of having more time at their disposal. They could offer repeat contact at the same place, instead of having to refer victims to other agencies and risk them dropping out on the way.

Overall, the November staff has a wider remit than the ordinary domestic violence police in that they are less restricted by the priority of severe and police-reported cases. The staff explained that cases which would otherwise be thought to fall outside the police priorities were "picked up" by them, including what are typically termed "difficult" or "lost" cases, such as those involving episodic and bilateral violence patterns in conjunction with alcohol abuse, for example.

In their typology of different collaborative models, Atkinson et al. (2007) differentiate between three dimensions of multi-agency activity: organisation, joint investment and integration. In terms of organisation, Project November is funded by one agency, the Ministry of Justice and Public Security, through the Police Directorate, and it is owned and managed by the same source. In this sense, the project is thus not multi-agency. In terms of joint investment, there have so far been limited efforts to create links with and to commit agencies outside the police. Integration is low in relation to other agencies but high within the project itself. The multi-professional staff work closely together on a day-to-day basis involving a mutual exchange of knowledge and skills. There is a flexible division of tasks, such as when it comes to the role as the main contact for a victim or perpetrator, and professional roles may overlap to a certain extent.

In short, the ambition of offering victims one door into the coordinated services of multiple agencies that are co-located under one roof has not (yet) materialised. November is not a multi-agency model in the sense of bringing agencies together and pooling resources. In Atkinson et al.'s (2007) terms, it is more a case of multi-professional or multi-disciplinary collaboration. At this stage of the implementation, there is thus a question of whether and how to proceed in terms of multi-agency integration. It seems that Project November will have to choose between moving towards a more truly integrated inter-agency model and settling with being a multi-professional support centre for adults involved in police cases about domestic violence, be they criminal cases or risk management cases.

In Karin, by contrast, social workers are employed in the municipal social service. Moreover, Karin offers a more extensive service in that they are co-located with a shelter and a version of Barnahus. As an inter-agency model, November thus seems to be more similar to the Norwegian Barnahus than to the Karin Project in Malmö.

Key Challenges for a "Barnahus for Adults"

So far then, we have established that Project November is a multi-professional support centre for adult victims and perpetrators of domestic violence in a police context. This model is still a preliminary outcome of a translation process in the making; however, the first phase of implementation has brought some key issues of general interest for the translation of practices that are complex, partly tacit and embedded in local structures. In the following discussion, we will focus on two sets of interrelated challenges.

Translating Across National Borders: Issues of Particular Contexts

Scholarship on multi-agency working stresses the need to be clear about roles and to conduct a needs analysis (Atkinson et al. 2007, 44–45). Analyses of needs should be context specific and may include questions such as: What is the particular need or gap to be filled? Who are the potential collaborating partners and are there any competitors or overlaps?

In the case of Karin, that particular model grew out of the process of developing a municipal action plan against domestic violence (BRÅ 2013). The Malmö municipality already had a specialised domestic violence police station on the one hand and a special unit for domestic violence within the social services on the other. Establishing Karin involved bringing these two specialist parts of two agencies together to create a multi-agency facility. In Norway, the Barnahus model was introduced by national authorities, but after much lobbying and pressure from NGOs, politicians and professionals (Bakketeig et al. 2012; Stefansen et al. 2012; Chap. 16 in this book). In the policy field of violence and abuse against children, there seems to have been a consensus that a coordinating mechanism was lacking. Barnahus thus filled a void, in terms of both providing enhanced and specialised police procedures and functioning as a multi-agency coordinating mechanism for the follow-up phase after the police interview.

The process in November has been more top-down and may prove to become more contentious. As already noted, the initiative came from the Ministry of Justice and Public Security, and the Oslo municipality was not involved until later and so far only to a limited extent. Norwegian municipalities are strongly encouraged to develop action plans against domestic violence as a key coordinating tool. In Oslo's case, there is both an overall plan for the city in general and local plans for all fifteen boroughs, reflecting the considerable degree of decentralised self-government in the Norwegian municipal system. The overall municipal action plan mentions November only briefly, under the heading "Cooperation with the police" (Oslo Municipality 2014, 8), and notes a health agency as the main coordinating agency for adult domestic violence cases, the Emergency Social and Medical Team, which is part of the Oslo municipal emergency ward (Sosial og ambulant vakttjeneste, Oslo legevakt) (Ibid., page 9). At the central municipal level in Oslo, there is, however, another specialist agency, the Oslo domestic violence shelter. Both the shelter and the Emergency Social and Medical team are 24/7 services and both are, to some extent, given coordinating roles in relation to adult victims of domestic violence. In other words, Project November was introduced into a local context which already had certain structures for coordination and where there seemed to be some degree of tension built into these structures. To illustrate the significance of such pre-existing structural conditions, we will use the shelter as an example.

The Oslo domestic violence shelter was established in 1978 as a refuge run by volunteers and based on the idea of peer support, but later developed into a professional support centre for domestic violence victims (Bakketeig et al. 2014; Jonassen and Stefansen 2003; Laugerud 2014; Stefansen 2006). Today, it consists of a residential section for women and an outpatient section providing counselling, advocacy and courses as well as a 24/7 telephone line. There are also three special accommodation units: one for young women exposed to honour-based violence, one for female victims of trafficking and a separate unit for male victims (Bakketeig et al. 2014). The shelter is in charge of their own intake procedure and has contracted working agreements with the municipal social services in all boroughs. According to these agreements, each social service office assigns a special liaison person to cooperate with the shelter. This coordinating arrangement follows from the shelter's role as Oslo's statutory municipal shelter provision, based on a 10-year contract in keeping with the shelter law noted above.

This role as a comprehensive public service provider is still relatively new, however, and in the shelter's own opinion, they have not yet been fully acknowledged by other municipal agencies. There is, for instance, limited reference to the shelter in the municipal action plan. In fact, there seems to be a certain tension between the role assigned to Oslo municipal emergency ward and the statutory role of the shelter. Moreover, there may seem to be some lingering prejudice associated with the shelter's NGO and self-help past, as well as a certain understanding that some women do not want to use the shelter.

Overall, these particular circumstances mean that the establishing of November coincides with a somewhat fluid situation when it comes to the roles of already existing specialist agencies in Oslo and to the question of coordination. Such structural circumstances could imply that existing agencies may see November as a competitor and not (only) as a partner. When it comes to the more generalist agencies, such as the social services, the structure of relevant municipal and state partners for November is a conglomerate of centralised, semi-centralised and decentralised agencies. Within November, there is an ambition to establish cooperation agreements with the social services and housing that belong to the borough-based services. As noted, social services are considered especially important, but difficult to include into the chain of support for domestic violence victims. Compared to Barnahus in Norway, where the child welfare service is the equivalent agency, the duties of social services in connection with (adult) domestic violence seem to be less developed and acknowledged by the agency itself.

In Karin, the social services are an integrated part of the collaborative model. Social workers were drawn from, and have retained their employment in, social services. It is notable, however, that they do not have the authority to make decisions about social benefits or any other economic support. To claim such support, Karin's clients still have to approach their local social service office, albeit with the help from Karin's social workers. To this extent, November and Karin might not be so different after all, although November's social workers are part of the police, while Karin's liaise with colleagues. Nevertheless, the evaluators of the Karin model point to this particular element as a major limitation of such police-based models centred on the judicial process, which is only one part of the victim's process towards a life free of violence. They stress the need to develop additional, well-functioning systems that take over when the judicial process is finished. This includes, for instance, housing, economy, and the social area. The social services need to cultivate the kind of skills and organisation that, in addition to initial support, can provide help based on a decision to offer public assistance; otherwise, there is a risk that the efforts of Karin—and other similar organisations—will be a temporary relief but nothing more (BRÅ 2013, 31).

A central challenge, therefore, in the next stage of implementation, is whether November can develop new and innovative working relationships with the social services. What should the aim and division of work for such cooperation be, in view of the perceived reluctant attitude of the social services in cases of violence? Will the social services welcome cooperation as a way of being relieved of "difficult" cases, or will more cooperation result in more competent and adequate social services for this group?

Translating Across Age: Issues of Autonomy

The demarcation of both Norwegian Barnahus and Project Karin is in police-reported cases, while November has taken a more open approach and includes cases that are not yet reported and perhaps will not be. The issue of police reporting is not just a matter of priority, however. It evokes a more general question of victim autonomy that is central to the difference between a multi-agency model for children compared to one for adults. To put it very briefly, as far as children are concerned, the suspicion of violence or sexual abuse would always result in some kind of police involvement. In the case of domestic violence against adults, the question of police involvement is more open and contested.

Arguments for collaborative arrangements in tackling domestic violence against adults often refer to the challenge of breaking the cycle of abuse. It is argued that prosecution needs to be supplemented by other types of support in order to create sustainable change in the lives of victims and perpetrators lives. Adding civil to criminal remedies is both an aim in itself and a tool to increase conviction rates. Some see psycho-social support primarily as a tool to improve and enhance the punitive process, by motivating victims to cooperate with the police, giving evidence and remaining "cooperative" witnesses. Others argue that psycho-social support is needed to improve victim autonomy and choice about how they want to live their lives. The latter set of arguments is often framed in terms of victim empowerment (Hoyle and Palmer 2014). In discussing what an empowerment approach means in a domestic violence context, Hoyle and Palmer define it as helping clients to understand the choices that are available to them and to make informed choices, as well as supporting them in the choices they make. According to Hoyle and Palmer, empowerment thinking is still relatively rare within the criminal justice system. They claim that focus is more on "providing services in the interest of the victim", than engaging with victims about what they see as the best solution to their problems (Hoyle and Palmer 2014, 3).

Such issues of autonomy and choice were also raised in the interviews with November staff. One of the informants pointed to differences between the police and the psycho-social professions when it comes to approaching so-called reluctant victims. She explained that the police tend to be action oriented and impatient, sometimes to the extent that they want to make choices on behalf of the victim. In contrast, her psycho-social training inclined her to give the victim more time. She said that she encouraged her police colleagues to think of tackling witness reluctance as planting a seed. By working with the person over time, their wish to participate in the investigation and to leave the abuser will often become stronger, she claimed.

Reinterpreting Barnahus to accommodate adult victims should consider how victim autonomy may represent challenges that are different from those at Barnahus. As noted, suspicions of violence against children will involve a more clear-cut procedure of criminal investigation and police involvement. Of course there are also empowerment and autonomy issues when children are victims; however, agencies have a more unambiguous duty to intervene. The agencies are also not the same for child cases and adult cases, and their remits reflect the different status of children and adults as victims. For instance, child welfare services are not conditional in the same way as the economic support and housing benefits issued by the social services for adults. Such provisions are crucial elements when adult victims consider their options in relation to the perpetrator, to stay or to leave. Social workers and the psychologist may motivate and work with the victim to overcome psycho-social barriers to reporting the violence but this choice is also contingent on more concrete alternatives.

The view of autonomy could also imply that, in contrast to child victims, adult victims may want to choose between agencies, depending on their specific situation. Typically, some women prefer to seek refuge or advice at a shelter but refrain from involving the police. As the question of punitive intervention in domestic violence cases is still an ambivalent issue, it may thus be argued that issues of autonomy and choice favour a range of services and agencies that do not necessarily merge into one coordinated whole.

Discussion

It seems that November was based on a rather generalised notion of the problem of fragmentation and a correspondingly generalised idea of what was needed as a solution. The Ministry of Justice and Public

Security decided that the project be housed in a police station in Oslo, with very little analysis of needs or the consequences in the particular local context. In other words, it seems like a rather top-down initiative that was nevertheless given an enthusiastic welcome by police leadership, both at district and at police station level. The involvement of agencies outside the police, including the central municipal authorities and boroughs, as such, has been limited, however.

In taking the pilot project forward, it seems that a project like November has a choice between two models: the present multidisciplinary police station or a more truly multi-agency organisation. In the case of the latter, there seem to be two ways of achieving such collaborative arrangements. The most ambitious is a co-located facility where specially dedicated personnel from several agencies work together in the same physical space, offering victims "one door" in literal terms. This would take the model in the direction of Karin but ideally add decision-making authority for social benefit and housing issues. A less ambitious solution would be that November personnel cooperate with specially assigned personnel in other agencies who mainly remain physically in their localities but work closely with November on a case-by-case basis, as in the Barnahus model.

It appears that the more ambitious the multi-agency intentions, the stronger the need for an assessment of the particular local context in terms of existing collaborative structures and unmet needs. In the case of November, on the one hand there probably is a real void when it comes to coordination mechanisms and structures, in particular for bringing the social services on board. On the other hand, the void is not clearly defined and there are already other specialist agencies geared towards trying to fill it. Accordingly, if November opts for a fully fledged inter-agency model, there is a risk of duplication and competition.

Moving towards a multi-agency model would also raise the question of location. Why a police station? When the Norwegian Barnahus was established, as part of the police districts, a point was made about locating it separately from ordinary police work and at a central, convenient place for users (cf. Chap. 2). Barnahus is already an established competent organisation specialising in domestic violence cases and multi-agency work. One could envisage the existing Barnahus being extended and adapted to include adult victims, although that would entail a much broader regional scope than planned for November. On the other hand, as noted there are already considerable elements of coordination within the mandates of both the Oslo domestic violence shelter and the Oslo municipal emergency ward.

Our analysis of this reinterpretation process shows how the outcome is determined by a translation in two dimensions. The idea of a Barnahus for adults draws on two quite divergent inspirational sources, consisting of a range of elements that are included or excluded, reproduced or modified as they are adapted in the recipient unit. Some combinations of elements may seem more feasible or difficult than others. For instance, issues of autonomy and choice pose different challenges in a model targeted at adults, compared to one developed for child victims, and vice versa. On a more general note, it seems necessary to specify the type of collaborative model that is envisaged, in terms of the scope and level of collaboration. For instance, there is a choice between a multidisciplinary model within one agency or sector and a more comprehensive inter-agency model spanning multiple sectors. In particular, the latter will require extensive multi-sector support from the top and concrete adaptation on the ground. This actualises the second dimension, the varied contexts that surround and impact the source and recipient models. There should be an acute awareness towards the particular recipient context, especially in terms of existing collaborative structures and unmet needs; otherwise, introducing a new multi-agency framework without analysing the local setting may end up as duplicating and competing effort.

Notes

1. The process evaluation is conducted within the framework of the Domestic Violence Research Programme (2014–2019) at NOVA. The programme is financed by the Norwegian Ministry of Justice and Public Security.
2. Oslo has a specialist treatment centre for perpetrators of interpersonal violence, Alternative to Violence.

Acknowledgements The chapter is written as part of the Domestic violence research programme at NOVA, funded by the Ministry of Justice and Public Security. We would like to thank Susanna Johansson for her instructive comments on draft versions of this chapter.

References

Atkinson, Mary, Megan Jones, and Emily Lamont. 2007. *Multi-agency Working and its Implications for Practice. A Review of the Literature*. Reading: CfBT Education Trust.

Bakketeig, Elisiv, Mette Berg, Trond Myklebust, and Kari Stefansen. 2012. *Barnehusevalueringen 2012, delrapport 1: Barnehusmodellens implikasjoner for politiets arbeid med fokus på dommeravhør og rettsmedisinsk undersøkelse*. Oslo: PHS Forskning.

Bakketeig, Elisiv, Elisabeth Gording Stang, Christian Madsen, Ingrid Smette, and Kari Stefansen. 2014. *Krisesentertilbudet i kommunene*. NOVA: Evaluering av kommunenes implementering av krisesenterloven. Oslo.

Blacklock, Neiland, and Ruth Phillips. 2015. Reshaping the Child Protection Response to Domestic Violence through Collaborative Working. In *Domestic Violence and Protecting Children. New Thinking and Approaches Nicky Stanley and Cathy Humphreys*, ed. 196–213. London: Jessica Kingsley Publishers.

BRÅ. 2013. Utvärdering av koncept Karin. En samverkansmodell i Malmö för personer som utsatts för våld i nära relationer, Rapport 2013:8. Stockholm: Brottsförebyggande rådet.

Grøvdal, Yngvil, Randi Saur and Are R. Skaalerud. 2014. En velvillig og oppmerksom tilhører. Mennesker som har vært utsatt for vold og deres møte med hjelpeapparatet og politiet. Oslo: NKVTS.

Hoyle, Carolyn, and Nicola Palmer. 2014. Family Justice Centres: A Model for Empowerment? *International Review of Victimology* 20 (2): 191–210.

Johansson, Susanna. 2011. Juridifiering som institutionell förändring. Om mötet mellan straffrätt och socialrätt vid interorganisatorisk samverkan. *Nordic Journal of Law and Justice* 34 (135): 38–59.

Johansson, Susanna. 2012. Diffusion and Governance of 'Barnahus' in the Nordic Countries: Report from an On-going Project. *Journal of Scandinavian Studies in Criminology and Crime Prevention* 13 (1): 69–84.

Jonassen, Wencheand Kari Stefansen. 2003. Idealisme eller profesjonstenking? Statusrapport om krisesentrene. Kompetansesenter for voldsofferarbeid, Høgskolen i Oslo. HiO.

Laugerud, Solveig. 2014. Juss og juks - igjen? Om uavhengighet og likestilling i krisesenterloven. *Tidsskrift for kjønnsforskning* 38 (3–4): 287–301.

Ministry of Justice and Public Security. 2013. *The Action Plan Against Domestic Violence for the Period 2014–2017*. Oslo: Ministry of Justice and Public Security.

Municipality, Oslo. 2014. *Action Plan against Violence in Close Relations, Byrådssak 80/14*. Oslo: Byrådet.

Percy-Smith, Janie. 2006. What Works in Strategic Partnerships for Children: A Research Review. *Children and Society* 20 (4): 313–323.

Røvik, Kjell. 2016. Knowledge Transfer as Translation: Review and Elements of an Instrumental Theory. *International Journal of Management Reviews* 18 (3): 290–310.

Shepard, Melanie F. 1999. Advocacy for battered women: Implications for a coordinated community response. In *Coordinating Community Responses to Domestic Violence: Lessons from Duluth and Beyond*, eds. Shepard, Melanie F., and Pence, Ellen L., 115–125. Thousand Oaks, CA: SAGE.

Stefansen, Kari. 2006. Krisesentrene i Norge – fra sosial bevegelse til profesjonaliserte hjelpetiltak. *Nordisk sosialt arbeid* 26 (1): 27–38.

Stefansen, Kari, Tonje Gundersen and Elisiv Bakketeig. 2012. Barnehusevalueringen 2012, delrapport 2. En undersøkelse blant barn og pårørende, samarbeidspartnere, ledere og ansatte. Oslo: NOVA.

16

Potentials and Challenges of the Barnahus model

Kari Stefansen, Susanna Johansson, Anna Kaldal and Elisiv Bakketeig

Introduction

The Barnahus model was introduced in the Nordic countries as a response to a growing recognition of the need for more integrated and child-centred services for children exposed to violence and sexual abuse. It has been

K. Stefansen (✉) · E. Bakketeig
Norwegian Social Research, Oslo and Akershus University College of Applied Sciences, Oslo, Norway
e-mail: kari.stefansen@nova.hioa.no

E. Bakketeig
e-mail: elisiv.bakketeig@nova.hioa.no

S. Johansson
School of Social Work, Lund University, Lund, Sweden
e-mail: susanna.johansson@soch.lu.se

A. Kaldal
Law Faculty, Stockholm University, Stockholm, Sweden
e-mail: anna.kaldal@juridicum.su.se

recognised as the most important reform related to child victimisation in the Nordic region (Johansson 2012). Evaluation studies (Åström and Rejmer 2008; Swedish National Police Agency 2008; Gudjonsson et al. 2009; Kaldal et al. 2010; Bakketeig et al. 2012; Stefansen et al. 2012; Landberg and Svedin 2013) have concluded that the Barnahus model in many respects represents a promising development towards meeting victimised children's needs and legal rights. The chapters in this book confirm that the Barnahus model is a step in the right direction, but also highlight the need for critical analysis of its potentials and challenges. Questions that arise from the book include: Under what conditions can the Barnahus model achieve its ideal potential of providing both child-friendly support and justice to victimised children? Are there developments in how Barnahus works, and the roles Barnahus are given, that challenge the key ideas behind the model and its potential benefits for children? Are there limits to what societies can achieve in these respects through the Barnahus measure, in its current form?

In our opinion, these are important questions to address in the Nordic countries, where the Barnahus model has become a permanent part of the welfare state, as well as beyond the Nordic context, given that the Barnahus model has been widely promoted outside the Nordic countries. In 2002, for instance, the Barnahus model was identified as "best practice" in a comparative study of nine European countries in the Save the Children publication: "Child Abuse and Adult Justice" (Diesen 2002), and in 2006, the Icelandic Barnahus received the "Multidisciplinary Award" from the International Society for Child Abuse and Neglect (ISPCAN). This is of course an indication of the model's success; however, there is also the risk of overlooking critical issues, limitations and potentials for improvement in the celebration and promotion of the model. As this volume has shown, the Barnahus model differs quite significantly among the Nordic countries. The model has also been the subject of evaluation and research to very different extents, and many outcomes and effects of the Barnahus practice are therefore yet unknown. Country-specific implementation and institutionalisation processes mean that it is possible to identify a variety of potentials and challenges, which this chapter discusses in the light of the book contributions.

The Role of the Institutional Landscape

A key perspective in this book, as outlined in the introduction, is that the Barnahus model will take on different forms when introduced in different institutional contexts. Following on from this perspective, we have highlighted how the Barnahus model's success in terms of its rapid diffusion and status as a model for collaborative approaches to child victims of abuse is linked to key and common characteristics of both the justice and welfare systems of the Nordic countries. Importantly, all the Nordic countries have a zero legal tolerance for child abuse, which includes acts that may be considered acceptable methods of disciplining children in other countries. Welfare systems in the Nordic countries also have in common a well-developed child welfare system characterised by a family service orientation (e.g. early prevention, voluntary measures, broad target group) and measures to protect children at risk, such as mandatory reporting systems (see Gilbert et al. 2011 and Chap. 1).

In the Nordic countries, the Barnahus model was thus introduced and moulded to fit into a particular institutional landscape relating to child welfare and criminal justice systems as well as already existing local welfare services. How the institutional landscape of the Nordic countries may further the potentials of the Barnahus model in terms of meeting children's needs and rights is an important issue for further research. It should be noted, however, that there are reasons to claim that there is a link between the effects of the Barnahus model and this particular institutional landscape. In the Nordic contexts, Barnahus operates within a landscape of broader welfare measures related to, for instance, childcare and education, social security and health services. These services and the potential for broader interventions for victimised children add to what is specifically offered at the Barnahus. The institutional premises for Barnahus are in this sense better than might be the case in several contexts outside the Nordic welfare states. It is important for agents promoting the Barnahus model as *the* instrument for dealing with the complex issue of child abuse to recognise this. The key message for countries discussing whether the Barnahus model, or similar collaborative multi-professional approaches, should be implemented is that the model's potential cannot be understood separately from the institutional landscape in which it is implemented.

The Diffusion of the Barnahus Idea, Modes of Governance and Implementation

Institutional theory offers important concepts for understanding diffusion and implementation processes. Røvik (2016), for instance, differentiates between *copying*, *modifying* and *radical* forms of translations between "source models" and "outcome models". What we have seen in the Nordic region may be interpreted as modifying processes that, as we will discuss further below, are still very much "in the making".Iceland adapted the US Children's Advocacy Centre model to fit the Icelandic justice and welfare system, while Sweden and Norway adapted the Icelandic model to their respective systems. Denmark drew on experiences from all the models. In Finland, in contrast, the Barnahus pilot project partly draws on existing specialised forensic psychology units at university hospitals, as described by Korkman and co-authors in this book (Chap. 7), and partly on the other Nordic Barnahus models.

As shown in Chap. 1, the Barnahus model "landed" quite differently among the Nordic countries. The implementation of Barnahus also followed partly different paths, where the varied role of state governance is especially worth addressing. In all the Nordic countries, the implementation of the Barnahus model, to larger or lesser extent, followed from an analysis of the institutional landscape. In Norway, for instance, a governmental committee described and discussed three different models for Barnahus and concluded that only one of the models fitted the core idea of Barnahus as offering integrated services under one roof (Norwegian Ministry of Justice and the Police 2006). This and other national reports were based on ad hoc criteria for evaluating the existing system and the possible improvements that would follow from implementing the Barnahus. In Sweden, a Barnahus pilot was commissioned at six locations by the government, with minimum criteria for the target group and involved agencies, but stressing that more detailed organisation, localisation and financing was to be solved locally and within each agency's existing budget (Swedish Ministry of Justice 2005). The commission also initiated a cooperative group of central governmental agency representatives to follow the pilot and to stimulate the diffusion of collaborative arrangements like Barnahus in Sweden. This resulted in the establishment of around 30 Barnahus at different times and places, through varied initiatives. Great variation developed between different local Barnahus. The differences are partly linked to the local institutional landscape and specific local needs, pre-existing collaborative arrangements and available resources, and partly linked to the main interests of varied local promoters (e.g. local Save the Children organisations, politicians, agencies, professionals).

The relatively vague state governance in Sweden subsequently allowed for agents outside the government to influence the development of the Barnahus model. At both national and local levels, Save the Children Sweden has been a promoter and driving force for the establishment, diffusion and steering of Barnahus. The organisation has, for example, organised a national network for professionals involved in the Barnahus work, issued criteria for the content of a Barnahus (Save the Children Sweden 2009), conducted a quality assurance study and developed a manual of quality assurance of Swedish Barnahus (Landberg and Svedin 2013). This manual drew on international law (CRC), national guidelines, standards from the US National Children's Alliance, Save the Children Sweden's Barnahus criteria as well as guidelines on child-friendly justice from the Council of Europe, what could be interpreted as a mix of international, national and transnational regulations (cf. Djelic and Sahlin-Andersson 2006; Cotterell 2012; Johansson 2016).

In Denmark, in contrast, the simultaneous start of five mandatory Barnahus followed from a large national law reform ("the abuse package"), as described in Chaps. 1 and 14 of this book. The law reform also included changes in social welfare legislation as well as the enforcement of a specific Barnahus regulation. The reform was in turn based on a ministerial commission that included the investigation of a number of individual cases in order to analyse how serious system failure could be prevented, which resulted in an expert panel report with recommendations to the Danish government on how to combat child abuse (see appendix).

The role of the state as well as other non-governmental actors has thus taken quite different paths within the Nordic region in the implementation process of the Barnahus model. This calls for further attention to be paid to the implications of different steering mechanisms and forms of regulation, which includes the role of both legal changes and soft regulations (such as guidelines, standards, manuals) for the ongoing translation and implementation process of the Barnahus model in both national and local contexts.

In this book, two chapters in particular offer insights into how and why institutional analysis should be carried out to provide a good framework for the implementation and follow-up of the Barnahus model. Friðriksdóttir and Haugen's chapter (Chap. 9) presents and discusses a method to assess the extent to which the justice system and the complex system of services and professional practises are set up in accordance with the principles of child-friendly justice. Bredal and Stefansen (Chap. 15), using the "Barnahus for adults" pilot project as their point of reference, highlight the importance of analysing not only the landscape of services at the national level, but also the landscape of (partly overlapping) local services in order to prevent professional conflicts and competition.

Professional Tensions

The Balancing Act of Competing Institutional Logics

The Barnahus model is not only introduced into an institutional landscape; this landscape is also in a sense institutionalised in the Barnahus model, as described, for instance, by Johansson in this book (Chap. 12). The Barnahus idea, as discussed in Chap. 1, revolves around a notion of the Barnahus as a safe and child-friendly place for disclosure but also as a neutral space for professional interventions. Neutral here refers to the idea of Barnahus as a mechanism for balancing the different institutional logics that the Barnahus model comprises: the criminal law-oriented logic on the one hand and the treatment-oriented logic on the other hand (Johansson 2011a, b). As several chapters in the book suggest, this should be understood as an idea and not an in-built feature of the Barnahus model in practice. The "power" of the different institutional logics within Barnahus is, as the chapters of both Johansson (Chap. 12) and Bakketeig (Chap. 13) show, partly related to the design of the model and to professional and collaborative negotiations and routines that evolve over time. Bakketeig also points to the role of external factors in shifting the power balance between different logics. In Norway, the rapid increase in the number of abuse cases and the new law on mandatory use of Barnahus when conducting child investigative interviews have led to serious overload problems in the Barnahus and a corresponding worry that this may lead the staff to prioritise the coordination tasks related to the investigative interview over providing treatment and support. Bakketeig argues that this is caused in part by the organisation of the Barnahus as a service within the police. As police employees, the Barnahus staff within the Norwegian model (social workers, psychologists) are obliged to work towards the goals of the police in terms of executing child investigative interviews according to the time limit set in the law.

In order to identify and protect children at risk, the need to collaborate and coordinate professional competences and resources when handling cases of suspected child abuse is often stressed (see, e.g. Steinkopf et al. 2006; Anning et al. 2010; Stanley and Humphreys 2015; Parton 2014). This book also shows the importance of critical analysis of how the collaborative work takes form. Since the Barnahus collaboration implies professional tensions and the balancing of competing institutional logics, an important research agenda concerns comparative analysis of power dimensions and professional identities in the Barnahus collaboration. Such analysis will further the knowledge and potential of collaborative multi-professional work against child abuse.

The Relationship Between Barnahus and Local Child Welfare Services

The Danish chapter in the book, written by Søbjerg (Chap. 14), describes a form of professional tension that to date has been less acknowledged compared to the tension between the criminal law-oriented logic and the treatment-oriented logic. Søbjerg focuses on tensions that in her interpretation result from two competing notions of holism. The Barnahus model represents a holistic perspective in the effort to integrate specialised professional services for victimised children through collaboration. Social work, in contrast, and as carried out by the local child welfare services in Denmark, departs from a perspective of holism that emphasises the child's welfare in broad terms that is also related to issues in the family other than violence or abuse, such as parental drug and alcohol problems, or poverty. As Barnahus both centralises services for victimised children and primarily deals with the abuse the child may have suffered, local child welfare workers in Denmark worry that their holistic approach will become more difficult to carry out and legitimise.

As discussed in Chap. 1, the Nordic Barnahus models show great variation in terms of the integration, involvement and role of local child welfare services in relation to the Barnahus service. In Norway, for example, the local child welfare services are not formally a part of Barnahus collaboration, while in Denmark the local child welfare services are the key responsible agency throughout the whole Barnahus process. These variations address the importance of further researching the potentials and challenges these differences represent, not least concerning the performance and outcomes of the child welfare investigations and the participation of children and families in such processes (cf. Willumsen and Skivenes 2005).

Dilemmas in Reaching Children's Rights by Child-Friendly Justice

A common feature in Nordic child law is the growing emphasis on children as holders of individual rights. The formation, ratification, transformation and in some cases incorporation of the CRC is one explanation and has contributed to a new way of looking at children. One element of children's rights highlighted in international law is the right of access to justice. This can be seen as an outflow of art. 12, the right to participation (CRC/GC/12, Council of Europe 2010), but also as a fundamental right that follows from being a right holder when fundamental rights have been violated (CRC/GC/12 and CRC/GC/2). According to the CRC, a fundamental right of any child is protection from sexual, physical and psychological abuse (e.g. art. 6, 19 and 34), which makes access to justice in cases of abuse crucial from a child rights perspective.

An important question is to what extent the Barnahus model helps to realise children's rights. As discussed by Friðriksdóttir and Haugen (Chap. 9), the aim of Barnahus is safeguarding several aspects of children's rights, and this is a challenging task. This is illustrated in the chapter written by Kaldal et al. (Chap. 10), which discusses the child's right to information in Barnahus in the light of the CRC art. 12 on the child's right to participation. According to the CRC, participation is a right, not a duty, and therefore, the child has a right to information in order to make an informed decision according to the best interests of the child.

In the Nordic countries, children's right to access to justice has been considered in legislative work for the past decades. The discussion has, for example, led to legislation where children, through independent representation, have been given rights to act autonomously in relation to a custodian in legal proceedings. This legislation can be found in areas where there is a potential conflict of interest between the child and the custodian, such as in child welfare cases and criminal cases with suspected abuse from a family member. See, for example, the chapter in this book written by Forsman, where she discusses the special representative for children in criminal cases and the special representative's role in Barnahus (Chap. 11). An emphasis on children's rights to access to justice, however, also requires a justice system that is child friendly (cf. Council of Europe 2010). Consequently, a child's involvement in legal proceedings must be adapted to the needs of the child. This is also the core of the Barnahus ideology. What makes a Barnahus child friendly is not a simple question, however, and can be approached in different ways. One aim of the Barnahus model is to provide a child-friendly environment. What child-friendliness means in this context is discussed in the chapter written by Stefansen (Chap. 2). Research into children's own experiences and perspectives from visiting Barnahus is limited, but the chapter written by Olsson and Kläfverud presents a study of children's own experiences of visiting Barnahus (Chap. 3). Both chapters highlight child-friendliness as a multidimensional phenomenon that is far from easy to achieve in practice.

A core aspect of children's rights to access to justice is the child investigative interview. As pointed out in Baugerud and Johnson's chapter (Chap. 6), the main evidence in the vast majority of criminal cases in Barnahus is the child's statement. As described by Myklebust (Chap. 5), a child's statement in a criminal proceeding is handled in a similar way in the Nordic countries, by using a video-recording of their statement from the criminal (pre-trial) investigation as evidence in the main hearing. The child witness, therefore, is normally not present in the court. This especially applies to particularly young or vulnerable children (e.g. preschool-aged children, or children with developmental difficulties or communicational problems). Traditionally, statements from children in abuse cases have also raised issues about children's credibility and suggestibility (see, for example, Doris 1991; Hershkowitz et al. 2007; Chap. 7 by Korkman et al.; Chap. 6 by Baugerud and Johnson). The consequence of this is that the demands on the quality of the child statement are high, and therefore so is the quality of the interview method, as well as the requirements of safeguarding the defendant's right to a fair trial. The context in which the child is interviewed, as well as the interview method as such, has been in focus for many years in the Nordic countries, among researchers, police and prosecutors, as well as courts. In Sweden, for instance, the Supreme Court has commented several rulings on aspects of the child investigative interview, such as the questions asked, the defendant's right to cross-examination and the quality of the documentation (Sutorius and Kaldal 2003).

The tension between children's capacity as witnesses and their right to a child-friendly approach on the one hand, and on the other hand safeguarding the rights of the defendant, is one of the dilemmas when it comes to the child's right of access to justice. As discussed above, this has led to the development and implementation of a specific method for child investigative interviews.

The methods used in the Nordic countries are, as noted by several authors in this book, interview protocols that resemble the NICHD protocol (described in, for example, Chap. 6 by Baugerud and Johnson). Whether results are better in terms of following the principles of the protocol, when used in the Barnahus setting, is not clear however and needs to be further studied empirically. The Barnahus has, however, as described by Langballe and Davik (Chap. 8), and referring to the Norwegian context, been a driving force in the development of new interview procedures for groups that are difficult to interview using the standard protocol, such as very young children. As described by Myklebust (Chap. 5), the implementation of specific interview methods has led to high demands on the competence of the interviewer and the development of specific educational programmes designed for child investigative interviewers.

The Debated Question of Treatment and Medical Examinations

Psychological treatment and medical examinations are areas that have caused professional tensions and debate. In the Swedish context, the debate regarding psychological treatment relates to the availability of treatment, both in the Barnahus and in the local treatment system. This is probably because emergency and short-term interventions for the child and family are offered only in about half of the Barnahus in Sweden (Landberg and Svedin 2013). In the Norwegian context, emergency and short-term interventions are part of the Barnahus model. Here, the discussion among staff has revolved around what types of psychological treatment should be offered. According to the evaluation of the Norwegian model (Stefansen et al. 2012) the staff seem to have had a high degree of professional autonomy in this issue and a relatively wide opportunity to use their professional judgement to decide what to offer children and families. This probably relates to the mandate of the Barnahus to make sure that the chain of services is well connected.

The Barnahus in Norway are responsible for offering emergency and short-term interventions, while the responsibility for long-term treatment normally lies in the local specialised treatment systems. If the child, for instance, is already seeing a local therapist when arriving at the Barnahus, the child will normally continue treatment there. If the child is in need of treatment but this is not available locally, the Barnahus will offer treatment, normally for a limited amount of hours. The Barnahus staff will also arrange hand-over meetings or consultations when a child is referred to specialised treatment locally. Barnahus also makes use of different methods of emergency and short-term interventions, and are testing methods for more long-term treatment (e.g. Circle of Security). The Barnahus would like to handle more of the long-term psychological treatment themselves as a result of accumulating special competence in the treatment of abused children and their families. We do not know whether this will be the case, but it does illustrate how potential challenges and tensions may arise regarding institutional boundaries and fields of responsibilities when establishing a new service within a landscape of existing services. In the Finnish Forensic Psychology Units, operating at university hospitals, it was, for instance, decided that psychological treatment should be clearly separated from the forensic psychologist investigative interviews undertaken by the units (see Chap. 7 by Korkman et al.).

Another professional tension, or discussion, one that this book does not cover, relates to the role of the medical staff and medical examinations in Barnahus. Most Nordic Barnahus are equipped for medical examinations, but few such examinations are carried out (Bakketeig et al. 2012; Åström and Rejmer 2008; Kaldal et al. 2010). Discussions regarding the medical examinations revolve around two main issues (Bakketeig et al. 2012). One issue is whether all children that visit Barnahus should be offered a standard medical examination as part of the Barnahus routine, or whether the medical examination should be reserved for cases where the police require a forensic medical examination as part of the criminal investigation. Norwegian Barnahus leaders have, for instance, argued that all children should be offered a medical examination (cf. Oslo Barnahus 2014). They contend that this can have a healing effect on the child and also lead to a documentation of abuse which can be used as evidence in court, which otherwise would be overlooked. A standard procedure would thus improve children's access to due process. Arguments against such a standard routine are seldom voiced explicitly, but one key issue would be resources. Most Barnahus do not have the capacity to perform medical examinations on all children.

Offering medical examinations to all children as part of the support services at Barnahus can in a sense be seen as placing emphasis on the treatment-oriented logic in the Barnahus. At the same time, if this service also provides more evidence for use in court proceedings, the routine also responds to the criminal law-oriented logic. Results from a Swedish Barnahus context have, for instance, identified how higher attendance of medical specialists at consultation meetings results in more medical examinations of children, as well as close connections between decisions about medical examination on the one hand and decisions about police reporting, as well as to prosecute, on the other hand (see Åström and Rejmer 2008; Johansson 2011a). This suggests the importance of the attendance of medical staff as well as undertakings of medical examinations at the Barnahus from a criminal law-oriented perspective.

Another discussion relates to whether or not the (forensic) medical examination should be carried out at the Barnahus with more limitations regarding specialised examination and consultation, compared to hospitals. Moving the medical examination out of the Barnahus would mean leaving aside the one door principle and thus one of the core components of the Barnahus model. Specially trained medical staff always carries out the examinations in Barnahus, while this may not be the case at hospitals. Still, several arguments have been presented against using the Barnahus for medical examinations in the Norwegian context (Bakketeig et al. 2012). One argument is that it would drain the hospitals of specialised competence and weaken an already limited field of specialised competence. This is a similar argument to the one Søbjerg finds among child welfare workers in the municipalities related to social work (see Chap. 14). The medical specialist would also lose the opportunity to be part of a broader medical environment at the hospital and specialists in other medical fields would be less available

(Bakketeig et al. 2012). Another argument is availability: the Barnahus has limited opening hours, while the hospitals are open 24/7. Since the capacity at the Barnahus would be more limited than in the hospitals, there may also be a risk of compromising the child's ability to present medical documentation of abuse in court. The research-based knowledge regarding the forensic medical examination is presently very limited, however, and it is important to initiate research to investigate the quality of the medical examinations as well as the implications of conducting the examinations at Barnahus or at hospitals.

Barnahus: A Field in the Making

The extensive and rapid diffusion of Barnahus throughout the Nordic region, and the creation and implementation of both national laws and transnational regulations concerning the model, indicates the emergence of a new organisational field within the Nordic welfare states. The notion of a specific Barnahus field implies that it represents a recognisable and distinguishable field constituted by organisations that produce similar services and that are bounded by shared institutional norms and rules (cf. DiMaggio and Powell 1983; Scott 2008). More recent contributions also suggest that "fields can develop not only around settled markets, technologies, or policy domains, but also around central disputes and issues" (Scott 2008, 184) that is not solely around shared conceptions and compatible structures. Fields are in this sense bounded by a duality of meaning and space (cf. Scott and Meyer 1983; Djelic and Sahlin-Andersson 2006), and represent constantly evolving structures of communication and meaning as well as spatial and relational boundaries. From this perspective, the Barnahus field can be seen as an evolving institutional structure that deals with the issue of child welfare and child justice in cases of suspected child abuse, in terms of both meaning and space formation. As the book demonstrates, and as we discuss below, the Barnahus field is a field in the making.

Branching Out: A Common Trend?

One example of an ongoing field development or trend is the Barnahus models' branching out in terms of defining its target group. Common target groups for all but the Greenlandic Barnahus models are at the moment children as victims of sexual abuse and violence. In a sense, this is also due to a process of branching out, as the first Icelandic Barnahus for many years only focused on sexual abuse cases, but under inspiration from, for example, Sweden and Norway, came to also include physical abuse. In addition, recent developments of branching out include discussion of whether to include young people who sexually abuse other children within the target group of Barnahus. This is currently debated in Norway and noted as a recommended target group when considered appropriate in the Swedish national guidelines (Swedish National Police Agency 2009). Iceland, in contrast, has taken a stance against including this target group, since it is regarded as problematic in relation to the central idea of Barnahus as a safe space for victims, free from offenders (see Chaps. 1 and 2). Similarly, there has been a parallel discussion regarding safety from offenders in relation to the Swedish "Karin-project" that physically moved a separate Barnahus into a building that integrated crisis centres for women, children and men under one roof (cf. Chap. 15 by Bredal and Stefansen). It was, for example, questioned whether it was appropriate to still regard this measure as a Barnahus or not, due to the collision with the idea of Barnahus as a safe space. As explained by Thulin and Kjellgren (Chap. 4), a treatment intervention in cases of child physical abuse is offered at several Swedish Barnahus, which is directed towards the whole family, including the offender(s). This is also an example of the tension between the idea of a safe space on the one hand and offering support and treatment in order to prevent continuous child abuse on the other hand.

Another example of branching out regarding the target groups of Barnahus is children as witnesses of violence. This is, for example, a challenge for Barnahus in Sweden, due to differences in "legal status" for children who have witnessed abuse and children who have been exposed to violence themselves. The former group of children are rarely seen in the Swedish Barnahus (Landberg and Svedin 2013). An explanation is probably that they are not regarded as parties in the criminal case and therefore lack the procedural rights of victims during the criminal case, which is regarded as problematic in relation to the parallel investigations coordinated within the Swedish Barnahus model (the criminal investigation and the child welfare investigation). In Norway, this is not an issue since it has been ruled by the Supreme Court (Rt. 2010/949) that children as witnesses of violence are covered by the statue[1] in the Norwegian criminal law that targets family violence.

This book has also identified other examples of branching out the target groups of Barnahus, for example, due to the legal regulation of mandatory use of the Barnahus which significantly increased the number of children interviewed (cf. Norway), or by including all criminal acts against children as part of the target group (cf. the Faroe Islands and the Åland Islands) . An important subsequent research question is what implications the trends of branching out in relation to the target group will have for Barnahus field development. It could possibly imply a process of criminalisation and potential juridification, with more police reports, child investigative interviews and increased focus on criminal investigations (cf. Chap. 12 by Johansson and Chap. 13 by Bakketeig), but it could possibly also imply more support and treatment for children not previously acknowledged and supported. The tension and balancing act between "justice" and "welfare" is evidently still an important question for research, policy implementation, as well as the ongoing collaborative work within Barnahus.

The Barnahus field is also branching out in terms of diffusion, space and location. This involves, for example, the establishment of a number of new Barnahus as has been the case in both Sweden and Norway. A similar trend is the establishment of satellites in order to complement already existing Barnahus (which is the case in Denmark, and currently being piloted in Norway). In Greenland, the Barnahus has developed complementary "mobile Barnahus" or travelling units of police who bring video equipment and interview children in their local settlement (see appendix). Common to all these branching out trends are geographical difficulties in reaching the target group nation-wide. A continuous and central discussion in several Nordic countries has involved how Barnahus should be dimensioned, staffed and localised in order to fulfil thc dcmands of serving the whole country in an equivalent manner (e.g. Kaldal et al. 2010; Bakketeig et al. 2012; Stefansen et al. 2012). This trend is also partly related to the case volume of Barnahus, which differs quite significantly both within and between the different Nordic countries. For example, in Norway the Barnahus in Oslo (the capital) conducted 1150 investigative interviews in 2015, while the Barnahus in Bodø, in the northern part of the country, conducted 263. In 2014, the Faroe Island's Barnahus received 20 notifications about child abuse in total. Another expression of branching out is in terms of size, for which the Stockholm Barnahus in Sweden is an apt example. This Barnahus is a centralisation of three original Barnahus locations into one larger building, dimensioned for more cases as well as staff. As illustrated by these examples of branching out, questions of dimension and locality could be identified as equally important to consider when evaluating needs and planning to implement Barnahus in countries outside the Nordic region.

New Professional Practices

The chapters in this book illustrate an important effect of the introduction of the Barnahus model in the Nordic countries: it has in many respects worked as a change maker, facilitating discussion of professional standards and procedures.

Langballe and Daviks chapter (Chap. 8), for instance, shows how the Barnahus staff are in the process of carving out a distinct professional role related to the child investigative interview through collaboration with police interviewers. This can perhaps be seen as a sign of a development towards a shared Barnahus identity for professional staff with training in different disciplines. To give an example, the Barnahus psychologist not only evaluates children's needs as a psychologist, but also as a Barnahus professional. In the Norwegian context, the coordination role related to treatment and support following the child investigative interview also seems to be constructed as a specialised task for professional Barnahus work (cf. Stefansen et al. 2012).

An important research area is thus how different Barnahus models affect the professional roles developing among Barnahus staff in relation to collaborative partners.

Another area where Barnahus have had a wider effect on the development of professional practice is related to treatment and interventions. As exemplified in this book, in the chapter written by Thulin and Kjellgren (Chap. 4), treatment models are tried out in Barnahus and with the help of Barnahus staff. Given the coordinating role that Barnahus staff takes in assuring support for the child and family after the interview, at least in the Norwegian model, it seems reasonable to suggest that the Barnahus model will, over time, increase the awareness of local services regarding providing support. This could counteract the negative effects of the centralisation of professional competence that Søbjerg (Chap. 14) suggests is an unintended consequence of the implementation of Barnahus in Denmark.

A third area, which we have discussed above, relates to the education of child investigative interviewers.

An Emerging Research Field

As an overall perspective, we suggest seeing the Barnahus model as at the core of an emerging institutional field that interlinks child welfare and child justice, in turn, two partly overlapping policy fields. Barnahus can thus be understood as a "hybrid organisation" positioned in an institutional tension field spanning the legal areas of welfare law and criminal law, and bringing together contrasting institutional logics (Johansson 2011a). This position subsequently implies dilemmas and challenges of special interest from an interdisciplinary and comparative research perspective, which we hope this book has demonstrated. While the chapters of the book are organised in broad themes that represent different scholarly traditions and specialised discussions, one aim of bringing them together has been the presentation of an emerging research field: *the field of Barnahus research*. With this book, we have aimed to further the understanding of what the Barnahus model is, how it works and what its potentials and challenges are, which can inform Barnahus policies and practices both in the Nordic region and beyond. We also hope to stimulate further research on Barnahus and to have demonstrated the many advantages of bringing together research from different disciplines and national contexts. Our aim throughout the book has also been to highlight how Barnahus research can take its outlook from within the Barnahus practice (e.g. from the perspectives of Barnahus staff) but also from outside the Barnahus practice (e.g. from surrounding actors, services, governance structures or relating processes).

The variations in implementation and institutionalisation processes, as well as the potential and challenges, identified in this volume, call for the initiation of more interdisciplinary and comparative Barnahus research. While in one sense being a specialised research field, Barnahus research is simultaneously inter-related with many broader research areas concerning child abuse, domestic violence, child welfare policy and practice, children's rights and child-friendly justice, integrated services and multi-professional collaboration, and governance, to mention the most central. From this perspective, the Barnahus research presented in this volume and the identified set of agendas for further research are also important for broader scientific discussions. In conclusion, we wish to stress the importance of dialogue among related research fields in order to further the development of interdisciplinary knowledge that may inform policy implementation and professional practice, with the overall aim of collaborating against child abuse.

Note

1. In the ruling from 2010, this was related to §219 in the Norwegian Criminal Code 22. May 1902 no 10. Norway now has a new Criminal Code of 20. May 2005 no 28 and the relevant statue is now §§282 and 283.

References

Anning, Angela, David Cottrell, Nick Frost, Josephine Green, and Mark Robinson. 2010. *Developing Multiprofessional Teamwork for Integrated Children's Services*. Berkshire: Open University Press.

Åström, Karsten, and Annika Rejmer. 2008. *"Det blir nog bättre för barnen…" Slutrapport i utvärderingen av nationell försöksverksamhet med barnahus 2006–2007.* Lund: Lunds universitet.

Bakketeig, Elisiv, Mette Berg, Trond Myklebust, and Kari Stefansen. 2012. *Barnehusevalueringen 2012, delrapport 1: Barnehusmodellens implikasjoner for politiets arbeid med fokus på dommeravhør og rettsmedisinsk undersøkelse.* Oslo: PHS.

Barnahus, Oslo. 2014. *Årsmelding.* Oslo: Barnehuset i Oslo.

Cotterell, Roger. 2012. What is Transnational Law? *Law & Social Inquiry* 37 (2): 500–524.

Council of Europe. 2010. *Guidelines of the Committee of Ministers of the Council of Europe on Child-Friendly Justice.* Strasbourg: Council of Europe Publishing.

Diesen, Christian. 2002. *Child Abuse and Adult Justice—A Comparative Study of Different European Criminal Justice Systems Handling of Cases Concerning Child Sexual Abuse.* Stockholm: Save the Children Sweden.

DiMaggio, Paul J., and Walter W. Powell. 1983. The Iron Cage Revisited: Institutional Isomorphism and Collective Rationality in Organisational Fields. *American Sociological Association* 48 (2): 147–160.

Djelic, Marie-Laure, and Kerstin Sahlin-Andersson (eds.). 2006. *Transnational Governance: Institutional Dynamics of Regulation.* Cambridge: Cambridge University Press.

Doris, John (ed.). 1991. *The Suggestibility of Children's Recollections. Implications for Eyewitness Testimony.* Washington: American Psychological Association.

Gilbert, Neil, Nigel Parton, and Marit Skivenes (eds.). 2011. *Child Protection Systems: International Trends and Orientations.* Oxford: Oxford University Press.

Gudjonsson, Gisli, Thorbjorg Sveinsdottir, Jon Fridrik Sigurdsson, and Johanna Jonsdottir. 2010. The Ability of Suspected Victims of Childhood Sexual Abuse (CSA) to Give Evidence. Findings From the Children's House in Iceland. *The Journal of Forensic Psychiatry & Psychology* 21 (4): 569–586.

Hershkowitz, Irit, Sara Fisher, Michael E. Lamb, and Dvora Horowitz. 2007. Improving Credibility Assessment in Child Sexual Abuse Allegations: The Role of the NICHD Investigative Interview Protocol. *Child Abuse and Neglect* 31 (2): 99–110.

Johansson, Susanna. 2011a. *Rätt, makt och institutionell förändring. En kritisk analys av myndigheters samverkan i barnahus.* (Diss.) Lund Studies in Sociology of Law 35, Lund University.

Johansson, Susanna. 2011b. Juridifiering som institutionell förändring. Om mötet mellan straffrätt och socialrätt vid interorganisatorisk samverkan. *Retfærd, Nordic Journal of Law and Justice* 34 (4/135): 38–59.

Johansson, Susanna. 2012. Diffusion and Governance of 'Barnahus' in the Nordic Countries: Report form an On-Going Project. *Journal of Scandinavian Studies in Criminology and Crime Prevention* 13 (1): 69–84.

Johansson, Susanna. 2016. Var finns välfärdsrätten i dag? Reflektioner kring en transnationalisering. In *Festskrift till Karsten Åström*, ed. Karl Dahlstrand, 271–285. Lund: Juristförlaget i Lund.

Kaldal, Anna, Christian Diesen, Johan Beije, and Eva Diesen. 2010. *Barnahusutredningen 2010*. Stockholm: Jure förlag.

Landberg, Åsa, and Carl Göran Svedin. 2013. *Inuti ett barnahus. En kvalitetsgranskning av 23 svenska verksamheter*. Stockholm: Save the Children Sweden.

Norwegian Ministry of Justice and the Police. 2006. *Barnas hus: Rapport om etablering av et pilotprosjekt med ny avhørsmodell for barn som har vært utsatt for overgrep m.m.* Oslo: Ministry of Justice and the Police.

Parton, Nigel. 2014. *The Politics of Child Protection. Contemporary Developments and Future directions*. Hampshire: Palgrave Macmillan.

Røvik, Kjell A. 2016. Knowledge Transfer as Translation: Review and Elements of an Instrumental Theory. *International Journal of Management Reviews* 18 (3): 290–310.

Save the Children Sweden. 2009. *Gemensamma kriterier! Innehållet i ett barnahus i 10 punkter*. Stockholm: Save the Children Sweden.

Scott, Richard W., and John W. Meyer. 1983. The Organisation of Societal Sectors. In *Organisational Environments: Ritual and Rationality*, eds. John W. Meyer, and Richard W. Scott, 129–153. London: Sage.

Scott, Richard W. 2008. *Institutions and Organizations. Ideas and Interests*, 3rd ed. Los Angeles, CA: Sage Publications.

Stanley, Nicky and Cathy Humphreys (eds.). 2015. *Domestic Violence and Protecting Children. New Thinking and Approaches*. London: Jessica Kingsley Publishers.

Stefansen, Kari, Tonje Gundersen, and Elisiv Bakketeig. 2012. Barnehusevalueringen 2012, delrapport 2. *En undersøkelse blant barn og pårørende, samarbeidspartnere, ledere og ansatte*. Oslo: NOVA.

Steinkopf, Heine, Ragnhild Laukvik Leite, Gunhild Gjedrem Spikkeland, Linda Karlsen, and Paul Magne Lunde. 2006. Kontroll, terapi eller begge deler? Samarbeid om familievold mellom politi, barnevern og familiekontor. *Fokus på familien* 04: 242–257.

Sutorius, Helena, and Anna Kaldal. 2003. *Bevisprövning vid sexualbrott.* Stockholm: Norstedts juridik.

Swedish Ministry of Justice. 2005. *Uppdrag att medverka till etablering av flera försöksverksamheter med samverkan under gemensamt tak vid utredningar kring barn som misstänks vara utsatta för allvarliga brott.* (Government decision). Stockholm: Swedish Ministry of Justice.

Swedish National Police Agency. 2009. *Delredovisning av regeringsuppdrag avseende gemensamma nationella riktlinjer kring barn som misstänks vara utsatta för brott och kriterier för landets barnahus.* Stockholm: The Swedish National Police Agency.

Willumsen, Elisabeth, and Marit Skivenes. 2005. Collaboration Between Service Users and Professionals: Legitimate Decisions in Child Protection—A Norwegian Model. *Child and Family Social Work* 10 (3): 197–206.

Appendix: Country Model Descriptions

This appendix presents short descriptions of the Barnahus models in each Nordic country. The countries are listed in the chronological order in which they implemented Barnahus. The Nordic autonomous regions, the Åland Islands, Greenland and the Faroe Islands, are presented together in the final section.

Iceland (1998)[1]

Implementation

Barnahus was established in 1998 on the initiative of the Government Agency for Child Protection (GACP). There is only one Barnahus in Iceland, in Reykjavik, the capital city.

Key Tasks, Agencies Involved and Collaboration

The overall goal of Barnahus is to coordinate the responsibility and functions of the child welfare services, the police, the prosecution and the medical services. Barnahus provides a child-friendly environment for investigative interviews conducted by child specialists trained in forensic interviewing (including court statements), medical examination and therapeutic services. Barnahus can also be used by child welfare services for exploratory interviews in cases of suspected abuse.

When a child is interviewed at Barnahus, the various professionals can follow the interview via video link in an adjacent co-hearing/observation room. Recent changes have been made in the setting up of pre-interview conferences between local child welfare services, the police and the forensic interviewer, addressing both the criminal and child welfare investigations, and where the role of the Barnahus staff as coordinators has been strengthened. Regular consultation meetings in Barnahus have also been held since autumn 2016, in order to coordinate and collaborate around complex cases, especially investigations of physical/domestic violence.

Target Group

Initially, Barnahus in Iceland handled cases of suspected child sexual abuse, but since 2015 children below the age of 15 exposed to sexual or physical violence have comprised the main group targeted at Barnahus. The police can also choose to use Barnahus for testimony in cases where children are aged 15–18, but children aged 15–18 will need to repeat this testimony during the main hearing (Criminal Procedure Act no. 88/2008).

Regulations

There is no specific Barnahus law, and Barnahus is not explicitly referred to in any legal provision, but there are regulations in both the Child Protection Act and the Law on Criminal Procedure that provide the legal basis for the Barnahus operation. The Child Protection Act mandates the Government Agency for Child Protection to run special service centres with the objective of promoting interdisciplinary collaboration, and strengthening the co-ordination of agencies in the handling of cases of child protection (Art. 7; Child Protection Act nr. 80/2002). In addition, the Icelandic Government Agency for Child Protection has issued guidelines and standard settings for the local child welfare services, which are not mandatory but normative for the practice of the local child welfare services. These guidelines and standards address, for example, explorative interviews, medical examinations and therapeutic services provided by Barnahus.

In 2015, there was also a legal change made in the Law on Criminal Procedure (nr. 88/2008), stipulating that investigative interviews of child victims up to 15 years old shall be conducted under the auspice of a court judge in a facility specially designed for such purposes (Art. 9) and with the support of a specially trained person (Art. 123). These provisions are generally interpreted by court judges as mandating the interviews of children below the age of 15 in Barnahus.

Organisation, funding and staff

The Government Agency for Child Protection funds the general operation of Barnahus, that is, they pay for the running of the facilities and employ child specialists trained in forensic child interviewing, counselling and providing therapeutic services. The child welfare services pay for a small portion of the costs of the therapeutic services. All agencies linked with the Barnahus pay for their own staff, as involved in each case.

The training of specialists in Barnahus is organised and funded by the Government Agency for Child Protection. The staff receives regular training in forensic interviewing and trauma-focused therapy. The training of law enforcement specialists is organised and funded by the police agencies when considered necessary. The specialists in Barnahus are required to use child investigative interviewing according to evidence-based protocols.

Sweden (2006)

Implementation

Barnahus was introduced in Sweden as a pilot project in six cities in 2006, on the initiative of the Swedish Ministry of Justice. A coordination group representing the Public Prosecution Authority, the National Police Board, the National Board of Health and Welfare and the National Board of Forensic Medicine was commissioned to lead the pilot and contribute to the further establishment of collaborative initiatives in this area. Since then, Barnahus has been implemented at around 30 locations, and in 2013, 160 of Sweden's 290 municipalities were connected to a Barnahus (Landberg and Svedin 2013). The Barnahus in Sweden started at different times and out of various initiatives, and are subsequently varied in terms of, for example, size, organisation and financing.

Key Tasks, Agencies Involved and Collaboration

Within Barnahus, two parallel investigations with different objectives are often coordinated: criminal investigation led by the public prosecutor and police, regarding the suspected crime, and child welfare investigation led by the child welfare services regarding the child's need for protection and support. The overall aim of the Barnahus model is to improve the quality of these investigations, and the protection and psycho-social support for victimised children (see, for example, Swedish Ministry of Justice 2005; Swedish National Police Agency et. al. 2008; Johansson 2011).

According to the minimum criteria to enter the pilot project, collaboration in Barnahus should involve the police, public prosecutors, child welfare services, child paediatrics and child psychiatry (Swedish National Police Agency et. al. 2008). Evaluation studies have concluded that collaboration is most intense or developed between the child welfare services and the police (and, to a different degree, prosecutors) but that healthcare agencies and professionals are more peripheral (even though local differences exist). Subsequently, the number of cases where medical and/or treatment measures are undertaken is quite low and varies between different Barnahus (see Åström and Rejmer 2008; Kaldal et al. 2010; Landberg and Svedin 2013).

Collaboration within Barnahus can be seen as a development towards a more structured form of collaboration that includes both overarching collaboration (through steering and reference groups) and the collaboration and coordination of specific cases (through consultation meetings and co-hearings of child investigative interviews). The Barnahus staff do not possess any investigatory responsibility for either of the two parallel investigations (i.e. the criminal investigation and the child welfare investigation), but they can sometimes perform some parts of the child welfare investigations on assignment by the child welfare services, as well as function as advisors for the child welfare caseworkers.

Target Groups

Initially, the Swedish Barnahus target group was children below 18 years who were suspected of being the victims of serious crimes directed towards the child's life, health, freedom or peace (i.e. Chapters 3, 4 and 6 in the Criminal Act [Brottsbalken], see also Swedish Ministry of Justice 2005; Swedish National Police Agency et. al. 2008, 12). The national guidelines, adopted in 2009, do not draw the line at serious crimes any longer, but state that the target group includes the above-mentioned crimes in cases where both the child welfare services and police and prosecutors initiate investigations (i.e. parallel investigations). Through the guidelines, the target group has also formally expanded to include children who are victims of female genital mutilation and children who are (direct or indirect) witnesses of violence, in addition to the above types of crime. Crime types are clarified to include crimes with motives of honour and also children who sexually abuse other children when appropriate (see Swedish National Police Agency 2009). There are also local variations in how the target group is more specifically defined.

In practice, most Swedish Barnahus have focused on physical violence within close relationships and sexual abuse cases with both intimate and unknown suspects, where cases involving physical abuse constitute the majority of those handled in Barnahus (Kaldal et. al. 2010; Åström and Rejmer 2008).

Regulations

There is no specific Barnahus law in Sweden, and Barnahus is not mandatory; however, there are national guidelines and criteria, issued in 2009 (see Swedish National Police Agency 2009). Hence, the agencies included in the Swedish Barnahus model are regulated by their respective legislations, primarily the Code of criminal procedure (SFS 1942: 740) and Social Services Act (SFS 2001: 453); however, collaboration between agencies that work with children at risk is emphasised in Swedish legislation, and the Act of Social Services explicitly states that the child welfare agency has responsibility for establishing such collaboration. Rules of secrecy apply as standard between governmental agencies, even though they collaborate in Barnahus, which means that the professionals need to assess rules of secrecy when exchanging information.

Organisation, Funding and Staff

In Sweden, Barnahus does not constitute a governmental agency per se, which means that all professionals working in Barnahus are employed by their respective agencies. The Barnahus staff is most often social workers employed by the municipality's child welfare services, although at some locations psychologists and/or police officers also work as Barnahus staff. The Barnahus staff primarily hold coordination roles that include receiving and guiding a child (and potential companions), summoning the respective professionals from the different agencies to the consultation meetings and co-hearings of child investigative interviews, leading the consultation meetings, and ensuring that the coordination of the parallel investigations is handled in a suitable manner. It is the municipality child welfare services that finance the local Barnahus to the greatest extent, although the collaborating agencies contribute to varying degrees with resources in terms of personnel, technical equipment and so on, which is often regulated in a collaboration agreement or contract between the agencies. The Barnahus pilot was commissioned by the government and coordinated by an interagency coordination group at state level. Since then there has not been any central administrative coordinating agency for Barnahus in Sweden, except for the national Barnahus network coordinated by the Save the Children Sweden and since 2016 by thc National Competence Centre in Child Abuse (Barnafrid) in cooperation with Save the Children Sweden.

Norway (2007)[2]

Implementation

The idea of establishing Barnahus in Norway was launched in 2004 in a report from Save the Children Norway (Skybak 2004). The first Barnahus was established in 2007, in Bergen, and over a two-year period, six Barnahus were established in different regions. In 2016, there are Barnahus in all regions of Norway, eleven in total. The implementation process in Norway has been top-down and led by the Ministry of Justice and Public Security, and the Police Directorate.

Key Tasks, Agencies Involved and Collaboration

The key aims of the Norwegian model are to facilitate investigative interviews in a supportive environment and to ensure that children and families receive the necessary support and treatment—at the Barnahus or from other agencies. In addition to the Barnahus staff, the key agencies and professions involved are the police and prosecution, and legal representatives for the child and suspect. Child welfare services are allowed access but are not formally part of the collaborative model. They can observe the investigative interview as part of the child welfare case and may be summoned to the Barnahus for risk assessment and emergency placement of the child.

Regulation and Target Groups

Barnahus was initially implemented as a trial project in accordance with the descriptions given in a ministerial working group report of key tasks and the different agency roles and responsibilities (Norwegian Ministry of

Justice and the Police 2006). Local working groups also wrote reports prior to Barnahus establishment (for instance, Bergen Police District 2007; Oslo Police District 2010), which set the standard for new Barnahus.

It was not mandatory to use Barnahus for investigative interviews in the early phase, but the majority of police districts used the facilities from the start, and in the majority of cases (Bakketeig et al. 2012).

In 2015, the Criminal Procedure Act ("Straffeprosessloven") was amended, and new regulations for facilitated interviews were brought into force (FOR-2015-09-24-1098[3]). The new main rule is that Barnahus should be used for facilitated investigative interviews with children under the age of 16 and other particularly vulnerable victims and witnesses in cases involving sexual abuse, direct and indirect physical violence, homicide and gender mutilation. The new regulation thus defines the target groups of the Barnahus model.

The new regulation also defines the roles and responsibilities of the Barnahus staff: they shall welcome the child, participate in consultation meetings, observe the investigative interview, advise the police interviewer, and support and offer treatment to the child and family. The staff must have child-related competence and competence in intellectual impairment and other disabilities.

Organisation, Funding and Staff

The Barnahus in Norway are coordinated by the Police Directorate on behalf of the Ministry of Police and Public Security. A national Barnahus committee was established in 2014 ("Barnehusrådet") to facilitate coordination. The members represent the agencies that are involved in the model: the Police Directorate, the Health Directorate, the Child-, Youth- and Family Directorate, the National Courts Administration, Barnahus and the police districts. Note that child welfare services are not represented. The committee meets twice a year (Norwegian Police Directorate 2015, 2016).

Barnahus is organised as separate units within the police district where they are localised, and a regular staff is employed as civilians in the police district. Funding is channelled through the general funding of the police districts, except for Barnahus in Oslo, which is funded directly from the central government budget.

The staff comprises social workers and therapists, usually clinical psychologists. In most Barnahus, the staff are generalists, meaning that the person designated to the case is responsible for both coordination related to the investigative interview and providing treatment (see Stefansen et al. 2012).

Denmark (2013)[4]

Implementation

The implementation of Barnahus in Denmark followed a broad law reform that was brought into force in October 2013, called the abuse package ("overgrebspakken" in Danish). The background to the law reform involved several reports from both governmental committees and NGOs.[5] From October 2013, it became statutory for Danish municipalities to create a Barnahus in each region to meet the needs of all children and young people in cases of the suspicion or knowledge of violence or sexual abuse (Consolidation Act on Social Services, §50a). Denmark has five Barnahus, one in each region, all established in 2013. Three Barnahus have local satellites to ensure that access to a Barnahus does not take too long.

Key Tasks, Agencies Involved and Collaboration

In Denmark, Barnahus is used in child welfare cases that also involve either the police or healthcare services. The Barnahus staff functions as coordinators in relation to the interaction between the municipality's local child welfare services, the police and the healthcare services. In these cases, the professionals involved meet at the Barnahus for consultation meetings and the child will meet the child welfare caseworker at the Barnahus. In police-reported cases, the investigative interview will take place at the Barnahus. Medical staff are connected to the Barnahus, but it varies between the five Barnahus to whether medical examinations take place at the Barnahus or at a hospital. Assessment of treatment needs will take place at the Barnahus, and short-term crisis interventions and consultations with a psychologist can be provided. The Barnahus can offer up to eight crisis consultations with the child and/or their family.

The main role of the Barnahus is to assist local child welfare services, which are the key agencies in the Danish Barnahus model and responsible for initiating the necessary and correct help for victimised children. In cases of sexual or physical abuse, a child welfare investigation has to be made. This is by the local child welfare service in the municipality in which the child lives, but when a case is referred to the Barnahus, the Barnahus will provide expertise which is to be included in the investigation.

Regulation

The abuse package included several legal changes within the Consolidation Act on Social Services No. 1284, which are of importance for the Danish Barnahus model. It was made mandatory for the municipality's child welfare services to use the Barnahus for child welfare investigations in cases of suspicion or knowledge of child abuse, and where at least one other sector, either police or health care, is involved (Consolidation Act on Social Services, §50b). The law reform also implicates the work within the Barnahus, for instance, related to rules of professional secrecy. In Barnahus cases, health professionals, the police and child welfare services, are allowed to share information without the consent of parents or legal guardians (Consolidation Act on Social Services, §50c).

As part of the abuse package, a specific law authorising the Barnahus and providing guidelines for the tasks and duties of the Barnahus was also passed (Order on Children Houses no. 1153 of 01/10/2013). The Barnahus law states that, in the above cases, the Barnahus is mandated to assist the local child welfare services in their child welfare investigation (Order on Children Houses no. 1153 of 01/10/2013 §1). In addition to the legal provisions, the National Board of Social Services has issued common professional quality standards for the Danish Barnahus model.

Target Groups

Children and adolescents under the age of 18, who have been subjected sexual abuse, physical violence or where there is suspicion thereof, are the target group of the Danish Barnahus model. The child or adolescent's closest caregivers and siblings also receive support in order to be able to handle the situation and take care of the child or adolescent (cf. Order on Children Houses no. 1153 of 01/10/2013).

Organisation, Funding and Staff

The five Barnahus are independent units that are supported and supervised by the National Board of Social Services ("Socialstyrelsen"). Each of the Barnahus is administratively placed in one municipality, but covers all municipalities within its region. The Barnahus is funded by the municipalities. The Barnahus staff are permanently employed by the municipality in which they are located. The Barnahus law specifies that the Barnahus must have permanent staff and that the staff must be qualified to work with cases of sexual abuse and violence. The Barnahus staff is experienced in dealing with child abuse and consists mainly of social workers and psychologists. The staff works as a multidisciplinary team in each case.

The National Board of Social Services provides administrative support, offers professional assistance and support, and ensures the nationwide equality of services provided by the Barnahus.

Finland (2014)[6]

Implementation

In 2009, a working group was commissioned to investigate how all abused children could be investigated in a more coordinated way, based on collaboration between police, prosecution, child welfare services and healthcare agencies. In the commission report, it was suggested that Finland should start a pilot of the Barnahus model, and that the pilot should be undertaken by an inter-administrative management and planning group. This group, in turn, was to create explicit national guidelines for a Finnish Barnahus model (Finnish Ministry of Social Affairs and Health 2009).

In 2014, a Barnahus pilot (called "LASTA") started in the city of Turku. It was coordinated by the National Institute of Health and Welfare and used the expertise of the Forensic Child and Adolescent Psychiatry Units and the Social Paediatrics Units (described below). At the national level, the Barnahus pilot was steered by the Ministry of Social Affairs and Health, the Ministry of the Interior/the National Police Board and the Ministry of Justice/the Office of the Prosecutor General. The pilot constituted a multiprofessional working group handling cases from the police. The starting point was suspicion of physical and/or sexual abuse of children and adolecents under 18 years of age. The pilot was located at the Turku University Hospital and aimed to further develop the Finnish model to ensure a multi-professional, integrated and child-friendly approach in cases of child abuse, and to cover the increased loads of allegations of abuse (Sinkkonen and Mäkelä 2017). The development work was ongoing from 2014 until the end of 2016.

Prior to the LASTA-pilot, Finland has also developed a system for investigative interviews of young children and children with special needs. Since 2008, Finland has had a set of Forensic Child and Adolescent Psychiatry Units operating in university hospitals in five districts. Upon request for assistance by the police or prosecutor, these units perform child investigative interviews. The interviews are performed by forensic psychologists in child-friendly settings (see Korkman et al., Chap. 7, for details on this arrangement).

In addition, there is also a strong clinical tradition in conducting somatic examinations in Finland, with specialised Social Paediatric Units in two university hospitals (Helsinki and Turku), as well as a tradition of cooperation between the police and child welfare services.

Experiences from the Pilot Project

The LASTA-pilot has developed and tried out a way to work, described as similar to the Barnahus model, through networking instead of through creating new physical units or centers. The pilot used existing professional networks in a more integrated and systematic way (Sinkkonen and Mäkelä 2017). The pilot has developed and tested a multiagency risk-assessment form to collect information on all cases of suspected child abuse reported to the police. The form is modelled on the multiagency risk-assessment conferences (MARAC) that have been used in Finland since 2010 to better identify high-risk adult victims and protect them from future abuse. The risk assessment form was used to support the police in identifying children with higher risk to be discussed in a multiprofessional meeting (see Sinkkonen and Mäkelä 2017).

In the pilot project, the police sent a request for each child abuse allegation to LASTA, requesting a multiagency risk assessment. A LASTA coordinator collected information on risk factors from health records both at the primary level and at higher levels and contacted the child's social worker to collect information about risk factors recorded in child protection and/or social welfare records. Both the LASTA coordinator and the social worker were able to record their wish for a multiprofessional meeting. The police received completed forms and decided on those to be discussed in the multiprofessional meeting. The forms thus functioned as a screening tool, and about half of the cases resulted in a meeting. In a weekly meeting, the police, prosecutor, somatic specialist, forensic psychologist, specialist social worker, child and family psychiatrist and crisis work specialist went through each case in a 30 minutes consultation. They assessed the facts, risk factors and protective factors, and created a common action plan about who and how to interview the child. The case follow-up was performed by the coordinator with a social worker and police.

Experiences are mainly reported as positive, for example resulting in faster handling of cases initially, more background information for the police, and more cases discussed in multiprofessional meetings (see Sinkkonen and Mäkelä 2017).

Further Plans for Barnahus in Finland

The experiences and models of collaboration developed in the pilot project will be integrated into the "Strategic Government Programme" (2016–2018), which includes a key reform of the child and family services. The project will model a new service structure, including the establishment of regional centres of excellence and support for persons in need of special support and assistance, and for children and adolescents with severe symptoms. These centres are planned to bring together mental health and substance abuse services for children and adolescents, child welfare specialists and child and adolescent forensic psychiatry expertise (see further Sinkkonen and Mäkelä 2017).

The Åland Islands (2007), Greenland (2011)[7] and the Faroe Islands (2014)[8]

Implementation

Initiated by the Police Agency, the Government of Åland decided to initiate an inter-agency committee to develop collaboration between relevant agencies, resulting in the Barnahus model starting in 2007 (Government of Åland 2007). The Barnahus model in Greenland was initiated as a pilot project in 2011. The Barnahus (locally called Saaffik) was placed in Nuuk, with the intention of serving the whole country and being further developed locally in all municipalities (Rust 2011). The Barnahus in the Faroe Islands started its operations in December 2014 and serves all the Faroe Islands.

Key Tasks and Agencies Involved

In all the Nordic autonomous regions, Barnahus aims at coordinating inter-agency investigatory and treatment/support processes for children who are the victims of abuse (see, for example, Rust 2011, 488). There is some variation, however, in which agencies are included in the collaboration. The Faroe Islandic Barnahus, for example, is a partnership between the police, the Child Protection Services and the Inter-Municipality Agency for Child Protection. In the Åland Islands, the Barnahus model involves coordination between the police, prosecution, child and youth health, child psychiatry, the child welfare services and

"Tallbacken" which is a protected residence for children and their mothers (Government of Åland 2007).

The primary tasks for Barnahus are also described with some variations. In the Faroe Islands, for example, the Barnahus coordinates the efforts between the agencies involved, supports child welfare services in their investigations, provides trauma-focused therapy for children and their families and ensures that the police are performing child investigative interviews in Barnahus. In the Greenlandic Barnahus, the overarching goal is described as contributing to examinations, investigations, crisis therapy and follow-up in cases of the sexual abuse of children and youth (see Rust 2011).

Regulation and Target Groups

The primary target group for the Barnahus in the Faroe Islands is children who have suffered sexual or physical abuse, or cases where there is a suspicion of abuse. It was later decided that all criminal behaviour against children was to be taken care of in Barnahus.

The Åland Islands Barnahus model generally targets crimes against children (Government of Åland 2007), although it has been pointed out that, in practice, it primarily deals with children who have been the victims of physical or sexual crimes (Diesen and Diesen 2015, 12).

In contrast to these broad target groups, the primary target group of the Greenlandic Barnahus model is children and youth aged 0–18 years and their families, where they have been sexually abused or been witnesses to sexual abuse (Government of Greenland 2009; Rust 2011). Parents, siblings and other potential resource persons in the child's network are offered counselling (Rust 2011, 493).

In the Greenlandic Barnahus, specially trained police interview children and youths. Investigative interviews with children from 3 years up to 12 years are video-recorded (Rust 2011). Initially, these interviews took place at the Barnahus; however, the geographical distances in Greenland resulted in the Barnahus in practice only being able to cover the capital of Nuuk.[9] Consequently, the police decided to develop travelling units which take video equipment and travel to the child in order to interview them in their city or settlement, either at the police station or in hired localities depending on what they regard as most appropriate.

In the Faroe Islandic Barnahus, children up to 12 years old, or with a mental age of 12 years or younger, can be interviewed and video-recorded, and the interview can be used in court. Children are interviewed in a special room at the Barnahus by a specially trained police investigator, and the interviews are observed in a co-hearing room by, for example, the child welfare services, the defence attorney and Barnahus staff, although it is not possible for the child to have an assistance lawyer assigned.

Organisation, Funding and Staff

In the Faroe Islands, the Barnahus is an integrated part of the Child Protection Agency. The staff of the agency is one part-time psychologist and a part-time social worker. Since spring 2016, the Barnahus in Greenland has been part of a larger Central Advisory Unit under the Ministry of Family, Equality and Social Affairs, which deals with child welfare in all of Greenland. Children and families undertake abuse-focused interviews with consultants and psychotherapists. The Barnahus staff in Greenland includes psychologists and other professionals with expertise in psychotherapy. It was concluded from an evaluation of the Åland Islands Barnahus model that in practice the collaboration primarily involved the child welfare services and police, and that attendance at consultation meetings was lacking, especially from child psychiatry/psychologists and paediatrics/forensic medicine (see Diesen and Diesen 2015).

Notes

1. Bragi Guðbrandsson has provided information on the Icelandic model.
2. A more comprehensive description of the model and the implementation process in Norway is found in Bakketeig et al. (2012) and Stefansen et al. (2012). See also the annual report on Barnahus from the Norwegian Police Directorate, 2014 and 2015.

3. Regulation on the investigative interview of children and other vulnerable aggrieved parties and witnesses (facilitated interviews) of 24 September 2015 no. 1098.
4. Lene Mosegaard Søbjerg and the National Board of Social Services in Denmark have provided information about the Danish model.
5. See, for instance, Report of the Working Group (2012): "Establishment of children houses in Denmark—strengthened framework for the interdisciplinary and intersectoral cooperation in cases of abuse of children", Report of the Expert Panel (2012): "On abuse of children", The Social Appeals Board (2012): "Thorough investigation of cases of abuse of children and adolescents", Ministry of Social Affairs and the Interior (2013): "Allocation of social reserve grants for 2013. Sub-agreement for social affairs and integration".
6. Minna Sinkkonen has provided information about the Finnish model.
7. Lene Mosegaard Søbjerg and Arnajaraq Poulsen have provided information on the Greenlandic model.
8. Oddbjørg Balle has provided information about the Faroe Islands model.
9. Greenland is a huge island of more than two million square kilometres and has a population of around 55,000 inhabitants, which makes it difficult to travel between cities and settlements.

References

Åström, Karsten, and Annika Rejmer. 2008. "Det blir nog bättre för barnen". Slutrapport i utvärderingen av nationell försöksverksamhet med barnahus 2006-2007. Lund: Lund University.

Bakketeig, Elisiv, Mette Berg, Trond Myklebust, and Kari Stefansen. 2012. *Barnehusevalueringen 2012, delrapport 1: Barnehusmodellens implikasjoner for politiets arbeid med fokus på dommeravhør og rettsmedisinsk undersøkelse.* Oslo: PHS Forskning.

Bergen Police District. 2007. *Barnehuset region vest. Rapport fra planleggingsgruppen.* Bergen: Bergen Police District.

Diesen, Christian, and Eva Diesen. 2015. Utvärdering av barnahus på Åland. Rapport angiven i september 2015, avseende barnahusets verksamhet 2014. Stockholm: Juristfirman.

Finnish Ministry of Social Affairs and Health. 2009. *Investigation of child sexual abuse.* Working Group Report. Helsingfors: Finnish Ministry of Social Affairs and Health.

Government of Åland. 2007. Samordningsmodell för myndigheterna vid misstanke om våld mot barn. Government of Åland.

Government of Greenland. 2009. *Anbefalinger angående børns og familiers trivsel.* Departementet for Sociale Anliggender ogTusagassiivik.

Johansson, Susanna. 2011. Rätt, makt och institutionell förändring. En kritisk analys av myndigheters samverkan i barnahus. Diss. Lund: Lund Studies in Sociology of Law 31, Lund University.

Kaldal, Anna, Christian Diesen, Johan Beije, and Eva Diesen. 2010. Barnahusutredningen 2010. Stockholm: Jure förlag.

Landberg, Åsa, and Carl Göran Svedin. 2013. *Inuti ett barnahus. En kvalitetsgranskning av 23 svenska verksamheter.* Stockholm: Rädda Barnen.

Norwegian Ministry of Justice and the Police. 2006. *Barnas hus. Rapport om etablering av et pilotprosjekt med ny avhørsmodell for barn som har vært utsatt for overgrep m.m.* Oslo: Norwegian Ministry of Justice and the Police.

Norwegian Police Directorate. 2015. *Statens barnehus årsrapport 2014.* Oslo: POD.

Norwegian Police Directorate. 2016. *Statens barnehus årsrapport 2015.* Oslo: POD.

Oslo Police District. 2010. Sluttrapport. Etablering av Barnehuset Oslo. Oslo: Oslo Police District.

Rust, Annalise. 2011. MeeqqanutIllu, KalaallitNunaat – Et grønlandsk Børnehus. *Paedagogisk Psykologisk Tidskrift* 2011(6): 487–497.

Sinkkonen, Minna and Jukka Mäkelä (eds.). 2017. LASTA project 2014-2016. Final report. Report 2/2017. Helsinki: National Institute for Health and Welfare (THL), Finland. (Online publication)

Skybak, Thale. 2004. *Barnas hus - et helhetlig og barnevennlig tilbud til barn som har vært utsatt for seksuelt misbruk.* Oslo: Redd Barna.

Stefansen, Kari, Tonje Gundersen, and Elisiv Bakketeig. 2012. *Barnehusevalueringen 2012, Delrapport 2. En undersøkelse blant barn og pårørende, samarbeidspartnere, ledere og ansatte.* Oslo: NOVA.

Swedish Ministry of Justice. 2005. Uppdrag att medverka till etablering av flera försöksverksamheter med samverkan under gemensamt tak vid utredningar kring barn som misstänks vara utsatta för allvarliga brott (Government decision). Stockholm: Swedish Ministry of Justice.

Swedish National Board of Health and Welfare, Swedish National Police Agency, Swedish Prosecution Authority and Swedish National Board of Forensic Medicine. 2008. Barnahus – försöksverksamhet med samverkan under gemensamt tak vid misstanke om brott mot barn. Stockholm: Swedish National Board of Health and Welfare.

Swedish National Police Agency. 2009. Delredovisning av regeringsuppdrag avseende gemensamma nationella riktlinjer kring barn som misstänks vara utsatta för brott och kriterier för landets barnahus. Stockholm: Swedish National Police Agency.

Permissions

All chapters in this book were first published in CACAENBM, by Springer; hereby published with permission under the Creative Commons Attribution License or equivalent. Every chapter published in this book has been scrutinized by our experts. Their significance has been extensively debated. The topics covered herein carry significant information for a comprehensive understanding. They may even be implemented as practical applications or may be referred to as a beginning point for further studies.

The contributors of this book come from diverse backgrounds, making this book a truly international effort. We would like to thank all the contributing authors for lending their expertise to make the book truly unique. They have played a crucial role in the development of this book. Without their invaluable contributions this book wouldn't have been possible. They have made vital efforts to compile up to date information on the varied aspects of this subject to make this book a valuable addition to the collection of many professionals and students.

This book was conceptualized with the vision of imparting up-to-date and integrated information in this field. To ensure the same, a matchless editorial board was set up. Every individual on the board went through rigorous rounds of assessment to prove their worth. After which they invested a large part of their time researching and compiling the most relevant data for our readers.

The editorial board has been involved in producing this book since its inception. They have spent rigorous hours researching and exploring the diverse topics which have resulted in the successful publishing of this book. They have passed on their knowledge of decades through this book. To expedite this challenging task, the publisher supported the team at every step. A small team of assistant editors was also appointed to further simplify the editing procedure and attain best results for the readers.

Apart from the editorial board, the designing team has also invested a significant amount of their time in understanding the subject and creating the most relevant covers. They scrutinized every image to scout for the most suitable representation of the subject and create an appropriate cover for the book.

The publishing team has been an ardent support to the editorial, designing and production team. Their endless efforts to recruit the best for this project, has resulted in the accomplishment of this book. They are a veteran in the field of academics and their pool of knowledge is as vast as their experience in printing. Their expertise and guidance has proved useful at every step. Their uncompromising quality standards have made this book an exceptional effort. Their encouragement from time to time has been an inspiration for everyone.

The publisher and the editorial board hope that this book will prove to be a valuable piece of knowledge for students, practitioners and scholars across the globe.

Index

www.ingramcontent.com/pod-product-compliance
Lightning Source LLC
LaVergne TN
LVHW051050220926
848485LV00001BA/55